THE LETTERS OF
RICHARD CUMBERLAND

AMS Studies in the Eighteenth Century, No. 13

ISSN: 0196-6561

Other titles in this series:

1. Modern Language Association of America. *Proceedings of the 1967—68 Neoclassicism Conferences.* Edited [and with a Selected Bibliography, 1920—68], by Paul J. Korshin. 1970.
2. Francesco Cordasco. *Tobias George Smollet: A Bibliographical Guide.* 1978.
3. Paula R. Backscheider, ed. *Probability, Time, and Space in Eighteenth-Century Literature.* 1979.
4. Ruth Perry. *Women, Letters, and the Novel.* 1980.
5. Paul J. Korshin, ed. *The American Revolution and Eighteenth Century Culture.* 1986.
6. G. S. Rousseau, ed. *The Letters and Papers of Sir John Hill.* 1982.
7. Paula R. Backscheider. *A Being More Intense: A Study of the Prose Works of Bunyan, Swift, and Defoe.* 1984.
8. Christopher Fox, ed. *Psychology and Literature in the Eighteenth Century.* 1988.
9. John F. Sena. *The Best-Natured Man: Sir Samuel Garth, Physician and Poet.* 1986.
10. Robert A.Erickson. *Mother Midnight: Birth, Sex, and Fate in Eighteenth-Century Fiction (Defoe, Richardson, and Sterne).* 1986.

THE LETTERS OF
RICHARD CUMBERLAND

Edited by
Richard J. Dircks

AMS Press
New York

10 0 000 6166

Library of Congress Cataloging-in-Publication Data

Cumberland, Richard, 1732—1811.
  The letters of Richard Cumberland.

  (AMS studies in the eighteenth century; no.13)
Includes index.
  1. Cumberland, Richard, 1732—1811—Correspondence. 2. Dramatists,
English—18th Century—Correspondence. I. Dircks, Richard J. II. Title. III.
Series.
PR3393.A44 1988   822'6 [B]   87-45799
ISBN 0-404-63513-X

All AMS books are printed on acid-free paper that meets the guidelines for performance
and durability of the Committee on Production Guidelines for Book Longevity of the
Council on Library Resources.

AMS PRESS
56 East 13th Street
New York, N.Y. 10003, U.S.A.

Manufactured in the United States of America

Contents

For George Winchester Stone, Jr.

Introduction

Richard Cumberland (1732-1811) is known primarily
as the leading sentimental dramatist of the second
half of the eighteenth century.[1] His interests, however, ranged far beyond the theatre, and he came to
be recognized as an important man of letters, publishing, in addition to his more than forty plays,
three novels, five volumes of essays, a sizeable
body of poetry, and two volumes of memoirs. His *Memoirs* are of particular interest to the cultural historian, for as a prominent man of letters he moved
with ease among some of the great political, literary, and social figures of his time. The often fascinating accounts provided in these reminiscences
are supplemented by his letters, which offer further
details about, and insights into, social and political history. Despite the fact that Cumberland rarely
retained copies of his correspondence, four substantial groups of letters have survived, those written
to Roger Pinckney, David Garrick, George Germain,
and James Bland Burgess. While these are of special
interest, they are often reinforced by letters to
other individuals.

More than a score of letters to Roger Pinckney,
Cumberland's representative in South Carolina, where
he held the patent for the office of Provost Marshal
from 1759 until 1770, provide rare insights into the
way placemen discharged their responsibilities in
the Colonies, and trace in Pinckney the transition
from a loyal Englishman to a dedicated American. A
substantial set of letters to David Garrick, the
great actor and theatrical manager at Drury Lane,
portray intimately the author-manager relationship
in the English theater of the time and include interesting footnotes to the stage history of the pe-

riod. From an historical point of view, the letters
from Cumberland to George Germain (Lord Sackville),
together with several to the Earl of Hillsborough,
Bernardo del Campo, and Abbé Hussey in connection
with the mission which he undertook to Spain in 1780
are the most significant. They are of special value
in tracing a picture of Spanish culture during the
eighteenth century and suggest some interesting
questions regarding the desire of Spain to acquire
Gibraltar at that time. Finally, the letters to Sir
James Bland Burgess contribute to our knowledge of
the society of Tunbridge Wells shortly after the
turn of the nineteenth century and provides details
of Cumberland's successful efforts to recruit volunteers in that section of the country against the
feared threat of Napoleon. For students of literature, a continuing record of Cumberland's collaboration with Burgess on the composition of the religious epic poem *The Exodiad* reveals the surprising
popularity of the epic at the turn of the century.
Further insights into the culture of the period may
be found in several letter to the painter, George
Romney.

I

As private secretary to Lord Halifax, Cumberland
began his political career in 1751 and subsequently
assumed various duties at the Board of Trade, of
which Halifax was President.[2] This association resulted in Cumberland's giving up a promising career
as a Cambridge scholar, and often throughout his
life he expressed his preference for the more peace-
ful and restrained life of the University.[3] On the
other hand, his choice of a political career enabled
Cumberland not only to support his family but also
to further his personal ambitions. It offered strong
hope of preferment in the service of one of the
leading political figures of the day. Halifax, on
his part, both obtained in Cumberland the services
of a brilliant and promising Cambridge scholar

and paid a political debt to Cumberland's father,
who in 1745 had enlisted two companies of men for a
regiment raised by Halifax and, three years later,
had supported the Whig cause in Northamptonshire.[4]
Cumberland soon learned to move with relative ease
in the company of the great, and his *Memoirs* contain
a number of interesting political portraits, perhaps
the most notable of which is that of Bubb Dodington,
with whom he spent several summers at La Trappe.[5]
When Halifax was made Lord Lieutenant of Ireland in
1761, he appointed Cumberland as Ulster Secretary,
but his failure to name Cumberland as an undersecretary when he was elevated to Secretary of State the
following year was a bitter disappointment to the
dramatist. It was the culmination of a gradual deterioration of their friendship that seems to have
begun when Cumberland imprudently turned down a baronetcy when it was offered him by Halifax, judging
that the offer was more show than substance.[6] Although Halifax failed to reward Cumberland with an
important political post, he had previously granted
him two valuable colonial sinecures, those of Crown
Agent of Nova Scotia and Provost Marshal of South
Carolina. Curiously, in his *Memoirs* Cumberland neither mentions nor alludes to the South Carolina appointment, which forms the subject of most of his
letters to Roger Pinckney.

The story of how these letters came to light is
itself an interesting one. After the dramatist's
death in 1811, William Mudford undertook to write
his biography, a work mainly based on the dramatist's *Memoirs* that had been published only a few
years before.[7] In April of 1812, Mudford received a
packet of letters from Charleston, forwarded by a
man identified only by the name Bee, with whom Mudford had had no previous acquaintance.[8] Bee, in an
accompanying letter, complains of Cumberland's having failed to mention the circumstances relating to
the Patent in his *Memoirs* and offers the letters as
proof of the fact that Cumberland did not suffer the
neglect from Halifax that he seems to imply in his

account of their relationship. Mudford somewhat a-
pologetically includes them in an appendix to his
biography, indicating in doing so his substantial
agreement with Bee's position: "I perfectly agree
with this sentiment, and it is rather with a view to
show that Cumberland was *not* wholly deserted by the
ministry, than from any peculiar impression of the
excellence or interest of the letters themselves
that I insert them here." The argument over the gen-
erosity of Halifax seems somewhat irrelevant from
the vantage point of the twentieth century, but the
historical relevance of Cumberland's effort to sell
the patent to the Colony of South Carolina for a
substanial sum of money is much clearer. In a very
intimate way the letters detail the method by which
authority was delegated by placeman, and they offer
insights into the interaction between the government
of South Carolina and that of the mother country
during the years immediately preceding the American
Revolution.

The first of Cumberland's letters, dated 30 September 1764, replies to several of Pinckney's, the
earliest of which is given as 14 July suggesting the
point at which the authority included in the patent
was transferred to Pinckney. In addition to the office of Provost Marshal, the patent also included
the lesser duties of Clerk of the Peace and Clerk of
the Crown, both of which Cumberland wanted Pinckney
to sell because they were not lucrative. Pinckney
assumed the full responsibilities of the Provost
Marshal's office and shared its revenues with Cumberland. The two men were family friends, and in
this first letter Cumberland conveys the good wishes
of Pinckney's father, mother, and sister, whom he
has recently seen. The letters frequently make reference to Cumberland's father, the Bishop of Clonfert, and other members of the family in a way that
suggests a close and cordial relationship between
them and Pinckney, who was, for this reason, a
trusted agent in whom Cumberland had complete confidence.

Cumberland soon had hopes of disposing of his patent in such a manner as to assure him an equivalent income for life with no further responsibility for the conduct of the office. In his letter of 1 October 1764, he reveals to Pinckney a proposal by George Saxby, Receiver-General of South Carolina, to sell the patent outright to the Province and by so doing grant them freedom to police their own territory. South Carlina would, under the plan which would require approval of the South Carolina Assembly as well as the release of the patent by the Crown, be free to appoint their own Sheriff "as their neighbours do" and to retain within the Province the revenues derived from fines and fees. Under Saxby's proposal, the Province would pay Cumberland five or six thousand pounds sterling for the patent, the income from which would equal the current value of the office to him. This was particularly attractive to Cumberland, for it would provide a permanent addition to his fortune. After assuring Pinckney that his interest will be fully protected, he asks his agent to "throw out a hint to some of the leading members of the Assembly." Recognizing that some bargaining may be involved, he cautions Pinckney: "I must not appear forward and eager in the offer, so that I could wish you would affect to speak of it at a distance, and as if without authority." A postscript to the letter reveals that Cumberland expects to achieve a revenue of £240. per year, his share of the £600. revenue then being divided between Pinckney and himself.

The sale of Cumberland's patent was accomplished during the summer of 1769 when the Crown finally approved the Circuit Court Act, releasing to the dramatist the £5000. sterling which had been appropriated the year before by the South Carolina Assembly. In the years that intervened between his initial efforts and his final success, the matter was frequently embroiled in political controversies between the Colony of South Carolina and England, and the bitter quarrels over the Stamp Act almost dashed the dramatist's hopes.

In his letter of 18 March 1765, Cumberland outlines to Pinckney the procedures he will follow in
obtaining the King's permission to transfer control
of the patent to South Carolina. He will first obtain a legal opinion regarding "the suitability of
the proposal" and then obtain "a recommendation of
the proposal from the Board of Trade, as a matter of
public utility in the Province." Finally, he will
entreat Lord Halifax, at that time his patron, "to
lay it before his Majesty, for his assent."

Cumberland had to rely on the good offices of both
Saxby and Pinckney, who, at the outset at least,
acted more as rivals than friends. Dealing with the
South Carolina Assembly, whose active interest in
the proposal was essential, raised other problems.
The measures Pinckney initially took met with
Cumberland's approval, but some members of the
Assembly questioned Cumberland's ability "to carry
the point" in England because of the "tenacity of
government." Responding to this objection in his
letter of 31 July 1765, Cumberland points out that
if the bill which the Assembly was then advancing
for the establishment of Circuit Courts were to
pass, it would "almost draw" his petition along with
it, and he expresses confidence in being able to obtain a favorable report from the Board of Trade to
the Secretary of State. Finally, he suggests that if
the South Carolina Assembly will grant him "full
powers for concluding and executing the agreement,"
he will be able to end the matter satisfactorily,
adding that Mr. Saxby, who will soon return to the
Colony, will convey these ideas to his friends
there.

By the following January, however, the question of
taxing the American Colonies and the passing of the
Stamp Act had created considerable tension between
the South Carolina Assembly and England. Cumberland
recognizes this fact in his letter of 15 January
1766, in which he speaks of William Pitt's declaration the day before condemning the taxation of the

American Colonies without representation, and offers his own opinion that "the Stamp Act will be absolutely revoked and rescinded," hoping that "the universal joy and good humour" that will occur in the Colonies will enable the legislature to return to Pinckney's project of building a public jail. Cumberland's optimism was to be short lived, however, and within six months his correspondence becomes increasingly pessimistic about the sale of his patent. Pinckney, moreover, had grown dissatisfied with his situation on two counts, the diminution of revenues due to the Stamp Act, and what he conceived to be Cumberland's preference for Saxby in negotiating with the South Carolina Assembly. In his letter of 2 July 1766, Cumberland strenuously denies favoring Saxby, asserting that he has not given Saxby, "or any man living, any power or authority to transact" the affair. He regrets the misunderstanding that has occurred, for by it he may be deprived of their "joint and cordial cooperations" in the effort to sell the patent, adding the afterthought that he is disappointed that Saxby "must lose the opportunity of making an agreeable friend." In regard to the Stamp Act, Cumberland expresses confidence that its repeal will correct the difficulties Pinckney has experienced in the reduction of his income.

Feelings over the Stamp Act created a thrust for greater independence in South Carolina, as it did in the other Colonies, and accelerated efforts to diminish the power of the Crown, particularly in judicial matters. Pinckney is disturbed by an effort of the Assembly to pass a law "empowering magistrates to issue warrants for the recovery of all sums" under £70. currency feeling that such a law would substantially diminish the value of the Provost Marshal's office. Cumberland, on the other hand, hopes that the repeal of the Stamp Act "will crush the thought in embryo," but he fears that the colonial reaction to the favorable news about the Stamp Act might have been extreme. "I make no doubt your joy on that occasion was as great as possible," he observes, adding the hope that Pinckney had not been betrayed into any excesses which might have prejudiced his position.

Cumberland's letter of 1 January 1767 provides evidence that Pinckney had been involved in activities against the Chief Justice. Although Cumberland is persuaded that Pinckney's action, "both from reason and conscience, was right and proper for him to take," his opinion is largely dictated by friendship and he notes that the issue involves "such a mixture and confusion of interests and sentiments, that different men will have different opinions upon the matter." He has interceded with Lord Shelbourne's secretary on Pinckney's behalf and has been assured that "an entire oblivion" of this and all other disputes will take place. An indication of the kind of incident in which Pinckney may have been involved is provided later in the letter when Cumberland explains the reason for the lapse in their correspondence: "I have been a long while without writing to you, but while you was burning governors and stamp collectors in effigy, I did not chuse to meddle with you, nor knew I what to say to you; now I expect some pleasure and satisfaction in your correspondence."

Improved relations between England and South Carolina soon heightened Cumberland's chances of bringing the affair of the patent to a close, and in a letter of 28 November 1766, Pinckney acquaints him with favorable actions that he has been able to take. Cumberland's reply of 30 July 1767 looks forward to dealing with an agent of the Colony. Although Lord Halifax's "retirement from business,"[9] has diminished his political influence, Cumberland is confident that he will be able to "summon strength enough to carry this point."

Details of the negotiations regarding the patent emerge in Cumberland's letter of 3 June 1767, in which he tells Pinckney of the arrival of the provincial agent, Garth, and of the fact that he has presented his memorial to Lord Shelbourne. Cumberland believes the plan will be approved if "the legislature of South Carolina are content to pass a bill of the same nature with those which have been passed in other colonies, for establishing sheriffs," and if they suspend its execution until "his Majesty's, (or the patentee's) consent is obtained." Such a procedure was finally followed, although instituting it was not without its difficulties.

Cumberland is certain in his letter of 8 July 1767 that only price is a factor, and he is convinced that his demands "will not be out of reason" and that "the Assembly will not be their own enemies" to such an extent that they will quarrel with him "upon a small sum." On 29 July 1767 he informs Pinckney that Lord Shelbourne has acted favorably upon the proposal and that he has informed Garth that his terms will be £5000. sterling. Cumberland, moreover, anticipates the possible argument of the opposition that the Colony simply could await Cumberland's death and the matter would be settled without expense. But aware of the value of patronage, Cumberland argues that even if the office were vacant, "it is not likely that a minister would forego the disposal of it merely to save the expense of the Province of South Carolina." To have awaited the event of Cumberland's death could, indeed, have been expensive, for he did not die until 1811, at the age of seventy-nine. On the other hand, the events of history would have served the Colony's cause had they waited, for the outbreak of open rebellion clearly rendered the patent worthless.

In pursuing his objective, Cumberland sought all the help he could, even to asking Pinckney to forward letters to friends who might assist him,[10] and to offering to write to the Committee of the Assembly directly if they should so desire. On 17 October 1767 he notes that "the Secretary of State has wrote to Lord Charles, empowering him to give his assent" to an act for the purpose of transferring the patent to the Colony.

All difficulties had not, however, been overcome.

The Act passed by the South Carolina Assembly regarding the establishment of courts was found to be defective in an important article, and its passage was delayed. "But the main question," Cumberland writes on 15 August 1768, "was the clause of granting salaries to the judges, whenever his Majesty should change the present form of their commissions, and establish them during *good behaviour*." According to Cumberland, this clause for altering the judges' commissions ran counter to a "particular instruction in the year 1760" that had been sent to the continental governors, "forbidding them to give their assent to any Act of Assembly for making alteration in the Commissions of the Judges." His fear that the act would be repealed because of this clause was well-founded, and the act to abolish the Provost Marshall's office was ultimately disallowed. Some hope remained, however, and Cumberland tells Pinckney in his letter of 12 October 1768 that at the time the King disallows the Act, "he will likewise instruct his governor to recommend the re-passing this Act...free from those objections." He assures Pinckney that "all has been conducted with tenderness and respect towards the Province and its legislature" and strongly emphasizes that the reason for the action was "principally upon the motives of their proposal for altering the judge's commissions."

The letters point to a reason for Colonial dissatisfaction that was largely rooted in the methods of administering justice. D. D. Wallace sums up the source of the complaint: "There had been but one provost marshal for the whole province, a capital grievance, which the Commons carried to the very foot of the throne. The officer was a royal patentee, and the office was personal property, transmitted, sold or gambled with under certain limitations."[11] Cumberland knew that this grievance in the Colony offered the best hope of divesting himself of the office, noting that "The spirit of *regulation* that obtains so vehemently, in your back settlements, the total subversion of the regular course of administering justice by the Provost Marshal, and the general outcry that obtains throughout the interior of your country for county courts and the establishment of sheriffs, will, surely, induce your legislature to repass the Act, upon such terms and conditions as the crown has thought fit to prescribe."[12]

Cumberland was correct in his estimate, for despite the dissolving of the Assembly which he complains of in his letter of 15 March 1769, the act, which was repassed on 29 July of that year without the objectionable provisions, obtained the approval of the King on the following 20 November.[13] The Assembly had the year before appropriated the necessary £5000. sterling to purchase the office from Cumberland, and the matter was concluded on amicable terms. On 1 May 1770 he writes to Pinckney thanking him for his good efforts in enabling him to vacate the office of Provost Marshal and accepting his congratualations "on that agreeable event."

Cumberland seems to have had less success in selling his other titles of Clerk of the Peace and Clerk of the Crown, but his overall profit was certainly substantial. Pinckney, who clearly served Cumberland well throughout, seems to have benefited considerably less and to have suffered from the increasing acrimony between the Colony and England. "I am sorry," Cumberland comments in his letter of 13 November 1770, "that unhappy step in your Assembly, by making a useless and irregular present to the Society, who call themselves the supporters of the Bill of Rights, has kept you out of so large a sum due you."

The five years during which Cumberland negotiated the sale of his patent were crucial ones in the escalation of Colonial aspirations for independence, and pinpoint, in the operation of the Provost Marshal's office, a source of dissatisfaction less obvious than the quarrel over taxation, but in may ways as irritating. The letters of Cumberland to

Pinckney illustrate the interaction between the Colonies and England in legislative matters and are evidence of the selfish interests and personal friendships that were frequently determining factors in Colonial government.

Of equally significant interest is the documentation of the progressive Americanization of Pinckney, whose loyalty shifts from England to South Carolina. The Stamp Act first drastically tested Pinckney's loyalty and Cumberland speaks of "the difficulties and dilemmas" into which he was cast by it.[14] Even its repeal poses a danger Cumberland warns his agent against. "For my own part," he cautions, "I think that the extreme of joy is almost as formidable a fury, as that of anger, and sometimes attended with as bad consequences; I hope no instance of such will appear upon this event."[15] But only six months later he is able to congratulate Pinckney upon "the restoration of peace and concord" in the Colony.[16] Cumberland never fully understood the spirit of Colonial aspirations for independence, nor the gradual effect that Pinckney's presence in America would have on his outlook. By 1769 Pinckney had become a sufficient force in the Colony to seek a seat in the Assembly, and he receives Cumberland's good wishes that he might be successful. It was an ambition, however, that apparently did not bear fruit.[17]

A long break in the correspondence between the two men occurs from 13 November 1770 until 28 July 1775, the date of Cumberland's last letter. Pinckney had written Cumberland on 10 May, and, although the letter does not survive, it was apparently a zealous defense of the American position. Cumberland sees Pinckney's attitude as one that is highly prejudiced in favor of the Colonial cause. "You are very particular and diffusive in your description of the action at Concord, and the inhumanity of your late countrymen, the English troops," he notes, and goes on to lament that his friend will not return home "till Mr. Hancock and Mr. Adams take lodging at St. James." There is apparent regret in his recognition of Pinckney's position: "...you are as true an American as ever I met with, so thoroughly have you assimilated yourself to the soil and sentiments to which you have been transplanted." Cumberland's chauvinistic instincts come into conflict with the claims of friendship. He blames much of the attiutde of the Americans on politicians in England who "have conceived the idea of disobedience and disorder in all its fatal extent." He answers the accusation of the cruelty of the English soldiers by asking, "Have not you known the temper and nature of your own brave countrymen in times past?" The acrimony of civil discord has left little room for moderation, and the Pinckney-Cumberland relationship may be viewed as a case history of the separating forces of war in which political reality takes its toll of personal friendship. In this it is a microcosmic view of the deterioration of Colonial affection for England.

II

While Cumberland was in the service of Lord Halifax, he pursued his interest in the theater. Despite the active backing of his patron, his tragedy *The Banishment of Cicero* was rejected by David Garrick, the manager of the Drury Lane theater. At the rival playhouse, Covent Garden, however, he was successful in producing *The Summer's Tale*, a slight musical play, which, despite its lukewarm reception, convinced Cumberland that his talents should be directed toward comedy. His first important drama *The Brothers* was presented at Covent Garden on 2 December 1769, after being turned down at Drury Lane. Despite Garrick's rejection, Cumberland complimented him in the Epilogue. With Garrick in the audience, this public offer of peace and the high quality of the drama itself led eventually to their profitable collaboration.

Cumberland had made other efforts to present his work to Garrick with little success. On 26 January

1768, he offered a version of Shakespeare's *Timon of Athens* altered for the contemporary audience. The accompanying letter reveals Cumberland's deferential attitude in dealing with important people, as well as an unattractively assertive pride, telling Garrick that he had submitted the play to George Colman, then head of Covent Garden, who "flattered it more than it deserves," and had cast the parts, but at length rejected it. Somewhat deferentially, but prophetically, he suggests that although he has "little doubt but that" Garrick's opinion will agree with Colman's, he still seeks his judgment.

Undaunted by the refusal of *Timon*, he submitted his next comedy *The Brothers* to Garrick. His letter of 21 March 1768 is an interesting portrait of the early Cumberland. With little prior encouragement of any sort, he feels impelled to lay down conditions. The drama will be submitted to Garrick's judgment, "upon the presumption that, in case of acceptance, it will be brought out between the periods of Christmas and Lent," adding that "some new decorations will be necessary." The refusal by Garrick, who seldom allowed actors or dramatists to make conditions, was inevitable, for, although he could be a willing and generous friend, he seldom compromised the flexibility that he felt was necessary for the proper managing of his theater. Garrick's reply that there would be no room for additional new productions in the ensuing season evoked a petulant response, in which Cumberland affirms that he had submitted the play without "any view to theatrical emoluments," declaring, "if I find the ensuing season shut against me before this is expired, I think it not improbable that before another succeeds, you may be tired of the trouble of receiving these performances, and I cured of the folly of writing them."[18]

Garrick's attending the performance of *The Brothers* indicates his interest in Cumberland as a dramatist, and perhaps some interest in the play itself. Cumberland's conciliatory lines in the prologue

points to his understanding of how important Garrick
would be in his pursuit of a theatrical career.
Clearly it was in the best interests of both men to
reconcile their differences, and by the winter of
1770 Cumberland was corresponding with Garrick regarding a new tragedy, "Salome". In letters written
on 25 January and 17 March 1770 he discusses details
of the drama, but it was never produced.[19]
No acrimony was involved in this exchange and they
closely cooperated in the production of *The West Indian*. The extent of their mutual effort is revealed
in Cumberland's letters to Garrick on 24 June and 2
July 1770 prior to production of the drama on 19
January 1771. The comedy firmly established Cumberland's reputation as a leading dramatist, and its
great success encouraged him to return to Ireland
the following summer to work on a new play, *The
Fashionable Lover*. His letter of 4 July 1771 suggests a relaxed and intimate relationship with Garrick, as he reveals the result of his investigation
of the Dublin "Jubilee" for the manager.
During the summer of 1769, Garrick prepared for
presentation at Stratford a three-day celebration of
Shakespeare's birth, including an elaborate "Jubilee." The spectacle ran into bad weather and other
mishaps, and it became a subject of controversy and
ridicule during the ensuing season. Garrick's response to the criticism was to compose a successful
afterpiece, predictably called *The Jubilee*. Meanwhile word reached Garrick that his "Jubilee" had
been plagiarized and was being performed at the Crow
Street Theatre in Dublin. Cumberland looked into the
matter while he was in Ireland and his account of
the affair reflects his sense of humor and the dedication with which he pursued his task, exonerating
those concerned from any substantial theft of Garrick's material.[20]
Writing from Ireland during the summer of 1771,
Cumberland, in great good humor and full recognition
of the value of Garrick's counsel, discusses the
progress he is making with *The Fashionable Lover*. As

he leaves Dublin for his retreat in Clonfert, Cumberland observes in his letter of August 5 that "when the West Indian gave me your regard and bestow'd all mine upon you, it did more for me than the best production ever did for it's author before." This is more than rhetoric, and it is clear that for Cumberland his friendship for Garrick meant much more than simply an entree into the theater.

Cumberland's association with Garrick was not consistently harmonious and the formal tone of Cumberland's letter of 26 June 1773 indicates that an estrangement has taken place. Garrick's reply is archly formal. After agreeing to read Cumberland's farce he adds in the formal third person that "at the same time he [Garrick] must confess himself as much surpriz'd, after so long a silence, to receive his [Cumberland's] Note of Yesterday, as he was to know the cause of it: indeed he little thought after he was inform's of his New Scheme, that he shoud have been honour'd again with his Commands--."[21] What Cumberland's new scheme was is not certain. Stanley Williams, in his biography of Cumberland, believes it to have been the dramatist's efforts to have Garrick engage the actor, Henderson, but discussions with Garrick about Henderson were to continue for two more years, and the remaining correspondence between Garrick and Cumberland concerning the actor, seems not to point to the kind of acrimony suggested in this letter. A more likely explanation is that during the spring of 1773, Cumberland together with Samuel Johnson and others of his literary circle were actively engaged in promoting Oliver Goldsmith's new comedy *She Stoops to Conquer*, which was produced successfully at the rival theatre, Covent Garden, on 15 March 1773. Cumberland's involvement in this activity could not have pleased Garrick and might well have been viewed as disloyalty. Although Garrick wrote the epilogue to Goldsmith's play, this fact alone does not argue convincingly against hidden resentment by the manager, and writing it might

have been motivated by a desire to appear cooperative as a friend of Johnson. Cumberland's lengthy
reply that attempts to explain his "scheme" seems
consistent with this view: "It is true, Sir, I have
been engaged in an undertaking, which had for it's
object the promotion of Genius; I have been tempted
to subscribe my Opinion at the instigation of
friends whose judgement I hold sacred, and amongst
them by some which you and I enjoy in common, who
like myself, did not apprehend you would have resented an effort founded in public spirit."[22] It is
unfortunate that Cumberland was not more specific in
detailing his activities, for whatever explanation
is advanced, conjecture rather than certitude remains. The letter is, however, a genuine, sincere,
and successful effort at reconciliation. Their correspondence continues, only to run into additional
difficulties regarding the production of *The Choleric Man.*

After three extremely successful comedies, Cumberland ran into problems with *The Choleric Man.* Whatever the reason, emotional, psychological, or simply
a temporary diminution of creative talent, the comedy was a problem from the start. In late August 1774
Garrick writes to Cumberland complaining of the delay in delivering the drama: "I could wish to have
the *passionate Man* in my hands, and also that you
would send me a Cast of the Parts, according to your
Notion of the Matter. The sooner the better...,"[23]
and he observes a week later "but my good friend,
not a word of the *Comedy?* I mean, of *when* I am to
have it."[24] No sooner was the problem of getting the
completed drama to Garrick solved than difficulties
in casting developed. The actors were dissatisfied
with their roles. On 23 October 1774 Cumberland
writes to Garrick regarding William Smith and Frances Abington: "I have thrown all my influence in the
scale of friendship for his [Smith's] coming to the
Theatre,...If you think the part worthy of him, you
have the means in your hands of engaging him to it,"
and he adds, "I only observe that Mr. Smith *ought* to

perform and Mrs. Abington *must*, or the play is undone." Some weeks later he continues his complaints:
"Two principal performers [Smith and Dodd] have already returned their parts in my comedy and parts
which, if I have any judgement, cannot so properly
be filled by any two men in either Theatre." Cumberland is ready to withdraw his comedy. "What is to
be done?" he declares, "Let us join in withdrawing
the object of contention, before the Evil spreads. I
am unfit for such Controversies, and it will operate
in the End for your ease and relief."[25] Cumberland
had read some scenes of the comedy to Dodd while he
was in Dublin, and the actor had formed the impression that he was to play Jack Nightshade, a role
subsequently given to Thomas Weston. Neither Smith
nor Dodd acted when the play was finally produced,
although Smith recited the Prologue. Garrick was not
easily ruffled by dissension in the ranks, and moved
ahead with the production. In Cumberland's next letter of 17 November, moreover, he fears the loss of
Miss Jane Pope from the cast, a loss that was never
to materialize, for she appeared as Lucy. Garrick
seems to have tried to calm the dramatist's mind,
attempting to reassure him that proper attention was
being paid to the production, and Cumberland acknowledges his error: "Obnoxious I called my peice
from the offence and Revolt of the performers; I beseech you to believe it coud point no where else;
for I do faithfully assure you I never did, (nay it
was impossible I ever coud) think otherwise for a
moment than that you was taking more pains than you
ought about me." In his letter of 24 November he expresses satisfaction with the cast, but would like
Garrick to consider playing the part of Charles Manlove himself. Garrick declined the request and assigned the role to Samuel Reddish.

The cast satisfactorily established, Cumberland
found himself unable to satisfy Garrick with a fit-
ting prologue. The death of his father provided a
plausible excuse for his failure, and when Garrick
found his dialogue prologue unsuitable, he hastily

wrote a serious one dealing with the classical ori-
gins of the drama. Garrick rejection of this as well
evoked a sharp response from Cumberland. "Your short
letter has been no cordial to me, I must confess, as
you speak so unpromisingly of the second prologue I
sent you, and which I flatt'red myself you would
warmly approve: I have strictly considered it, and I
have nothing to alter or suppress, so that I beg it
may be spoken literally as it is wrote."[26] Garrick
decided to substitute one of his own, a decision
which Cumberland reacts against in his next letter
on 17 December. "My reasons do not turn upon comparative Merit in our Poems; that I am well content to
yeild, but I could wish my words to be heard and
seen, especially as my foes have never ceased objecting against a flippancy in my first prologue."
Cumberland's prologue was apparently used and printed with the published version of the comedy, but
contemporary accounts of the performance reserved
their praise for the epilogue written by Garrick,
presumably the poem previously intended for the prologue.[27] Cumberland apparently thought better of the
tone of his letter and a day or two later apologized
for his sharpness: "I find every thing affects me
too sensibly, and being much wounded of late, I am
easily hurt--Dont misinterpret my impatience about
the prologue; and above all things dont think I can
misunderstand the friendly motives of your writing
it; nothing could be kinder--but I am very anxious
to avail myself of the conciliatory turn which my
prologue has taken by your advice, and as I am apt
to wish ardently, when I do wish, I have written to
you perhaps too warmly on the Subject;..."[28]

Cumberland's correspondence over the *Choleric Man*
reveals his highly sensitive, easily offended,
proud, and determined personality, while suggesting
an unflatteringly subservient and apologetic aspect
of it. The humble tone of his letter of 19 December
failed to reconcile him fully to Garrick, who a week
later wrote to George Colman at Covent Garden: "It
was impossible for you to satisfy Cumberland, had

the rack forc'd from you as much falsehood, as he
has vanity--I am very glad you have prepar'd him for
Me, had you been as Mischievous, as you were sincere
with him, You might have sent him so high Season'd,
and stuff'd so full with conceit, that I should have
had much ado to lower him; he has behav'd so disa-
greeably with me, that I must have a pluck at his
feathers, whether they belong to Terence, Shadwell,
or are of his own growth."[29]

During this period Cumberland was unsuccessfully
attempting to bring Garrick and the actor Henderson
to mutually satisfactory terms. Moreover, within a
month, Mrs. Abington, who was playing Laetitia in
The Choleric Man, became a catalyst that further aggravated relations between the dramatist and Garrick. She sought Cumberland's permission to withdraw
from the comedy, and, without consulting the manager, he granted it. Her note to Garrick, telling him
that the matter had been settled with Cumberland,
brought an angry reply. Writing to her in the formal
third person, Garrick declares that "without saying
a word to Me, did she not send back her part in the
new Comedy, and say that she had settled the matter
with Mr. Cumberland? could a greater affront be offered any Manager?"[30] He apparently also vented his
wrath on Cumberland who was compelled to write to
Mrs Abington. He explains to Garrick: "I have written her a Letter to the Effect you wished. I have
told her the very unpleasant situation I was thrown
into by having exceeded my powers from a wish to
gratify her Inclination, and I have represented the
high displeasure you had conceived both against her
and myself from the attempt upon what is justly inherent in you alone."[31]

The Choleric Man was in trouble from the beginning. William Hopkins wrote to George Garrick on 14
December 1774: "The Cholerick Man is to come out on
Monday--I have my fears about its success. I can't
say I am charm'd with it."[32] Despite the problems
and gloomy predictions, the comedy was performed
thirteen times during the season, a respectable suc-

cess. Following Cumberland's previous triumphs, however, it was a disappointment.

Unfortunately, the relationship between Cumberland and Garrick had been so strained that only a brilliant performance might have provided sufficient common interest to restore it to its former state, and they drifted further apart until Garrick announced his impending retirement. Only then did Cumberland feel sufficiently secure to take the first step toward reconciliation.

Writing on 20 January 1776, Cumberland pays tribute to Garrick's generous help and friendship in the past and makes it clear that his effort to renew their association is free from motives of personal gain: "While you continued in the Administration of the Theatre, I shoud have continued to have esteem'd you, without telling you so: Now that you have quitted your Vocation, I throw off my reserve and seize the first opportunity of wishing you all possible happiness."

Garrick was receptive to the overture and was soon assisting Cumberland once more. Early in 1776 Cumberland offered Covent Garden *The Battle of Hastings*, which the multiple management of the theatre refused. Writing to the former manager of that theatre, George Colman, Cumberland complains about its rejection, asserting his confidence in the drama's worth: "My tragedy cost me great pains and much attention; hath been many years in hand; is entirely original in plan, popular in it's subject and free of all Imitation. The Opinions of Men exceeding high in the Republic of Letters have been unanimous and more than warmly in it's favour." He adds that the piece had been accepted by Garrick for the current season but had been withdrawn by the dramatist "for reasons not worth troubling you with."[33] Cumberland's pride had clearly gotten the better of his judgment in withdrawing the play from Garrick, for upon the manager's retirement, he had to deal with his young, brilliant, and brash successor, Richard Brinsley Sheridan. Cumberland soon sought the opinion and advice of Garrick in reconstructing the play and wrote to Sheridan on 9 January 1777 offering him the revised *Battle of Hastings.* In a letter to Garrick, he criticises Sheridan for not replying to his letter sent nine days before. A postscript, however, tells of his receipt of a note from Sheridan and of arrangements to meet with him.[34]

By the following November, the drama was being prepared for the stage, with Cumberland frequently implementing suggestions from Garrick. On 12 January 1778 he warmly thanks the actor for his help, observing that "there is nothing gratifies like the candid censures of a real judge, and on the score of criticism you know I am more endebted to you than to any man living." He confides that he has been guided by him in dealing with Sheridan. "I called yesterday on Mr. Sheridan and quickened him, but all in good humour and perfect harmony," he reports. The successful tragedy was acted twelve times with Cumberland's protege, Henderson, in the leading role of Edgar. Garrick had served his friend well, and although the production did not meet with the marked success of Cumberland's great comedies, it was not without its merits. With it ended their cooperative efforts on the London stage. Garrick's death the following year, moved Cumberland to record in his *Memoirs* a sympathetic and moving portrait of perhaps the greatest actor-manager that the English stage has known. He is seldom more convincing than when he describes Samuel Johnson at the grave of his former pupil, Garrick: "I saw old Samuel Johnson standing beside his grave, at the foot of Shakespeare's monument, and bathed in tears: a few succeeding years laid him in earth, and though the marble shall preserve for ages the exact resemblance of his form and features, his own strong pen has pictured out a transcript of his mind, that shall outlive that and the very language, which he laboured to perpetuate."[35] Johnson and Garrick, who came up to London together and whose lives met on frequent occasions, are here appropriately linked.

The letters reveal other aspects of eighteenth-century life, people, and places that are of interest to the social historian. Through his political connections Cumberland gained entrance into a wide circle of London society. As his reputation in the theatre grew, he became a celebrity and had an opportunity to make use of his unusual conversational skill. At the Board of Trade he knew William Fitzherbert, then Commissioner and a friend of Johnson. Soon Cumberland became a regular member of the brilliant society that surrounded Johnson. He was always acutely conscious of position and wealth, and although he could, when the occasion offered, summon elements of self-righteous pride, as in his rejection of a baronetcy offered by Halifax, he was for the most part aware of the social necessity of not offending the great. Moreover, he took every opportunity of advancing the interests of his family. His letter of 24 June 1770 tells Garrick that he has arranged for a dinner between the manager and Fitzherbert and that he has presumed to include himself and his wife in the party: "I hope Mrs. Garrick and you will forgive me when I desire leave to accompany him and to bring Mrs. Cumberland with me who wishes much to improve her acquaintance with you and be made known to Mrs. Garrick." The Cumberland and Garrick families knew each other well, and, in his *Memoirs*, the dramatist speaks with affection of the actor's friendliness toward his children, characteristically mixing his praise of Garrick with recognition of his wife's disciplinary achievements, observing that "though Garrick could charm a circle of them [Cumberland's children] about him whilst he acted the turkey-cocks, and peacocks and water-wagtails to their infinite and undescribable amusement, yet at the word or even look of the mother, *hi motus animorum* were instantly composed and order reestablished, whenever it became time to release their generous entertainer from the trouble of his exertions."[36]

Cumberland's lack of political sophistication is

apparent in his dedication of *The Brothers* to the
Duke of Grafton when he published the comedy in
1770. In his *Memoirs*, he explains that although he
did not know Grafton, he had been motivated to make
the dedication because the Duke was the Chancellor
of the University of Cambridge. If this was the
dramatist's sole motivation, it suggests an almost
incredible unawareness of the political implications
of the tribute. Curiously, Cumberland did display
such unawareness from time to time, and his expression of surprise at the reaction of the politically
oriented *Morning Chronicle* may be genuine enough: "I
casually took it up some time ago and found my name
at full length with an assertion directly false as
to the department in which I am concerned, and motives ascribed to me for my Dedication to the Duke
of Grafton which I utterly disavow." This letter of
17 March 1770 supports subsequent observations to
the same effect in his *Memoirs*.[37] Grafton was a
highly controversial figure at the time, with his
liberal policies toward the American colonies coming
under constant fire. He was one of the chief objects
of the attacks by Junius, and ultimately was compelled to resign as First Lord of the Treasury to be
succeeded by Lord North on 10 February 1770. A few
months later, on 2 July 1770, Cumberland very likely
refers to the same matter when he tells Garrick, "I
am very glad so unfavorable an Impression is effaced
from Mr. Burke's mind. I am doubly anxious it shoud
be cleared to Lord Rockingham, and I am happy to owe
these kind offices to your friendship." Lord Grafton's succeeding Lord Rockingham as Lord of the
Treasury on 2 August 1766 explains Rockingham's unfavorable reaction to the dedication.

Cumberland's letters to Garrick from Ireland during the summer of 1771 give a picture of the Crow
Street Theatre recently purchased by the energetic
William Dawson, who had previously organized a company at the Capel Street Theatre to rival Henry Mossop, then in control of both the Smock Alley and
Crow Street theatres. Cumberland provides firsthand

information about the theatre during its initial summer under Dawson's control, particularly regarding the important acting couple, Spranger and Ann Barry. "The Barrys are here acting to thin Theatres," he tells Garrick, "the weather being very hot and the Town empty."[38] He expresses the wish that Barry would act the role of O'Flaherty in *The West Indian* and his wife that of Charlotte Rusport. In his letter of 13 July, he mentions a young actor by the name of Lewis and observes that, although he had overacted the role of Belcour, he had been well received. He asks whether or not he should make overtures to him on Garrick's behalf, explaining that "he woud be an accession under your Government, as he is young, handsome and volatile." Cumberland did not find Lewis receptive, and was convinced that the actor had deliberately avoided meeting with him. While noting that Lewis's salary in Ireland is greater than that which Garrick would pay him, he praises his ability: "I am firmly of opinion the Lad has faculties to make a figure in Comedy...He has a strong tone which breaks occasionally into the humorous with great success, and is capable of variation in his cadences; his Eye is quick and his modesty does not stand in his way."[39]

Cumberland provides brief glimpses into the life and customs of the time. He describes his journey by sea to Ireland, "a calm and pleasant passage of 36 hours," in which he made the trip pleasant for his family by avoiding contact with the mass of passengers. "My Dear Woman and the little Boys, who had been charming Companions on land to me," he relates, "did not lose their spirits by sea and as I lash'd my Chariot on deck, we sate in it with great state and composure and sav'd the nauseous smell of human sickliness, which infests the lower regions of a Ship full of passengers."[40] He is characteristically romantic as he looks forward to his retirement to the country: "I am going with a resolution not to stir out of the demesne lands of Clonfert, but to court the Muse naked from the Bog and catch a glimpse of unsophisticated Nature." Cumberland had written *The West Indian* in Ireland and attributed much of the success of the character of O'Flaherty to hints he took from observing the Irish character. During the summer of 1771, he was completing *The Fashionable Lover*, which met with similar success, although its chief character, Colin Macleod, is a Scotsman.

Occasionaly Cumberland's discussion of personal details illuminates the political or social realities of the day. His revelation of his father's hopes for preferment describes the tenuous nature of ecclesiastical appointments: "A vacancy being now made on the bench by the Bishop of Limerick's death," he writes, "my father puts in his plea for a Remove; the general report of the Town sends him to Elphin or Kilgore, both which woud be agreeable Exchanges, but I fear this matter will not be decided before I leave Dublin, as Lord Townshend generally keeps those Destinations a long time secret."[41] There is an unattractive tone of self-praise in his references to his attendance on Lady Germain in the winter of 1778 during an attack of measles which she had contracted from her children. "Lady George continues most dangerously ill," he tells Garrick, "and I have little hopes of her recovery; nothing can exceed the distress incident upon her loss; her Truth of character, Charity and domestic Virtues are almost without parallel, but being a latent character without any brilliancy they are only known to those who feel her merits and live under their influence: My time is painfully employed in continual attendance on Distress."[42]

Several of the Garrick letters describe events of special interest. The dramatist's letter from Kelmarsh in Northamptonshire on 23 October 1774 describes the private theatricals conducted there, among them a drama in which Cumberland, himself, acted. Garrick had been invited to participate, but had declined. Perhaps the most interesting revelation for the student of Cumberland is his laudatory evaluation of his own performance.

An especially important letter describes in detail the dinner at which Goldsmith probably first read his poem *Retaliation*. Cumberland's *Memoirs* reveal how the "Friday's Club" originated following a proposal by Burke that those who had dined together at Sir Joshua Reynold's and Cumberland's homes decided to meet at the St. James's Coffeehouse.[43] In the letter of 14 March 1774, Cumberland describes Goldsmith's contribution to one of these meetings: "Dr. Goldsmith's Dinner was very ingenious, but evidently written with haste and negligence. The Dishes were nothing to the purpose, but they were followed by Epitaphs that had humour, some Satire and more panegyric." He has little to say of his own poem, which was apparently recited by Goldsmith: "My wine was drank very cordially, though it was very ill pour'd out by Dr. Goldsmith, who proved himself a Recitator acerbus."[44] In his *Memoirs* Cumberland lists the regular members of the group and describes the meeting immediately before the one recorded in this letter.[45] Taken together, the two accounts interestingly portray the Club's activities.

Cumberland's letter of 18 January 1777, describes a four-hour visit to Court. His eye for detail reveals that "the richest habit at Court was Lady Warwick's," that "the King and Queen both spoke particularly long to Mrs. Montagu," and that "Sir George Warren had his order snatched off his ribbon, encircled with diamonds to the value of 700*l.*"

A keen sense of incident supported Cumberland's gossipy temperament. As a result, the letters to Garrick are products of a sensitive and interested observer of social history and go beyond providing insights into the theater and the life of the great actor-manager to enlarge our view of the society of the day. The end of the Garrick era at Drury Lane did not end Cumberland's work in the theater, but it does mark clearly the apex of his career. Not until late in the century was he again to become one of the leading playwrights of the day. His dramatic ca-

reer was interrupted by a unique, and, in many respects, fascinating diplomatic venture to Spain.

III

Lord George Germain elevated Cumberland to the position of Secretary of the Board of Trade, and their
association developed into a close friendship. Cumberland became a capable and dedicated associate to
whom Germain entrusted the responsibility for providing intelligence about England's conflict with
Spain. Cumberland, acting for Germain, employed William Wardlaw as an agent and discovered that a secret treaty had been signed between Spain and Portugal. At the time, Abbé Hussey, an Irish priest in
the service of Spain as Chaplain to the Spanish embassy in London, was also a political agent. Wardlaw, acting as a double agent employed by both Hussey and the English, reported directly to Cumberland. This multiple intrigue led to discussions between Cumberland and Hussey concerning the possibility of the English achieving a separate peace with
Spain.[46]
The choice of Cumberland an emissary to Spain was
based on his close involvement in developing the intelligence that peace with that country might be
possible, while holding a sufficiently low official
position that his presence in Spain would not suggest the real purpose of his mission. About thirty
of Cumberland's letters on the subject survive,
written mostly to Germain and to Lord Hillsborough,
then Secretary of State for the the Southern Department. In addition, letters to Bernardo Campo, a
Spanish sub-minister, and Abbé Hussey serve to fill
in the picture of what took place. Cumberland's
sketchy and guarded account of the mission in his
Memoirs is not substantially altered by his letters,
but is enhanced by them.[47] Equally important is the
first hand account of the mission which Cumberland
prepared for Lord Shelbourne, dated 4 June 1781.[48]
This account largely evaluates the reasons that led

to the failure of the mission that had begun with some prospects of success.

Cumberland writes to Shelbourne in his *Particulars of the Secret Negotiation between Great Britain and Spain, Carried on at Madrid in the Years 1780 and 1781* that "at the close of the year 1799, the Minister of Spain, Count Florida-blanca, manifested a disposition for treating with Gibraltar upon terms of peace, secretly and apart from France.[49] Further details regarding the means by which Florida-blanca expressed this view may be gleaned from the Stopford-Sackville papers, which include the Cumberland letters to Germain. Although a summary of them is provided in the *Report on the Manuscripts of Mrs. Stoppford-Sackville of Drayton House, Northamptonshire*, a full picture of the events requires an examination of the letters themselves, along with those available from other sources. They reveal that Gibraltar, which had been in the possession of Great Britain since the early eighteenth century, was the initial reason for Spain's interest in negotiation. The fortress was at the time under siege by Spain, but was in no real danger of falling. However, Spain had possessions in America that she felt might be of equal value to the British and could be offered in exchange. Cumberland discusses Abbé Hussey's willingness to accept the role of mediator between the two nations in his letter to Germain of 19 November 1779. Hussey apparently emphasized the need for haste, explaining that there was danger of "some reciprocal Article or Treaty with France...by which Spain might bind herself not to make peace without France," and that "he had secret Intelligence that it was now in Agitation to send a Man from Spain to the Congress." Hussey also, although unofficially, had made it clear to Cumberland that Gibraltar was the central issue. Although Cumberland was not permitted to discuss the future of the fortress, he transmits Hussey's opinion that Gibraltar was "the Sine qua non of Spain," and that, on the strength of the word of Florida-blanca, Britain might be given in exchange "a strong footing on the Mosq shore, and upon the Coast of Barbary Oran." In his next letter, Cumberland adds the following remarkable evaluation of the situation: "Spain seems to dread offensive Operations next year upon her Colonies, and thinks we shall withdraw from America with the whole force of the well-affected on that Continent to descend upon the Settlements of Spain in South America; and Mr. H[ussey] says she despairs of Gibraltar—and he even insinuated that the Kings obstinacy in persisting to reach that unattainable object might throw His Majesty into a Convent for Life, or end in an assassination—Nay, he pointed at the parties, but this I don't commit to a letter."[50]

Although by the time Cumberland's mission took place Gibraltar had been relieved by the British fleet, his report to Lord Shelbourne indicates that the principal difficulty remained "the perseverance of His Catholic Majesty in continuing his attempts against Gibraltar, the pretensions founded upon certain unwarranted propositions for it's Surrender fabricated in Lisbon, and the requisition of some qualifying expedient for saving His Catholic Majesty's good faith with France, and preventing the consequence of a direct rupture with that Power."[51] In any event, Cumberland was enjoined not to treat of Gibraltar "on any terms," and, without obtaining Spain's agreement on this point, he decided to enter the country against the advice of the British representative in Lisbon, who cautioned him against doing so without first obtaining firm guarantees.

Writing to Hillsborough on 6 June 1780, Cumberland explains his dilemma. He has received a letter from Hussey that does not contain a firm statement that the future of Gibraltar will or will not be treated of. Under the circumatances, Cumberland notes, "I do not consider myself under orders to return; on the other hand as he does not tell me that she will treat without it, I am doubtful whether I am warranted to advance." Informal assurances and the early actions of Spain in the negotiations that finally got under way suggested that there was a possibility that an accommodation without Gibraltar might have been possible. Unfortunately England's strong posture at sea deteriorated as Spain took steps to strengthen her own position. Cumberland reports the situation as it appears to him. Spain had "fit out a considerable fleet and body of troops from Cadiz for the West Indies; the blockade of Gibraltar was now resumed, and in the meantime the stability of the British Ministry became questionable in the opinion of the Spanish Court on account of the powerful division of opposition in the House of Commons."[52] The last opportunity for success seems to have been lost when word of the Gordon riots in London reached Spain. Cumberland conveys his reaction to the news in writing to Germain on 5 July 1780: "I forebear to attempt a description of what I have felt upon the intelligence of your dreadful commotions in London." He observes more force-fully in his report to Shelbourne that the "tumults in London...put a full stop to the Negotiation; and, altho' these alarming Commotions were soon happily composed with circumstances highly honorable to Government, yet my business, whose success so evidently depended on dispatch, receiv'd thereby very inopportunely a critical delay."[53]

The delay allowed France to interpose and to develop diplomatic initiatives. All aspects of secrecy in the discussions were lost, and evidence of British weakness seemed to be mounting. Talks that had begun with the British responding to a peace initiative on the part of Spain now found England in a position of relative weakness. Cumberland's correspondence and reports shed light on the diplomatic moves of France. Count Montmorin, the French Ambassador, had grown suspicious of Cumberland's presence, and it seems clear that the question of his mission was a serious concern at the French court. "A quick succession of Couriers and Instructions from Paris now ensued," Cumberland affirms to Shelbourne, "Count de Aranda and the remains of the Grimaldi party join'd in support of the Family compact; the Minister Galvez had now a leading influence in public Affairs, and he employ'd it for the interest of France."[54]

France's strategy took the form of convincing Spain that peace might better be achieved through the mediation of Russia than through direct negotiations with England. Bernardo Campo on 22 July 1780 indicated that intimation had been received from the Spanish minister at the Court of Russia of "a formal overture made on the part of that Court proposing to his Catholic Majesty the good Offices and mediation of the Empress" in the Spanish quarrel with Great Britain.[55] In his reply, Cumberland takes the offer at face value and inquires whether or not mediation with France was included in the proposal and where the negotiations might take place. On the following day he suggested to Campo that if it "should be inconvenient to Spain to wait the return of my Answer by the circuitous Channel of Lisbon," it might be advisable "to advertize Lord Hillsborough of the proposal of Russia by special express thro France."[56] On 4 August 1780 Cumberland dispatched a message to Hillsborough suggesting that "If the Wisdom of the British Cabinet should decide for accepting the mediation now offered by her Czarist Majesty, it may perhaps be held adviseable to communicate with the Imperial Court on that Subject." Cumberland was in a difficult position, faced by delaying tactics on the part of Spain and, what was perhaps more difficult, Hillsborough's neglect. Cumberland complains that "I have been near 4 months absent, and have not yet heard from the Minister. The intervention of the riots was critical against my business. A communication of their issue from authority woud have been a very useful exhibit. I have in the meantime not omitted by every post writing to the Minister besides special conveyances, and shoud communicate more, if my letters were secure, and to send expresses upon every occasion wou'd be an insufferable expense."[57] Nothing came of the supposed Russian offer of mediation, and in his letter to Hillsborough on 3 February 1781, Cumberland maintains that the Spanish Court has been guilty of trickery: "as for the *formal overtures* of Russia, fabricated by the Minister of this Court, the proofs of that Chicanery are too gross to escape detection, and the purpose of it too apparent to require an explanation."

France moved quickly to strengthen the appearance of her power. Admiral D'Estaing arrived in Spain, ostensibly to take command of the French fleets then gathering at Cadiz, and used the occasion to emphasize French sea power. Cumberland gives Shelbourne a full account: "About this time Count D'Estaing arrived at San Ildefonso under plea of taking command of the french Squadron, which had now rendezvous'd at Cadiz, and which was afterwards join'd by Monsieur de Guichen's fleet from the West Indies, composing jointly with the Spanish ships in that port the most respectable force that probably had ever anchor'd there before."[58] When the combined fleets subsequently intercepted the British East and West India Convoy, there seemed little reason for Spain to seek peace with England. At the very least Spain saw this as an opportunity to bargain for Gibraltar. Cumberland remained true to his instructions not to allow the subject to be discussed in his dealings with the Spanish, but when Abbé Hussey brought back to England an ultimatum concerning Gibraltar from Count Florida-blanca, negotiations broke down and Cumberland was recalled. Cumberland tells Shelbourne that the combined French and Spanish fleets sailed from Cadiz under the joint leadership of D'Estaing and the Spanish admiral, but difficulties at sea, resulting in substantial damage to the Spanish ships, gave D'Estaing an opportunity to head for the port of Brest. Although the stage had seemed set for a battle at sea, the French admiral had, in reality little confidence in his ability to meet the British fleet. "Count D'Estaing," Cumberland observes, "before his departure, had given a formal opinion by Letter, touching the impracticability of preventing the English fleet from releiving Gibraltar, or annoying them in the operation." The Spanish, disenchanted with D'Estaing, spoke of "the probability of his suffering by an Encounter with the English fleet." Cumberland was now received graciously, and at the Escorial he was treated to "many marks of grace and condescension from the Royal Family." The expected battle at sea did not take place: "A long period of anxious suspense elaps'd before any news arriv'd of the fleets; at length we were inform'd of Admiral Darby's return to England without any attempt against the French. It is needless to describe the Effects of this intelligence."[59] Cumberland felt, rightly or wrongly, that England had a major victory in its grasp and failed to take advantage of its opportunity. England's failure to act at sea, for all practical purposes, brought negotiations to an end.

Before leaving Madrid, Cumberland claims to have obtained "authentic proof that no formal overture of mediation had been made on the part of the Empress of Russia, as was pretended by the Minister of Spain. This appear'd, not only by the positive declaration of the Minister of Russia at Madrid, but more particularly from the copy of a Letter written by Count Florida Blanca to the Spanish chargé d'affaires at Petersburgh. By the same letter it also appear'd that he had confidentially communicated to the Russian Minister at Madrid the State of the Negotiation separate and immediate with the Court of Great Britain."[60] Cumberland discusses this matter fully in his letter to Hillsborough of 3 January 1781, enclosing translations of letters from Florida-blanca to Normande, the Spanish chargé d'affaires in Russia, and to the Minister of Russia in October and November of 1780.

Much vivid and personal information about Cumberland's visit to Spain may be gleaned from his letters, and his interest in society makes his account of considerable interest to the social historian. Writing to Germain on 25 May 1780, he describes the

intense heat of Portugal. "The thermometer," he complains, "for several days has never been below 80
degrees in the shade, and the Sun's action is intense: Lisbon is built of the whitest stone and
without the shade of trees, the soil also is white
and the hills are steep, with deep vallies, where
Circulation of aire is scarce perceivable." Cumberland details the Portuguese royal family's participation in a religious spectacle amidst the severe
heat: "Yesterday exhibited His Majesty of Portugal
with the Prince of Brazils walking the streets,
bareheaded in the flaming meridian sun, without a
canopy, following the Cardinal Patriarch of Lisbon
bearing the Host, in vestments of white damask and
silver embroider'd with gold and spangles underneath
a cloth of gold supported by six mitred abbots and
preceeded by the Knights of Christ with all the religious Orders bearing Crucifixes, Images and
chaunting as they walk'd." This five-hour procession, participated in by both religious and military
groups, fascinates Cumberland who is particularly
moved by the prostration of the military before the
Host: "Two entire Regiments pass'd me under arms,
which to my judgement, as to men and accoutrement,
were excellent, the whole Corps was prostrated in
the dust at the passing of the Host, and the attitude of the men with the action of the musquets with
fixt bayonets resting over the arms, and pointed
into the earth, had a touching effect." The Queen
did not take part in the procession, "but sat very
stately and erect in the Church."

Cumberland's accounts are often detailed and sometimes petty such as his observation that the Queen's
attire is "fine in jewels, particularly pearls," and
his noting that she was dressed "in an ill stile
both of cloathes and headdress."[61] Cumberland's a-
wareness of such details is not surprising since he
was accompanied by his wife and two daughters. In a
subsequent letter to Germain, he writes with pride
of the Spanish taking to English styles and admiring
his family. There is fatherly pride in his account

of their reception: "The girls enjoy themselves tolerably, but Sophia the best. They are much carest, and are the spectacle of the place, and have set the English fashions for every tittle of their dress from the Princess of Asturias downwards."[62]

Lisbon and its heat distressed Cumberland. "I wonder at myself for standing the heat, as I do," he observes. "The flies cover the table as we sit at our meals, and the bugs and fleas are another plague of Egypt." The city provided few comforts and lacked suitable shops: "Lisbon affords no one article that can be convey'd to the young ladies; its fruits and flowers woud perish and as for manufactures, it has none; the scourings of our shops form the chief ornament of their's, but they are not shops, they are hogstyes hung with penny ribbands."[63] As the Cumberlands moved on to Madrid, the heat was still oppressive, remaining at eighty-six degrees through the night, but they had suitable accommodations. "My house is very spacious," he writes, "well adapted to the climate, stands high and faces the north gate of the city and opens to the mountains. This has been the saving of our lives." While in Madrid his daughters went to the bull fights, and he was disturbed by the unaccustomed violence of the "shocking spectacle." One bullfight, in which three combatants and seven horses were killed, caused his daughters to suffer "more than words can relate."[64]

In Madrid Cumberland explored the cultural side of Spanish life, and, after returning to England, published a small two-volume history of Spanish painting. Moreover, the account in his *Memoirs* of his visits to the Escurial and its vast art treasures is fresh and interesting. He finds no beauty in the externals of the edifice, concluding that the architect had to sacrifice beauty and proportion to the security needed to protect it from the winds sweeping down from the mountains. But the "immense edifice" contained "abundant food for curiosity in paintings, books and consecrated treasures exceeding all description."[66] Cumberland plays the art critic as he appraises the work of Raphael, Titian, Rubens, Velasquez and Coello. Of special interest is his description of his visit on a second occasion to the Escurial when the King was in residence. Among other anecdotes, he relates how, while walking through the King's apartments, he inadvertently surprised the monarch in his bedroom "on his knees before his private altar." The King, whom Cumberland characterizes as "one of the best tempered men living," asked him to stay, and took the trouble to show him "some very curious South American deer, extremely small and elegantly formed, which he kept under a netting; and amongst others a little green monkey, the most diminutive and most beautiful of its species" he had ever seen.[67]

Cumberland's *Memoirs* fill out our knowledge of the reception he received in Spain. The letters point to an uneven welcome, varying in its warmth in proportion to the state of the diplomatic situation. But his recollection of events years later suggests a more uniform cordiality on the part of the King and members of the nobility he met. Writing to Germain on 30 August 1780 he notes that "My girls have visited in the houses of Osuna and Benevento, but I was present at only one visit." He is more effusive in his account of such contacts in his *Memoirs.* On good terms with the Prince of Asturias, he enthusiastically describes his family's reception on a formal visit to the Prince's "elegant pavilion," which was a short distance from the Escorial. "The Dukes of Alva, Grenada, Almodovar and others of high rank" accompanied them through the building and asked his opinion of the decor. Cumberland's vanity was generously fed when the Prince completely redecorated the principal room at Cumberland's suggestion.[68]

The friendship Cumberland had developed with Count Kaunitz, the Austrian ambassador to Spain, encouraged him to suggest that he be the English representative at any "Congress of the Belligerent Powers at Vienna or elsewhere." Kaunitz, who was romantically attracted to Cumberland's oldest daughter, was a

constant visitor to the dramatist's residence while
he was in Spain. Speaking of his possible service on
a peace commission, Cumberland observes to Germain:
"I should not offer such an idea to your Lordship,
if I did not know in what place the report of Count
Kaunitz had put me with his Father and his Court,
and what had passed between them and him on that occasion. The daily intercourse of Count Kaunitz in my
family, and his personal Correspondence with the Emperor, warrants me to say what otherwise I shoud not
have said."[69]

The bulk of Cumberland's letters concerning Spain
were to Hillsborough and Germain, and there is an
easily discernible difference in his attitude toward
the two men. Although each had been his superior at
the Board of Trade, only Germain, who elevated Cumberland to Secretary, became a close friend.   There
is always a practiced respect and distance in his
correspondence with Hillsborough, but with Germain
the clear marks of friendship are evident. Cumberland had first come into contact with Germain when,
as a young man, he acted as an observer for Bubb
Dodington at Germain's trial for his conduct at the
battle of Minden.[70] In that battle, Prince Ferdinand
of Brunswick had been able to achieve victory over
the French in an engagement that was largely fought
by six English infantry regiments. Germain, then a
Colonel and Commander of the English cavalry, refused an order to advance and took no part in the
battle. Convicted by court-martial, he suffered total disgrace when the decision of the Court was read
out at the head of every regiment, asserting that
Germain was unfit to serve the King in any capacity.

After years of being shunned by society, Germain
returned to public life following the accession to
the throne of George III and, as Secretary of State
for the Colonies from 1775 to 1782, was further
criticized for his part in the conduct of the war in
America. Cumberland eulogizes his friend in a pamphlet published after his death in 1785,[71] defending
him against the allegation that he was a cunning

person by attributing his lack of cummunicativness to a naturally reserved temper and thoughtful disposition. He praises Germain's benevolent instincts, which made him a "friend and father to his servants," and his practical and unostentatious charity, which was "no less the excercise of judgment than of the heart" and directed to the spiritual as well as physical needs of the poor.[72] Cumberland recalls Germain's final words at their last meeting, two days before the statesman's death: "You see me now in those moments, when no disguise will serve, and when the spirit of a man must be proved; I have a mind perfectly resigned, and at peace within itself: I have no more to do with this world, and what I have done in it, I have done for the best; I hope and trust I am prepared for the next. Tell me not of all that passes in health and pride of heart, these are the moments in which a man must be searched;-- and remember, that I die, as you see me, happy and content."[73] These are such words as Cumberland's moral sense and feeling for the dramatic could appreciate. As Germain's neighbour at Tunbridge Wells he had learned to admire him, and the public conduct of the American war or the actions taken years before at Minden were less significant than the the moral equation the man represented.

Cumberland's friendship for Germain, however, did not help him achieve adequate compensation for his Spanish mission. On his journey home, he found his credit cut off, and he might well have been imprisoned for debt in France had not a Spanish friend come to his aid with a loan of five-hundred pounds to enable him to complete his journey. Signs of trouble emerged while Cumberland was still at Madrid and he complains to John Robinson that "my banker informs me of a difficulty, which has arisen in replacing the bills, which I have had occasion to draw upon him for the expences of my commission at this court."[74] His detailed defense of his expenditures emphasizes the economy with which he handled his affairs. But the plea brought no help, and on his re-

turn journey through France, he writes to Germain
from Bayonne on 28 April 1781 asking for help. He
has been at "death's door with a violent fever," he
notes, and his credit has been stopped at both Paris
and Bordeaux. "What effect this may have on a skeleton, scarce convalescent; God only knows," he comments, adding that, although "providentially" he has
"found a friend to answer for" him and he will be
able to pass to England, he desires Germain's help
in adjusting matters with the government.

Cumberland's *Memoirs* contains his "Memorial" to
Lord North, unsuccessfully seeking compensation for
his journey.[75] A similar memorial to Lord Rockingham
on 5 April 1782 includes interesting details of the
dramatist's predicament and reveals matters not
found in that to North. Cumberland had supported the
activities of Abbé Hussey in the amount of £518. and
had defrayed the cost of special messengers with
dispatches to London, costing £156. He had obtained
information and transfered papers and records for
which he advanced the sum of £350. In addition, following the capture of the East and West India
fleets, he had obtained through Florida-blanca the
liberation of prisoners, and through the Bishop of
Burgos the freedom of "certain British Seamen who
had settled in that Capital embracing the Roman
Catholic Religion." He complains of North's neglect,
observing that "Your Memorialist during a most painful soliciatation of ten Months was but once admitted to the presence of Lord North and never favored
with any answer to his Letters or Petitions." Although he understands that a decision had been made
to pay him as an "Envoy Extraordinary" at a sum of
five pounds a day from the time he left until he returned, he has received no such remuneration. Cumberland calculates the sum of his individual dis-
bursements to be £1058., and requests payment of
that amount, together with "such Allowance for the
extraordinary Expenses of his Journies, as to your
Lordship's discretion may seem meet."[76]

Cumberland never felt he had been fully compensated and as late as 5 January 1801, he was still trying to obtain justice from the Fourth Earl of Buckinghamshire, the then Secretary of War and a brother of the widow of his son, Richard. He emphasizes that following his journey "there was not the smallest charge against me, the King was graciously pleas'd to approve of my service, and to accept of the Royal Horses." Lord North and his successor, Shelbourne, ignored his pleas, but Fox, as Secretary of State and acting on the advice of the Duke of Portland, authorized payment of about £1300., "which was all I then ventur'd to pray for, intimidated and desponding as I was by such a course of disappointments." Cumberland recalls details of his desperate financial situation. He had been forced to sell his "wife's jointure" to replace his overdraft at his bank and his position at the Board of trade had been abolished with a settlement worth only half its previous value. "I have been from that period to the present," he complains, "tho' divesting myself of everything that can be call'd superfluity, been struggling to uphold myself and family against the pressure of the time, with the painful reflection ever present to my mind, that at the advanc'd age of near seventy years, I am departing out of life without leaving any provisions for a wife, whose jointure I was oblig'd to Sacrifice in the extremity of my unmerited distress." Cumberland was to survive his wife and to live for another decade, faced with a constant struggle for survival in which he poured out plays, essays, and a novel in his effort to ward off disaster. His final estate, which he left mainly to his youngest daughter, Marianne, who cared for him in his declining years, was less than £450.[77]

Despite the personal disappointment, diplomatic failure, and financial problems that resulted from his Spanish journey, Cumberland found that it indirectly brought him a measure of social reward. His monetary reverses forced him to retrench and move to Tunbridge Wells, where as part of its interesting society he came into intimate contact with Germain, developed a close association with Lord North, and began a strong friendship with Sir James Bland Burgess.

IV

From Tunbridge Wells Cumberland continued his work for the stage, but his correspondence contributes little to our knowledge of his dramatic activities. At the end of the century he achieved great success with the production of *The Jew* (1794) and *The Wheel of Fortune* (1795), both of which capitalize on the intensification of literary sentiment at the end of the century. Cumberland found himself once more one of the leading dramatists on the London stage. But the intervening years had not been kind, and, although his theatrical pen had been consistently active, the taste of major success had eluded him.

Two letters to George Colman, then manager of the Little Theatre in the Haymarket, reveal the tenuous state of the dramatist's fortunes. On 30 April 1787 Cumberland wrote to Colman regarding his projected comedy, *The Country Attorney*, which was acted first on 7 July 1787 and performed only four times. Cumberland's deferential appeal concludes, "If your opinion shoud revolt against it, I repeat to you my assurances, that however I may be disappointed in my wishes to enlist myself as your author, I shall not cease to be your friend and very faithfull servant." Once the play had been accepted Cumberland began to have problems with the leading lady, Elizabeth Farren, and he reluctantly submitted to her suggestions about the role of Lady Rustic, which she was scheduled to play. "I have just received your letter dignifying Miss Farren's commands for transposing her Introductory Scene to the Second Act. Be it so!" he later writes, and adds, with unmistakable annoyance: "For Heaven's sake write her an Epilogue; I have plung'd from thought to thought in the profound of nonsense and can fix upon nothing--"[78]

The Country Attorney is one of the few laughing

comedies that Cumberland attempted. He found himself uncomfortable away from his usual themes of sensibility, and two years later tried to salvage the play by recasting it along lines more congenial to his romantic instincts, working closely with the great actress Frances Abington. Mrs. Abington and Cumberland were concerned about offering *The School for Widows* to one of the theatres in view of the failure of its source, *The Country Attorney*. Mrs. Abington apparently wanted to offer it anonymously, but with her committed to act the leading role. Cumberland questioned the omission of his name: "I submit to you," he observes, "if it may not be proper to let Mr. Harris [of Covent Garden] know his Author, and if he will meet me on Tuesday Night...the business might be put in trim, and the copy delivered to the transcriber."[79] The play was finally acted on 8 May 1789, but withdrawn after only three performances.[80] Cumberland protests, perhaps too vehemently, that he neither does, "nor ever did, experience any real vexation for the treatment" he received from Harris, and finds comfort in Mrs. Abington's encouragement of his efforts: "I have had a piece well approved, and you have been the supporter of it's introduction, representation and success."[81] Although Mrs. Abington continued her support of the drama, and Cumberland expresses his gratitude for her "kind and zealous negotiation" in his letter of 21 May 1789, his hopes for the play's successful presentation again that season were not realized.

During this period, Cumberland wrote, in addition to his dramas, two novels, *Arundel* (1789) and *Henry* (1795), five volumes of essays, *The Observer* (1786-1790), and an epic poem, *Calvary* (1795), drawing in all of these tasks great strength from his neighbours at Tunbridge Wells. Although his friendship with Germain ended with the statesman's death in 1785, he continued to enjoy associations with political figures, notably Lord North who had retired to Tunbridge Wells at the end of his long career in government. Before North's death in 1792, Cumberland

had come to know him well. "Some hours (and those
not few) of his society," Cumberland notes regarding
North in his *Memoirs*, "he was kind in bestowing upon
me: I eagerly courted and very hightly prized
them."[82] The dramatist was impressed by the equanim-
ity with which North endured his blindness and by
the vitality of his intellectual interests in the
waning years of his life. In view of his conviction
that North had not treated him justly after his
Spanish mission, Cumberland's characterization is
all the more remarkable: "To his acquaintances and
friends he was all complacency; to his family all
affection: he was generous, hospitable, open-handed,
and loved his ease infinitely too well to sacrifice
any portion of it to a solicitude about money."[83]
Perhaps Cumberland's attitude is best indicated in
his observation that "the minister indeed has
wronged me, but the man atones."[84]

Although Lord North was the most famous of Cumberland's friends among Tunbridge Wells society at the
end of the century, he found, in addition, "many
valuable characters, many candid and engenius
men."[85] He is strongly touched in these later years
by the sadness of old age, and he laments, "What a
multitude of past friends can I number amongst the
dead! It is the melancholy consequence of old age;
if we outlive our feelings we are nothing worth; if
they remain in force, a thousand sad occurrences remind us that we live too long."[86]

Cumberland's letters record his enduring and sat-
isfying friendship with Sir James Bland Burgess, who
for a time lived near him in Tunbridge Wells. Burgess was just the type of man to appeal to Cumberland, studious, retentive of memory, and possessed
of wide and varied knowledge. His education at Westminster School and at Oxford had provided good prep-
aration for his study of the law, and he served in
Parliament and in a number of minor public offices
before becoming an amateur author in his retirement.
In this endeavor he found a strong supporter in Cumberland.

Burgess's first major effort was a long epic poem
Richard the First, which received a careful reading
and some technical help from Cumberland.[87] Writing
to Burgess on 30 January 1801, the dramatist con-
gratulates his friend on his success and characteristically adds reflections on fame: "I rejoice to
hear well of your Richard in his outset; contemporary praise is not always the lot of Merit to obtain.
Your claim is of so striking a sort, that I little
doubted of your gaining present fame, and I was perfectly sure your work would secure future fame to
itself, when jealousy and cavil had exhausted their
spite."

The critical acceptance of *Richard the First*'s did
not last, but it was sufficient to encourage the two
men to collaborate on a joint poetic venture, *The
Exodiad*. Its evolution can be traced through Cumberland's letters to his friend. The plan for the poem
seems to have been largely that of Burgess, although
the final execution of it was likely the result of
the persistent concern of Cumberland who had a-
chieved recognition some years before with the
publication of *Calvary*, a continuation of the Biblical story developed in Milton's two epic poems. *The
Exodiad* seeks to dramatize the journey of the He-
brews from Egypt to the promised land. Serious work
on the poem must have begun in the fall of 1805, for
in a letter to Burgess, noting the near completion
of his work on his *Memoirs*, Cumberland urges his
friend to take up the effort once more: "If I live
to see you I wish you woud prepare yourself by a revision of our *Exodiad* to put that work in further
train, for I am within two or three days of closing
up my book..."[88]

Within a year Cumberland is well into the second
book of the poem and has already discussed its publication with George Lackington, who was at the time
producing Cumberland's *Memoirs*. In his letter of 3
November 1806, he discusses matters of copyright and
contract with Burgess, expressing his hope that the
appearance of the *Memoirs* will help them: "The Octa-

vo Memoirs with the supplement will be out in a fortnight, and I hope will prove instrumental as advertisers of the poem, and smoothe the way in some degree for its appearance."

As the writing of the poem continued, Cumberland expresses his growing weariness with the work: "To confess the truth the task of the Exodiad is no light one...Composition of this sort is laborious, and, as I have not been in high health, requires the relief of lighter studies, which offer themselves in the person of De Lancaster."[89] Cumberland's change of pace was work on his third novel *John de Lancaster*, which he published three years later in 1809.

The Exodiad was produced despite all difficulties, although its success was endangered by the almost simultaneous appearance of William Sotheby's epic, *Saul.* Cumberland tries to be optimistic about the news in his letter of 31 December 1806: "I receive this welcome news with joy, as I doubt not but the production of Sotherby's Saul will reflect honour on the age we live in, which from the date of Calvary will have given birth to as many epics as the world can number for I know not how many generations." Out of touch as Cumberland's sensibilities are with the emerging force of Romantic poetry, he interestingly focusses on the curiously anacronistic resurgence of epic poetry when he observes that "the proper character of our National Genius is the Epic, and the proper tone of our language is heroic blank verse. Sotherby has found it out; Bowles possesses it, but Madoc has no ear."

The element of competition was very much in Cumberland's mind as the time of publication approached. By 30 January 1807 he has learned that another poet is at work on a poem dealing with the same subject. He unconvincingly tells Burgess that he hopes their rival will succeed, suggesting that "there are more bay-trees on Parnassus, than there are heads to be crowned by their branches." Moreover his advice to Burgess "to keep the work warm, whilst we are upon it" betrays more concern than is evident from his later observation that he sees "no spur to quicken us beyond our natural speed, that can have any reference of the Exodus of Mr. Hoyle."

The publication of *The Exodiad* on "the very same day and hour" as Sotheby's *Saul* prompts Cumberland to observe of *Saul*, "You was right in your conjecture--too right, for I find the metre horrible, and the diction infinitely below par." The appearance of their own volume, "one of the most beautiful samples of the Art of Mr. Wright, that was ever exhibited,"[90] however, pleases him. Although the reception of the poem was disappointing, Cumberland is not surprised: "We have had little circulation as yet, but not less than I expected; for the Town has had something else to do besides reading sacred poems." The Scotch critics ignored *The Exodiad* while reviewing the rival poem. Cumberland's account of their comments betrays a trace of envy: "Saul has been review'd by the Edenboro Critics, and tho' it has not escaped censure, yet it has been treated with lenity, and the author prais'd for his other works; so that it is plain he was in favour with them, of which I was aware. Of us they say nothing."[91]

The composition of *The Exodiad* fell largely on Cumberland because of Burgess's preoccupation with writing for the stage. Perhaps on Cumberland's suggestion that "the moment is seasonable for the production of your Rhodian at Covent Garden,"[92] Burgess unsuccessfully submitted the drama to that theater. Cumberland assures his friend early in November, 1805, that he is not a theatrical rival: "I must write to you again," he emphasizes, "to say you are not correctly inform'd as to my tendering any thing to Mr. Harris, which coud be put into competition with your drama, or coud in any degree bias his judgement with respect to it."[93] Cumberland had indeed sent Harris *The Sicilian Banditti*, "an old comic opera" based on "The Armorer", a musical play produced unsuccessfully years before, and a slight, patriotic eulogy of Admiral Nelson's victory and death that could in no sense be regarded as a drama.

Neither work was a threat to Burgess.[94]

Burgess was experiencing the unusual difficulties of a new name in the theater, and although Cumberland is prepared to do battle for his friend, he is pessimistic about the play's chances: "My expectations on the subject point naturally to the repelling pole;...and tho' I am prepar'd to hear him [Harris] on one side, I am resolv'd he shall hear my full opinion on the other." But he still holds out hope of eventual success at the rival theater: "If Mr. Harris returns your play, and I live till next season, I shall hope to see it on the stage of Drury."[95] Burgess, despite his lack of success with the tragedy, was not deterred from trying again with a comedy, *Welcome Home*. Cumberland is still not optimistic: "Whilst you have the consciousness of writing such a play as *Welcome Home*, you ought on no account to concern yourself about any measures, which the proprietors of a stage, devoted to spectacle alone, may take either against it, or for it. I am very glad they don't act, for I don't think it quite ripe for acting, and, if it was, I do not think they are quite the people to perform it. You will complete it, and what is it to you how they estimate your production."[96]

Theatrical practices had changed substantially as the eighteenth century came to an end, and Cumberland, both in his *Memoirs* and elsewhere, laments the disintegration of taste and the movement away from legitimate comedy and tragedy toward a growing emphasis on spectacle. Drury Lane was greatly enlarged to accommodate about 3500 patrons. A theatre of that size militated against intimate comedy or tragedy and placed emphasis on music and visual effects. Although the popularity of plays had increased substantially throughout England, the economic state of the theater in London was poor, particularly after both Drury Lane and Covent Garden burned in 1808 and 1809. In a letter to Burgess, Cumberland reflects on the gloomy outlook for Sheridan at Drury Lane. "When he talks of re-building Drury Lane, and erecting a third theatre, if occasion call'd for it, he must first extinguish or compromise a debt, which lies upon the ruins to the amount of £300,000., before he can execute the first object." At the major rival theatre the situation was little better. "I can form no guess about the fate of Covent Garden, Cumberland notes. "Every day sinks them deeper in decay. The popular rage against Kemble seems to shut him from the stage for a length of time, perhaps forever. I think the private boxes must be given up, and they produce £12,000. per annum. They cannot now receed from their new prices, and whilst the mob persists, their treasury is starv'd. The Lyceum is the only theatre, that gentle folks can go to; but the government is of that mixt sort, which cannot act with decision, and such in fact as no man of talents can trust, or be concern'd with." He concludes in a mood of despair: "Well may genius appear to be inert in a period like this."[97]

In 1802 Cumberland and Burgess were associated with an unsuccessful weekly newspaper, *Pic Nic*, which was tangentially associated with the creation of the Pic Nic Society, a dining club that put on private theatrical entertainments. Opposition from the legitimate theaters, that saw in the growth of the society a serious financial threat, ultimately forced its dissolution but provided satiric grist to the mill of the journal which was founded by Colonel Henry Greville and which included among its contributors, in additon to Cumberland and Burgess, John Wilson Croker and James and Horace Smith. William Combe, one of the most experienced writers of the time, despite his virtual anonymity, was employed as its editor. The newspaper lasted only twelve issues, but was continued briefly by Greville as *The Cabinet.* Its dissolution was not effected harmoniously, as Cumberland suggests in a consolatory letter to Burgess: "Pray don't demean yourself to waste a word of anger or resentment upon Greville, such follies are but feathers in the scale of a substantial mind. I never knew a wise man right in arguing with a silly one."[98]

Cumberland discusses the death of *Pic Nic* in a letter to Burgess on 27 June 1803. "We had a meeting last Night," he notes, "at which Mr. Greville attended, and signified his intention of carrying the Cabinet on upon his own account, and at his own risque. He brought an Irish man with him, who wrote the Essay in the last No. sign'd N., who seems likely to be his chief coadjutor. With the ensuing Number therefore we conclude: It was the sense of *The Committee* to fill it up on the spot, and it is full. Combe is dismiss's from being Editor, Mr. Herries is exonerated from any future pledge on the part of Government,...."

In a previous letter to Burgess, Cumberland anticipates the demise of the paper and asserts his fundamental loyalty to his friend. "I think myself bound in common with the amiable Smiths to the twelve papers,..." he notes, but "Beyond that, my answer to any speculation will be simply, that I will do as Sir Jas. Burgess does." He joins Burgess in his distaste for Greville: "With Greville I cannot act any more than you can, so it is no compliment to say I am as you are in that connection."[99]

Cumberland shared with most of his countrymen their great concern over the threat of an invasion of England by Napoleon during the early nineteenth century. Always an intense patriot, he anticipated the possibility of a need to defend the English countryside and discusses with Burgess, in a letter on 30 January 1801, his recently formed company of volunteers: "The Corps is just now in the crisis of receiving their second supply of arms and second lot of officers, when my presence becomes useful at least, if not necessary." During the first few years of the century, the government disputed the relative value of voluntary militia versus regular troops for the defense of England and support was withdrawn from the volunteers in a crucial vote in 1803.[100] Cumberland tells Burgess of his change in attitude: "I beg leave to say in confidence to you that I have

no wish to turn out again upon such Propositions, as
are now made; and I see the business of Volunteering
in so different a light from what it was before we
broke up, and am so perfectly unable to uphold the
outgoings of the Corps at my own expence, that if
the men are not resolute to stand forward and as a
full company, I shall be most entirely content to
stay at home."[101] Cumberland did, however, remain
involved with the volunteers and two years later
speaks of his pleasure in their local efforts: "I
beg my respects to Lady Burgess, and be pleas'd to
tell her that when I turn'd out the Corps, whom she
has honour's with her patronage, not a single man
hesitated to stand by their Colours,..."[102]

Cumberland reflects the way ordinary Englishmen
reacted to military and naval events during the summer of 1805 when the threat of invasion was particularly acute. In a letter postmarked 26 August 1805,
Cumberland conveys something of the uncertainty felt
in London. "The Naval Manoeuvres of our Enemy seem
to puzzle us," he writes to Burgess, "and opinions
here seem prevalent for invasion; the majority expecting it in Ireland, and some, but not many, on
our own shores." Earlier in the month, the French
admiral, Villeneuve, had been ordered to sea in an
effort to clear the Channel preparatory to a possible invasion. Fortunately for England, although she
was unaware of it at the time, the entrance of Austria into the war against France and Napoleon's decision to move against her temporarily ended the
threat.

Writing again to Burgess a month later, about 18
September 1805, Cumberland describes military and
naval activity at Ramsgate. "The sight of the Downs
has been wonderful and is still a wood of Masts; in
short the whole sea is alive, and my windows embrace
one of the greatest spectacles that can be conceiv'd. We have lost our friendly West Kents, and
the regiments of Perthshire, Lanerk and Renfrew are
now quarter'd with us and about us: Lord Mansfield
commands the Perth, and lodges within a few doors of

us. The 13th Drag., who live with us as friends, are on the wing, being under orders to be ready."[103]

The immediacy of these accounts is seen as well in his relation of the movement of German mercenaries, basing his information on a letter from his daugher, Marianne: "I am concern'd to find that 1400 of our Hanoverians embark'd yesterday from Ramsgate pier, and 1500 this day from the same spot. The whole a-mount in the course of the week will be 7000."[104] Cumberland's poetic and detailed letter of 31 December 1806 reveals the resentment underlying the hospitality shown the mercenaries at Ramsgate: "The old year is now taking leave of us in one of the brightest gleams of sunshine, that ever winter sky could boast of. The Sea is cover'd with ships; Above 300 sail are within our peer, and the Spectacle of the Downs is amazing. A German General commanding 900 mercenaries occupies this important post, and it justly gives offence: His band is now serenading Lord and Lady Edward Bentinck, and the compliment is justly due, for every officer finds hospitality and kindness there."

While Cumberland's letters to Burgess are more valuable to the literary and social historian than to the biographer, they still have value in revealing the depth of Cumberland's friendship for Burgess and the range and extent of his activities. The dramatist, who has often been regarded as ridiculous because of Sheridan's attribution of pettiness and self-concern to the character of Sir Fretful Plagiary in *The Critic*, a character widely accepted as a portrait of Cumberland, is seen in these letters as a man of considerable social dimension and strong patriotic instincts.

Cumberland's letters span half a century and carry the reader through different worlds: the fascinating panorama of the eighteenth-century stage, the world of foreign diplomacy and intrigue, and the cultivat-ed society of Tunbridge Wells. Cumberland provides a continuity that links these different aspects of late eighteenth-century life. He represents that

stolidity of the British character that permitted it
to survive the threat of revolution, the spectre of
invasion, and the reality of defeat in America. In
literature, Cumberland seems largely unaware of the
growing pressures and shifting tides of the Romantic
movement. But despite his political and literary
conservatism, he shared the instinct for benevolence
and social reform that was moving England toward the
great social changes that would take place before
the mid-nineteenth century. Unchanged in his basic
perspective, he lived to become, instead of a typi-
cal representative of his age, something of an
anachronism. The survival of the old in men like
Burgess and Cumberland perhaps permitted the revolu-
tionary changes of the new to take place without destroying order and peace at home. In this respect
his letters provide a record of personal continuity
and social evolution.

Endnotes

1. The most complete study of the entire corpus of Cumberland's works is Richard J. Dircks, *Richard Cumberland* (Boston, 1976). Stanley William, *Richard Cumberland, His Life and Dramatic Works* (New Haven, 1917) contains much detail regarding the plays and their production. The most important earlier sources of information are Cumberland's *Memoirs*, 2 vols. (London, 1807), and William Mudford, *The Life of Richard Cumberland*, 2 vols. (London 1812). There are, in addition, numerous references to him in contemporary letters, diaries and similar material, especially *Horace Walpole's Correspondence*, ed. W. S. Lewis, *et al.* (New Haven, 1937-), *The Letters of Samuel Johnson*, ed. R. W. Chapman, 3 vols., (Oxford, 1952); and *The Letters of David Garrick*, ed. David Little and George Kahrl, 3 vols. (Cambridge, Massachusetts, 1963).

2. Cumberland's duties under Halifax were for the most part routine. Disappointed at not being appointed an undersecretary when Halifax was named Secretary of State, Cumberland sought and obtained from Lord Hillsborough, Halifax' successor at the Board of Trade, the position of Clerk of Reports. Subsequently, when Lord George Germain headed the Board of Trade, he made Cumberland Secretary.

3. Cumberland seems to have been obsessed with the indignity of being a "dependent," and in his first novel, *Arundel*, he portrays the life of a young man compelled to serve as secretary to an overbearing nobleman. He observes in his *Memoirs* concerning his situation with Halifax: "I was not fitted for dependence; my nature was repugnant to it; I was most unfortunately formed with feelings, that could ill endure the assumed importance of some, or submit to take advantage of the weakness of others" (*Memoirs of Richard Cumberland*, I, 130).

4. *Memoirs*, I, 117-118; 76-77. Halifax bestowed one of the companies on Cumberland, who was at the time too young to take command.

5. Cumberland's impressions of Dodington and the society surrounding him are recorded in the *Memoirs*, I, 181-195). Cumberland is not mentioned in Dodington's *Diary*, which the dramatist had read: "I was...acquainted with his *diary*, which since his death has been published, and I well remember the temporary disgust he seemed to take, when upon asking what I would do with it, should he bequeath it to my discretion, I instantly replied that I would destroy it" (*Memoirs*, I, 194)

6. "I certainly did not make my court to him by this refusal," Cumberland notes in his *Memoirs* (I, 223).

7. William Mudford, *A Critical Examination of the Writings of Richard Cumberland*, 2 vols. (London, 1812).

8. D. D. Wallace in his *Constitutional History of South Carolina* (Abbeville, South Carolina, 1899) mentions a Mr. Bee who was a practicing attorney in South Carolina in 1766 (p. 40).

9. Although Cumberland parted from Halifax in 1762 on terms that have generally been regarded as less than amicable, he still felt, as late as 1767, that he could count on him for political support.

10. He asks Pinckney in his letter of 29 July 1767 to forward letters to Lord Charles Greville Montagu, the Provincial Governor, to George Saxby, and to "young" Guerard. Guerard is mentioned several times in the letters but is not further identified by Cumberland. Cumberland states in his covering letter regarding Guerard: "I have forgot his Christian name, so I must desire you to fill it up."

11. D. D. Wallace, *Constitutional History of South Carolina*, pp. 29-30.

12. 29 October 1769.

13. Wallace, *Constitutional History*, p. 29; Wallace, *The History of South Carolina*, 4 vols. (New York, 1934), I, 269.

14. 2 July 1766.

15. *Ibid.*

16. 1 January 1767.

17. Cumberland speaks of the possibility of Pinckney's taking a seat in the Assembly in his letter of 15 March 1769. No further mention of it is made in the remaining correspondence, including three letters written in 1770, when the two men were still on most amicable terms.

18. After 21 March 1768.

19. Always one to husband his material, Cumberland produced a

play dealing with the same topic and containing many of the same characters some years later on 8 March 1785 as *The Arab*, but it survived only one performance. He seems to have tinkered with the play most of his life, and a further development of it is found among his *Posthumous Dramatic Works* (1813) as *Alcanor*.

20. In his letter to Garrick 4 July 1771.

21. Garrick to Cumberland, 27 June 1773. In *The Letters of David Garrick*, ed. David Little and George Kahrl, 1963, #781, Vol. II, 882.

22. 30 June 1773.

23. *Letters of Garrick*, 29 August 1774, #856, Vol. III, 952.

24. *Letters of Garrick*, 5 September 1774, #860, Vol. III, 956.

25. 11 November 1774.

26. 14 December 1774.

27. *The London Stage*, Part IV, ed. George Winchester Stone, Jr., (1962), Vol. III, 1857.

28. 19 December 1774.

29. *Letters of Garrick*, 28 December 1774, #875, Vol. III, 973.
30. *Letters of Garrick*, 28 January 1775, #890, Vol. III, 987.

31. The letter from Cumberland to Garrick is undated, but clearly was written about 28 January 1775, the date of Garrick's letter to Mrs. Abington.

32. *Letters of Garrick*, "Appendix F," Vol. III, 1360.

33. 17 February 1776.

34. Garrick's intercession with Sheridan on Cumberland's behalf is made clear in the letter to Sheridan of 9 January: "I am informed by Mr. Garrick that you have been so obliging to express a readiness to receive a tragedy of my writing...."

35. *Memoirs*, II, 210.

36. *Memoirs*, I, 332-333.

37. "I was silly enough to send this comedy into the world with a dedication to the Duke of Grafton, a man, with whom I had not the slightest acquaintance, nor did I seek to establish any upon the merit of this address: he was Chancellor of the University of Cambridge, and this was my sole motive for inscribing my first comedy to him" (*Memoirs*, I, 268).

38. 4 July 1771.

39. 5 August 1771.

40. 4 July 1771.

41. 2 October 1771.

42. 12 January 1778.

43. *Memoirs*, I, 369-370.

44. 14 March 1774. Goldsmith's "dishes," published under the title of *Retaliation*, appeared in 1774. See Richard J. Dircks, "The Genesis and Date of Goldsmith's *Retaliation*," *Modern Philology* (August 1977), 48-53.

45. *Memoirs*, I, 369-372.

46. On Cumberland's mission to Spain see Samuel Flagg Bemis, *The Hussey-Cumberland Mission and American Independence* (Princeton, 1931) and J. Homer Caskey, "Richard Cumberland's Mission to Spain," *Philological Quarterly*, IX (1930), 82-86.

47. *Memoirs*, I, 414-432; II, 1-172.

48. The account prepared for Shelbourn and the letters to Germain are located in manuscript in the Clements Library at the University of Michigan.

49. Shelbourne manuscript, p. 1.

50. 20 November 1779.

51. Shelbourne manuscript, p. 2.

52. Shelbourne manuscript, p. 3.

53. Shelbourne manuscript, p. 4.

54. Cumberland suggests that Galvez had personal motives for his actions: "assuring himself of a successful issue to his projected attack upon West Florida, to which he had destined a powerful armament and obtain'd the Command for his Nephew, he form'd high Expectations from a continuance of the War" (Shelbourne Manuscript, p. 5).

55. Cumberland to Campo, 23 July 1780.

56. 24 July 1780.

57. 4 August 1780.

58. Shelbourne manuscript, p. 7.

59. Shelbourne manuscript, pp. 10-11.

60. Shelbourne manuscript, pp. 12-13.

61. 25 May 1780.

62. Germain, 4 August 1780.

63. 26 May 1780.

64. Germain, 4 August 1780.

65. *Anecdotes of Eminent Painters in Spain*, 2 vols. (London, 1782).

66. *Memoirs*, II, 78.

67. *Memoirs*, II, 80.

68. *Memoirs*, II, 84-85.

69. 11 February 1781.

70. *Memoirs*, II, 245-246.

71. *Character of the Late Viscount Sackville* (London, 1785).

72. *Character of Sackville*, pp. 14-15.

73. *Character of Sackville*, pp. 22-23.

74. 8 March 1781.

75. *Memoirs*, II, 166-171.

76. The "Memorial" to Rockingham is in manuscript in the Clements Library at the University of Michigan.

77. Cumberland's will was published in Mudford's *Life of Cumberland*, pp. 597-600. In addition to its cash value, the estate included rights to his unpublished plays which appeared as *The Posthumous Dramatic Works of the Late Richard Cumberland* (London, 1813).

78. Before 7 July 1787.

79. Before 8 May 1789.

80. John Genest, *Some Account of the English Stage* (Bath, 1832), VI, 551.

81. 17 May 1789.

82. *Memoirs*, II, 174.

83. *Memoirs*, II, 350.

84. *Memoirs*, II, 349.

85. *Memoirs*, II, 359.

86. *Memoirs*, II, 359.

87. *Richard the First: a Poem*. By Sir James B. Burgess, "containing corrections and emendations by R. C." (1800).

88. On or Before 18 September 1805.

89. Before April 1806.

90. 24 March 1807.

91. May 1807.

92. Fall of 1805.

93. 1 November 1805.

94. *The Sicilian Banditti* was never produced, but the "Melodramatic Piece" eulogizing Admiral Nelson was performed at Covent Garden on 7 November 1805.

95. After 14 November 1805.

96. Late 1806.

97. After 18 September 1809.

98. About July 1803.

99. 26 June 1803.

100. J. Steven Watson describes the situation following the passage of the second militia bill in 1803: "The patriotic vol-

unteers found, therefore, that when they rushed to help their
country they were coldly received, their expense allowances reduced, and a pike at most put into their hands" (*The Reign of
George III*, p. 416).

101. 26 June 1803.

102. 3 September 1805.

103. On or Before 18 September 1805.

104. 5 November 1805.

Editorial Procedure

The text of the letters included in this edition
is based on manuscripts in Cumberland's hand, on a
few manuscripts in other hands but clearly copies of
original letters of Cumberland, and on previously
printed texts. In all cases the source of the material has been indicated. In letters reproduced from
manuscript, I have, where clarity required it, mod-
ernized Cumberland's use of certain marks of abbre-
viation, such as "&" for "and", and "y^e" for "the."
In a relatively few instances, I have completed some
words abbreviated by Cumberland, but where I have
done so, I have indicated the addition in brackets.
In most cases I have not altered Cumberland's punc-
tuation, even in those instances where it is unusual
according to modern custom. Letters drawn from previously printed sources have been reproduced without
change.

Many of Cumberland's letters are only partially
dated by him, or not dated at all. I have either established the exact date, conjectured it, or indicated the approximate year or month as closely as
possible from the content of the letters. In all
cases I have given the basis for my editorializing.
In the very few cases in which it has been necessary
to conjecture the name of the correspondent, I have
supplied my reasons for doing so. In a few cases I
have had to leave a letter unidentified as to either
correspondent or date. The source of each letter is
indicated in the notes in an abbreviated form, but
full acknowledgement is given in the list of sources
preceding the text of the letters.

Sources

The letters in this collection have been drawn
from manuscripts in the following collections and
are published with permission:

The Beinecke Library, Yale University
The Berg Collection in The New York Public Library
The Bodleian Library, Oxford, England
The Boston Public Library
The British Library
The British Science Museum
The Clements Library, University of Michigan
The Columbia University Library
The Folger Shakespeare Library
The Harvard University Library
The Historical Society of Pennsylvania
The Library of Congress, Washington, D. C.
The Massachusetts Historical Society
The Princeton University Library
The Sheffield City Library, Sheffield, England

Additional letters have been drawn from the following published books:

The Cumberland Letters, ed. Clementinia Black,
(London, 1912).
The Memoirs of Richard Cumberland, 2 vols., (Lon-
don, 1807).
Mudford, William. *A Critical Examination of the
Writings of Richard Cumberland*, 2 vols., (London,
1812).
The Private Correspondence of David Garrick, ed.
James Boaden, 2 vols., (London, 1831-1832).

Letters in this Collection

1. Charles Jenkinson. 28 May 1764. BL.
2. Roger Pinckney. 30 September 1764 M.
3. Roger Pinckney. 1 October 1764. M.
4. Roger Pinckney. 8 February 1765. M.
5. Roger Pinckney. 27 February 1765. M.
6. Roger Pinckney. 18 March 1765. M.
7. Roger Pinckney. 31 July 1765. M.
8. Roger Pinckney. 30 August 1765. M.
9. Roger Pinckney. 15 January 1766. M.
10. Roger Pinckney. 2 July 1766. M.
11. Roger Pinckney. 1 January 1767. M.
12. Roger Pinckney. 30 January 1767. M.
13. Roger Pinckney. 3 June 1767. M.
14. Roger Pinckney. 8 July 1767. M.
15. Roger Pinckney. 29 July 1767. M.
16. [Benjamin] Guerard. 29 July 1767. M.
17. George Saxby. 29 July 1767. M.
18. Roger Pinckney. 17 October 1767. M.
19. David Garrick. Before 26 January 1768. BSM.
20. David Garrick. 26 January 1768. BSM.
21. David Garrick. 7 February 1768. BSM.
22. David Garrick. 21 March 1768. BOA.
23. David Garrick. After 21 March 1768. BSM.
24. Roger Pinckney. 15 August 1768. M.
25. Roger Pinckney. 12 October 1768. M.
26. Roger Pinckney. 27 October 1768. M.
27. Roger Pinckney. 15 March 1769. M.
28. David Garrick. 25 January 1770. BSM.
29. David Garrick. 17 March 1770. BSM.
30. Roger Pinckney. 1 May 1770. M.
31. Roger Pinckney. 11 June, 1770. M.
32. David Garrick. 24 June, 1770. F.
33. David Garrick. 2 July 1770. BSM.

34. George Romney. 30 September [1770]. Y.
35. Roger Pinckney. 13 November 1770. M.
36. George Romney. 30 March 1771. Y.
37. David Garrick. 4 July 1771. BSM.
38. David Garrick. 13 July 1771. H.
39. David Garrick. 5 August 1771. BSM.
40. David Garrick. 8 September 1771. BSM.
41. David Garrick. 2 October 1771. BSM.
42. David Garrick. After 28 October 1771. BSM.
43. Elizabeth Cumberland. 27 November 1771. B.
44. Richard D. Cumberland. 16 February 1772. B.
45. George Ashby. 16 November 1772. B.
46. George Ashby. Probably 23 December 1772. BL.
47. David Garrick. 26 June 1773. BSM.
48. David Garrick. 30 June 1773. BSM.
49. David Garrick. 14 March 1774. BSM.
50. George Romney. 14 August 1774. Y.
51. David Garrick. 23 October 1774. BSM.
52. David Garrick. 11 November 1774. BSM.
53. David Garrick. About 18 November 1774. BSM.
54. David Garrick. 24 November 1774. BSM.
55. David Garrick. 27 November 1774. BSM.
56. David Garrick. 1 December 1774. BSM.
57. David Garrick. 2 December 1774. BSM.
58. David Garrick. 3 December 1774. BSM.
59. David Garrick. 10 December 1774. BSM.
60. David Garrick. About 12 December 1774. BSM.
61. David Garrick. 13 December 1774. BSM.
62. David Garrick. 14 December 1774. BSM.
63. David Garrick. 17 December 1774. BSM.
64. David Garrick. 19 December 1774. BSM.
65. David Garrick. About 28 January 1775. BSM.
66. Roger Pinckney. 28 July 1775. M.
67. George Romney. July or August 1775. Y.
68. [Henry Wilmot]. After 16 January 1776. HSP.
69. David Garrick. 20 January 1776. BSM.
70. Sir Grey Cooper. 1 February 1776. LC.
71. George Colman. 17 February 1776. HSP.
72. David Garrick. 16 June 1776. BSM.
73. John Robinson. 11 November 1776. LC.
74. Henry Wilmot. 19 November 1776. HSP.

75. [Thomas Cadell]. 29 December 1776. HSP.
76. [Thomas Cadell]. After 29 December 1776. BPL.
77. Ozias Humphry. Probably about 1777. P.
78. Richard Brinsley Sheridan. 9 January 1777. BSM.
79. David Garrick. 18 January 1777. BOA.
80. Edmund Burke. 15 February 1777. SCL.
81. David Garrick. 23 May 1777. BSM.
82. John Robinson. 23 July 1777. LC.
83. William Woodfall. 8 November 1777. Y.
84. David Garrick. About 15 December 1777. H.
85. David Garrick. 19 December 1777. F.
86. David Garrick. 22 December 1777. BSM.
87. David Garrick. 4 January 1778. BSM.
88. David Garrick. 12 January 1778. BSM.
89. David Garrick. 13 January 1778. BSM.
90. George Germain. 21 January 1778. MI.
91. William Eden. 1 April 1776. BL.
92. George Germain. 31 August 1778. MI.
93. Decimus Reynolds. 13 January 1779. *Mem.*
94. Samuel Farr. 26 January 1779. BL.
95. Gen. Frederick Haldimand. 1 April 1779. BL.
96. George Germain. 19 November 1779. MI.
97. George Germain. After 19 November 1779. MI.
98. George Germain. 21 April 1780. MI.
99. Lord William Hillsborough. 19 May 1780. *Mem.*
100. Lord William Hillsborough. 20 May 1780. *Mem.*
101. George Germain. 25 May 1780. MI.
102. George Germain. 26 May 1780. MI.
103. Lord William Hillsborough. 6 June 1780. *Mem.*
104. Lord William Hillsborough. 7 June 1780. *Mem.*
105. Abbé Hussey. 16 June 1780. *Mem.*
106. Lord William Hillsborough. 26 June 1780. *Mem.*
107. Lord William Hillsborough. 26 June 1780. *Mem.*
108. George Germain. 5 July 1780. M; C.
109. Bernardo Campo. 23 July 1780. BL.
110. Bernardo Campo. 24 July 1780. BL.
111. George Germain. 4 August 1780. MI.
112. Lord William Hillsborough. 4 August 1780. BL.
113. Lord William Hillsborough. 11 August 1780. C.
114. George Germain. 30 August 1780. MI.
115. George Germain. 24 Semptember 1780. MI.

116. Lord William Hillsborough. 3 January 1781. BL.
117. Lord Wm. Hillsborough. 18 January 1781. *Mem.*
118. Lord William Hillsborough. 31 January 1781. BL.
119. Lord William Hillsborough. 3 February 1781. BL.
120. George Germain. 3 February 1781. MI.
121. Abbé Hussey. Before 11 February 1781. BL.
122. George Germain. 11 February 1781. MI.
123. George Germain. 2 March 1781. MI.
124. John Robinson. 8 March 1781. *Mem.*
125. Lord William Hillsborough. 15 March 1781.*Mem.*
126. Bernardo Campo. 20 March 1781. *Mem.*
127. George Germain. 28 April 1781. MI.
128. William Petty. 29 March 1782. LC.
129. George Germain. 3 December 1784. MI.
130. Richard Sharp. 5 December [1785]. Y.
131. Richard Sharp. 13 December 1785. Y.
132. George Colman. 30 April 1787. Y.
133. John Banister. 14 July 1787. Y.
134. George Colman. Before 7 July 1787. F.
135. Frances Abington. Before 8 May 1789. BL.
136. Frances Abington. 17 May 1789. BL.
137. Frances Abington. 21 May 1789. BL.
138. Rev. John Romney. 18 April 1790. Y.
139. Edmund Burke. 11 November 1790. SCL.
140. Lady Edward Bentinck. About 1 December 1798. Y.
141. Unidentified. 20 January 1799. H.
142. Richard D. Cumberland. 6 February 1799. BL.
143. Richard D. Cumberland. 21 August 1799. BL.
144. Sir James Bland Burgess. 10 January 1800. F.
145. Sir James Burgess. Before 10 January 1800. H.
146. Sir James Bland Burgess. 22 May 1800. H.
147. Mr. Barker. 10 October 1800. F.
148. George Cooke. 4 January 1801. HSP.
149. Robert Hobart. 5 January 1801. NYPL.
150. Sir James Bland Burgess. 30 January 1801. H.
151. Sir James Bland Burgess. 10 February 1801. F.
152. George Lackington. 31 March [1801]. P.
153. Sir James B. Burgess. June or July 1801. H.
154. Sir James B. Burgess. Probably early 1801. F.
155. Sir James Bland Burgess. 1 January 1802. H.
156. Sir James Bland Burgess. Probably 1803. H.

157. Sir James B. Burgess. Before 8 January 1803. H.
158. Richard Sharp. 31 January 1803. H.
159. Sir James B. Burgess. After Mid-April 1803. H.
160. Thomas Greene. Before June 1803. BO.
161. Sir James Bland Burgess. 26 June 1803. H.
162. Sir James Bland Burgess. 27 June 1803. H.
163. Sir James Bland Burgess. About July 1803. H.
164. Robert William Elliston. 11 October 1803. F.
165. George Hardinge. 30 October 1803. Y.
166. Unidentified. About 1803. F.
167. Sir James Bland Burgess. Late 1803. H.
168. Sir James B. Burgess. Probably 1803-4. HSP.
169. Sir James Bland Burgess. Probably 1804-5. H.
170. George Cumberland. 23 January 1805. BL.
171. George Cumberland. 30 January 1805. BL.
172. George Lackington. Before 24 March 1805. H.
173. George Lackington. 24 March 1805. MI.
174. Sir James Bland Burgess. 29 March 1805. H.
175. Sir James Bland Burgess. 26 August 1805. H.
176. Sir James Bland Burgess. 3 September 1805. H.
177. Sir James Burgess. About 18 September 1805. H.
178. Sir James Burgess. After 18 September 1805. H.
179. Sir James Bland Burgess. 4 October 1805. H.
180. Sir James Bland Burgess. Fall of 1805. H.
181. Sir James Bland Burgess. Late 1805 (1). H.
182. Sir James Bland Burgess. Late 1805 (2). H.
183. Sir James Bland Burgess. 1 November 1805. H.
184. Sir James Bland Burgess. 5 November 1805. H.
185. Sir James Bland Burgess. 6 November 1805. H.
186. Sir James Burgess. After 14 November 1805. H.
187. William Smith. 27 March [1806]. Y.
188. Sir James Bland Burgess. Before April 1806. H.
189. Sir James Bland Burgess. Spring 1806 (1). H.
190. Sir James Bland Burgess. Spring 1806 (2). H.
191. Sir James Bland Burgess. Spring 1806 (3). H.
192. Sir James Bland Burgess. 5 May 1806. F.
193. Sir James Bland Burgess. About 8 May 1806. H.
194. Sir James Bland Burgess. Mid-1806. H.
195. Sir James Bland Burgess. After 23 June 1806. H.
196. Sir James Bland Burgess. Late 1806. H.
197. Sir James Bland Burgess. September 1806. H.

198. Sir James Bland Burgess. 3 November 1806. H.
199. Sir James Burgess. Before 22 December 1806. H.
200. Sir James Burgess. About 22 December 1806. H.
201. Sir James Burgess. About 24 December 1806. H.
202. Sir James Bland Burgess. 31 December 1806. H.
203. Sir James Bland Burgess. 8 January 1807. H.
204. Sir James Bland Burgess. 30 January 1807. H.
205. Sir James Bland Burgess. Early 1807. H.
206. Sir James B. Burgess. Before 24 March 1807. H.
207. Sir James B. Burgess. 24 March 1807. NYPL.
208. Sir James Bland Burgess. 26 March 1807. H.
209. Sir James Bland Burgess. May 1807. H.
210. Sir James Bland Burgess. 18 June 1807. H.
211. Sir James Bland Burgess. 30 June 1807. H.
212. Sir James Bland Burgess. 8 July 1807. H.
213. Sir James Bland Burgess. 3 September 1807. H.
214. Elizabeth Walker. 26 March 1808. MHS.
215. C. W. Ward. 1 August 1808. BL.
216. George Townshend. 21 December 1808. P.
217. Mr. Pratt. July 6, [1809]. Y.
218. James Asperne. About 1809 (1). BO.
219. James Asperne. About 1809 (2). BO.
220. Sir James Burgess. After 18 September 1809. H.
221. Sir James Bland Burgess. 6 January 1810. F.
222. Celia Fry. 14 January 1811. F.
223. Browne (Unidentified). After 25 March 1811. Y.
224. Elizabeth Walker. Undated. BPL.

Abbreviations

B	Black, *Cumberland Letters*	LC	Library of Congress
BOA	Boaden, *Cor. of Garrick*	*Mem*	*Memoirs of Cumberland*
BO	Bodleian Lib. Oxford Univ.	M	Mudford, *Cumberland*
BL	British Library	MHS	Massachusetts Hist. Soc.
BPL	Boston Public Library	MI	Clements Lib. Michigan.
BSC	British Science Museum	NYPL	N. Y. Pub. Lib. Berg Col.
C	Columbia Univ. Lib.	P	Princeton Univ. Lib.
F	Folger Shakes. Library	SCL	Sheffield City Library
H	Harvard University Library	Y	Yale Univ. Beinecke Lib.
HSP	Hist. Soc. of Pennsylvania			

The Letters of Richard Cumberland

I   Charles Jenkinson   28 May 1764[1]

Downing Street
May 28th

Sir

I beg leave to inclose to you my Memorial for the Nova Scotia Grant.[2] I was with Lord Hillsboro[3] this Morning, and stated to His Lordship the necessity there is of redeeming the Public Credit of the Province, by enabling the Agent to accept and discharge such Bills of Exch[ang]e, as are properly drawn and duely authenticated by a voucher from the Secret[ar]y of the Board of Trade: This can only be done by the Treasury advancing to the Agent the Grant of Parliam[en]t; for without Effects you well know, Sir, that no Ag[en]t can safely accept Bills of Exch[ang]e, upon the mere presumption that Treasury will give Orders for payment within the time limited for their Discharge. The other Agents have received their Grants by a Surprize upon Their Lordships, which I am told has received Reprehension; thought it my Duty and a necessary Respect to the Board of Trade not to take such a step without their sanction; and I am heartily glad I did not partake of the Rebuke my fraternity have met with--I presume therefore I shall not now be made an Example of Displeasure, by the Lords of Treasury refusing the Petition of my Memorial; but that the Grant will be

2

issued to me, as their's has been to them: Lord
Hillsboro fully accedes to the reasonableness of
their Request, and I dare say, Sir, woud give you
further Satisfaction in the matter upon discourse
with his Lordship. I have lodged with Mr. Tompkins
the proper voucher signed by Mr. Pownall,[4] recommending my Memorial for Cap. Holland's[5] Grant; which
I most cordially thank you for expediting.

I am ashamed of the Length of this Letter, but I
hope it will interrupt you at a less unseasonable
Time, and for a shorter space of it, than if I was
to trouble you in person. I am with great Respect,
Sir,

Your most obedient
and oblig'd Humble Servant

Richd Cumberland

Cha[rle]s Jenkinson Esquire[6]

Source: British Library

1. The year is determined by the date of the Memorial for Captain Holland. See the *Journal of the Commissioners of Trade and
Plantations, January 1764-December 1767*, (London, 1936), p. 60.

2. Cumberland was Crown Agent for Nova Scotia.

3. Among the various periods that Lord Hillsborough was President of the Board of Trade was September 1763 to July 1765.

4. John Pownall, Secretary of the Board of Trade.

5. Samuel Holland, Surveyor of the Lands in America.

6. Secretary of the Treasury between 1763 and 1765.

II Roger Pinckney   30 September 1764

Downing-Street, Sept. 30, 1764

Dear Sir,

I am favoured with your letters of July 14th, 16th, and August the 1st.[1] I have likewise received the two hundred dollars by the Union, Captain Smith; and shall to-morrow send to enquire after the pipe of Madeira, by Captain Muir, the bill of lading for which I have received in your letter of August the 1st. I heartily congratulate you on your safe arrival, and the reception that you met with from all people with whom you are to be concerned: I think myself much bound to Mr. Doyley[2] for his politeness to you, and I wish I could render him any services in return; so I beg you will assure him. I condole with Mr. Guerard[3] on the loss of his worthy father, and I make no doubt that he will inherit his virtues. You have stated my account with Mr. Guerard perfectly right, and he is now discharged from any further demands from me. I have not yet sold the dollars; I hear, however, at the Carolina Coffeehouse, that 4s. 6d. will be as much as I can possibly get for them, nevertheless. I like them better than bills of exchange, both because they are present cash, and principally because you suffer no discount upon them. I am glad you was in receipt of this money immediately, on your arrival, as cash must, undoubtedly, be of use to you in the set out; my time of wanting money is about the latter end of January, or in the month of February; and what remittance soever you can make me by that time, with tolerable convenience to yourself, I shall be thankful to you for, as I have a particular account this year to settle, which will, for the future, make me a much less troublesome solicitor to you. I am to thank you for the account you have hitherto collected of the nature and advantages of your office, as likewise for the table of fees; I wish from my soul (nor am I purely self-interested in that wish), that you may find it more lucrative than we apprehend it to be; your ingenuous declaration of those profits, (be they what they will) shall never be turned a-

gainst you. I need not press you to push the matter
of the gaol with all your interest and attention;
you tell me that you pay 300l. currency per annum
for Mr. Doyley's house; if you can remove that in-
cumbrance, the advantage shall not singly be mine,
but we will jointly benefit ourselves by the event;
I think now is the time for this point, during the
lieutenancy of Mr. Bull,[4] who is an affable, easy,
and upright gentleman, and well beloved in the province. I have consulted my patent; the offices it re-
cites are, *Provost Marshall, Clerk of the Peace and
Clerk of the Crown*; it mentions not *Clerk of the
Pleas.*[5] You remember that I told you I could wish
you would let the offices of Clerk of the Crown and
Clerk of the Peace to any person who would pay down
a reasonable fine for them, and hold them free of
any deductions on account of fees, during the term
of your lease of Provost Marshal, or longer, if you
think fit. The salary arising therefrom, you know I
reserve; and you will likewise remark, that the said
salaries are paid only to Lady-day last, which, I
presume, is the time of payment from the Receiver-
General. I have now the satisfaction to acquaint
you, that I saw your father, mother, and sister, in
good health at Peterborough this week, who desire
affectionately to be remembered to you; your father
talks of sending your brother to you sometime or
other, and I think he will make you a nice clerk.
Pray present Mrs. Cumberland's and my compliments
and good wishes to Mrs. Pinckney, and thank her for
her designed favours to my little ones. I enclose
you a receipt for the amount of the wine and dollars. I beg you will ever persist in believing me,

Dear Sir,

Your sincere friend and
Faithful humble servant,

Richard Cumberland.

P.S. All alarms of a rupture with France and Spain are now terminated, as each power has receded from their unjust attempts, and ordered indemnification for them.[6]

Source: Mudford.

1. The date of July 14th probably indicates the approximate date of Pinckney's arrival to assume the post of Provost Marshal. Cumberland first received the patent in 1759. His predecessor was probably Thomas Lowndes, who had succeeded Hugh Watson (cf. Esla Williams, *The Charleston Stage in the Eighteenth Century*, II, 62). Mr. Guerard, mentioned later in the letter, was undoubtedly Cumberland's previous representative. One of Pinckney's first acts appears to have been to straighten out and complete Guerard's account with Cumberland. Mr. Doyley probably rented his house to Guerard for the conduct of the official business of the Provost Marshal, and for this reason, the savings involved in eliminating it would jointly benefit Pinckney and Cumberland.

2. Probably Daniel Doyley, a member of the South Carolina Assembly.

3. John Guerard, an eminent Charleston merchant and a member of the Council of Provincial South Carolina, had died on 14 May 1764. Benjamin Guerard, probably his son, was a member of the South Carolina Assembly.

4. William Bull (1710-1791) was Captain of a South Carolina Company during the war with Spain and became Lieutenant Governor in 1759. In this position he acted as Governor on several occasions, one of which was 1764-1766.

5. Cumberland never succeeded in disposing of the offices of Clerk of the Peace and Clerk of the Crown.

6. In July 1764, Ambassadors were withdrawn by England and Prussia. George Greville, Chancellor of the Exchequer and First Lord of the Treasury from 16 April 1763 to 13 July 1765, concentrated on defensive measures against France and Spain. His firm stand against those nations succeeded in forcing concessions from them that preserved the peace. See Steven Watson, *The Reign of George III*, p. 108.

III Roger Pinckney 1 October 1764

(Secret and Confidential).

Downing-Street, Oct. 1, 1764

Dear Pinckney,

I write to you now on a subject of a very nice and delicate nature, in a matter where my interest is deeply concerned, and in consequence of a hint which has been thrown out to me this morning, since my writing of yesterday's letter to you. I should not do justice to your heart, if I scrupled your friendship to me, and I should pay an ill compliment to your judgment, if I doubted your discretion in the managemant of the affair I am now to submit to you. Mr. Saxby,[1] the Receiver-General of South Carolina, in conversation with me this morning upon the subject of your employment, suggested to me a proposal, so palpably advantageous to me, and so feasible withal, that I embrace the first opportunity of communicating it to you, and entreating your good offices on the occasion. I do not believe that it is a necessary inducement to engage your services in the affair, that it will be no interruption to your interest and advantage; but I think it needful for my own justification to assure you, that I would engage in no plans where you should be excluded from the benefits you justly deserve. Mr. Saxby tells me that the Province of South Carolina are extremely desirous of purchasing my patent of Provost Marshal, and annexing it to their government, whereby they may appoint their own sheriff, as their neighbours do; and that he is confident, they will give me such a price for it as shall not leave me the least room for hesitation about parting with it; nay, he suggests to me, that they will vest as much money in the English funds as shall bring me in the same revenue as my office now produces me; which, you see,

is turning my annuity into a perpetuity. It is superfluous to tell you that this would be such an accession to my large and growing family, such a relief to a father's mind, as would make my pillow,
for the rest of my life, easy to me; the thing is
too obvious to need explanation. He persuades me
that the Assembly would give me five thousand, nay,
perhaps, six thousand pounds sterling, which, you
know, would not lessen my income, and be an accession to my fortune of so much money. Now I make no
doubt that I could procure his Majesty's consent to
annihilate the patent, and vest the power of ap-
pointing their own sheriff in the Government of
South Carolina; the reasonableness of the request,
and the expediency of the measure, so salutary to
the province, and so economical with regard to the
public, would I dare say, when supported by the influence of my patron,[2] carry me through the measure.
Your lease you know could not be dissolved; nay, in
that case, you would have an opportunity of improv-
ing the conditions on which you hold it, or sell the
remainder to advantage. The part, therefore, I now
wish you to act, is to throw out a hint to some of
the leading members of the Assembly,--*that you have
no authority from Mr. Cumberland to suppose he
would part from his employment to them, but, however, that you do conceive he would listen to advantageous terms; that those terms should be to vest as
much money in the English funds as should produce an
equivalent to him for his present* reservation.* In
consequence of such an agreement with the patentee,
the province may build a gaol at public expence, and
appoint their own sheriff for ever after; by which
means, you see, that, although I sell only an annuity, they, in fact, purchase a perpetuity, and therefore should pay me accordingly. Mr. Saxby (who is a
very temperate, judicious man), in consequence of
this idea, proposes to me not to push the affair of
the public gaol, because, if they were to grant
that, he thinks they would be more indifferent about
the purchase. I think there is good sense in this

opinion, and therefore wish you would be easy upon
that subject, till we see the result of this affair.** I must not appear forward and eager in the
offer, so that I could wish you would affect to
speak of it at a distance, and as if without authority. In short, let your wisdom, your friendship, and
the present face of men and things, dictate your
part to you. I can give no instructions at this
distance, except in the general. I throw myself upon
your discretion. You can conceive what happiness it
would bestow on my life, if I could accomplish a
point of such consequence, and I know you will feel
for me, and act for me accordingly. I beseech you to
lose no time nor conveyance in writing to me, and
to write fully, freely, and confidentially in all
points. Think not I can ever betray or neglect your
interest, while you are serving and promoting mine;
in short, believe me as much yours as you could wish
a friend to be.

Richard Cumberland.

Oct. 2. P.S. It occurs to me that you might make
good terms with the province (in case this project
takes place) for the term in your lease; as they
would be glad to come into absolute disposal. I consider likewise, that though *I sell it* on the ideal
of its bringing to me a revenue of no more than
£240. per annum; yet, *they would buy it* as an employment worth the whole amount of it on the spot,
and, consequently, would have it extremely cheap.
For call the whole amount of the revenue (divided
now between you and me) to be £600. per annum, if
they give £6000. for it, they have a perpetuity at
ten years purchase.

* Or suppose the terms hereafter to be proposed were
these, viz. Ten years purchase of the whole amount
of the office, which would certainly be sufficiently
advantageous to the Province, and abundantly so to
the Patentee.

** Upon second reflection I dont see the force of this objection of Mr. Saxby's, and think the jail is a measure not to be waved.

Source: Mudford.

1. George Saxby, a merchant planter and royal official, was Receiver General of the Quit Rents (1742-1774) and a member of the Royal Council (1752-1760).
2. Cumbeland's patron was the Second Earl of Halifax, George Montagu Dunk (1716-1771), who was Secretary of State for the Southern Department from 9 September 1763 to 12 July 1765. Although Cumberland was disappointed when Halifax, late in 1762, was made Secretary of State for the Northern Department and failed to name him Under-Secretary, he obtained employment at the Board of Trade under Lord Hillsborough with the approval of Halifax. In his letter to Pinckney of 30 January 1767, he comments on the retirement of Halifax in such a way as to indicate his dependence on him.

IV Roger Pinckney 8 February 1765

Downing-street, February 8, 1765

Dear Pinckney,

I have just received your favour of the 17th of December, which I heartily thank you for; I am likewise to acknowledge the receipt of the bill of exchange for one hundred pounds, which was duly honoured, and 130 dollars, by the Two Friends, which together, leave a balance as you state it; and I believe, in a former letter, I have particularized all my receipts, and corrected a little mistake in your own disfavour; let this suffice on the present occasion. The dollars which you charge at 4s. 6d.

(though, when I first received them they were rather below price) yet I contrived to lose nothing by them; and silver is now risen, so that by the last parcel, which are yet undisposed of, I shall gain about 1¹/₂d. per dollar; so that you need not be out of humour with them, as I think them the best returns you can make. Your Madeira, which I did not speak highly of at first, will, I believe, turn out better than I apprehended, and come reasonable to me.[1]

I cannot sufficiently express my grateful acknowledgements to you for your friendly attention to my interest and hap-piness, and the kind manner in which you receive the proposal I submitted to you in my private letter. Indeed, Sir, I must confess to you, that I am exceedingly anxious to bring a point of such vast advantage to me to bear; and I believe I may venture to say, I should not miscarry in the attempt, if the Assembly were as willing to treat as I am told, and believe that they are. I am rejoiced to hear that you are likely to carry the measure of a public jail, which was so strongly recommended by the Board of Trade. It will be an event very favourable to my office, and to us both; and at the same time will entitle me to better terms in the disposal of it. Mr. Saxby has this moment left me; I have had a long conversation [with] him; he encourages me to hope that the Assembly will acceed to my terms, which shall simply be these: "So much money vested in the English funds, as will produce the net income remitted to me from my employment." This I mean to make the ground-plot of the transaction, and though these are conditions extremely favourable to a life-holder, yet you see that they purchase a perpetuity, and one not of the reserved value, but of the entire. Mr. Saxby has been so kind as to say, that if I can bring matters to no conclusion till he returns to Charlestown, which will be in August next, that he will take my power of attorney, and negociate the business for me; he at the same time says there is no doubt of your being preserved in the office. I shall therefore make no further movement, than in submitting the affair, as I now do, to your judgment, to open it as you think best, and to whom you think best, either entirely, or in part; but if you think it wiser to reserve it for his arrival, you will act according to your own discretion. In the mean time I think that the business of the public jail should be pushed with all your influence; for let the event be what it will, that must be a favourable circumstance.

I do not wonder that the Province are dissatisfied with their chief justice,[2] for the little I saw of him did not give me advantageous impressions. I entirely recommend your conduct with respect to him, and I make no doubt of your making both yourself and your office respectable. I rejoice at the account you give me of your health, and I hope you will observe the same cautious attention to it, and not endanger it either by excess of fatigue or conviviality. Your journey must have been very new and grotesque; and I heartily wish I could have been present at the scenes of wild original nature, which you must have met with, without the pains and labour you must have taken in arriving there.[3]

I shall attend to the matter of the fees, and as I have just now taken an office in the Board of Trade,[4] it is possible I may be able to assist you in them. The West-India Governments have some of them made a horrible reduction of fees. Heaven forbid that their example should be followed on the Continent!

You will direct to me at the Plantation Office, in White=hall, London. Your friends at Petersborough were well, when I heard last; and I shall take care to convey your compliments to the bishop and family.[5] Mrs. Cumberland joins me in respects and sincere good wishes to Mrs Pinckney and yourself.

Believe me, most truly,
Dear Sir,
Your faithful and most obedient

Humble Servant,

Richard Cumberland.

Feb. 11, 1765. P.S. I open my letter again to tell
you that I have this day paid to Messrs. Robert Harris and Co. your draft for twenty-seven pounds,
which was drawn at twelve months date.

R. C.

Source: Mudford.

1. See 30 September 1764: "I enclose you a receipt for the a-
mount of the wine and dollars."

2. Chief Justice Charles Shinner was appointed in March 1761
and removed on 11 May, 1767.

3. Pinckney's duties took him to the interior of the Province,
which was still very primitive, and offered "scenes of wild original nature."

4. Cumberland joined the Board of Trade as Clerk of Reports under the Earl of Hillsborough who became President on 9 September
1763. "Thus I entered upon an office, the duties of which consis-
ted of taking minutes of the debates and proceedings at the
Board, and preparing for their approbation and signature such reports, as they should direct to be drawn up for his Majesty, or
the Council, and, on some occasions, for the Board of Treasury or
Secretaries of State" (*Memoirs*, I, 248).

5. Denison Cumberland, the dramatist's father, was Bishop of
Clonfert, Ireland. The Pinckney family was from Petersborough,
where Cumberland's great grandfather had been a distinguished
bishop.

V Roger Pinckney 27 February 1775

Downing Street, February 27, 1765

Dear Pinckney,

I wrote to you by the Little Carpenter, Captain Muir, and I now beg your care and furtherance of the inclosed letter to General Shirley,[1] which has a paper in it of considerable consequence. With respect to your draft of office fees, taken by the Provost Marshal, I have abstained from laying them before the Board of Trade, because that enquiry is dropt, and to revive it might be of prejudice to your office, but could not be any benefit. I acquainted you in my last that I had paid your bill, at twelve months date, for £27.; and when you remit any more money, I shall be glad to receive it in dollars, for they bear a premium. I am, Dear Sir,

Most faithfully your's,

Richard Cumberland.

Source: Mudford.

1. Probably William Shirley (1694-1771), who was a General in the Canadian wars. He was made Colonian Governor of the Bahamas on 24 July 1761.

VI Roger Pinckney 18 March 1765

Downing-Street, March 18, 1765

Dear Pinckney,

I cannot let your brother depart without writing a line to you, though I have nothing to add to my last pacquet, by the Minerva. As I am likely to pass my summer here, in London, till the time of Mr. Saxby's departure,[1] I shall, before that period, hope to accomplish my point with respect to the office you now execute, as far as relates to the procuring his Majesty's permission to make over the patent to the assembly of South Carolina. The process I intend to follow is this, first to get council's opinion upon the legality of the measure, of which, I believe, there is no doubt; secondly, to get a recommendation of the proposal from the Board of Trade, as a matter of public utility to the Province, and then entreat of Lord Halifax to lay it before his Majesty, for his assent. By Mr. Saxby I will send over full powers, and your assistance and concurrence will lay me under lasting obligations.

I hope you will carry your point about the erecting a public gaol, which I think will not only be a mutual benefit, but will enhance the value of my post upon sale.

Your brother is a very promising youth, and under your eye, will, I dare say, fix advantageously in Charles Town; as he seems likely to be handsome, you must look out for a girl of good fortune, and see if you cannot lay him in; which, I suppose, in your climate is more practicable than with us.[2]

All happiness and success attend you and your's.

I shall be glad of my remittances in dollars, as there is something gained by them. I told you I had paid your bill of £27.--Let me hear frequently from you. I am, Dear Sir,

Your most faithful,
Humble servant,

Richard Cumberland.

I hope you forwarded my letter to General Shirley.[3]

Source: Mudford.

1. In his letter of 8 February 1765, Cumberland indicates that Saxby will leave for the Colony of South Carolina in August.

2. In 30 September 1764, Cumberland speaks of Pinckney's father

thinking of sending Roger's brother to South Carolina.
3. See 27 February 1765.

VII   Roger Pinckney   31 July 1765

Parliament-Street, July 31, 1765

Dear Pinckney,

I am favoured with your letter of the 9th of May
last, and with it have received the bag of dollars
and doubloons of gold which accompanied it, the a-
mount of which you will see stated at the bottom of
this letter. I am sorry you have suffered any uneas-
iness at not hearing from me in acknowledgement of
former remittances, which have come duly to hand; I
hope your apprehensions have been long since removed
by the arrival of my letters; and, for the future, I
wish that no alarm may be given on this account, as
there is so long a passage between us, so uncertain
a communication, and I am afraid I must add, to my
own discredit, so irregular a correspondent. However, suffer me now to acknowledge the receipt of mon-
ies you have received on my account, prior to your
commencing my deputy, in full; for which this shall
be your further discharge.
I know, very well, there was a small balance due
to you upon your former remittances, which was properly stated in one of my letters to you, and credit
given you for it; but as I have no copy of that letter, I cannot so easily make out the exact account,
as refer you to my letter and your own accounts,
which I dare say, are kept clearer than mine are.
The dollars I sold at 5s. 3¼d. per ounce, and was
told it was a good price; I disposed of them to Mr.
Bland, a banker of good reputation at the corner of
Birchin Lane; but he would allow no more than £3.
6s. for the doubloons, which you expected would

have bore a premium; however, you have saved freight, and that is something: in a separate paper enclosed you will see my account and receipt.

With respect to the measures you have taken, and the discourse you have held with the leading persons in the Assembly, both relating to the affair of the sale of the patent, and to the erection of a public gaol, I persuade myself the steps you have taken in both matters have been perfectly prudent and friendly. It gives me great pleasure to hear you say that the business of the public gaol is in such forwardness; nothing can add more to your comfort and security, and of course to mine; and it will give me the highest satisfaction to hear that, upon the meeting of the Assembly this month, the Act has been passed; I can assure you, and them, that it will be highly agreeable to government here.

Your conduct, your integrity, and your friendship, in the other article relating to the patent, I rely upon with the utmost tranquillity. As we set forth in this undertaking upon principles of honour and confidence, so, I dare say, no motives of self–interest will divert either of us from the sentiments of friendship we entertained for each other at the outset. I see every thing open and sincere in your conduct, and as this point is an object of such vast importance to me and my family, I am sure you will serve me in it faithfully and to the best of your power; and, at the same time, I hope you will believe that I shall ever have too much honour to allow you to be a sufferer by your good services to me.

The leading men of the Assembly, you tell me, doubt of my being able to carry the point, from the tenacity of government: I will not say positively I can, but presumptively I will affirm to them that I can; and especially if their bill for the establishment of Circuit Courts passes into an Act, it will almost draw my petition along with it. The method I shall propose to take, (if they will join with me in it) is this: to procure a favourable report to be made from the Board of Trade to the Secretary of State, in consequence of a joint memorial both from their agent and myself; such a report, I flatter myself, I shall find little difficulty in obtaining from my station in that office,[1] and if they will empower their agent to co-operate with me, (as I know him very well)[2] and, at the same time, will furnish him with full powers for concluding and executing the agreement, I make no doubt of carrying the measure through, and of putting them into possession of the patent. I have talked this language to Mr. Saxby, and he is so good as to say he will convey my sentiments to his friends in the Province, and will support the design to the best of his power; he thinks of leaving England in about a month; by him you shall hear from me again.

I wish you all satisfaction in the execution of your Province, and should have been heartily glad had it exceeded your expectations in point of profit and ease, as much as I fear, by what you tell me, that it is likely to fall short of them. With respect to the office of clerk, I must leave that entirely to your management, and am sorry it is so poor an office: if I can give the chief a lift, you may depend upon it I will.

Mrs. Cumberland and my family, as well as the bishop[3] and his, are in good health. I heartily wish that Mrs. Pinckney's health may be re-established, and that you may enjoy all happiness and prosperity, being with great truth,

Dear Sir,
Your most faithful and
Sincere humble servant,

Richard Cumberland.

P.S. I hope you received the bill of exchange I sent you, on Mr. Tucker, of New Providence, for £100. sterling. I sent a duplicate soon after. I beg of you to find a conveyance for the inclosed letters, and to charge to my account the expenses thereby incurred.

R. C.

Source: Mudford.

1. Cumberland was Clerk of Reports at the Board of Trade. The office was worth some £200 a year, but not one of prestige as suggested here.

2. Charles Garth (b. 1730?) had been made Crown Agent of South Carolina in 1762. See 3 June 1767.

3. Cumberland's father.

VIII Roger Pinckney 30 August 1765

Parliament-Street, August 30, 1765

Dear Pinckney,

I have just now received your favour by the Beuffain, Captain Daniel Curling, containing an invoice for 500 dollars, and inclosing a draft for £50. sterling. As I am unwilling to lose the opportunity of acknowledging this to you by the conveyance of Mr. Saxby,[1] I write immediately before I have received the dollars; but, however, this acknowledgement for the present will serve as my receipt and your discharge; and if the dollars turn out as well as the last did, (which I believe there is no doubt of) you will be creditor to me in a larger sum than you state. However, by the first subsequent opportunity you shall have my state of the account drawn out. I thank you most heartily for your expedition and punctuality, and am not only better, but much speedier, paid than ever I was before.

With respect to the measure of selling my patent

to the Province, my short conception is, that if the Assembly will empower their agent to co-operate with me, the business may be effected; and, if they will likewise authorize him to conclude the bargain, we shall not disagree upon the matter: my terms are, "as much money vested in the English funds, as shall produce to me a sum equal to my reserved rent." If the Assembly pass an Act for the erection of a public gaol, I should think such a step would forward an accommodation between us.

As Mr. Saxby started the suggestion to me, and has promised to support it in the Province to the best of his power, I have possessed him of so much of my resolution as is needful for his information. I shall, however, not only pay due regard to every hint and advice of your's, but do greatly and principally depend upon your kind offices for success. Indeed, I cannot sufficiently thank you for the assurances you give me; for nothing had I ever more at heart than the present affair.

I sincerely hope your fatigues will not be attended with any ill consequences to your health, and wish that they may answer every purpose of your interest. I should be obliged to you, if you will pay an attention to Mr. Saxby, as far as is compatible with your own sentiments. I have inclosed to you a letter to Governor Shirley,[2] which I will beg you to provide a conveyance for. I likewise trouble you with an official letter to Lieut.-Governor Bull,[3] which you will please to deliver to him.

My wife and family are in good health. The bishop[4] and his were well, when I heard last of them; accept my constant good wishes, and ever believe me, Dear Sir,

> Your most faithful and
> Obedient humble servant,
>
> Richard Cumberland.

Source: Mudford.

1. George Saxby.
2. Governor William Shirley of the Bahamas.
3. Lieutenant Governor William Bull was in 1765 acting as Governor of the Province. Governor Thomas Boone had embarked for Great Britain on 11 May 1764, leaving Bull in charge. Boon was succeeded by Lord Charles Greville Montagu.
4. Cumberland's father.

IX Roger Pinckney 15 January 1766

Parliament-Street, Jan. 15, 1766

Dear Pinckney,

It was yesterday asserted, by the great Mr. P--t,[1] in the House of Commons, that the British Parl-----t had no right to tax the American Colonies, who were not therein legally represented. It is universally concluded, from what past on the part of administration, in consequence of this gentleman's opinion, that the Stamp Act will be absolutely revoked and rescinded.[2] If so, amidst the universal joy and good humour which will prevail throughout America upon that event, perhaps the interrupted measure of a public gaol may be resumed by your legislature; and the bill, already twice read, may be past, and as soon as it is transmitted hither, I will procure it a speedy confirmation. I send you this early notice, hoping you may put matters into a train against a proper opportunity.

I need not repeat to you the thing I have so much at heart, which is the sale of my patent. I may venture to promise that I can procure an absolute transfer of it to the Assembly, if they will purchase it upon reasonable terms: I hope you will confer with Mr. Saxby upon this matter, to whom I write by this opportunity. Forgive my frequent iteration of this subject, but consider the importance of it to me, and you will, I am sure, promote my interest to the best of your power.

I am, Dear Sir,
Your most faithful friend, and
Sincere humble servant,

Richard Cumberland.

Source: Mudford.

1. William Pitt (1708-1778), the Earl of Chatham.

2. Pitt's expression of his view that representation in taxation was necessary for political liberty was a factor in the repeal of the Stamp Act. Unfortunately, the assertion of Parliament through the passage of the Declaration Act that it had a right to tax the Colonies did much to diminish the effect of the repeal. Moreover, an act requiring the Colonies to repay those whose property had been destroyed in the riots resulting from the Stamp Act further aggravated the situation.

A letter from Lieutenant Governor Bull of South Carolina to the Board of Trade on 3 November 1765 details the commotions in South Carolina over the Stamp Act. It is printed in *English Historical Documents* IX, ed. Merrell Jensen (New York: Oxford University Press, 1955), pp. 680-683.

X Roger Pinckney 2 July 1766

Plantation-Office, July 2, 1766

Dear Pinckney,

I am now to thank you for your favours of Feb. 21st, April the 28th, May 1st, 14th, and 21st; these letters came all in the course of last week; I will beg leave to answer them in their order. The first of them principally relates to Mr. Saxby, and my proposal of selling my patent of Provost Marshal.

You seem hurt by a preference, which you conceive I have shewn to Mr. Saxby in this business, by commissioning him to negociate the disposal of my patent; I must beg to assure you, that you have not the least shadow of reason to complain of any such preference; nor to suspect that I entertain the smallest scruple of diffidence, either of your disposition to serve me, or of your ability so to do; I have not given Mr. Saxby, or any other man living, any power or authority to transact this affair for me; I dare not, and cannot, convey any such commission, while my patent is yet in the disposal of the crown, which I have not yet solicited the release of; for, till the Assembly of South Carolina show a readiness to treat with me, I think it would be premature in me to make any motions on my side; all that I requested, (or, if you will, all that I commissioned) Mr. Saxby to do for me was, to sound the Assembly, to prepare the leading members for the proposal, and to be kind enough to use his interest, as far as it would go, in my behalf: what his interest may be I know not; it is possible, from what you tell me, that it may operate rather to my prejudice, than in my favour; but it was he who first started to me the idea of selling my patent; and you must not wonder, if I was glad to catch at every assistance and help towards so beneficial a proposal. This is my situation with Mr. Saxby; and sorry I am that his behaviour appears to you to be so supercilious, that I may be deprived of your joint and cordial co-operations, and he must lose the opportunity of making an agreeable friend. With respect to the mode of treating with the Assembly, I should conceive the proper channel would be for them to empower their agent to negotiate a bargain with me; the outlines of which might be, that they should vest as much money to my use, as would bring me in an income, equal to what the office pays me here in England. This is my object; the attainment of which

is of the utmost importance to me; and which you
will not be surprized that I should try every method
and employ every instrument to obtain. As the rest
of this letter respects the difficulties and dilemmas which you are thrown into, by the Stamp Act,
and as your latter letters acknowledge the repeal of
it, I shall make no observations upon that subject,
but hasten to assure you that I take a sincere part
in your concern on Mrs. Pinckney's account; the relation you give me of her state of health, and your
silence upon that subject in your subsequent letters, make me apprehend the worst. I beg I may be
informed what the result of her situation has been.[1]

Your second letter, dated April the 28th, further
relates to the effects which the Stamp Act has upon
your place, and the diminution it has occasioned in
its revenue. I am much concerned at this account,
and do equally with you regret the consequences
which have attended it; your reasonings upon the office and duty of the Provost Marshal are, I dare
say, perfectly right, but I am the most wretched
lawyer in the world, and know nothing of the matter.
The repeal answers this part of your letter, as it
did the former, and I have only to add, that I hope
now the Province has got into good-humour again,
that the Assembly will be induced to take up their
measure of erecting a public gaol; I need not urge
you to use your best endeavours towards this work;
and I hope my Lord Governor[2] will not be averse to
it.

Your next letter, of the 1st of May, relates to an
alarm you are under concerning a motion for passing
a law, "empowering magistrates to issue warrants for
the recovery of all sums under £70. currency." This
would, indeed, be prejudicial to my office; but I
hope the inexpediency of the Act itself, the opposition which the gentlemen of the law will of course
make to it, and, above all, the repeal of the Stamp
Act will crush the thought in embryo, and we shall
never see it on this side the water; should that be
the case, you must think I would leave no stone un-

turned to get it repealed: you say nothing of it in your subsequent letters, so I conclude the motion is dropt.

Your letter of May the 14th, by the Hillsborough, gives an account of your having received news of the repeal; I make no doubt your joy on that occasion was as great as possible, but I hope not such as to betray you into any excesses, which may prejudice your health. If America, which has been so heated and inflamed with resentment against the contrivers and abettors of the Stamp Act, will but make a sober and temperate use of it, it may be happy for her, that the measure was taken, as far as it is a proof of the just attention which this country pays to the remonstrances of her colonies; for my own part, I think that the extreme of joy is almost as formidable a fury, as that of anger, and sometimes attended with as bad consequences; I hope no instances of such will appear upon this event.

By the Argo, Captain Cutter, I receive your letter of May the 21st, together with a bill of lading for 540 Spanish dollars, of which £94. 8s. sterling, is to be put to the credit of Mr. Rush Tucker; I have not yet received the dollars; if I do, and sell them before I part from this, I will give you the state of our account current at the foot of this, if not, by the next conveyance. This goes by the Two Friends, Captain Ball.

July the 7th. Having not yet received the dollars, I am obliged to close this, and refer you to my next, which shall speedily follow this, for our account. In the mean time this letter will serve as an acknowledgement of their receipt.

Accept my good wishes, and
Believe me your's,

Richard Cumberland

Source: Mudford.

1. Cumberland speaks of Mrs. Pinckney's illness and eventual death in several other letters, specifically 1 January 1767, 8 July 1767, 17 October 1767, and 27 October 1769.
2. Lord Charles Greville Montagu.

XI Roger Pinckney 1 January 1767

Plantation Office, January 1, 1767

Dear Pinckney,

I am to thank you for various letters and papers relative to your conduct and the state of your affairs. The part which you have taken, during the late unhappy situation of men and things, was such, I dare believe, as you was persuaded, both from reason and conscience, was right and proper for you to take: I have nothng to object to it, nor would now wish, (was I able so to do) to enter into a discussion of it; but I must fairly confess to you, I am entirely ignorant of the question; it is a point of law too hard for me to decide; you may be sure, in such a mixture and confusion of interests and sentiments, that different men will have different opinions upon the matter; but happily, both for you and for me, an Act of total oblivion is now passed, which buries all these matters in silence, and cancels, as I hope, all enmities and animosities that have so much agitated and enflamed the minds of men:[1] I do not mean, by this to say your conduct stood in need of pardon; I rather believe that it needed only to be understood in order to be approved; but it is always better not to be engaged in controversy, though one should come off victorious from the engagement With this in view, I put your defence into the hands of my friend Mr. Maclean,[2] Lord Shelburne's secretary, to be used by him if occasion should require; I am now informed from him,

that the measure is, to recommend an entire oblivion
of this and all other disputes; so that government
here will pass over, and take no cognizance of the
matter, and of course, I suppose, recommend the same
conduct to be observed on your side the water. I
beg, therefore, you will be silent upon this head;
let the matter stand; be perfectly at ease relating
to yourself, and molest no one else in their opinions; do not use any hostile terms or expressions
towards the Chief Justice,[3] but act as if this dispute had never occurred; I shall think myself much
obliged to you, if you will pursue this conduct, and
I dare say, you will find it best calculated for
your own credit and repose. With respect to the
young man at the head of affairs in your Province,[4]
I hope you will take no part pro or con; your remarks, I dare say, are just, and they shall never
transpire; but I would wish you, if possible, to a-
void being a party man, and, on the contrary, to
conciliate all faction in a good opinion of you;
such is the report and character I have ever received in your favour, and such I dare say, it will
continue to be. It was impossible for a person in
your post, let his precaution be what it would, not
to offend one set of men; you have been on the con-
quering side; contented with victory let your passions subside.

So much for the sermonizing part of my letter, let
us now turn to more agreeable topics, I rejoice to
hear of your welfare, and happy I am that I have an
opportunity of congratulating you upon the restoration of peace and concord amongst you; I have been
a long while without writing to you, but while you
was burning governors and stamp collectors in effigy, I did not chuse to meddle with you, nor knew I
what to say to you; now I expect some pleasure and
satisfaction in your correspondence. You tell me
nothing of your family affairs; I have great reason
to apprehend that you have lost Mrs. Pinckney, but
you have never satisfied my enquiries upon that subject.[5] Mrs. Cumberland and my little ones, (thank

God) are in good health, and the good bishop, my mother, and sister are now in England, settled at Tyringham, which I have made over to them during their abode on this side the water; my father always makes kind enquiries after you, and rejoices to hear of your welfare.

If I can procure a power of attorney, entitling you to sell my place of Clerk of the Peace, &c. for my life, or such term as may be fixed upon, (which I believe is preferable) I will send it by this conveyance; if not, it shall follow as soon as possible. Is there no news of a public gaol? nor any hopes of the Assembly purchasing my patent? I wish to hear from you on this subject.

I am your's,

Richard Cumberland

Source: Mudford.

1. While the rise of Pitt to power in 1766 was cheerful news to the Colonies, the irritations that prevented peace between England and America were to continue. The Mutiny Act of 1766 authorizing military leaders to require local communities to support the troops was widely disregarded, particularly in New York and Massachusetts. The administration of Pitt, now the Earl of Chatham, passed an act prohibiting New York's Assembly from passing any Act until they had complied with these orders. Chatham found that the pacification of American aspirations was not easy. Moreover, the question of obtaining revenue from America still persisted. See Steven Watson, *The Reign of George III* (Oxford, 1960), pp. 122ff.

2. Lauchlin Macleane (d. 1777) was Governor of St. Martin's in the West Indies in 1765, and later Secretary to Lord Shelbourne and a member of Parliament. The Second Earl of Shelbourne (1737-1805) was at this time Secretary of State for the Southern Department.

3. Charles Shinner.

4. Lord Charles Montagu.

5. See 8 July 1767 and 27 October 1769.

XII Roger Pinckney 30 January 1767

Plantation Office, Jan 30, 1767

Dear Pinckney,

I just now receive your letter of the 28th of November, by the ship Friendship, and am made exceeding happy by the hopes you give me of putting my affairs in a train for success, respecting the surrender of my patent: I shall wait with impatience for
the event of their report, and shall be glad to
treat with their agent, whom I am somewhat acquainted with.[1] Though I have lost some political support
by Lord Halifax's retirement from business,[2] I yet
think I can summon strength enough to carry this
point. I shall be particularly happy if you can get
agreeably established in the office, and will make
no terms in which your interest is not made a condition.

With respect to my place of Clerk of the Crown and
Pleas, you know I have for a long time past touched
nothing from it but my salary; if therefore you can
sell it, together with the salary for the term of my
life, I desire you will; and as I think you can do
it by virtue of your power of attorney, I desire you
will make a bargain for me, the best you can in the
case, and let me know by the first opportunity.

Accept my best thanks,
And believe me your's,

Richard Cumberland

Source: Mudford.

1. Charles Garth
2. Halifax had been replaced as Secretary of State for the Southern Department by General H. S. Conway on 12 July 1765.

XIII **Roger Pinckney** 3 June 1767

Queen Anne-Street, June 3, 1767

Dear Pinckney,

Captain Ball being on the point of sailing, I cannot let him depart without writing you a line, though I have not yet received a word from you since your letter inclosing that bill which I sent you back protested. Many ships are now arrived, and I am still frustrated in my hopes of hearing from you, so that I am under no small concern, lest your health should have prevented you. The Little Carpenter, I am told is soon expected, and I hope I shall not be disappointed when she arrives.

Mr. Garth,[1] your provincial agent, has represented his memorial to Lord Shelbourne, relative to the purchase of my patent.[2] The result of this application is yet in suspense, though I am very much inclined to think that government will accede to our proposal; provided the legislature of South Carolina are content to pass a bill of the same nature with those which have been passed in other colonies, for establishing sheriffs, and will accompany that bill with a clause, suspending its execution till his Majesty's, (or the patentee's) consent is obtained. You shall have the earliest intelligence of our proceedings, and I beseech you to help my interests with your leading Assembly men, towards disposing them to advance in their offers; ever considering that they are purchasing a perpetuity, and for the value which my place brings on the spot, not its rent to me as residing here in England.

I write in haste; but am ever,

My dear Sir,
Most sincerely and faithfully yours,

Richard Cumberland.

Source: Mudford.

1. Charles Garth.

2. A copy of a "Report from the Lords of Trade" to the Earl of Shelbourne, Secretary of State for the Southern Department, is included in the Pinckney letters in Mudford ("Appendix," pp. 43-44). It indicates the content of Garth's "Memorial": "...we have taken into our consideration the memorial of Mr. Garth, Agent for South Carolina, petitioning, that County Sheriffs may be appointed in that Province in lieu of a Provost Marshal...." The report recommends favorable action: "We do not hesitate, therefore, to recommend it to your lordship to advise his Majesty to instruct his Governor of South Carolina, to give his assent to an Act of Assembly for instituting County Sheriffs in lieu of a Provost Marshal (provided proper compensation be made to the present Patentee for his interest in the said office), in like form and manner as has been done in other Colonies...."

XIV Roger Pinckney 8 July 1767

Plantation Office, July 8, 1767

Dear Pinckney,

I again trouble you with an inclosed dispatch for General Shirley,[1] of which I entreat your particular care. I am this morning favoured with your letter of the 10th of May, in-closing the drafts of agreement; I have had scarce time to run my eye over the contents of your letter, being much hurried when I read

it, much less have I had time to consider the purport and requisition of it, but I always feel myself
heartily disposed to do every thing that, in reason
and justice, I possibly can for your interest and
benefit. The business of the sheriffs is not yet
brought to a conclusion, but from circumstances I
have no manner of doubt that Government will consent
to their establishment, and gladly consent, as it is
an institution more approved of than that of a Provost Marshal, upon various very substantial reasons.
Nothing therefore but price can part us, and I think
the Assembly will not be their own enemies so much
as to differ with me upon a small sum; and my demands I am sure will not be out of reason.

I thankfully received your turtle safe and sound,
and a marvellous fine one it was; we celebrated the
founder of our feast with great festivity, and nothing could be more acceptable than your favour was. I
thanked you for it by the first opportunity: and am
glad to do it again by this occasion; as well as to
tell you how much I think myself beholden to you for
your further designs.

I am much disappointed at the state of your affairs in Charlestown, neither money nor bills to be
had. I am glad you got the bad bill for 100*l.* in a-
gain. Gold would be pretty near as good as dollars,
but either gold, silver, or good paper, would be
very acceptable.

I am truly concerned to hear of Mrs. Pinckney's
deplorable state of health. How you must suffer on
this occasion! so dreadful a disorder, and so cure-
less an one; surely it would be advisable to send
her home.[2] Command my services on this business, for
indeed I feel for you and her most cordially.

My wife and little ones are all well, and she desires to be kindly remembered to you; the good bishop and family are also in perfect health; he is
still in England, but is on the point of setting out
on his return to Ireland.[3]

Accept my constant good wishes, and ever believe
me,

Dear Sir,
Your's most faithfully,

Richard Cumberland

Source: Mudford.

1. Governor William Shirley of the Bahamas.
2. Cumberland mentions Mrs. Pinckney's death in his letter of 27 October 1769.
3. Cumberland's father.

XV Roger Pinckney 29 July 1767

Plantation Office, July 29, 1767

Dear Pinckney,

I beg you will deliver the inclosed letter, together with my best respects, to Lord Charles;[1] I need not tell you that it refers to the subject of the patent.

I was in some doubt whether I should not write to the Committee upon the same subject, but as it occurs to me that their agent, Mr. Garth, may not take the thing well, if I communicate with his constituents immediately, I shall entreat of you to signify to them the following particulars:

"Mr. Garth having, with my concurrence presented a Memorial to Lord Shelburne, Secretary of State, proposing the establishment of County Sheriffs, in lieu of a Provost Marshal, his lordship has favourably received the said Petition, and referred it to the consideration of this Board. The Report, which has been made in consequence thereof, recommends it to his lordship to advise his Majesty to instruct his Governor of South Carolina to give his assent to an

Act of Assembly for instituting County Sheriffs in lieu of a Provost Marshall, provided proper compensation be made to the present patentee, and provided a clause be inserted therein, suspending its execution till his Majesty's pleaure thereupon shall be known.[2]

"This Report having been accordingly made, in a conference I had yesterday with Lord Shelburne upon this subject, his lordship was so good to promise that he would forward the business in council, and cause a very speedy order to be issued to this Board for preparing an additional instruction to the Government, according to the above purport and effect."

The business, therefore, being in such forwardness, and the security that we may be considered to be in as to the Crown's assenting to the patent's being vacated, I have thought it a proper season for declaring to Mr. Garth what my terms definitively are: five thousand pounds sterling is the sum I have demanded, and, all things weighed and considered, I am persuaded that my demand is just and reasonable.

If they assent to this proposal, and will empower Mr. Garth to conclude with me upon these conditions, I will then cause the additional instruction to be transmitted agreeably to the order in Council; but, if they will not close upon this bargain, it will be of no use to transmit the instruction while our negociation remains open.

I beg of you to signify to the Committee of Correspondence, what I have now written, and if they urge an argument which I have heard suggested, I beg you will answer it on my part. The argument I mean is this, viz. that having obtained this sanction to their proposal for abolishing the office of Provost Marshal, they have only to wait the event of my death, and then it will be adjusted without any expence.

To this I answer, that the Assembly being an immortal body, may no doubt wait the determination of my life; but that it will by no means follow that his event is to put them in possession of their wishes. Different ministers may adopt different measures; a strict attention to prerogative, or a mere natural regard to their own patronage, may effect a change of sentiment with respect to the matter in question. Supposing that the office was vacant, it is not likely that a minister would forego the disposal of it merely to save the expences of the Province of South Carolina; when, after having bestowed it as he thought fit, it would then be favour enough to consent to the disposal of it, by sale, to them.[3]

These, I think, are natural conclusions, and such as it is not likely the Assembly will trust to; however I must, besides, observe, that it would be rather ungenerous to urge that prospect of success, which is entirely owing to my concurrence and solicitation, as an argument for reducing me in my terms.

I beg, therefore, you will oppose any argument of this sort, with reasoning of the nature above-mentioned, or such better as your own judgment suggests. I rely absolutely upon you in this matter, and have no doubt of your friendship and assistance; in return for which you may depend upon every attention to your interest that is in my power to give.

I wish much to hear what you have done relative to my other employment of Clerk of the Peace, &c. I should be glad if you could dispose of it for my life, to any reasonable advantage; and I conceive you are sufficiently empowered for that purpose.

I have as yet received no remittances whatever, since the protested bill; I can assure you they would be very acceptable, and though I am satisfied you do all in your power to forward them to me, yet I must confess that I am not a little distressed for want of them. Gold would be very acceptable in failure of dollars.

I thank you for the trouble you have taken in procuring me another turtle. I have heard nothing of it at present, but shall be very thankful to you for it, whenever it arrives.

I am, with great esteem,
Dear Sir,
Most faithfully your's,

Richard Cumberland.

Pray deliver the enclosed letter to Mr. George Saxby and young Guerard; I have forgot his Christian name, so I must desire you to fill it up.

I think it may be useful to transmit to you a copy of the Report to Lord Shelburne,[4] though I make no doubt Mr. Garth will send it to his constituents; however you will have it first, and may communicate it with some advantage to me.

If you think the Committee would like to hear from me immediately, pray inform me, and I will write to them.

R. C.

Source: Mudford.

1. Lord Charles Greville Montagu, Governor of South Carolina.
2. See 3 June 1767, note.
3. Had the colony awaited the event of Cumberland's death it would have lost the gamble, for he lived until 7 May 1811. However, the events of the American Revolution would have rendered the patent worthless much earlier.
4. Printed in Mudford, "Appendix," pp. 43-44.

XVI [Benjamin] Guerard[1] Guerard   29 July 1767

Plantation Office, July 29, 1767

Dear Sir,

Allow me to enquire after your welfare by this

conveyance, and to assure you of the grateful remembrance I preserve of the politeness and favours I have received both from your father and yourself.

I am now in treaty with the Assembly of your Province, through the intervention of their agent, Mr. Garth,[2] for the surrender of my patent of Provost Marshal. The situation to which I have now brought that affair, gives me an almost certain prospect of success, if they do but approve the terms and conditions which I have proposed. I persuade myself that these terms are just and honest, and in no respect exorbitant, at least if I thought so I would not propose them; my demand, Sir, is five thousand pounds sterling. This board has made a Report favourable to the proposal, and it only remains now for the King in Council to direct an instruction to be prepared for his Governor, for assenting to a bill, instituting County Sheriffs in lieu of a Provost Marshal. As soon as Mr. Garth and I have agreed upon terms, I will cause this instruction to be transmitted, and till then it will be better on all accounts to keep it suspended.

As I know you are capable both of private as well as public friendship, and as I flatter myself you would wish well to my interests when they do not clash with those of the Province, I think I may hope for your services in the present case, where, undoubtedly, the public convenience and advantage is as much concerned as mine is. Allow me, therefore, to entreat your favour for assistance towards inducing such of your friends as are concerned in this negociation, to close with me upon the present proposals I have made, and from which I shall not depart.

Accept my constant good wishes for your welfare and prosperity and believe me,

Dear Sir,
Your most obedient
And faithful humble servant,

Richard Cumberland.

Source: Mudford.

1. Probably Benjamin Guerard, a member of the South Carolina Assembly, who served on the Committee of Correspondence. John Guerard, probably his father, was a Charleston merchant.
2. Charles Garth.

XVII George Saxby 29 July 1767

Plantation Office, July 29, 1767

Dear Sir,

As I owe the original suggestion to you, I have all along used the freedom of making you acquainted with the steps I have taken relative to the disposal of my patent of Provost Marshal.

The situation in which the matter now stands, ensures a favourable and speedy issue to the business, provided the Assembly think fit to acceed to my terms. I ask no more than five thousand pounds sterling, and I flatter myself that, when all things are considered, they will not be thought hard or unreasonable.

The Report which the Lords of Trade have made in favour of this measure, to his Majesty, and the disposition that the present Secretary of State[1] is in to complete the exchange, leave me no room to doubt the success of the affair. Lord Shelburne has assured me, that an Order of Council shall speedily be sent for preparing an instruction to the Governor, to pass an act to this effect, but this instruction I shall detain here in England till Mr. Garth and I are agreed.

If you think my demands are just and reasonable,

as I persuade myself you will, from what passed between us before your departure, I hope and trust you
will contribute all in your power to forward an accommodation, in doing which you will no doubt have
the satisfaction of serving the Province, which cannot fail of receiving great use and benefit from the
institution of County Sheriffs in lieu of that of
Provost Marshal.

An opportunity so favourable as the present may
not happen again for a long term of years. I think,
therefore, that the Assembly will not object to the
proposal I have made, when they consider it maturely
and fully.

I have the honour to be, with great esteem and respect,

Dear Sir,
Your most obedient and faithful humble servant,

Richard Cumberland.

Source: Mudford.

1. Lord Shelburne, Secretary of State for the Southern Department.

XVIII **Roger Pinckney**   17 October 1767

Queen Anne Street, October 17, 1767

My dear Sir,

I wrote a few lines to you by a young man who has
served me in the capacity of coachman for two years,
and has now hired himself to Mr. Gibbs,[1] of your
Province. I have promised the man that, if he be-
haves well, you will, if occasion requires, protect

him: and allow him to lodge in your hands any little matter he may have the good fortune to save. I am not in the least acquainted with Mr. Gibbs, so that I look upon it as possible that he may need your countenance and assistance. He has stipulated to serve him for three years, at the rate of 40*l.* sterling per annum.

I have wrote fully to you on the subject of my treaty with Mr. Garth, relative to my patent. The Secretary of State[2] has wrote to Lord Charles,[3] empowering him to give his assent to an Act for that purpose, provided it is passed with a suspending clause, and that compensation is made to me. My terms are fixed at 5000*l.* sterling, and I have the satisfaction to find that they are thought here to be very reasonable.

I have been favoured by you with a bill from Lord Charles of 50*l.* with 340 dollars by the same conveyance, and since that with 600 dollars, the amount of which is as follows:

	£.	s.	d.
Aug. 20--By Lord Charles Montagu's draft.	50	0	0
By 340 dollars.....................	78	6	1
Sept. 14.-By 600 ditto...................138		6	0
	266	12	1

A thousand thanks to you for a turtle. It is now late at night, and the servant waiting for this scrawl. The agreement was but made this morning with Mr. Gibbs, and early to-morrow he sets off for Gravesend, otherwise I would have thought of something that would have been agreeable to you. I sincerely wish to hear a better account of Mrs. Pinckney.[4] Mrs. Cumberland joins me in good wishes to you and your's; the Bishop[5] and family are well in Ireland.

> I am, dear Pinckney,
> Most faithfully your's,

Richard Cumberland.

Source: Mudford.

1. Possibly William Gibbes, a merchant, and father of the historian Robert W. Gibbes.
2. Lord Shelburne of the Southern Department.
3. Governor Charles Montagu.
4. See 27 October 1769 for the death of Mrs. Pinckney.
5. Cumberland's father.

XIX David Garrick Before 26 January 1768[1]

My dear friend,

Such you have been, are, and ever shall be. I will take an early opportunity to obey your wishes, when I can meet you without that flutter, which I now feel.

I am Yours,

R. C.

Source: British Science Museum. The manuscript is not in Cumberland's hand.

1. The manuscript records Garrick's endorsement of the letter as follows: "Mr. Cumberland's 2d Letter to me." The date of the earliest other letter from Cumberland to Garrick is 26 January 1768, the tone of which is such that Cumberland is well recovered from "that flutter" which he speaks of in this letter. Cumberland's first letter to Garrick has not been located.

XX   David Garrick   26 January 1768

Queen Anne Street Cavendish Square
January the 26th 1768

Sir

I beg leave to enclose an alter'd Copy of Shakespeare's *Timon*, with the Addition of a New Character,[1] which I dare say you will be polite enough to read. This Act of Civility I am confident you will not refuse, tho I must inform you that the Copy has been a long time in Mr. Colman's Hands,[2] who after having flatter'd it more than it deserves, and, as I was told, cast the Parts, has at length rejected it. I have little doubt but that your Opinion will agree with Mr. Colman's, however as I am totally disinterested with respect to profit in the offer, and as I hope the perusal will not involve you in any extraordinary Trouble, I take the Liberty of submitting it to your Judgement, and am, Sir

Your most obedient
Humble Servant

Richd Cumberland.

You will be good enough to return it to me according to the above Direction.

Source: British Science Museum. It is endorsed by Garrick: "Letter from Cumberland about Timon before our Correction."

1. Cumberland added the character of Evanthe, Timon's daughter. The play was not acted until 4 December 1771, at Drury Lane.
2. George Colman (1732-1794), then manager of the Covent Garden Theatre.

XXI David Garrick 7 February 1768

Queen Anne Street
February the 7th 1768

Sir,

I give you many thanks for the trouble you have taken in the perusal of Timon and your speedy Return of it; Had it met with your Approbation, it would have been entirely at your service without any reserve.[1] It was the unreasonable time Mr. Colman detained it, not his refusal, gave me offence. In the latter particular he did justice to himself, in the former he neglected what I thought was justly due to me and to every one, who makes a disinterested offer of his performance. Your conduct, Sir, has indeed confirmed my opinion of Mr. Colman's judgement, but convinced me that it woud have been no empeachment to his *Management* if he had had a little more politeness.

I shall be glad to see the Time when Simplicity is a recommendation to any Dramatick piece. It was in conformity to the depravity of modern Taste that I alter'd Shakespear, and conceived that when I robb'd him of the beauties of his native Simplicity, I made him less venerable indeed, but more suitably equipt for the Company he was to keep.

I hope your ideas are better founded, than mine.

I am, Sir,
Your most obedient
Humble servant

Richd Cumberland.

Source: British Science Museum. It is endorsed by Garrick: "Letter from Mr. Cumberland about Timon before our Correction."

1. Garrick changed his mind about *Timon* after Cumberland's reputation had been established by *The West Indian*. *Timon* was acted and favorably received at Drury Lane on 4 December 1771.

XXII   David Garrick   21 March 1768

Queen Anne Street, March 21, 1768

Sir,

I have a comedy in my possession which has never been in any hands but my own, and is, both in plot and execution, entirely new and original.[1] If your engagements for the ensuing season admit, and the offer of this piece will be agreeable to you, it shall be submitted to your refusal, upon presumption that, in case of acceptance, it will be brought out between the periods of Christmas and Lent next. The characters are numerous, and some new decorations will be necessary.

If these proposals are acceptable, it shall be got ready for your perusal as soon as a correct copy can be made out; but as this must fall singly upon myself, it will be some little time before I can send it to you; in the mean while you will favour me with your answer.

I am, Sir, your most obedient humble servant,

Richard Cumberland

Source: Boaden.

1. *The Brothers*. Garrick did not accept the comedy, but it was successfully produced at Covent Garden on 2 December 1769.

XXIII **David Garrick   After 21 March 1768**[1]

Queen Anne Street,
Thursday Morning

Sir,

I am favoured with your letter, and as the piece[2] which I have now Offered to you was such as I flatter myself would not have disgraced either you or myself, and was particularly in the walk of some of your principal comedians, I am sorry it cannot have a representation at your Theatre, and that what I thought a very early application finds you absolutely engaged for the whole ensuing season.

I readily believe that I should have no cause of complaint was you to accept any production of mine; 'twas in this presumption that I tendered the piece in question, not with any view to Theatrical emoluments; but how to arrive at favours so long in anticipation, I am utterly at a loss; for if I find the ensuing season shut against me before this is expired; I think it not improbable that before another succeeds, you may be tired of the trouble of receiving these performances, and I cured of the folly of writing them.

If you find yourself at leisure to make any subsequent engagements for next season, I presume I shall have the preference, which in point of time is due to my application.

I am, Sir,
Your most obedient
humble servant,

Richd Cumberland

Source: British Science Museum. The manuscript is not in Cumberland'd hand.

1. The date is determeined by Cumberland's letter to Garrick of 21 March 1768, in which he offers the comedy.

2. *The Brothers.* The comedy was acted on 2 December 1769 at Covent Garden with Garrick in the audience. Cumberland complimented him in the epilogue, and this offer of friendship together, with the obvious high quality of the play, led to a lasting association between them.

XXIV   Roger Pinckney   15 August 1768

August 15, 1768

Dear Pinckney,

I put off writing to you till I could inform you of the fate of the Act for the establishment of courts, &c. which, on account of the importance of it, and delicacy to my interest, has been some time under examination of the Lords of Trade. Sir Matthew Lambe[1], one of his Majesty's Counsel, to whom the Board refers all Plantation Acts, had objected to some clauses in the Bill; particualrly to the summary jurisdiction of the judges in their Circuit Courts, which he stated as an extent greater than obtained in any other Colony, and for less than which acts had been heretofore repealed. He observed, that the salary to the Attorney-General and the Clerk of the Pleas was granted to them personally, while in office, and not annexed to the offices. But the main question was the clause for granting salaries to the judges, whenever his Majesty should change the present form of their commissions, and establish them during *good behaviour*, against this clause the chief force of his objection was directed, and it was submitted by him whether it would not be derogatory to the King's dignity to pass an Act with such a clause in it. This was Sir Matthew Lambe's Report to us, upon the Act in question. In

answer to these objections various arguments were
used, both by your humble servant, and particularly
Mr. Garth,[2] who, at a solemn hearing of the Board,
and on a day singly set apart for this business,
spoke for two hours to the question, with great a-
bility and spirit. The sense of the Board upon the
event was, that the objections on the one part, and
the advantages of the Act on the other, should be
fairly stated, and the matter left to the decision
of the King and Council. The Lords were of opinion,
that no objection laid against the summary jurisdic-
tions being extended to 20*l.* sterling; particularly
as both, or either, of the parties might resort to
the ordinary forms of common law, or equity, if they
thought fit; a law of the same sort obtains in Ireland, and the convenience that would result from it,
was thought a full balance for the uncommon extent
of it. The Attorney-General's clause was stated as
exceptionable in a degree, but not fatal against a
bill productive of such general benefit. It had been
urged by Mr. Garth, that these officers (viz. the
Attorney-General and Clerk of the Pleas) would be
put to great extra trouble in carrying the measure
of this Act into operation, and therefore these appointments were given them as a personal compensation for that trouble, and this was done by salary
rather than by grant at once, as it was possible
those officers might quit their employs before the
whole business was conducted to an issue, and they
entitled to their full reward.

As to the clause for altering the judges commissions, that was not got over with such ease. A particular instruction in the year 1760 had been circu-
lated to all the continental governors, forbidding
them to give their assent to any Act of Assembly
for making alteration in the Commissions of the
Judges, and this was done on account of some steps
of that nature taken by New York; this particular
instruction is since incorporated into the general
body of instructions given to all governors, and
makes the 42d article of Lord Charles Montagu's. In

the face of such an article, it is not possible for
government to pass over this regulation, which
should have come by way of separate application, and
not been tacked to an Act of this high importance.
To make the judges removable only by writ of *scire
facias* in the Provinces, without subjecting thenm to
parliamentary jurisdiction, will, I conceive, never
be adopted by this country. Upon the whole, therefore, I conclude that the council will repeal the
Act on account of this clause. The advantages of the
general regulation will be stated in the report of
the Lords of Trade, in a very full and explicit
manner, and as I think Mr. Garth will speedily
transmit a copy of that report to his constituents,
and I hope the temper and moderation of government
will appear so conspicuous throughout the agitation
of this question, that the Assembly will find no
difficulty in passing it without this exceptionable
clause.

I have now only to request the favour of you to
continue your kind services to me in this affair, in
the same disinterested manner you have hitherto proceeded; to move every friend you have in government,
not to let a measure of such public convenience fall
to the ground from a false punctilio, when this
country is disposed to grant them evey indulgence in
the general affair that can be wished for, and the
crown has consented to abrogate its patent. I should
hope your Assembly will see it in this light, and
let it be one of the first acts of their session, to
re-enact this useful law in a manner less objectionable, in case it should be repealed. With respect to
my office of Clerk of the Crown and Peace, I should
hope you will be able to part from it to advantage
for the term of my life; you have had powers for
that purpose; which, I believe, are sufficient, and
I dare say, you will take the first good opportunity
of doing it.

I inclose a little abstract of our account current, which I believe you will find right. You state
Joliffe's[3] bill at £65. in yours of March 6th.; I

48

have entered it at £60. only, but as I have not my banker's book, I cannot correct it now, but will in my next. Farewel.

Believe me most faithfully
And obediently your's,

Richard Cumberland.

Source: Mudford.

1. Counsel to the Board of Trade. See Richard Maxwell Brown, *The South Carolina Regulators* (Cambridge, Massachusetts), pp. 79-80.

2. Charles Garth.

3. The identity of Joliffe is obscure. There seems to be no connection with the Jollife family of Virginia, details of which are given in *The Historical, Genealogical and Biographical Account of the Jollife Family of Virginia 1652-1893* (Philadelphia, 1893).

XXV Roger Pinckney 12 October 1768

Tyringham, Oct. 12, 1768

Dear Sir,

I am here partaking of a few holidays, and am just now informed by my friend Mr. Pownall,[1] that the council have advised his Majesty to disallow the Act for the abolition of the Provost Marshal's office. The objections which have occasioned this repeal you are acquainted with, by a former letter from me,[2] and indeed, in great part from your own suggestions; I shall not, therefore, repeat them; the clause concerning the judge's commissions, had the most weight against it. At the same time that his Majesty will

signify his royal disallowance, he will likewise instruct his governor to recommend the repassing this
Act, for the above general purposes, free from those
objections; and as all has been conducted with tenderness and respect towards the Province and its
legislature, I cannot but sanguinely hope and expect
the return of the Bill in an unexceptionable shape.
Your good offices will, I dare say, be exerted on
this occasion; and as the Secretary of State[3] stops
the sailing of the pacquet singly for this purpose,
of instructing the governor[4] relative to the return
of this Bill, I should hope the Assembly will take
it up in their first meeting, and as there is so
little to be done to it, it may very well be got
through before Christmas. Mr. Garth, their agent,
is, I believe, at the Devizes; if so, perhaps he
cannot write officially by this pacquet, nor send
over a copy of the Board's representation, which you
will see was very favourable and indulgent. In that
case, I must entreat of you to converse with the
Speaker and leading men of the Assembly, and to soften their minds towards the measure, by assuring
them, (which you truly may) that the repeal of this
Act has not been hastily or captiously decided on,
but upon full and temperate deliberations, and principally upon the motives of their proposal for altering the judge's commissions, which certainly
should not have been made a clause in an Act, and
from which the governor was, by express instructions, particularly restricted.

I write in the greatest haste, hoping that this
letter may find a conveyance, together with the Secretary of State's dispatches, for which purpose I
enclose it to Mr. Pownall, but I think I need use
but few words to induce you to use your best offices, and as to the manner how, you are doubtless a
far better judge than I can pretend to be.

I will write more fully to you by the next conveyance of a merchant ship, and in the meantime, (as
always) am your very affectionate friend, and

Obliged humble servant,

Richard Cumberland.

The bishop and family are expected here from Dublin every day.[5] Mrs. Cum. sends compliments, she and the little ones are all well.

Source: Mudford.

1. John Pownall, Secretary of the Board of Trade.
2. 15 August 1768.
3. Lord Shelburne.
4. Lord Charles Montagu.
5. Cumberland's father.

XXVI **Roger Pinckney   27 October 1769**

Queen Anne-Street, Oct. 27, 1769[1]

Dear Pinckney,

By the pacquet, which was detained in order to convey the Secretary of State's[2] dispatches to the governor,[3] touching the repeal of the Act for instituting sheriffs, &c. you was troubled with a letter from me. The reasons upon which that Act was repealed, and the conditions on which the crown will give its assent to another for the same general purposes, are fully explained to the governor, and the copy of this Board's report on the law is likewise annexed to the letter, which conveys those reasons. What will be now the fate of this important measure remains with time to discover: the spirit of *regulation* that obtains, so vehemently, in your back settlements, the total subversion of the regular course of administering justice by the Provost Marshal, and the general outcry that obtains throughout the interior of your country for county courts and the establishment of sheriffs, will, surely, induce your legislature to repass the Act, upon such terms and conditions as the crown has thought fit to prescribe.

There is one stipulation, however, which may in some degree check the progress of this Act, and, perhaps, endanger its safety; that is, the condition that his Majesty's governor shall not be bound to nominate one of the three persons returned by the judges. People disinclined to the measure, may possibly make this a plausible handle for opposing it, but surely the crown, which has now the absolute nomination of the Provost Marshal, may retain to itself the power of naming a pocket sheriff through the means of its governor, when the king voluntarily consents to abolish his patent. The practice in England justifies the crown in this exertion of its prerogative, and I cannot think the Province will be put upon worse ground, by having a sheriff appointed *de novo* by the sole authority of the king's governor, than they would by having one of his election out of three recommended by the judges; for these judges, you know, are as much in the power of the crown, as the governor is, and so they seem likely to remain. Upon the whole, what can be more just and equitable than for the crown to make its own stipulations, when it is conferring a favour? The whole question is, whether the institution of sheriffs, upon such reasonable terms, is, or is not, more advantageous to South Carolina than the present establishment of a Provost Marshall; if they think so, they will reenact their law; if they do not, nothing that you and I can say will signify a straw.

I read with much concern, in our papers, of the death of Mrs. Pinckney;[4] the long state of ill health she has laboured under, must have inured you to the loss you have endured; I have now only to hope that, when your grief has subsided, you will look out for yourself a good rich planter, and make

52

up your fortune with her assistance for life.[5]

Pray write to me frequently and fully; I need not tell you that a few dollars will be acceptable.

I am, my dear Pinckney,
Most faithfully yours,

Richard Cumberland.

I much wish to hear what you have done with my office of Clerk of, &c. &c. I beg your furtherance of the enclosed letter to Colonel Shirley.[6]

Source: Mudford.

1. The date here is unquestionably a misprint in Mudford on the basis of the suggestion of Mrs. Pinckney's death. The next letter, 15 March 1769, speaks of Pinckney's plans to marry again.

2. Lord Shelbourne.

3. Lord Charles Montagu.

4. Cumberland had expressed concern over Mrs. Pinckney's health in a number of previous letters, 2 July 1766 and 1 January, 8 July and 17 October 1767.

5. The marriage of Roger Pinckney and Susannah Hume (widow) on 26 March 1769 at Charleston, South Carolina, is recorded in *North and South Carolina Marriage Records from the Earliest Colonial Days to the Civil War*, compiled and edited by William Montgomery Clemens (New York, 1927).

6. General William Shirley, who was Governor of the Bahamas, succeeded in having that post turned over to his son in 1769 (*The Correspondence of William Shirley*, ed. Charles Henry Lincoln [New York, 1912], I, xxx).

XXVII   Roger Pinckney   15 March 1769

Queen Anne-Street, March 15, 1769

Dear Pinckney,

I am to thank you for the favour of both your o-
bliging letters, the last of which (dated Jan. the
27th) came to hand this very day. It gives me so
much pleasure, and of so sincere a sort, that I cannot withstand the satisfaction of writing diretly in
answer to it; the prospect you set before me, of the
happy and advantageous alliance you are now upon the
point of forming,[1] has given me inconceivable delight; I have always felt myself in a manner responsible for your good or ill fortune, and this event
has relieved me from all anxiety on your account.
Mr. William Strong happening to be in town, and
bound to Peterborough to-morrow, I seized the occasion of communicating the good tidings to your
friends in that place, which, for what I know, may
be new intelligence to them. The Bishop of Clonfert,[2] with whom I dined this day, joins with us all
in congratulating you on your aproaching good fortune; he charges me to assure you of his constant
regard for you, and his wishes in your behalf. I beg
you will make my respects, and those of Mrs. Cumberland, to your lady, and assure her, that we shall
remember the day, and wear wedding favours upon the
occasion. I need not assure you how happy we shall
be to see you in England next spring, and shall
study to make London as agreeable to Mrs. Pinckney,
as it will be in our power; I hope nothing will prevent your design taking place, and I have no doubt I
shall find your fair choice as amiable, and as full
of accomplishments as you think her.

I esteem myself highly beholden to you, for your
disinterested and friendly support of my interests
in the negociation of my patent. That fatal and unfortunate measure for dissolving the Assembly has
thrown every thing back; what it arose from is past
my comprehension;[3] I have yet to hope that every
thing will turn out well at last; I think your Assembly will be called together upon amicable terms,
and I persuade myself they will meet with friendly
dispositions; nothing, I believe, can be less hostile than the sentiments of government towards them,

and I think, amongst other marks of their regard to the requisitions of the mother country, and the dictates of their own interest, this Act, (as recommended by the crown) will take place; it is surely a gracious tender on the part of his Majesty, and the pressing necessity of your internal police makes it highly expedient for the welfare of the Province. I wish you may take your seat in the Assembly, and I dare say, your voice and support will greatly forward this salutary proposal.

I am preparing, (and I hope to send you by this conveyance) a prolongation to your lease; in which, for the sake of accommodating myself to the convenience of the Province, I have taken the liberty of making it a condition in the said lease, that upon six months notice, I may be released from the engagement. I am sure your candour will see the necessity of this measure, and look upon it in the right light. With respect to security, I refer myself to your honour; I will not apply to any third person to transact that business for me, but I rely, with confidence, that you will send me over such an obligation as shall be satisfactory and sufficient.

I am sorry you cannot dispose of my other office[4] to advantage, for, in the state it is, it lies quite profitless and fallow: by the time you come to England, you will, I dare say, conclude upon something beneficial.

Never entertain a moment's thought that I have suffered myself to doubt of your friendship, punctuality, or integrity; so many proofs as you have given me in each respect, must have put that matter long since out of doubt. I am perfectly satisfied with your conduct in every particular, and have never heard a report that has not been to your honour. I am now to acknowledge the receipt of £150. sterling, by bill of exchange, which I have no doubt will be duly honoured, and of which, upon that presumption, I now discharge you. The money resulting from the legacy you mention, I have not as yet heard of;[5] it is most probable a few days will inform me of it, and I will then give you credit to the amount by the first opportunity, and, at the same time, transmit the abstract of our whole account. I thank you, likewise, for the promise you make me, of remitting to me upon sale of your rice; it is a favour more than I can expect, to be paid in advance, but I think myself obliged to you for the intention, and will take care to make myself properly responsible when such an event takes place.

I think I have little to add on this occasion, more than to re-assure you of the cordial participation I feel in your approaching happiness, and to make an offer of my best services, in case you have any commissions to execute here in England. In return for your good news, I hope soon to send you tiding of my promotion to considerable advantage in my present occupation.[6]

I am, dear Sir,
Your most faithful servant,
And sincere friend,

Richard Cumberland.

Source: Mudford.

1. Pinckney's marriage to Susannah Hume.

2. Cumberland's father.

3. The passage of the Townshend duties by Parliament in 1767 angered the Massachusetts Assembly which urged all the other Assemblies to unite in opposition to it. Lord Hillsborough, Secretary of State for the Colonies, ordered the Colonial governors to prevent their respective Assemblies from supporting Massachusetts. When Governor Montagu ordered the Assembly of South Carolina not to support Massachusetts, they defied him and did so. His reaction was immediately to dissolve the Assembly (*South Carolina Regulators*. p. 63).

4. Clerk of the Peace and Clerk of the Crown.

5. There is no subsequent mention of this legacy in the letters.

6. Cumberland remained in a subordinate position at the Board
of Trade until he was elevated to Secretary by George Germain
(Lord Sackville), who became Secretary of State for Colonial Affairs in 1775.

XXVIII   David Garrick   25 January 1770

Jan. 25th 1770

Sir,

I am as ready to adopt unfavourable sentiments of
my own performances, as any man living and therefore
do not allow that we differ in opinion about Salome.[1] I gave it to you (as I have done every other
performance of mine)[2] as the best I coud write, but
I did not insist upon it that you was to approve of
it. I fear now it is not within the bounds of my
genius to give you satisfaction. However as these
points are soon settled in conversation, and read
very ill upon paper, I hope you will not think it
much trouble to indulge me with a few minutes conversation tomorrow morning, and that I maynt interrupt better business I will call between ten and e-
leven.

The motives of Salome (if I mistake not) are revenge, ambition and disappointment. These are strong
principles for guilty action; perhaps they are not
so forcibly marked in her character as they might
be, but a very few touches might finish that part of
the peice as highly as you please. Her life twice
attempted by Mariamne, her ambition defeated by Antipater and her revenge frustrated by Alexander, I
know no other principle but love that coud add to
the motives that she has for what she commits. You
see I have still a little partiality left, a small
feeling for a performance which has been many years
under my pen, and which hitherto no friend (nor even

Mr. Colman himself) has assisted with an objection. With your leave I will wait upon you, and I dare say I shall submit my prejucices to your better judgement. I can by no means wish to have any peice put into a performers hand, which a manager disapproves, and therefore beg it may not be shewn to Mrs. Barry,[3] unless it is honour'd with your recommendation.

I am, Sir, Your most obedt
Humble servant
Richd Cumberland

Source: Victortia and Albert Museum.

1. "Salome" was never produced or published. Cumberland discusses it further in his letter to Garrick of 17 March 1770. A play, "The Arab", containing many of the characters mentioned by Cumberland in the letter of 17 March, was acted on 8 March 1785 at Covent Garden. It has generally been thought to be an altered version of "Salome". The manuscript of "The Arab" is included in the Larpent Collection at the Huntington Library. Cumberland's *Posthumous Dramatic Works* (London, 1813) includes *Alcanor*, a substantially altered version of "The Arab".

2. Through the intercession of Halifax, Cumberland had offered Garrick *The Banishment of Cicero*. It was never produced but was published in 1761. Subsequently he offered Garrick *Timon of Athens*, a modernization of Shakespeare's play, which was initially rejected, but eventually produced in 1771. There is no evidence that Cumberland offered Garrick *The Summer's Tale*, a three-act musical, produced at Covent Garden on 6 December 1765 and in a two act version as *Amelia* in 1768. He gave Garrick an opportunity to produce *The Brothers*, which Garrick refused, but the play was acted with great success at the rival theatre, Covent Garden. Cumberland's first play to be produced by Garrick was *The West Indian* on 19 January 1771.

3. Anne Barry (1734-1801), one of the leading actresses at Drury Lane and the wife of the famous actor, Spranger Barry. Mrs. Barry, later Mrs. Crawford, retired from the stage in 1798.

XXIX David Garrick 17 March 1770[1]

March 17th

Dear Sir,

I send you my Tragedy[2] in obedience to your desires. I scarce expected you coud find time to give
it a Hearing, but I was not guided in that proposal
by any other motives than extreme solicitude for
your Judgement, and I am apt to think that many minute Observations strike upon a Reading which the
memory loses when they are to be related.

I am exceedingly anxious to produce such a peice
under your protection as shall serve our mutual
Fame. No labour therefore will deter me from giving
this every finishing, that my pen can give it. I
therefore present it to you not as perfect and compleat, but as much improved. Your Objections bring
so much amendment with them, that if you are not
tired with making them, I can never be weary of receiving them. In the present Copy the character of
Doris is not soften'd in point of Terror, rather
heightened; her Tone and Language is much raised,
but her Wickedness is much abated, by the strengthening that is given to her motives; the real injuries she has received, the Connection between her
and Antipator, and the non-perpetration of the Murder meliorate her Character exceeding. If yet the
Catastrophe is too shocking, by the danger in which
Glaphyra is kept, I have a plan for softening that,
tho' I am humbly of opinion it has a very great effect as it is.

The Character of *Antipater* I now venture to deliver to you as compleat in all parts and principles.
Glaphyra is introduc'd with much more eclat, and is
made altogether more reasonable and important. I
flatter myself you will approve the turn I have giv-
en to that of *Bethanor*, the use I have put him to,
and the great accessions that he is to the peice.

The softenings that his Character give to the Play will I think be a great releif to the general Cast of Terror that prevails throughout.

I said this to you, Sir, not to puff my performance, but to explain my meaning. Pray keep it without troubling yourself about an Answer as long as ever you please, and till you have full Leisure: for I shoud earnestly wish that you did not take it up till you coud read it fairly thro' at one sitting.

I can't conclude without telling you that my friend in the *Morning Chronicle*[3] has not forgot me. I casually took it up some time ago and found my name at full length with an assertion direcltly false as to the department in which I am concerned, and motives ascribed to me for my Dedication to the Duke of Grafton[4] which I utterly disavow. As you saw the Letter I wrote on a certain occasion,[5] I mention this to you as being the only return which I have ever received to it.

I am with great truth, Dear Sir,

Your most obedt
and faithfull Servant

Richd Cumberland.

If Mr. B.[6] is not Compiler of the Morn. Chronle. he is no ways responsible for what I refer to. But this is by no means worth your mentioning.

Source: British Science Museum.

1. The year is determined by the previous letter of 25 January 1770 dealing with "Salome."

2. "Salome."

3. The *Morning Chronicle* was an anti-ministry political organ. Cumberland, who was employed at the Board of Trade, was closely linked to the government.

4. Cumberland had dedicated *The Brothers* to the third Duke of

Grafton (1735-1811). In his *Memoirs*, he notes: "I was silly e-
nough to send this comedy into the world with a dedication to the
Duke of Grafton, a man, with whom I had not the slightest acquaintance, nor did I seek to establish any upon the merit of
this address: he was Chancellor of the University of Cambridge,
and this was my sole motive for inscribing my first comedy to
him" (I, p. 268).

5. Probably to Isaac Bickerstaffe (c.1735-1812), a writer of
popular musical plays, who had accused Cumberland of plagiarism
following the production of *The Summer's Tale* on 6 December 1765
at Covent Garden. In his *Memoirs*, Cumberland observes: "I was no
sooner put in possession of the proofs against him, than I remon-
strated by letter to him against his uncandid proceeding; I have
no copy of that letter;..." (I, p. 251). Cumberland maintained
that Bickerstaffe had shown Garrick the letter (I, 253).

6. Likely Bickerstaffe, but also possibly the journalist, Sir
Henry Bate (1745-1824), an early editor of *The Morning Post*.

XXX   Roger Pinckney   1 May 1770

Queen Anne-Street, May 1, 1770

Dear Pinckney,

I am to acknowledge your favours by the London,
Alexander Curling, and the Beauffair, Daniel Curling, by the former of which, I had your order for
the produce of 93 barrels of rice, and by the latter, which I have very lately received, have your
order for the produce of 19 barrels of ditto. The
amount of the first you will find specified in a
little account inclosed, signed by Geo. Curling.
Since the receipt of the second, I have not seen
Geo. Curling, so can say nothing to that at present;
you have, likewise, inclosed an account of debtor
and creditor, continued since the conclusion of the
year 1765, when I stood indebted to you in the balance of £4. 11s. 9d. and carried down to the day of

my vacating the Provost Marshal's office.[1] I receive your congratulations on that agreeable event, with the utmost thankfulness, for all your kind and friendly offices; but as I have already conveyed my thanks to you on that subject, I won't punish your delicacy by repeating them too often. I now look to you for some assistance in the case of my remaining office of Clerk, &c. &c. which I think may be advantageously disposed of, upon the plan that I pointed out in my last letter. The Province must feel the use of taking these offices into their own management, and the appointment of clerks for the circuits cannot but be an object to the legislature, in the constitution of their courts; without they agree with me for my life in those offices, it cannot be expected I can appoint and furnish separate deputies for the respective circuits, when only one deputy cannot, or will not, afford to pay me any acknowledgement for the whole amount of the fees.

I sincerely congratulate you and Mrs. Pinckney on your birth of a son, and hope, upon her recovery, you will think of a trip to England; where Mrs. Cum. and I shall be happy to see you. Accept our joint compliments, and believe me,

Dear Pinckney,
Most faithfully your's,

Richard Cumberland.

Source: Mudford.

1. Stanley Williams, in *Richard Cumberland* (New Haven, 1915), is incorrect in assuming, in regard to the Provost Marshal's office, that "the desired change was not effected" (p. 59). Cumberland succeeded in selling the office for £5,000. See D. D. Wallace, *Constitutional History of South Carolina*, p. 29, and D. D. Wallace, *The History of South Carolina*, I, 269.

XXXI **Roger Pinckney** 11 June 1770

Queen Anne-Street, June 11, 1770

Dear Pinckney,

What is become of you, and how has this sleep fallen upon our correspondence, that I have not seen your hand writing this age. I was not without hopes that the spring would have brought you over to England, and I can scarce now persuade myself but that you are on the water with your fair wife at your side, looking out for English land. If it should not be so, and that this meets you at Charlestown, you well know I have yet some interests under your care, which I am anxious to bring to some good conclusion; I mean the sale of my post of clerk, &c. which, with the salary payable by the king's receiver, might, I should think, in the present circumstances of the colony, be sold to considerable profit, for I do not know how their county courts can well exist without deputies in my offices, and I am sure I have neither means nor meaning to appoint any such. I have given you regular accounts of our balance, and of the proceeds of your rice, which I should fear did not entirely meet your expectations; I shall hope to hear from you very shortly, or which will be much better to see you.--Accept my sincere wishes for yourself, and present them to your lady and believe me,

Dear Pinckney,
Most faithfully yours,

Richard Cumberland,

Source: Mudford.

XXXII   David Garrick 24 June 1770[1]

Dear Sir

I have deliver'd your letters, and your message to your friend Mr. Fitzherbert, who, with his son,[2] will wait upon you on Tuesday next to Dinner.[3] I hope Mrs. Garrick and you will forgive me when I desire leave to accompany him and to bring Mrs. Cumberland with me who wishes much to improve her acquaintance with you and be made known to Mrs. Garrick. Mr. Fitzherbert speaks uncertainly whether he is to go on with you to the Duchess of Portland's[4] or to return with us at night, but you will best know how to fix him.

The truth of your remarks strook me so strongly that I have nearly executed all your corrections,[5] so that when you have a chancery suit, remember to subpoena me for your judgement in dramatick performances. I know no objection to it, but your partiality to a very imperfect sketch. I beg to present my compliments to Mrs. Garrick, and hope she will excuse the freedom I take on Mrs. Cumberland's account.

I am, Dear Sir, most faithfully yours

Richard Cumberland

Queen Anne Street
June the 24th.

Source: Folger.

1. The year is determined by reference to *The West Indian.*

2. Mrs. Cumberland attended the dinner, as is indicated in Cumberland's letter to Garrick on 2 July 1770.

3. William Fitzherbert (1712-1772) was Commissioner of the Board of Trade. His youngest son, Alleyne, was at this time a

student at St. John's College, Cambridge. Fitzherbert killed himself on 2 January 1772.

4. Dorothy Cavendish Bentinck (1750-1794), third Duchess of
Portland. Cumberland's eldest daughter, Elizabeth, married Edward
Bentinck, the brother of William Bentinck, the Duke of Portland.

5. Cumberland had shown Garrick a preliminary draft of *The West
Indian* before leaving for Ireland in the summer of 1770.

XXXIII David Garrick 2 July 1770

Queen Anne Street
July 2nd. 1770

Dear Sir

I do indeed receive your letter[1] and the one inclosed with singular pleasure; I am very glad so unfavourable an Impression is effaced from Mr.
Burke's mind. I am doubly anxious it shoud be
cleared to Lord Rockingham, and I am happy to owe
these kind offices to your friendship.[2]
I have twice the pleasure in following your Corrections that I had in composing the piece, and if
your patience does not give out, mine never will.[3] I
entirely adopt your Observation on the first scene
and have already executed it in a manner that I hope
embraces your Ideas. I wished to have sent you the
new Scenes I have put in place of those, where Ful-
mer is Caned and the Constable is brought in. It is
the greatest Amendment that coud be made, but they
were too long for my time to transcribe. I will get
a proper Copy of the whole made in Ireland and
transmit it to you; perhaps I shall be able to
recruit the Character of O'Flaherty with some natural Touches from the County of Galway. I have
heightened it very much in the new Scenes and tied
him in closer to the plot, as you advised. The money
is given to Dudley in a way that satisfies all scru-

ples and casts a strong light on Belcour's Character.

Mrs. Cumberland desires her Comp[limen]ts and respects to Mrs. Garrick and yourself; she joins me in thanking her and you for a most delightfull day on Tuesday and hopes Mrs. Garrick will allow her to renew her Acquaintance on her return from Ireland. You see, Sir, you not only protect my fame, as Manager, but add to my Happiness, as a Friend.

I coud very much wish, that if this Comedy comes out next Season at your Theatre, it might steal quietly and silently into the world. There are but two men, yourself excepted, that ever heard a word of it, and they only in part. I don't know whether you will think me ridiculous in wishing to conceal the Title of it The *West-Indian* but I think it robs it of its novelty in some degree by announcing it under that Character.

> Farewell, and beleive me Your
> Most faithfull and obliged
> Humble Servant
>
> Richd Cumberland

Source: British Science Museum.

1. This letter apparently has not survived and is not included in Little and Kahrl, *The Letters of David Garrick*.

2. Edmund Burke (1729-1797) might have been disturbed by the dedication of *The Brothers* to the Duke of Grafton, which is mentioned in the letter of Cumberland to Garrick on 17 March 1770. Charles Watson-Wentworth (1730-1782), the second Marquis of Rockingham, was First Lord of the Treasury from 13 July 1765 to 2 August 1766. He was succeeded by the Duke of Grafton, who held the post until succeeded by Lord North on 10 February 1770. Cumberland's publication of *The Brothers* early in 1770, with its dedication to the Duke of Grafton, might well have been misunderstood by Rockingham.

3. Corrections to *The West Indian*.

66

XXXIV   George Romney   30 September [1770][1]

I am perswaded, Dear Sir, you will pardon my vanity, when I offer my thoughts to you upon the subject
of an historical picture for the Noble person we
were speaking of. A Composition that can at once involve beautiful forms in the nude, magnificent Scenery, with rich tints and a splendid Variety is not a
very easy story to collect. I submit to you the following Groupe as comprising all the above qualities
with the advantage of perspicuity in the characters
and fable superadded.[2]

I

Apollo descends to meet Thetis in her Grotto; He a-
lights from his Chariot and is welcom'd by the Goddess, whilst a groupe of her Nymphs raise up a beautifull drapery in the background, that discovers the
couch prepar'd for his repose. His Horses and, Chariot make part of the Scene, all the hints of Sun-set
illuminate the Sea and Coast, Some of the Groupe un-
yoke the Horses, which are panting with their diur-
nal Journey; the beaming Locks of the God light the
whole peice, and the ruddy hues are reflected on the
face and flesh of Thetis and her Nymphs; Boys or
Tritons may be introduc'd, and the Night may arise
at one [of] the extremities; the Evening Star will
mark the Sun's descent, and every other Emblem of
Evening; Shapes of Dolphins, Corals or Shells may be
introduc'd to enrich the Scenery.

II

If the morning Scenery be prefer'd; the Departure of
Apollo may be altogether as picturesque; more tender, but not so glowing: The characters of the Horses will be entirely different, and the hues will be
softer and not so ruddy. I conceive the Deity in the
act of ascending his Chariot, pointing to the Morn-

ing Star, and excusing the necessity of his departure to Thetis; the Solicitation of fondness will mark her Character, and the action of her nymphs in lifting up the drapery may be the same. The peice must be litt from the Tresses of Apollo in both cases, which idea strikes me as beautifull in the Extreme.

III

A Groupe of Bacchants are assisting at the Initiation of a Rustic Nymph: They assail her senses with Wine, Music and the Dance; She hesitates; and in the moment betwixt the allurem[en]ts of pleasure and the scruples of bashfullness, accepts the Thyrsis in one hand and seizes the goblet with the other: Triumph and revelry possess the whole Groupe, and every attitude of gayety, every luxuriancy of scenery enriches and enflames the compositon.

IV

Clodius in a female disguise finds admission into the mysteries of Ceres.

I am yrs affecty

R Cum

Tunbridge Wells
Sunday Evening
30 Sept.

Source: Yale.

1. Although no year can with absolute certainty be assigned to this letter, 1770 is very likely correct since Cumberland was discussing Romney's painting with the artist during that period of time (see 30 March 1771) and 30 September fell on a Sunday that year.

2. Eleven designs on the subjects suggested here by Cumberland were presented by Rev. John Romney, the painter's son, to the Fitzwilliam Museum, Cambridge, in 1817 (Chamberlain, p. 366).

XXXV Roger Pinckney 13 November 1770

Queen Anne-Street, Nov. 13, 1770

Dear Pinckney,

I have your favour of the 6th of July and with it a draft for sixty pounds sterling, which was duly paid, and for which I have given you credit. I had before acknowledged the receipt of the amount of the twenty-nine barrels of rice, the proceeds of which I fear have disappointed your expectations, though I am totally ignorant of those matters. I am sorry that unhappy step in your Assembly, by making a useless and irregular present to the Society, who call themselves the supporters of the Bill of Rights,[1] has kept you out of so large a sum due to you. It has been your lot to fall into troublesome and uncertain times, but by great good providence and prudent conduct I hope and trust you have weathered the storm, and I shall be heartily glad to hear that you are likely to bring your vessel to anchor in your own country once for life. I was not without hopes of seeing you and your lady this year, as you intimated such a design to me. I make no doubt you have staid upon good reasons, and I hope it will prove to good purpose. I depend upon your kind attention to me in the disposal of my place of Clerk of the Crown, &c. and give you full powers to do it in your own way; perhaps a term of years would be preferable to a lease for my life, as revolutions may rise to give it a future value, greater than it now has. The salary you know is 25*l*. sterling per annum, and cannot alter; the value of that, therefore, is determinate, and may easily be rated in a bargain for the whole. I sent the cheeses, which I hope arrived safe, and met your approbation.

Since my return out of Ireland, where I have lately been on a visit to the good bishop,[2] I have had the misfortune to lose my sister Hughes, who died in childbed of her eighth child, and left seven living behind her.[3] This has been a hard blow to the good people in Ireland, but my last accounts represent them better than I could expect. My younger, and now only sister, has lately married in Ireland, to Mr. Alcock,[4] a young gentleman of good family, fortune, and preferment; but even this event presents us with little present prospect of happiness to balance against the above misfortune, as the health of this gentleman seems to be of the most precarious sort, arising from a violent nervous affection on his spirits, to which people in these climates become more and more subject.

Parliament met yesterday. You will see the King's speech, and will not be able to draw any positive conclusions from it relative to the events of peace or war. The messenger who is expected to bring the definitive answer from the Court of Spain is not yet returned.[5]

Pray let me hear from you soon, and as often as your leisure and convenience allows, for your letters are great comforts to me, and to hear of your domestic happiness and prosperity, most agreeable intelligence.

My wife and children are all, thank God, in perfect health, and join in compliments and good wishes to you, your lady and child.

I am, dear Pinckney,
Most faithfully yours,

Richard Cumberland.

70

Account Current.

	£.	s.	d.
Debt upon balance of last year........	238	9	11
Rent from June 8, to Nov. 29,.........	95	1	10
Salary from Lady Day to ditto, at 40 l.	26	0	0
Salary of Clerk's place to Lady Day,.. 1770	25	0	0
Bill of Exchange to Collier...........	12	3	6
	396	15	3

	£.	s.	d.
April 6th, Received for rice..........	180	19	0
June 22d, Received for ditto..........	38	10	1
Sept. 1st. Bill of Exchange...........	60	0	0
	279	9	1
Due on balance	117	6	2
	£.396	15	3

Source: Mudford.

1. In February 1769, John Wilkes and others formed The Society for the Defence of the Bill of Rights. Its main objective seems to have been to get Wilkes into Parliament and to be a force of opposition to the government. Wilkes succeeded in formulating what amounted to a political party by 1770, and one point of its program was support of the Americans. An instruction from Lt. Gov. Bull of 14 April 1770 observes "that the House of Representatives, or *Lower House* of Assembly in South Carolina, had lately assumed to themselves a power of ordering, without the concurrence of the Governor and Council, the Public Treasurer of the said province, to issue and advance out of the public treasury, such sums of money and for such services, as they thought fit; and in particular, that the said Lower House of Assembly did on the 8th day of December last past, make an order on the said Public Treasurer to advance the sum of £10,500. currency, out of any money in the Treasury to be paid into the hands of Mr. Speaker, Mr. Gadsen, Mr. Rutledge, Mr. Parsons, Mr. Furguren, Mr. Dart,

and Mr. Lynch, who were to remit the same to Great Britain for the support of the just and constitutional rights and Liberties of the people of Great Britain and America." (John Drayton, *Memoirs of the American Revolution*, 1821, I, 66-67.

2. While visiting his father in Ireland during the summer of 1770, Cumberland completed the writing of *The West Indian*.

3. Cumberland's sister, Elizabeth, had married John Hughes.

4. Cumberland had four sisters. The eldest, Joanna, died while he was in school. Little is known of the others, one of whom married Alcock.

5. War with Spain was possible in 1770 as a result of the Spanish response to the demand by England that Spain leave her outpost in the Falkland Islands. Despite the humiliating defeat of the small English garrison there, subsequent negotiations by Lord North avoided war, with both sides secretly agreeing to leave the Islands.

XXXVI   George Romney   30 March 1771[1]

Saturday Night 30 March

Sir

Since I waited upon you this morning, my mind has been wholly occupied with reflecting upon your fine Compositions, which you are preparing for public Exhibition.[2] You will receive it only as a mark of Ignorance, which means to be friendly, when I suggest to you a doubt of the Title which I understand you intend to give to your Characters: If they are to be described under the terms of *L'Allegro e Penseroso*, I think your Dramatis personae will be liable to the following objections. In the first place the titles are not classical, they are modern, barbarous and affected; I am not master of so much Italian as to know whether they are proper, but I conceive not; they are borrowed from poetry, and by bringing Milton's descriptions to our minds they rob your Ideas of their originality; Descriptive poetry has been frequently assisted by Painting, but I think the latter Art has seldom excell'd when the pencil has copied after the Pen; Mr West[3] is now transcribing an Ode of Horace upon Canvass, and has flagrantly failed; I fancy he did not take his *Death of General Wolfe* from the paltry Poem call'd *Quebec* or the *Conquest of Canada*. No, Sir, let the Poets wait upon you and give your Figures their natural titles in their own language, or in establish'd classical Terms. The solemn Figure is strictly that of the Muse *Melpomene*; and Mr Reynolds[4] has led the way in calling the other *Euphrosyne*. I think I shoud render those into English by the titles of *Meditation* and *Mirth*.

You will receive this as nothing more than a suggestion entirely submitted to your better Judgement, and of very little importance upon the whole; but it is the subscripion of my mite, and you are richly welcome to it.

I am Sir,
Yr most obedient
Humble Servant

Richd Cumberland

Source: Yale.

1. During 1770, Romney contributed the pictures discussed in this letter to the exhibition of The Incorporated Society of Artists in Spring Gardens. March 30 fell on a Saturday in 1771.

2. "These were whole-length figures representing 'Mirth' and 'Melancholy,' suggested by Milton's *L'Allegro* and *Il Penseroso*" (Chamberlain, p. 55).

3. Benjamin West.

4. Sir Joshua Reynolds.

XXXVII   **David Garrick   4 July 1771**

Kildare street, July 4th

My Dear Sir

One of the first offices, following those of Duty,
is to give myself the importance with you of ac-
quainting you of my safe Arrival in this place on
the night of the 30th inst. after a calm and pleasant passage of 36 Hours in a Parkgate Ship, which on
my Arrival at Chester I found with her topsails un-
bent and ready to catch the first favourable breeze.
My Dear Woman and the little Boys, who had been
charming Companions on land to me, did not lose
their spirits by sea and as I lash'd my Chariot on
deck, we sate in it with great state and composure
and sav'd the nauseous smell of human sickliness,
which infests the lower regions of a Ship full of
passengers. We found our Friends were here almost
sinking under repeated family sorrows and losses,
and my Mother in particular suffering infinite pain
and illness from a disorder, which the faculty have
in vain attempted to remove. I much doubt if she is
recoverable, but I hope I shall give Comfort, if not
Cure. You will believe I lost no time in obeying
your Desires, and the second day I deliver's your
Letter into George Falkener's hands.[1] As you had anticipated the very words he saluted me with, I need
not repeat them; he rehears'd your epistle with
great dignity and energy, and we proceeded forthwith
to summon parties and witnesses relative to the Ju-
bilee-Cause before the Alderman,[2] Dean Bayly, and
the Author of the West Indian, assisted by a Jury of
Printers, Compilers, Devils, Hawkers and Raps of all
sorts, which compose the train of George the Great.
I have long known what conseq[uen]ce is to be expected from trying a Cause in Ireland; it was verified
on this Occasion; oaths, depositions, affidavits,
and all kinds of Evidence were attested to clear the

parties suspected, and as these proofs had been transmitted to you by Mr. Wilks[3] (Whom also I have seen) I hope you have form'd your opinion on the matter. It is said Mr. Dawson extracted *his* Jubilee,[4] (for it is not *your's*) from Magazines, Songbooks, papers &c. and that he compiled it from these publications as well as he coud; the Sparkes's[5] being entirely innocent of the plagiary. It seem'd probable that they had no hand in it.

The Barrys[6] are here acting to thin Theatres, the weather being very hot and the Town empty. She has play'd with reputation and is allowed to be much improved. She is at this moment acting Sir Harry Wildair for her own benefit, and on the same night that Firchar the Hautboy[7] has his, which is resented in gen[era]l. I am wishing that Barry woud get up the part of O'Flaherty and she that of Miss Rusport, and tho' I shall not signify my wish to them after what has passed from Mr. Barry on the same Subject, yet as Dr. Leland[8] in particular and many more are of the same opinion and they seem likely to ensure several full Houses from the Experiment, I am privately told, they will probably get it up. If they do I will let you know. Mossop is silent.[9] Miss Young[10] is well spoken of, and I beleive our friend Gibson[11] has as good a set at Liverpoole, as Dublin can show; wretched indeed and ill attended. They are very angry with Moody[12] and never knew his real Story till I gave 'em some intimation of it, on the contrary George and others believed him mad, and indeed between us he committed some wanton frolics under the name of O'Flaherty. I have bought your Linnen and shall send it over this week. Adieu, my Dear Friend, Yrs. R Cum.

Source: British Science Museum. The letter is endorsed by Garrick, "Mr. Cumberland's from Dublin July 4th. 1771."

1. George Faulkener (1699?-1775), the Irish publisher.

2. George Faulkener, who had been made Alderman. Garrick jests with William Burke about this in his letter of 16 July 1771 (Little and Kahrl, #640, II, 748-9).

3. Thomas Wilkes (d. 1786), a friend of Garrick's in Dublin.

4. William Dawson had gained control of the Crow Street theatre in Dublin in the spring of 1771. The "Jubilee" performed there seemed to suggest plagiarism of Garrick's "Stratford Jubilee." John Moody (c.1727-1812), the actor, had brought it to Garrick's attention, and Cumberland was asked to look into it while in Dublin (Moody to Garrick, 6 June 1771, in Little and Kahrl, #635, II, 743-4).

5. Isaac Sparks and his son, Richard, both actors.

6. Ann Barry and her husband, Spranger Barry (1719-1777).

7. John Abraham Fischer, a composer, played the hautboy at Covent Garden.

8. Dr. Thomas Leland (1722-1785), an important classical scholar.

9. The actor, Henry Mossop (c.1729-c.1774).

10. The actress, Elizabeth Young (c.1744-1797).

11. William Gibson (c.1713-1771), an actor at Covent Garden, who managed the Liverpool theatre during the summer.

12. John Moody.

XXXVIII David Garrick 13 July 1771

Kildare Street. July, 13th

My Dear Friend

It's well the Snarlers at home now and then give me a Snap, else I shoud swell like the frog in the fable, not only with Irish hospitality, but with Irish flattery. It is not only Individuals of the first rank in this Kingdom that have caress'd your undeserving friend, but the University of Dublin have of their own mere motion and bounty conferr'd upon me an honorary degree of Doctor of Civil Law at the public Commencement.[1] I am bound to report all these flattering Circumst[an]ces to you who are the friend and father of my fame, and to whom I owe an account of every thing relating to it. It has been a spur in the way of the growing Comedy,[2] which comes out purified by your fiery trial and less drossey than it woud otherwise have been. It will be ready in time, if it pleases God I have my health, and I flatter myself *Timon* will open the Season success-fully and brilliantly.[3] I wish to hear that you are at your ease about the Jubilee.[4]

There is a young man here of the name of Lewis,[5] who play'd *Belcour*. I have not yet seen him, as Bar-ry[6] is forever in the tragic vein. He seems to prom-ise good matters; he has person and spirit, and they tell me is quite at home in the Coxcomical and gay walk of Comedy. He overacted Belcour, but was liked, and that is a good fault, if any fault can be such. I shall write to you further particulars when I have seen him, but in the meantime tell me if I shall sound him about engagements, or hold out any over-ture to him in your behalf. I conceive he woud be an accession under your Government, as he is very young, handsome and volatile.

Adieu, my Dear Sir; accept mine and Mrs. Cum's best wishes and present them to your amiable wife.

I am ever most faithfully and affectly yrs.

Richd Cumberland

Source: Harvard. The letter is endorsed by Garrick: "Dr. Cumberland's first letter since his taking hi [sic] degree rec'd the 22d. of July 1771."

1. *Alumni Dublinenses*, ed. G. D. Burtchaell and T. U. Sadlier, London, 1924, records: "Cumberland, Richard. LL. D. (honoris cau-sa) Aest. 1771" (p. 201).

2. *The Fashionable Lover*, produced at Drury Lane on 4 December 1771.

3. *Timon of Athens* was produced at Drury Lane on 4 December

1771. It did not open the season. Hopkins' diary records its reception: "This play is alter'd by Mr Cumberland was very well receiv'd Mr & Mrs Barry play'd very well Alcibiades was perform'd
by Mr Crofts being his first appearance upon any Stage bad figure, bad voice & Play'd bad." Quoted from *The London Stage*, Part
IV, ed. Stone, p. 1590.

4. See 4 July 1771.

5. William Thomas Lewis (1748?-1811). He seems not to have been
employed by Garrick, but ultimately became a deputy manager of
Covent Garden in 1782.

6. Spranger Barry.

XXXIX David Garrick 5 August 1771[1]

Dublin Augst 5th

I can't leave Dublin, my dear friend, without bid-
ding you farewell, for the Solitude I am going into
naturally disposes my mind to take leave of those
friends which the world's Society have bestow'd upon
me; amongst them my chief accession lies in your
breast, and when the West Indian[2] gave me your regard and bestow'd all mine upon you, it did more for
me than the best production ever did for it's author
before.

I am going with a resolution not to stir out of
the demesne lands of Clonfert,[3] but to court the
Muse naked from the Bog and catch a glimpse of unsophisticated Nature. I woud fain do something for you
that shoud live. I write with double zeal because I
think I am in some degree serving your fame as well
as my own, and I proceed with confidence because I
know my production, if it can pass your scrutiny,
must make it's way with the public. Let me cast one
dart at Prejudice (national prejudice) and I shall
call it victory, if it pierces no further than the
stroke which Abdiel gave to Satan.[5]

I am not happy about this Lewis.[6] I am leaving him
behind, and I am not quite satisfied in so doing.

The fellow a voided an Interview with me, as I beleive contrivedly; for I understand he is connected,
or related, to Dawson[7] and has besides so great a
Salary (viz eight guineas a week) that if his ambition to be made an Actor did not generate more forcibly than his avarice, there would be no probability of detaching him; for I sup- pose you woud hardly
give him a moiety of such pay. I am firmly of opinion the Lad has faculties to make a figure in Comedy; and not in Mr. King's or Dod's worth only,[8] but
of the fine Gentleman, as that higher kind of Comedy
which hardly now exists, which Smith[9] has in the ex-
terior, and which Obrien[10] might perhaps have at-
tained if he had not medled with real instead of ar-
tificial, Upper Life. He has a strong tone which
breaks occasionally into the humourous with great
success, and is capable of variation in his cadences; his Eye is quick and his modesty does not stand
in his way. I lost the opportunity of seeing him in
Mercutio and *Dick* the Apprentice[11] for Dawson's Benefit, because Madam Barry chose to be *ill*-disposed
and so the benefit was laid aside. I beleive indeed
it woud not have lit the Candles. I have written my
foolish Sentiments about the Barry's[12] with the sincerity that I shall always use to you. As far as my
poor judgement goes it is confirm'd by reflection,
and when you have once shown them and the world you
can do as well without them as with them, they will
no longer be Tyrants and Coquettes. Miss Young[13] you
well know how to husband and not spend what powers
she may have with the profligate waste that the little man of Covent Garden used in Mr. Savigny's Instance.[14] I hear her [   ][15] Comedy, and am not
much edified by the ac[counts of her] tragical performances. I have not ab[so]lutely lost sight of
Lewis, if you chuse to give [me] any instruct[ion]s
peremptory about him, for I have left a word or two
in a friend's Ear, which may work upon him, but have
not committed you in the business--After all I have
said you woud frighten me, if you gave me full contracting powers, because I shoud distrust my judge-

ment from the short trial I have had of him.--I need not entreat my friend to equip my offspring *Timon*[16] with all due splendor and magnificence, for if he does not glitter in scenery and dress the words will come unrecommended to the Ear--Adieu, my dear Sir, and beleive me ever most faithfully and truly Yrs

R Cum

Source: British Science Museum.

1. The year is determined by the reference to *The West Indian* and to Cumberland's interest in the actor Lewis.

2. *The West Indian*, produced the previous season.

3. Cumberland retired to his family home at Clonfert.

4. In *The Fashionable Lover*, Colin McLeod is designed to present a Scotsman in a favorable light.

5. *Paradise Lost*, VI, 189. Abdiel's stroke begins the battle between Satan and the loyal angels in Heaven.

6. See 13 July 1771.

7. William Dawson.

8. Thomas King (1730-1805); James William Dodd (1740?-1796).

9. William (Gentleman) Smith (1730?-1819).

10. William O'Brien (d. 1815).

11. Mercutio in *Romeo and Juliet* and Dick in Arthur Murphy's *The Apprentice*.

12. Ann and Spranger Barry.

13. Elizabeth Younge.

14. George Colman had employed the actor Savigny at Covent Garden starting with the 1770-71 season.

15. The manuscript is defective at this point.

16. *Timon of Athens*, acted at Drury Lane 4 December 1771.

XL David Garrick 8 September 1771[1]

Clonfert Sept. 8th

I have been watching the posts, My Dear Sir, with more than usual impatience for some time--I wrote to you the day before I quitted Dublin the sum total of my thoughts, and I went out of my province by following the zeal of my friendship in talking about matters that respected the internal government and police of your Theatre. I mean with regard to the Barry's:[2] I own I wish to hear from you on that among other accounts. My little Major[3] says you have passed your time agreeably amongst the Great ones of this world in the paradise of West Mount Edgecombe. I rejoice in your felicity, and I envy them their's in having you. I have looked for you amongst our bogs, and sometimes in a brighter moment I have seen you. It is then I have pleas'd myself; it is then my Muse has been my favorite, and at length I have compleated my work.[4] You ask, does it please me?--I tell you with a sincerity that does not fear the imputation of vanity, that it does please me, and very highly. I have an internal plaudit that sanctifies my effort, and I am satisfied I shall put into your hands a work more worthy your protection than any I have yet committed to the public--*Mortimer* has gained upon me in the working up. Occasions given upon my plan that I did not foresee, and the intervention of *Aubrey* the father comes in with all the higher powers of Comedy, and carries *Mortimer* and *Mcleod* up along with it. I have kept these two pure and steady to their Character. I have not let *Mortimer* sink into mere good humour, as Dr. Smollet has let Mathew Bramble in Humphry Clinker. I think with the assistance of Doctor Druid, a Welch (instead of Dutch) Antiquarian, there is enough of Comedy, and the other parts go much deeper to the heart, than our last did. By putting out *Lady Carolina* and *Fairfax*, as you advis'd I have had elbow room, and without moving the Peice into Length, have been nowhere crampt or distrest. Enough is said to satisfy Morality and the Times, and the touches are light and pleasant, tho' they cut deep--To combat a National Prejudice[5] of a pernicious sort is the avow'd design of the play, and is the closing Moral. I think the world will be with us in the attempt. Give me pardon for this long digression upon the subject of self; but I really write with your approbation ever in view, and as I now flatter myself I enter into your sentiments, I am always in high spirits when I think I have hit upon your Taste. I write in a House of sickness, for my Mother has been, and still is, in a very dangerous state. I am looking homewards; but if accident or illness either to self, family or friends, clogs my chariot wheels in my return towards you, farther I beseech you to favour my half begotten Brat, call'd Timon,[6] give him a good Coat on his back, and send him into the world like a Gentleman's son. Cast the parts entirely to your own taste--but what shall I say about correcting the press--? Surely Backet[7] can do that--and then prologue and Epilogue--you know my wishes you see my wants and your friendship will provide for both--It shall be then my turn to propose my poor services to you in the way you hinted to me, as an office chore Hoadly was to have engaged in,[8] and if you think me capable of the task, I will hold myself vacant from any other pursuits, and give my thoughts entirely to the undertaking for your sake. I left word that any Turtles that might come in my absence shoud be sent to you, and I understand one has been at your door.[9] I hope you found it on your return, and that it was a good one. Adieu, my dear friend, I am going to the West Indian perform'd by a party of Pagan Irish at Eyre Court.[10] Bessy joins in good wishes and best Comp[limen]ts to you and Mrs. Garrick. Beleive me ever your's

Richd Cum.

Source: British Science Museum.

1. The year is determined by the reference to *The Fashionable Lover,* which Cumberland was writing during the summer of 1771.

2. Ann and Spranger Barry.

3. Probably Cumberland's eldest son. Cumberland was proud of the discipline of his family: "My young ones stood like little soldiers to be reviewed by those, who wished to have them drawn up for inspection, and were dismissed like soldiers at a word" (*Memoirs*, I, 332).

4. *The Fashionable Lover*.

5. Prejudice against Scotland was combated by the favorable characterization of Colin McLeod.

6. *Timon of Athens*.

7. Thomas Becket (1721?-1831), a bookseller and publisher. *Timon of Athens* was published by "The Proprietors of Shakespeare's Works," London, 1771.

8. John Hoadly (1711-1776), an amateur writer and actor, who was a close friend of Garrick, had written to him with criticisms of *The West Indian*, which the manager promised to pass on to Cumberland (John Hoadly to Garrick, 9 May 1771, in Little and Kahrl, #632, p. 739). There is no record of Cumberland's having taken a position with Garrick similar to that suggested here.

9. Roger Pinckney from time to time sent turtles, a rare delicacy in eighteenth-century England, to Cumberland from South Carolina.

10. Cumberland describes his father's friend, Lord Eyre of Eyre Court, in his *Memoirs* (I, 278ff.). He attributes features of the character of Major O'Flaherty in *The West Indian* to a gentleman encountered during an excursion with Lord Eyre.

XLI David Garrick 2 October 1771[1]

Dublin Octr. 2d

My Dear Sir

Your last kind Letter[2] reached me on the very day I had wrote to you and tho' I am now on the point of taking my departure from hence, I cannot turn my back on Dublin without thanking you in the most

affectionate manner for it and all your kindness. I
am glad you have passed your time so agreeably and
with such excellent Company. I am only afraid of
your Spirits misleading your Constitution a little
and laying in for a gouty winter. Indeed you have a
female Mentor at your elbow, but you have a great
deal of gayety at your Heart--Well, you are now come
home and your Campaign commenced. I watch your operations with a friendly eye, and I see my poor West
Indian receive early honours from your choice, and
as I had rather flatter my heart than my head, I
tell myself that your friendship to the Author leads
you to the preference of his works--I now recollect
that I never thank'd you for the paragraph you sent
me from the Public Advertiser relative to the Degree,[3] and I beleive I am to thank you not for the
sending it only. I have labour'd industriously not
to defeat your Expectations in the Comedy,[4] and the
more I weigh it in my mind, the more I am enclined
to stake myself upon it. I think it in my conscience
that it is greatly preferable to the West Indian.
With respect to *Timon*[5] you make me very happy to receive your approbation of it, and I hope it will
meet your Expectat[ion]s. I think you will not want
me in the getting it up, in case you shall see proper to bring it on before I can get to you; shoud
that be so, Mr. Roberts[6] a clerk in the Plantation
office has a Copy of it, and will give it to your
Servant upon sending for it; his Copy probably woud
do for the Prompter, and your Copy might be given to
Mr. Becket;[7] pray tell Mr. Beckett that my Lines are
to be printed between hooks (thus ") and the original left plain; as he is a sensible man I am sure he
can superintend the correction of the Press without
any trouble to you, who must have more than enough
to do. If your young Actor succeeds in *Alcibiades*,[8]
it will greatly strengthen the representation, and
one glance of your Eye at Rehearsal will decide upon
that. You are busily employed about your *Installa-*
tion I take for granted; may you be as superior in
that, as you was in the *Jubilee*.[9] I suppose however

that Cov[en]t Garden will put forth all it's strength and hand out all its Colours. The Wits will abuse you both but these are Sacrifices, which must be made, and their success speaks for them. I cannot forego this opportunity of returning by the North of Ireland and so through Scotland. I mean to take Glasgow and Edinburgh in my way, and I look to reap advantage from my reading my *Highlander*[10] to Doctor Robinson and the Coterie of Wits at Edinburgh. It is that principally which determines me to this long journey on friday next. I purpose to set out from hence, that is, the day after tomorrow, and probably shall kiss your hands the last week in the month. I shall write to you on the road, but it will be to no purpose for you to be at the trouble of an Answer. I have done a great deal of family business since my coming, and have at length closed the uneasy transaction of my Sister's marriage much to my satisfaction, and to that of all my family.[11] A vacancy being now made on the bench by the Bishop of Limerick's death, Dr. Averall, my father puts in his plea for a Remove; the general report of the Town sends him to Elphin or Kilmore, both which woud be agreeable Exchanges, but I fear this matter will not be decided before I leave Dublin, as Lord Townshend generally keeps those Destinations a long time secret.[12] Lord Hillsborough[13] came out of the North with his Lady and family last night, and I have this morning settled office matters with Him to my entire Satisfaction. My dear woman desires to be affectionately remember'd to you and Mrs. Garrick. She says she wishes for a chearfull dinner with you, and the more so as her spirits are greatly struck down at this particular time; and she seems losing the good Effects of her Country air and Exercise a great pace. I trust in God that the Journey will bring back her spirits and health, as it seldom or never fails to be a great Specific in her Case. I came hither only the day before yesterday, and find the Town quite Empty. I dined yesterday with the B[isho]p of Kildare,[14] who met you at my House, and drank your Health in a very chearfull company with the Primate[15] and several others. Farewell my dear friend, continue to believe me, what I shall ever continue to be, your most sincere and affectionate friend

Richd Cumberland

Source: British Science Museum.

1. The year is determined by reference to *The West Indian*, acted at Drury Lane during the 1771-72 season on 24 September 1771.

2. This letter is not included in Little and Kahrl and is probably not extant.

3. The honrary degree of Doctor of Laws was awarded by the University of Dublin on 22 July 1771.

4. *The Fashionable Lover*.

5. *Timon of Athens* was first performed at Drury Lane on 4 December.

6. Possibly John Roberts (1712?-1772), earlier private secretary to Henry Pelham and manager for Newcastle. He was M.P. for Harwich from 1761 on.

7. Thomas Becket. See 8 September 1771.

8. A young actor, Henry Croft, made his first stage appearance as Alcibiades, and it was disappointing (*The London Stage*, ed. Stone, IV, p. 1590). Garrick had warned him against undertaking a career as an actor in a letter on 6 August 1771 (Little and Kahrl, #644, p. 752).

9. From 6 to 9 September 1769 Garrick conducted a three day celebrarion or "Jubilee" in honor of Shakespeare at Stratford. Subsequently, Garrick brought to the stage an afterpiece called *The Jubilee* (14 October 1769), which was the most frequently performed piece of the century, being acted ninety times during its first season alone (*The London Stage*, ed. Stone, IV, pp. 1419, 1430). *Installation* may refer to Garrick's masque *Institution of the Garter; or Arthur's Round Table Restor'd*, acted on 28 October 1771.

10. Colin McLeod, the chief comic character in *The Fashionable Lover*.

11. Cumberland's only remaining sister had married a Mr. Alcock.

12. Thomas Townshend Sydney (1733-1800) was Lord Lieutenant of Ireland from August 1767 to October 1772.

13. William Hill (1718-1793), Second Viscount Hillsborough, then President of the Board of Trade, and Cumberland's superior there.

14. Dr. Richard Robinson, a close friend of Cumberland.

15. The Rt. Rev. Dr. John Craddock (d. 6 December 1778) was Archbishop of Dublin and Primate of Ireland.

XLII   David Garrick   After 28 October 1771[1]

Queen Ann Street
Thursday Morning

My Dear Friend,

Accept the print[2] of a Man who loves you, and whose chief Merit is in so doing. You will find it a less troublesome Visitor than the original, nor will it offend you with any idle Sallies of passion about Theatres and Hisses and Installations. But you shall love me not the worse for those Sparks of Impatience, and I will love you the better.

Farewell

Source: British Science Museum. The manuscript is not in Cumberland's hand, but Garrick's endorsement is recorded on the manuscript as "Mr. Cumberland."

1. The date is conjectured from the reference to the print being presented to Garrick. See Note 2 below.

2. A portrait of Cumberland painted by George Romney was engraved by Valentine Green on 28 October 1771. See "Catalogue Raisonné of the Works of George Romney," in Volume II of Humphry Ward and W. Roberts, *Romney*, 2 vols. (London, 1904).

XLIII   Elizabeth Cumberland   27 November 1771[1]

Dear Madam,

   I read with much concern an   Account of my poor
Relation's death, I have waited some time, thinking
it not improbable that one of the young men[2] might
have wrote or come to me, but I conclude the melancholy news is true, and I sincerely condole with you
on the Occasion. If anything in my power can be done
to alleviate your sorrow I shall gladly contribute
my best assistance: your eldest son is designed for
Orders, & I understand has a living under promise to
him; should that hope fail, & my father live, I dare
say he would prefer him in Ireland.[3] Pray desire him
to dine with me, as soon as conven[ien]t, & let me
hear how you all are.

I am, Dear Madm,
Yr sincere friend
and Relation,[4]

Richd Cumberland.

Queen Ann Street,
Nov. 27th.

Source: Black.

   1. The year is determined from that of the death of Elizabeth
Cumberland's husband, George, who was buried at St. Dunstan's,
Stepney, on 21 November 1771.
   2. Her sons, Richard Dennison and George.
   3. Cumberland's father was Bishop of Clonfert, Ireland, at this
time.
   4. Richard Dennison and George Cumberland were distant cousins
of the dramatist, members of a lateral branch of the family, the
connection dating back four generations.

XLIV Richard Dennison Cumberland 12 February 1772[1]

16 Feb. Q. A. Street

Dear Sir,

I hope you find yourself plac'd to your entire satisfaction and that ye short experience you have had of a College Life & studies gives you no prospect, but what is flattering & cheerful. I find my friend & relation Mr Ashby[2] has help'd to enliven your situation by his acquaintance, & I dare say you are very happy to cultivate it in ye manner most agreable to him. Your Mother & George[3] dined at my house yesterday sennight & were both well & in spirits; much depends upon your success in Life for ye comfort and support of your good Mother in the latter end of hers, and I hope & beleive that you will lose no effort, which assiduity, frugality & discretion can make, to attain ye means of being ye friend of your family. If there is any thing wanting, necessary to ye comforts of your Life; which your present establishment cannot readily accomplish, I insist upon your letting me know--or if your Finances fall short make me acquainted with it, and you shall on every laudable occasion find me,

Dear Cousin, yr most faithfull
friend & Servt,

Richd Cumberland.

Source: Black

1. The year is determined from Richard Dennison's taking up residence at Cambridge.
2. George Ashby, the son of the sister of Cumberland's father, who married Waring Ashby, High Sheriff of Leichestershire.

3. The recently widowed Elizabeth Cumberland and her son.

XLV   George Ashby   16 November 1772[1]

Queen Ann St. Nov. 16th.

My dear Cousin,

I hope I may congratulate you on your safe arrival
at Cambridge & I have the pleasure to inform you of
my having landed my charge in Health and Safety
within Her own House & in Her children's arms, who
are very well both they at Home & those at Westminster. If I had met anything worth communicating to
you I shoud before now have troubled you with a letter, but London is for what I know of it as dull &
vacant as the town of Leichester may be, except indeed you ventured into the Company of Aldermen &
Councilmen where you might meet with noise enough,
who in point of dulness you woud not mend your market. I hope you are getting thro' your Business, I
should be happy to hear you had brought it to an
agreable & profitable issue.
    A Letter has arrived from D. Cumberland of Magda-
len[2] which has produced a conversation between his
Friend Mr Balchen[3] & me upon the subject of the
young man's finances, which seem to stand in need of
some little assistance. In what manner best to apply
this assistance on the Part of my Father[4] is a matter of some little debate in my mind: Mr Tapp[5] a
worthy trader here in town, pays His Tutors Bills, &
by how much He exceeds His College Exhibitions etc.
supplies them from a small fund arising from the Amicable Society of Annuitants; the Bills come quarterly & I am of opinion the best method upon the
whole will be to throw in the Bishop's blessing into
the Hands of Mr Tapp in aid of the slender fund, by
which means I shall see the particulars of His ex-

pences & can proportion my aid[6] to the nature of the Demands & the situation of the fund, which if it holds out long enough to land Him in Holy Orders will have done all that we require of it: This being the case provided the youth is not in personal want, I think you need do no more on our behalf than signifie my design to Him; & as his Tutor supplies His pocket & other necessities I shoud expect there would be no call upon you of that sort.--We join in Love and good wishes to Mrs Ashby & you & desire you ever to believe me, Dear Sr,

Most affec. & truly yours.

Source: Black.

1. The year is determined from that in which Richard Dennison Cumberland entered Cambridge. On Ashby, see Letter #41.

2. Richard Dennison Cumberland.

3. Probably a distant relation, John Balchen, Senior. Richard Dennison Cumberland's father, George, had married Elizabeth Balchen in 1747.

4. Dennison Cumberland, Bishop of Clonfert.

5. W. Tapp, a local merchant.

6. Cumberland had offered aid to the young man in his letter of 16 February.

XLVI **George Ashby?**[1] **Probably 23 December 1772**[2]

Dear Cousin

You have sent me a very fine and acceptable present of a brace of Woodcocks and three brace of Snipes, for which I beg you will accept mine and Mrs. Cumberland's sincere and hearty thanks, together with those of all the young ones, who are now at home with me for the holidays and will partake of the good fare; for in my life I never saw such fine and fat birds. The fens however do produce some good things, tho' the Essentials of Life come very slowly and sparingly from that Quarter; as we have nothing from thence but Rates and Taxes for repairing Banks instead of Rents; which together with the great Drain of that Fatal Connexion with Mr. Hughes[3] has contributed with other great Out-goings to dry the good Bishop[4] as well as his Son; I mention this for reasons, which will occur to you, but which in delicacy I suppress. Tell me however in what state the finances are,[5] and perhaps

(Things may be   Non si male nunc
better by and by)   Et olim sic erit.

                    I am most   faithfully Yrs

                        Richd Cumberland

Queen Anne Street. 23d Decr.

Source: British Library

1. The cousin to whom the letter is sent is probably George Ashby, the son of Waring Ashby, who had married the only daughter of Cumberland's paternal grandfather.

2. The year is conjectured from the reference to finances at the conclusion of the letter. George Cumberland of a parallel branch of the Cumberland family had died in November 1771, leaving his immediate family in a difficult financial state. Cumberland had offered to help George Cumberland's son, Richard Dennison, attend Cambridge, largely through the good offices of the dramatist's father.

3. One of Cumberland's sisters, Elizabeth, had married a John Hughes.

4. Cumberland's father.

5. Probably regarding Richard Dennison Cumberland then attending Cambridge.

XLVII   David Garrick   26 June 1773[1]

Mr. Cumberland presents his Compliments to Mr. Garrick, will take an Opportunity of sending him the Peice of Two Acts,[2] agreable to his promise, as soon as he has compleated the Alteration which Mr. Garrick recommended. He will transmit it from Ireland before the Season commences in time for any purpose Mr. Garrick may have for it, tho' ever so early. Mr. Cum. leaves Town in very few days.[3]

Queen Ann street
Saturday 26th June

Source: British Science Museum. It is endorsed by Garrick: Mr. Cumberland's Letter of June 30th. 1773.

1. The year is determined by Garrick's endorsement. 30 June 1773 is probably the day he received it.

2. *The Note of Hand*, a farce, was produced at Drury Lane on 9 February 1774.

3. The formal tone of this letter is matched by that of Garrick's reply of 27 June 1773. In it he agrees to read the play, but expresses surprise at hearing from Cumberland, having been "informed of his new Scheme" (Little and Kahrl, #781, p. 882). What this scheme was is uncertain. Stanley Williams suggests that it may have been Cumberland's efforts to promote the interest of the actor, Henderson (*Richard Cumberland*, pp. 106-108). However, there is a more likely source of the difficulty, Cumberland's promotion, with Samuel Johnson and others, of Oliver Goldsmith's comedy, *She Stoops to Conquer*, at Covent Garden during the previous spring on 15 March 1773.

XLVIII   David Garrick   30 June 1783

Queen Ann Street

30 June 1773

Dear Sir

When I have used every Effort to preserve your friendship and to render myself understood by you, I shall have fulfilled the duty I owe to the professions that have been in use between us and shall bring myself to acquiesce in the consequences of my miscarriage, tho' they rob me of your Society forever.

I perceive you write to me under resentment, and it is plain you allude to the Cause when you tell me of the *New Scheme* I have been engaged in;[1] weak as the foundations are on which you build your anger, I am yet well content you shoud have some plea for your neglect of me, and I had rather that excuse shoud spring from passion (tho' Self-interest be the root of it) than be found to proceed from lassitude in friendship and that insensibility of nature which is more unconquerable than aversion itself.

It is true, Sir, I have been engaged in an undertaking, which had for it's object the promotion of Genius; I have been tempted to subscribe my Opinion at the instigation of friends whose judgement I hold sacred, and amongst them by some which you and I enjoy in common, who, like myself, did not apprehend you woud have resented an effort founded in public spirit, and which neither aim'd nor aspir'd to affect a fortune and a fame, which your unequall'd merits have long made secure and promise to transmit without empeachment to posterity. Why then do you express surprize that I write to yo to signify my readiness to fulfill an Engagement, enter'd into at our last meeting, and which, unless it is your wish to revoke, I cannot honourably recede from?[2] Indeed, as you say, our silence has been long; so long as almost to warrant your fogetfulness of the trifling production, which has interrupted it, and all that relates to it; but has the intercourse dropt in my hands? You are too ingenuous to suppose it. I am sure you can recollect nothing of me for the last eight months of our lives, which I have not obtruded upon you; and yet in that period I have had more claims upon the sensibility and politeness of my friends, than in all my Life before.

There is a time, Sir, when self-respect will tell us we have done enough; the last public testimony I set my hand to was in your just applause; the last private Encomium which my pen ever passed on any living person was dedicated and deliver'd to you, with whom rests the silence then, with yourself or me?[3]

I have been repeatedly at your door to converse with you on this very scheme you allude to; in short I am conscious of having neglected no occasion of deserving and maintaining your friendship upon fair and equal terms, but if I am to hold your favour upon conditions which must degrade me with myself, or if I am to incurr your displeasure, whenever I chance to crop your interest in a laudable pursuit, the wider and more public our breach is in that case the better.

I have troubled you with a very long Letter, because I woud be loth to lose any friend for want of a little Seasonable Explanation, and if my time allowed I woud have come to you myself, but I depart tomorrow, or at farthest on friday.[4] I therefore send my Servant with this, to receive your Answer which the post woud not bring me.

I am, Dear Sir, Yr faithfull
and most obedt Servant

Richd Cumberland

Source: British Science Museum

1. See Note 3, 26 June 1773.

2. Apparently a commitment to write The Note of Hand, a farce produced at Drury Lane on 9 February 1774.

3. In his "Advertisement" to *The Fashionable Lover* (London 1772), Cumberland observes: "I am both in the instance of this Comedy, and in that of The West Indian materially indebted to his [Garrick's] judgment, and owe the good effect of many incidents in both to his suggestion and advice." The private encomium might have been the message accompanying a print of his portrait. Cumberland clearly did not desire a breach with Garrick. See After 28 October 1771.

4. Cumberland was leaving for Ireland. In his letter to Garrick of 26 June 1773, he had indicated that he would send the "Piece of Two Acts" from there.

XLIX   David Garrick   14 March 1774[1]

Queen Ann Street
Monday Evening

Your Letter My Dear Sir, finds me now in the Middle of the Evening so that I cannot obey your wish by writing on the first Occasion, which I should else have done; for I would lose no time to express, what I sincerely feel, my real Anxiety on account of your Indisposition. I had heard something of it and went in search of Intelligence to your door.[2] We missed your Society much on Wednesday last, and I may say to me in particular it was a singular loss for in your place there came Mr. Whitefoord with his pockets crammed with epitaphs.[3] Two of them did me the honour and by implication yourself, as the turn of both was a mock lamentation over me from you with a most severe and ill natured Invective principally collected from the Strictures of Mr. Bickerstaff and thrown upon me with a Dungfork[4]--But of myself and him enough--Dr. Goldsmith's Dinner was very ingenious, but evidently written with haste and negligence. The Dishes were nothing to the purpose, but they were followed by Epitaphs that had humour, some Satire and more panegyric.[5] You had your Share of

96

both, but of the former very sparingly and in a strain to leave no sting behind, not at all in the character of Mr. Whitefoords Muse.

My wine was drank very cordially, though it was very ill pour'd by Dr. Goldsmith, who proved himself a Recitator acerbus.[6] The Dean of Derry[7] went out and produced an exceedingly good Extempore in answer to my Wine which had an excellent Effect. Mr. Beauclerc[8] was there, and joined with every one else in condemning the tenor of Mr. Whitefoords Invective, who I believe was brought maliciously enough by Sir Joshua[9]-- Mine was of such a sort that I have cut my name out of the friday's Club, and what is worse out of the Wine Merchant's Ledger.[10]

I am sorry we shall not see you on Wednesday and sincerely wish you a speedy re-establishment.

Lord North moves a Bill for dismantling the Port of Boston this day.[11]

I am ever Yrs most faithfully
and Affectionately

Richd Cumberland

Source: British Science Museum. The manuscript is not in Cumberland's hand.

1. The date is determined by Lord North's moving for the dismantling of the port of Boston on 14 March 1774, a Monday.

2. Garrick left London because of illness on March 8, and went to his home at Hampton. In a letter to George Steevens of that date, he tells of having contracted a fever at the House of Commons on the previous day (Garrick to Steevens, Little and Kahrl #823, p. 923).

3. Caleb Whitefoord (1734-1800) was not a regular member of the group. The origin of the club is described in Cumberland's Memoirs: "It was upon a proposal started by Edmund Burke, that a party of friends, who had dined together at Sir Joshua Reynolds and my house, should meet at the St. James's Coffee-House, which occasionally took place, and was occasionally repeated with much

festivity and good fellowship" (I, 369-370). Cumberland lists the regular members, and gives details of the meeting before that described in this letter in *Memoirs*, I, 370-371.

4. Isaac Bickerstaffe (1735?-1812), a writer of musical plays, had begun his attacks on Cumberland when the latter produced *The Summer's Tale*, a musical, in 1765.

5. Oliver Goldsmith's poem was published posthumously as *The Retaliation* later in 1774.

6. Cumberland's "Wine" was probably that published as "Poetical Epistle to Dr. Goldsmith; or Supplement to his Retaliation" in *The Gentleman's Magazine* for August 1778.

7. Rev. Dr. Thomas Barnard (1728-1806). Barnard's name appears on the "Round Robbin" that recommended revisions in Johnson's epitaph for Goldsmith (James Boswell, *Life of Johnson* [1776], III, p. 84).

8 Topham Beauclerk (1739-1780), a friend of Samuel Johnson.

9. Why Sir Joshua Reynolds would have been antagonistic to Cumberland at this time is not clear, although the dramatist was friendly with George Romney, a rival portrait painter. See Cumberland's letters to Romney elsewhere in this volume. Years later Reynolds had occasion to quarrel with the dramatist over references to him in Cumberland's *Anecdotes of Eminent Painters in Spain* (1782), (*Memoirs*, II, 187-192). Cumberland is probably in error in seeing Reynolds as behind Whitfoord's invective, since the latter addressed a verse apology to Reynolds (James Northcote, *Memoirs of Sir Joshua Reynolds*, Philadelphia, 1817, pp. 106-7).

10. Cumberland's resentment was inconsequential, since Goldsmith soon died. There was only one concluding meeting at Cumberland's home at which it was decided to publish the *Retaliation* (*Memoirs*, I, 371-2).

11. Following the Boston Tea Party on 16 December 1773, Lord North moved to retaliate by closing the port of Boston. The Boston Port Bill was enacted on 31 March 1774.

L   George Romney   14 August 1774[1]

Warwick Castle 14th Augst.

Dear Romney

I hope this letter will reach you before you quit
Rome and convey to you my gratefull acknowledgements
for your obliging favour, which came to hand yesterday and found me in this delightfull Castle, where I
have been sometime on a Visit to Lord Warwick[2] with
my wife, daughter and Eldest Son. It gives me true
satisfaction to hear that you have passed your time
in Italy so much to your wishes; your Country is
much interested in your Success, and amongst your
friends no one more faithfully than I am; I have
been very inquisitive from every quarter where I
thought I coud approach you, and I have always heard
what gratified my ambition in your behalf; Still I
wanted the Confirmation of your own testimony, and
this being had, leaves me compleatly happy. The Art
has stirr'd very little, since you left us; this
year exhibited no Advances in taste and execution:
Barry[3] fell into the false Sublime and became ridiculous; West[4] was in the wane and our friend Sir
Joshua,[5] tho' very voluminous, had nothing supremely
capital; coarse and flaring in his stile and colours, he seems tired with nature and is bringing in
Vagaries to hide his want of Improvement--How unlike
to the godlike Simplicity of the Antients before
your Eyes, and their Copyists of Modern Antiques,
the Heroes of the 16th Century. Dance[6] painted a
single figure of Orpheus--*mulcentem tigres*-- and did
well, in point of truth, but was vulgar; He carried
the palm however from his Contemporaries and hangs
now in the Music Room of Sir Watkins Williams,[7] com-
panioning a St Caecelia of Sir Joshua. Rely upon me
when I assure you, you are not forgot, on the contrary your fame rises, as the Expectations of your
Country encrease, and we shall demand great things

from you on your return; The Designs of M Angelo
with the Colouring of Titian will have been your
study and the fruits of it will build you both fame
and fortune. When I received your Letter I was in
the midst of your friends, and am charged by Lord
Warwick to assure you of his cordial wishes; Mr.
Greville[8] is now writing to you and inclosing a Letter to Sir Wm Hamilton[9] to prepare you a reception
equal to y[ou]r merits when you arrive at Naples.
What shall I say to you in return for the Head of
Sappho? did you paint without Genius, still the
friendship with which you bestow woud recommend your
works to me; and did you give without friendship,
still your Genius woud stamp a value on the present;
when both unite I am highly flatter'd and delighted
with this fresh testimony of your Remembrance of me
and shall keep it with those performances of your's
which are for ever in my eye and encrease in value
every day. I have got back my wife's picture with
the boy out of Ireland, and prize it inestimably--[10]
I must now say a few words to you from the Amiable
Lord of this Mansion; he has a few wishes about pictures which perhaps you coud gratify.   There is a
magnificent Room in this Castle, where a picture of
Consideration is wanting according to the proportion
of 63 inches by 43 wide, or near upon, (not to be
nice to a few inches) the subject historical, where
more than one figure is employed. Lord Warwick knows
too much of Italy and Pictures not to know how difficult it is to fall in with such a purchase upon
reasonable terms, for he does not mean to dedicate a
great sum to the purpose, but rather wishes to have
a picture of Effect & Genius, which perhaps may
cross you in your travells, out of the beat of our
Collectors, and not exceeding £100. sterling--He
likewise entreats the favour of you, if it falls in
your way, to buy him a few pourtraits for a Collection he is making; they must be Heads only (which we
call 3 Q[rs]) of spirit and effect; Titian or Guido,
if they can be met with in Compass of moderation;
mark'd Characters or dignified persons, and your

kind Compliance with this Request will gratify him most highly--He likewise says that if you bring home any Copies, which you mean to dispose of, or if it falls in the way of your Studies to make any Copies from Capital picts: which you will part from at your return, he begs he may be consider'd the first place; and any Drafts you may make on him in St James's Square for purchases he will duely honour-- Having said this I am to assure you of his sincere regards and good wishes, and how glad he shall be to see you here at your return. Accept my best love and that of my good woman and all my young ones, who, I bless God, are perfectly well--Bear me in remembrance and write again in answer to this. I am ever most affecty Yrs

Richd Cumberland

Lord Warwick desires me to add that if you can find any little Heads of good Hands, answering to the above Idea, he will be very glad of them. He does not mind Masters so much as Characters in the Pieces.

Source: Yale.
Addressed to: Monsieur Romney. Anglois
au Caffee Anglois
sur La Place dEspagne
Rome

1. George Romney (1734-1802) was in Rome during August 1774.
2. Fulke Greville, the Earl of Warwick.
3. James Barry, the painter.
4. Benjamin West (1738-1820), the artist.
5. Sir Joshua Reynokds, the portrait painter.
6. Sir Nathaniel Dance Holland (1734-1811), the artist.
7. Sir Watkins Williams
8. Charles Francis Greville, brother of the Earl of Warwick and a nephew of Sir William Hamilton, was introduced to Romney by Cumberland and they became close friends.

9. Sir William Hamilton(1730-1803), English Ambassador to the Court at Naples.

10. Regarding Romney's paintings of Mrs. Cumberland and her family see Arthur B. Chamberlain, *George Romney*, 1910 (Reprinted, Books for Libraries Press, Freeport, N. Y., 1971) p. 95.

LI   David Garrick   23 October 1774[1]

Kelmarsh Oct 23

Dear Sir

I waited the Event of our Play before I woud answer your kind favour, hoping that I might have the pleasure to tell you (what I now truly can) that the success was such as we coud wish it.[2] The Effect of both tragedy and Comedy was infinitely beyond my hopes and the performance in all the prime parts prodigiously applauded.   Mrs. Thursby[3] was Excellent, she spoke with a feeling, attention and Propriety that I never saw an example of. The pitch of her voice was wanderfully sweet, but not capable of very strong exertions, her actions gracefull with a dignified deportment perfectly in character; the tricks she had last year totally laid aside and she herself a new personage. I am sensible I flatter my own performance, when I tell you this, but it is true that my voice was more accordant to her's, (than Jaffier's was) and my attention without remission. The Death of Egmont was particularly approved of; the Gradations of his Madness as derived from the effects of poisons, with the Interval of reason in the moment before Death, wherein he stops the princess hand in the act of self destruction, had great effect; those broken tones that grief and pain impress on the approach of Death, but above all the Leap from Madness to immediate Reason on the Attempt of the Princess to destroy herself were the better executed for having never been practised except in Idea--I wish I coud have it resolved from the first of Actors, (Antient or Modern) whether this position be not true That when the mind has decided the action and fixed it in Idea, it is better left to the happy Genius of the moment, than practised in cold blood at preparatory Rehearsals--In my attempt I thought it so, and I perceived my spectators subscribing to it--I shoud tell you that I alter'd the Catastrophe entirely and made it very dramatic indeed. Mr. Hanbury[4] performed surprizingly well--And in the Entertainment everything was prosperous and Cradock[5] excellent. We had an exceeding brilliant audience--the House of Spencer[6] and of Warwick the Duke of Dorset[8] and the Lord Chancellor[9] with other illustrious persons were amongst our audience. Mr. Hanbury and Mrs. Thursby join with me in returning you many thanks for the assistance of your Dresses, of which however as it happen's we used but one. I shall return all the things to Blackmore by tomorrow's conveyance.

With respect to Mr. Smith's letter to Mr. William Cumberland,[10] I think it woud be best for William Cumberland to answer it and I wish he had sent it to Westm[inste]r School for that purpose. I have thrown all my influence in the scale of friendship for his coming to the Theatre, the first act of gratitude he pays me is rehearsing his part. If you think the part worthy of him, you have the means in y[ou]r hands of engaging him to it, if you do not, give it to anybody else. For my particular, was my play in any other hands but your's, I shoud make it a condition of the performance, but I started with a resolution of referring it absolutely to you, and with you it absolutely remains. I only observe that Mr. Smith *ought* to perform and Mrs. Abington *must*,[11] or the play is undone.--Accept on this and all occasions my sincere good wishes and beleive me ever most sincerely and faithfully yrs

R Cumb.

I shoud have sent you a Copy of our *Election*[12] but that I see you have one of your own; it was sent down to Mrs Thursby by Lord Robt. I think mine too seasonable and too full of Humour not to give it a display.

You must excuse my writing to Mr. Smith, for what can I say in such an unexpected case.

Source: British Science Museum.

1. The date is determined by Garrick's letter to Cumberland on 29 August 1774, declining to perform in the private theatricals (Little and Kahrl, #856, pp. 951-953).

2. The play, "The Princess of Parma," was performed privately at Kelmarsh, Northamptonshire but was never published. The part of Cardinal Granville, however, has survived in manuscript and is at the Folger Shakespeare Library.

3. Anne (Hanbury) Thursby (d. 1778).

4. William Hanbury (d. 1807), a brother of Anne Thursby.

5. Joseph Cradock (1742-1826).

6. John Spencer (1734-1783), after 1765 the first Earl Spencer.

7. Fulke Greville (1716-1806), Earl of Warwick.

8. John Frederick Sackville (1745-1799), the third Duke of Dorset.

9. Henry Bathurst (1714-1794) was made Baron Apsley in 1771. He became Lord Chancellor on 23 January 1771.

10. Cumberland's youngest son, then a student at Westminster school. Mr. Smith is the actor, William Smith, who had appeared at Covent Garden since 1759, but moved to Drury Lane in 1774.

11. Smith did not act in Cumberland's *The Choleric Man*, but Frances Abington (1737-1815) played the part of Laetitia. Smith, however, read the "Prologue" when the comedy opened at Drury Lane on 19 December 1774. Mrs. Abington's reading of the "Epilogue" was highly applauded (*The London Stage*, ed. Stone, Part IV, p. 1857).

12. A portion of the "Election," a brief humorous entertainment, is with the manuscript of "The Princess of Parma" at the Folger.

LII David Garrick 11 November 1774[1]

Kimston Nov. 11th.

I have long foreseen, Dear Sir, that the public must either withgo their theatrical Amusements, or provide some remedy against the capricious punctilio of the Actors. Two principal performers have already returned their parts in my comedy,[2] and parts which, if I have any judgement, cannot so properly be filled by any two men in either Theatre. Their Renegation will probably draw on more. What is to be done? Let us join in withdrawing the object of contention, before the Evil spreads. Iam unfit for such Controversies, and it will operate in the End for your ease and releif. Full of resources as your Management ever is, and possest of a Spectacle in the last new production which will satisfy the public thirst for novelty and splendor,[3] release, I earnestly beseech you, my obnoxious peice. Your Interest will probably not suffer for this sacrifice, and if the Town (who have sometimes been amused with my Trifles) shall think they have lost any thing by it's suppression, let them look to Mr. Smith and Mr. Dodd for the Causes of it.

The latter of these Gentlemen conceives I made a promise of the part of Jack to him. I have never understood it so. It is true when he called on me for the prologue I wrote for his speaking in Dublin, that I read a few desultory pages in my Comedy in the scenes between Jack and Dibble and Old Nightshade and the Merchant, but in no order, nor to the amo[un]t of 3 Acts, nor as I think of one. If I coud call to mind any word that had fallen from me at that time, on which a promise coud be grounded, I woud certainly use all means in my power to fulfill the just Expectations of a deserving performer--As it is, I am only to lament that either he has mistaken me, or that I was not sooner apprised of his Claim upon me. The Part cannot now be revoked--Nor

can I tell how Mr. Dodd's Vacancy coud be filled--
Mr. Baddeley[4] woud probably as little chuse to succeed to Mr. Dodd's leavings, as Mr. Reddish[5] woud to
Mr. Smith's--And yet there do not occurr to me any
two Gentlemen in the Company, except the above, to
whom those parts coud with any propriety be trans-
ferr'd. It is therefore on all hands safer and better both for you and for me to suppress the Piece
upon these Circumstances, and supply its place with
something wherein the Company shall be more unani-
mous--And I sincerely hope you will approve of this.

What it is in which the Company joined at the
Reading you do not mention; perhaps you will not now
think it necessary, tho' at all times I shall pay
due deference to the Opinions of persons so intitled
to have a Judgement in their own profession. Whether
in general You or they approved of the Reading I am
at a loss to guess, but from your Silence on that
Head I beleive I have fallen into an Error very common to Authors of building too much Expectation on
my own productions--And yet if I know my heart there
are few men in whose esteem my trifles hold a lower
Rank than in their Author's.

I have watch'd your favorite *Maid* in the papers,
and am rejoiced to find her so successful.[6] I make
no doubt of her holding on thro the Christmas Holidays with the occasional Releif of your own excellent performances. I am afraid the New Managers at
Cov[en]t Garden have slept in their outset;[7] I see
nothing new or brilliant and nothing that the Barrys
have done.[8] My Health has suffer'd so much from the
fatigues of Northamptonshire, that I am setting out
directly by advice for Bath, pray write me there,
and be assured I carry with me the best wishes for
your Health and Happiness, being most sincerely
Your's

                    Rich Cumberland

Direct to me at The Pump Room.

Source: British Science Museum.

1. The year is determined by the reference to *The Choleric Man*, produced 19 December 1774.

2. William Smith and James Dodd quarreled about their parts in *The Choleric Man*. Neither finally acted in the comedy, although Smith recited the "Prologue."

3. *The Maid of the Oaks* by General John Burgoyne (1722-1792) was first acted on 5 November 1774. The play was built around the extravagant fête champêtre given to celebrate the Marriage of Lord Stanley to Lady Elizabeth Hamilton at the Oaks in Surrey on 9 November 1774.

4. Robert Baddeley (d. 1794) acted Dibble in *The Choleric Man*.

5. Samuel Reddish (1735-1785) played Thomas Manlove in the Comedy.

6. *The Maid of the Oaks*.

7. Thomas Harris (d. 1820 was the principal manager, with Thomas Hull (1728-1808) acting as supervisor of rehearsals. George Colman, the previous manager, had sold his share in the theatre to Hull.

8. Anne and Spranger Barry.

LIII David Garrick About 18 November 1774[1]

You have wrote to me, my Dear Sir, with all the Explicitness that Good Sense and Friendship can inspire; and I shoud have less feelings of general Goodwill to Mankind, or partial affection for you, if I lost a moment's time in putting my poor stock of fame absolutely in your Hands--Do in all things I beseech you as you think best, or in other words, as may best contribute to the public Amusements, which are your object and ought to be mine--But as a general Direction may probably be not altogether so agreeable to you, as receiving my opinions in the particulars referr'd, I must tell you that I am satisfied as to the Alternative of Smith or Reddish,[2] tho' I think if Mr. Smith be wise he will not refuse--I think he wont--I hope Miss Pope will not revolt upon the defection of Mr. Dodd,[3] she is certainly an important Accession; we have never met yet on the stage, and I hope we shall not part in the outset; but if it shall so unluckily prove, do as you say and tutor whom you please; if they carry off any of their Instructions they cannot be far from right. The Young Man, whom you call the Sosia Obrien,[4] let him be the Lawyer's Clerk, and when you tell me it will avail in the fortunes of a young beginner you say the thing that ought to decide with me in his favour.--*Obnoxious* I called my peice from the offence and Revolt of the performers; I beseech you to beleive it coud point no where else; for I do faithfully assure you I never did, (nay it was impossible I ever coud) think otherwise for a moment than that you was taking more pains than you ought about me, and as I found you had got a Circle of Discontent about you, I wished for that reason to remove the obnoxious bone of Contention. Now as to the Observations--

If the piece drags at the Catastrophe give it a lift by a judicious attention to the Rehearsal, but do not cut deep till you hear distinctly.

The Warfare with Newspapers is an inglorious warfare; where there is hostility without humour let it be withdrawn, but where the laugh can be raised don't let us fear the Event. I am doom'd before hand to abuse, and this will not make it more or less--*He wrote most of the Articles in the Morning Chro[n-ic]le himself*, may be withdrawn if you think fit--but *the Circulation of Abuse* I think is quaint enough--Surely Jack's description of the picture of Action is comic enough, the City wives must have it; their Husbands will forgive us, besides they are all here at this moment and most of them in the *very Act. I wish he had been an Alderman, for then his Horn woud have warded off the blow* must have the author's stet, and I give it *meo periculo.* The play in general is long and where you can ease without castration pray do it, I cannot put the Incision knife into a more friendly or judicious hand.--Your Critic[ism] upon Andrew's betraying Stapleton to his wife is just. I never adverted to the Circumst[an]ce of the saving him on the broken stead, I think by all means it shoud be trimed as you say, and the reason given; *Come, he saved me with the postman*--But hold, what am I saying?--it was his brother Manlove that saved him, and it was Stapleton that humbugg'd him. I was speaking my memory and had not consider'd it-- Upon the whole I don't know what to say; I leave it with you, turn it as you like, th[ose]⁵ words do it if you think it better as you propose.

I am writing with a Head foul with the waters, and scarce compos; I don't remember w[ha]t I said about Dodd, only that it was truth; if it was angry don't show it; if it was said suaviter in modo, do show it; for I know I spoke my Heart. I will see Henderson;⁶ they play the Note of Hand tomorrow,⁷ but he does not play. Adieu, beleive me more than ever most faithfully and affect[ionatel]y y[ou]rs.

R Cum

Source: British Science Museum.

1. The postmark on the letter is 18 November. The year is 1774 because of the reference to *The Choleric Man*.

2. William Smith; Samuel Reddish. Reddish acted Charles Manlove in the comedy.

3. James Dodd. Jane Pope (1742-1818) did not defect but played the part of Lucy.

4. Probably Francis Waldron (1744-1818) who joined the Drury Lane company in 1769 and played Frampton. Sosia Obrien (d. 1815), was an actor and dramatist who had made his debut at Drury Lane in 1757, but was no longer a member of the company. The name of Sosia was taken from the character in Plautus' *Amphitryon* in whose guise Mercury appears. Plautus' play was performed at that time in John Hawkesworth's version, *Amphitryon; or the Two Sosias.*

5. The manuscript is defective at this point.

6. John Henderson (1747-1785), a popular actor at Bath.

7. *The Note of Hand*, a farce by Cumberland, had been produced at Drury Lane on 9 February 1774.

LIV   David Garrick   24 November 1774[1]

My dear Sir

I thank you for your obliging letter--I think that the cast of the Comedy will be strong in the parts of Jack, Andrew Nightshade, Letitia, Lucy, Dibble and Gregory; and that being the case   I   beg you will please yourself in the part of   Charles; I rather lean to Reddish,[2] as thinking his figure tallies better in some respects with that of Weston,[3] than Brereton's,[4] and as Jack is to wear his cloathes, it seems more consistent--but I beleive we have Comedy enough and to spare, without being exact about it;   I entreat you will fill it up most to your own ease and content.

I approve much of Baddeley[5]--I beg you will favor me in your next with the Bill of fare, and tell me when you think it will come out.[6] I cannot help persuading myself it will be highly successfull.

I have attended Mr. Henderson once in the part of Benedict,[7] and am greatly disposed in his favour, if he pleases me as well in other casts I shall write very warmly--I sent for him to me and desired him to play his princ[ip]le Tragic part and he has chosen Hamlet, in which I hear he excells. I am thinking of going to him tonight to see him in Posthumous[8] and on Saturday he takes you off in the prologue to the Rehearsal;[9] I advised him ag[ain]st it, but it was too late, and printed in the bills. Nature has not been beneficent to him in figure or in face, a prominent forehead, corpulent habit, inactive features and not a quick eye; nevertheless he has great sensibility, just elocution, a perfect Ear, good Sense and the most marking pauses (next to your own) I ever heard; in the latter respect he stands next to you and very near you. His memory is ready to a surprizing degree, and he is (as he tells me) sober and regular. I shall be able soon to speak more particularly to you, but I am confident he woud at all events be a great accession to y[ou]r Theatre--and what is more; he is to be had, and will give the preference to you, tho' he thinks you do not esteem his performance. Mr. Palmer[10] has this morning very politely sent me the Entrance into his Theatre.

As for Lord Camden[11] it is a long story, and it is a losing one on his side; every voice here is against him. The place is in confusion; the Rooms in separaton. I am at present too ill to write particulars, I am so fatigued by attending the whole morning to the business of accommodation, on the part of the New Rooms, that I am grievously reduced. I spoke long and often, gave in a string of qualifying Resolutions to sheathe the angry spirits which Lord G has inflamed, and received the thanks of the Meeting. These things are too ridiculous in the latitude[12] of London, but there they are Mountains, and indeed much may depend upon them.--The worst is, I am ill, weaken'd very much by medicine, and not releived from my disorder; I have a heavy cold besides, and the waters lye heavy, and must I doubt be suspended. In short I have just strength to tell you I am ever most faithfully yrs

R Cum

Bath thursday 6 oClock

Source: British Science Museum.

1. The date is determined by the postmark which, although blurred, shows clearly "2" as the first of the two numerals, with the month of November clear. Since the letter was written on Thursday, it had to be the 24th. The year is determined by reference to The Choleric Man, and confirmed by the reference to Hen-

derson's acting Posthumous.

2. Garrick followed Cumberland's suggestion and Samuel Reddish played Charles Manlove.

3. Thomas Weston (1737-1776) acted Jack Nightshade.

4. William Brereton (1741-1787) did not act in the comedy.

5. Robert Baddeley.

6. The play was produced on Monday, 19 November 1774.

7. In Shakespeare's *Much Ado about Nothing*.

8. Henderson acted Posthumous Leonatus, the husband of Imogen, in Shakespeare's *Cymbeline* at Bath on 24 November 1774 (Genest, V, 473).

9. Henderson played Bayes in *The Rehearsal* at Bath on 26 November 1774 (Genest, V, 473).

10. John Palmer, Sr., the owner of the Theatre Royal at Bath.

11. Lord Camden. Charles Pratt (1714-1794) was the first Earl.

12. The manuscript is blurred at this point. Only the last three letters are clear.

LV   David Garrick   27 November 1774[1]

Bath, Sunday Evening

My Dear Sir

I think that Mr. Reddish's Acceptance of the part of *Charles* is another Buttress to our Comedy.[2] His figure and his consequence are certainly good Auxiliaries, and consort better with the other Characters.

I have seen Mr. Henderson in Bayes, and do not depart from my favourable Opinion of him.[3] I think indeed he suffers in the Character on this Stage, but the Audience does not suit, and the play is so out of date that it can only be held up by your Acting, and the Tradition of the London theatre. Here it is Caviar to the Multitude.

The Good Bishop of Worchester[4] died this morning of the bruises occasioned by a fall from his Horse on Thursday last. Though covered with wounds and Contusions he would certainly have recovered but for the bursting of an internal Vessel, which was lacerated by the fall and gave way. He was an exemplary man, gentle and humane, by constitution as well as principle a philosopher; and in all respects a most valuable Man. He had been my Schoolmaster at Westminster and had honoured me with his friendship and esteem ever since. I suffer greatly.

I have a letter from the Secretary of the Society for the Relief of Debtors; he tells me you have given them a benefit, and that it is proposed to repeat my Epilogue.[5] I beg you will look it over, and if there be anything local to the other Theatre, render it conformable to yours; it is out of my mind. I need not request of you to put it into the hands of respectable performers.

I am ever most truly yours

Richd Cumberland

Source: British Science Museum. The manuscript is not in Cumberland's hand.

1. The date is determined by the reference to Henderson's performance as Bayes in *The Rehearsal*. See note 3 below.

2. Samuel Reddish.

3. Henderson acted the part on 26 November 1774 at Bath.

4. Mr. James Johnson (1705-1774), the second master at Westminster School when Cumberland was a student there.

5. On 17 December 1774, *Cymbeline* was acted at Drury Lane as a benefit for the relief of persons imprisoned for small debts. Cumberland's *Occasional Epilogue* was recited at the performance. (*The London Stage*, ed. Stone, Part IV, p. 1856).

LVI   David Garrick   1 December 1774[1]

Thursday Evening

My Dear Sir,

All you have done and all you have wrote is highly pleasing to me; the time and manner of bringing out my very inconsiderable production is perfectly agreeable,[2] and I thank you most affectionately for the natural and unstudied warmth with which you write to me.

It is but a reasonable demand to require a prologue, to ask a good one is not so well adapted to my Genius as to your occasions--I shall send you something tomorrow. Heaven knows what it will be, for can any Harmony proceed from a Heart that is wounded with the severest Sorrow; the death of a most excellent father;[3] fatally critical to his family and to me--But would it be grateful for one who has received far far above his measure of blessings, now to repine? I praise God, I have never given way to one murmur, for I have a better measure of my deservings. I take the dispensation with complacency; I oppose all my resolutions against it; I yield nothing to the affection of sorrow; I trouble my diligence in attending to my own Health; I withdraw myself entirely from a disagreable public and I retire into the bosom of my Friends--desire you to receive me for one. Say nothing to me, (or but little) on this Subject;   write as usual, and treat me like a Man who has understanding enough to comprehend upon what terms he lives and has his being. Adieu; may you be happy and believe me most affectionately yours

R. Cumberland.

Source: The British Science Museum. The manuscript

114

is not in Cumberland's hand.

1. The manuscript is endorsed 3 December, very likely from the postmark. The preceding Thursday was 1 December. The year is determined by reference to *The Choleric Man*.

2. *The Choleric Man*.

3. Cumberland must have learned of his father's death subsequent to his previous letter to Garrick on 27 November. His mother also died soon afterward (*Memoirs*, I, 375).

LVII **David Garrick 2 December 1774**[1]

friday evening

Dear Sir

Before my misfortunes[2] met me I had designed to have a dialogue prologue, in which I meant our friend Johnson to have supported a humorous part;[3] if the mirth has expired, you will not wonder, nevertheless I send it to you such as it is, because I consider your Expectations in the light of my own promises.

Mr. Johnson crosses the stage--Mr. King enters--[4]
"Harkye, You Johnson!--Answer me I say--
"*Well, what's your will* A box for the new play--
"*Box, there's no box.* Tis evermore the case,
"A front now then--*Zounds, Sir, there's not a
                             place.* exit.
How, not a place! This fellow's hir'd to puff,
I'll bet the Knave a crown there's room enough.
Let me look round--So, so; you're pretty full,
And under favor reasonably dull.
How is it, Sirs? What have you all yet wives,
Debts, mortgages, and Riders upon Lives?
Give me the sturdy Loon with broad face grin
Mantling behind a tripple row of Chin,
His laughing sides with stout October lin'd,

A healthful body in a happy mind:
Such were your fathers, and I can't divine
What food has train'd their sons so very fine.
It moves my spleen to see you sit so very wise,
Sipping your Coffee with your half-shut Eyes--
Any news, Doctor?--Sir, I've heard it said--
And then one whispers, to'ther shakes his head,
Winking like owls in sunshine--Oh, tis folly
To be so politic and melancholy.

Come, clear your brows; for, if report says
                                    right,
I'll promise you a merry tale tonight,
Something to chace away that angry spleen
Which forms the mirth and moral of our Scene;
A plot transplanted from the Roman stage,[5]
A drama fashion'd to the present age;
Something for father and for sons to hear
A tale for noble and ignoble Ear,
Bound to no partial no provincial plan
But wide and general as the scale of Man.

And spare, ye Critics, the superfluous blow
Grief's heavy hand has laid your poet low;
Nor think his Errors to himself unknown,
You cannot spy more faults, than he shall own
If the appearance of Johnson had in your opinion
be better omitted, or is unacceptable to him, it
will begin with the 5th verse.--What not a place!
this *Johnson's* hir'd to puff

        &c &c &c

I dare say it wants Correction, tho' I hardly
think Correction can cure it--in short there is no
music in my [dis]position,[6] but when I tell you how
sincer[ely][7] I esteem and love you. Adieu

        R Cum.

I rely upon your delicacy for prefacing the appearance of my play with a paragraph respecting the Death of my father and my being at Bath on acco[unt] of my Health, in the plainest and most unaffected words.

Source: British Science Museum.

1. On the preceding evening, Thursday, 1 December 1774, Cumberland had promised to send a prologue to Garrick "tomorrow." The letter is postmarked 5 December.

2. The death of Cumberland's father.

3. A Johnston, probably Alexander Johnston, served at different times as box-book and housekeeper at Drury Lane.

4. Thomas King who played Nightshade in *The Choleric Man*.

5. The *Choleric Man* was based on the *Adelphi* of Terence.

6. The manuscript is defective here.

7. The manuscript is defective here.

LVIII   **David Garrick   3 December 1774**[1]

Saturday Night
Rupel Street Bath

My Dear Sir

If it is consistent with the practise and interests of the Theatre to accommodate these provincial Stages by letting them in for a Copy a few days earlier than the publication entitles them to, I find myself disposed to interceed with you on behalf of Mr. Palmer of this place.[2] He has been exceedingly polite and obliging, and I shoud be glad to return his Civility, if it was in my power.

I have often thought there was something unfinished in the departure of *Dibble* in the 5th Act, after his being discover'd by *Charles Manlove*--I think it woud be in character for *Charles*, after having brought him to confession to dismiss him thus--vis.

> "*Charles*
> "You know, Mr. Dibble, it is in my power to pun-
> "ish you Severely; therefore, Sir, I shall re-
> "venge myself upon You--by forgiving you--Go." &c
> &c. (exit Dibble)

I think the prologue may be a little amended in the concluding Lines, thus, vis--

> "And spare, Ye Critics, the superfluous blow,
> "Not meanly stab an unresisting Foe;
> "Think not his errors to himself unknown,
> "You cannot spy more faults than he will own."[3]

I have never yet spoken to you about the publication of the Comedy; Becket[4] and I have had no words about it, so that I am not assured whether it will be acceptable to him or not; I presume however that it will upon proper conditions, I have never had more or less than £150. for all my Copies from Mr. Griffin,[5] and there would be this consideration in going to him again, that the property in that case being in one man's hands, I coud publish the four Comedies in one volume with a treatise which I have prepared upon the Greek Comedy, of which I have had an opportunity of collecting more fragments, and some Information that may be new to the Generality of Readers; and I propose by deduction to throw some lights upon the practise of the English Stage, which I think is now under great misconstruction--It would be foolish to affect importance about such a trifle as my idle play, which after all will probably bilk him, so that he shall take it, if he likes it, or leave it, if he don't.

But as he has been dealing with me in a trifling dilatory manner, I think (if you approve it) to drive a peremptory bargain for £150., to be positively paid in on the third night of it's performance if it shall reach that Night--but if it shall touch the twentieth Exhibition within this Season, I shall in that case require the purchase to be made £200., by the payment of £50. more on that Event. He

118

may probably agree to this, without much risque of exceeding the first payment--If these terms are not acceptable, be kind enough to inform me, and I will cause it to be tender'd to Griffin. I am ashamed to put you to this sorry office, but I trust you will not despise any office for a friend; and I submit it to you, that if you do not think it reasonable, you shoud tell me so--He may send down the sheets for Correction under franks, and it is only letting him have the copy a few days sooner to allow for the delays of postage.

I am most affecty   R Cum.

Source: British Science Museum.

1. The date is determined by the postmark, 6 December, and the year by references to *The Choleric Man*.

2. John Palmer, Sr., manager of the Theatre Royal at Bath.

3. See the prologue for *The Choleric Man* contained in Cumberland's letter to Garrick of 2 December.

4. Thomas Becket (1721?-1813), bookseller and publisher. He published *The Choleric Man*.

5. William Griffin, bookseller and publisher.

LIX **David Garrick   10 December 1774**[1]

Saturday Evening, Bath

My Dear Sir

I join with you so entirely in condemning the prologue I sent you, that prest as I am with a variety of untoward affairs and ill disposed to poetry, I have nevertheless begun and compleated an entire new prologue. Being new, perhaps I am the more pleased with it, but if I don't mistake it is better than the prologue to Dow's tragedy,[2] and the best of a bad market.

Prologue to the Choleric Man

In Athens once, as classic Story runs,
Thalia number'd fifty living Sons:
But mark the waste of Time's destructive hand,
One Bard survives of all this numerous band;
Yet human Genius seem'd as t'woud defy
Time's utmost rage by it's variety,
For t'was no wondrous harvest in those days
From one rich stock to reap a hundred plays:
Ah, coud we bring but one of those to light,
We'd give a hundred such as this tonight.

Rome from her Captive took the Law she gave,
And was at once her Mistress and her slave;
Greece from her fall immortal triumphs drew,
And prov'd her tutelar *Minerva* true;
She, goddess like, confiding in her charms,
To Mars resign'd the barren task of arms'
Full well assur'd, When those vain toils were
         past,
That Wit must triumph over strength at last;
Then smiling saw her Athens meet it's doom,
And crown'd her in the Theatres of Rome.
Nor murmur'd Rome to see her *Terence* shod
With the same Socc in which *Menander* trod;
Nor *Laelius* scorn'd, nor *Scipio* blusht to sit.
And join their plaudits to Athenian wit:
Micio's mild Virtues and mad *Demea's* rage
With bursts alternate shook the echoing stage.
And from these Models tis your poet draws
His best his only hope of your applause;
A Tale it is to chase that angry spleen,
Which forms the mirth and moral of his Scene
A Tale for noble and ignoble ear,
Something for fathers and for sons to hear.
And shoud you on your humbler Bard bestow

That Grace, which Rome to her's was pleas'd to
show,
Advantage with the Modern fairly lies,
Who, less deserving, gains as great a prize.

I have seen your Brother repeatedly,[3] and just now
I think he is on the recovering side, but certainly
in great danger; He has got into his Lodgings, and
wants no advice or assistance, nor shall he want the
services and attention of a friend, while I am here.
His head was very wandering just now, and I flatter
myself I have much composed his spirits. If his danger encreases, I shall send in Dr. Moysey, but I
hope there will be no occasion, and he is greatly
attach'd to his physician Dr. Falkner.[4] If he can
once drink the Waters I flatter myself he will be
saved; I have exacted his promise not to write to
you, as I am sure it will hurt his head.
Was I to come now to attend the Comedy, it woud
demolish me. I am sure you will stand by it. Mrs.
Cum will be in Town on Wednesday night and thankfull
if Mrs. Garrick will give her a Seat in her box at
the first night. Adieu

R C

Source: British Science Museum.

1. The date is determined by the postmark, 12 December, the indicated day of the week, and reference to *The Choleric Man*.

2. Alexander Dow (d. 1779). His tragedy, *Sethona*, had been produced on 19 February 1774 at Drury Lane. *The Public Advertiser*
commented on its prologue as follows: "The *Prologue* is a very
classical Performance, and well delivered by Mr. Reddish, notwithstanding the noise and frequent Interruption usual on these
occasions" (*The London Stage*, Part IV, ed. Stone, p. 1787).

3. George Garrick (1723-1779), David Garrick's brother, had become ill in the spring of 1774 and was considered near death. He
recovered, however, and went to Bath during the summer. By Decem-

ber, he was apparently well on his way to restored health. Frequent references to his illness are made in Garrick's letters.
    4. William Falconer (1744-1824).

LX   David Garrick   About 12 December 1774[1]

    I am delighted to hear of you so frequently on the stage, not only for the public, but as I take it for a testimony of your Health, especially so strong a part as Hamlet.[2] I fear you are greatly hurried and overwhelmed with Business, now particularly in your brother's absence. And you must give him Time, for he has been at the door of Death.[3]

Source: British Science Museum. This appears to be a fragment of a letter from Cumberland to Garrick, and is not in Cumberland's hand.

    1. The date is determined by the reference to Garrick's perfor-
mance in *Hamlet* and to Garrick's brother's illness. See 13 December 1774.
    2. Garrick acted Hamlet on 2 December and 12 December 1774.
    3. Cumberland's first reference to George Garrick's illness is
in his letter of 10 December 1774.

LXI   David Garrick   13 December 1774[1]

Bath Tuesday 6 oClock

    When your brother, my Dear Sir, first met my Eyes, I never beheld such a Spectacle of sickness and de-spair.[2] His Death appear'd inevitable and near; I was shocked. Behold the Change of two or three Days, he is now safe as you and I; has been out in his Chair, drank the waters, and is established. So that I have laid down my Charge and my Care.

I leave this town on Saturday Evening next, or Sunday morning; but I beg you will give me a Line on Thursday night from the Theatre directed to me hither to inform me how the Comedy went off,[3] and pray write without flattery, faithfully.

Henderson is on the point of agreeing for a new Contract with Mr. Palmer;[4] If you woud take my Judgement, you shoud engage him; the more I see of him the more I am persuaded he woud be the most valuable Accession you coud possibly make. His Agreement with Mr. P woud have been made this day, if I had not stopt it; I think you shoud by all means empower your brother to strike a bargain with him.

I am most sincerely

R Cum

Source: British Science Museum.

1. The date is determined by the postmark, 15 December, the reference to Tuesday, and to the illness of George Garrick.

2. George Garrick. See note to letter of 10 December 1774.

3. The Choleric Man was not acted on Thursday, but the following Monday, 19 December.

4. According to John Ireland, John Palmer, Sr., of the Theatre Royal at Bath, had employed the actor, John Henderson, in September 1772 under a three year contract as a result of a letter from Garrick (Letters and Poems by John Henderson, 1786, p. 66).

LXII   David Garrick   14 December 1774[1]

Wednesday Bath

My Dear Sir

I don't think I should have troubled you with a letter today if it had not been to have saved your brother the fatigue of writing;[2] I do not find him quite so well today, as he was yesterday tho he had a very good night. However the Weather is so relaxing that in bilious habits it is easily accounted, and I am sorry to say that I have not had a worse day myself these three months, than I have now after five weeks drinking. My Spirits are oppressed and my habit loaded to a great degree, with a foe that is forever grumbling within. Your short letter has been no cordial to me, I must confess, as you speak so unpromisingly of the second prologue I sent you, and which I flatt'red myself you would warmly approve.[3] I have strictly considered it, and I have nothing to alter or suppress, so that I beg it may be spoken literally as it is wrote. It is indeed for the Few, and many will not follow where it comes, but I thought you would be amongst the Few, and I still persuade myself you will when you reconsider it, but the fatigues of Hamlet[4] and the confusion of Dibdin's farce in a state of Damnation[5] (as I am told was the case) might not put you in a favourable disposition.

You did not mention to me what day you proposed to bring on the Comedy, but I learn from your brother that it is moved to Monday next,[6] which will be the day preceding my Arrival in Town and approaches very near the Holidays.

I fear Mr. Henderson will be lost, and (speaking as an Author) I esteem it a great loss.[7] I remain in my opinion, and I find it confirmed by those of whose judgments I think well. Lord Nuneham[8] tells me this morning, that he had wrote to Mr. Whitehead[9] in the highest terms of him, having seen him in the Characters of Hamlet and Lorenzo in the Spanish Friar.[10] I have seen him in Don John,[11] and Approved of him highly--As you was entirely silent on his Subject in your letters to me, I could say nothing to him, when he came for an Answer. Adieu my dear Sir, believe me

124

Yrs affectionately

Richd Cumberland

Source: British Science Museum. The manuscript is not in Cumberland's hand.

1. The date is determined by reference to the opening of *The Choleric Man* the following Monday, December 19.

2. George Garrick. See letter of 10 December 1774.

3. The text of this prologue is included in the letter of 10 December 1774.

4. Garrick had acted Hamlet on 12 December.

5. Charles Dibdin (1745-1814) had his farce, *The Cobler*, acted to an unfavorable audience reaction on 9 December 1774.

6. *The Choleric Man* was acted on Monday, December 19, 1774.

8. George Simon Harcourt (1736-1809), second Earl Harcourt after 1777. Prior to this he was Lord Viscount Nuneham.

9. William Whitehead (1715-1785).

10. John Dryden's *The Spanish Friar* (1681). Genest does not record a performance by Henderson as Lorenzo until 3 January 1775 (V, p. 474).

11. Genest records that Henderson acted Hamlet, Posthumous in *Cymbeline*, and Don John on December 1-6 and 10, 1774, at Bath. Don John was the leading character in the Duke of Buckingham's version of Fletcher's *The Chances*.

LXIII   David Garrick   17 December 1774[1]

Bath Saturday 4 oClock

My Dear Sir,

I hope this Letter will arrive in a happy time and salute you with Congratulations on the Success of the Choleric Man.[2] I dare say you have postponed it on good reasons and am perfectly satisfied on that score. I shall not disguise from you that it is a disappointment to me that you have superceded my prologue.[3] It is in all respects such as you desired, serious, classical and conciliatory, it acknowledges the use I have made of Terence and it speaks with due modesty of my own deservings. You certainly have not considered it when you call it heavy; grave it is, but that is a recommendation, as a merry prologue robs the play. I stake myself upon it, and if by good Chance the Piece is alive, I must earnestly desire to annex the prologue to it. Surely Mr. Reddish[4] could get up a prologue in a whole week; mine arrived on Monday and was to be spoken on Monday Se'nnight; Yours could only be a Night older--I should be highly ungratefull if I was insensible of your great kindness to me in taking such a trouble on yourself, so fully employed as you must be; It is amongst the many acts of Service you do your friends, for which we are as much obliged to your Heart as to your Genius; but my reasons do not turn upon comparative Merit in our Poems; that I am well content to yield, but I could wish my words to be heard and seen, especially as my foes have never ceased objecting against a flippancy in my first prologue.[5] I would sheath that objection, and this does it effectually--more to my entire Content, (as I told you in my last) than anything I ever wrote. But perhaps I am talking of a Joint Stool, when the House is burnt down.

I am, Dear Sir,

affectionately yours

Richd Cumberland

If this arrives before the play is acted, I beseech you to let the Prologue be read, and give the reason which is my Absence. I am very materially interested that it should be spoke. In your Tuesdays Letter[6] you make no mention of the Prologue you had written on the Sunday before, but say that you will make mine do as well as you can.

If this does not come in time for Mondays Reading, I beg most earnestly mine may be spoken or Read on Tuesday Night, if the piece survives.[7]

Source: British Science Museum. The manuscript is not in Cumberland's hand.

1. The date is determined by reference to the day, Saturday, before the Monday on which The Choleric Man was acted.

2. The play was acted with moderate success on 19 December 1774.

3. Included in his letter of 10 December 1774.

4. Samuel Reddish did not read the "Prologue." It was read by William Smith, and the "Epilogue" by Mrs. Frances Abington (1737-1815).

5. Included in his letter of 2 December 1774.

6. This letter does not survive.

7. Cumberland's "Prologue" was probably read, with Garrick's piece serving as "Epilogue": "...a most excellent *Epilogue* was written by Mr. G. & spoken by Mrs Abington which gave a great Lift to the play Uncommon Applause to the Epilogue (Hopkins Diary)" (*The London Stage*, Part IV, ed. Stone, p. 1857). Cumberland's "Prologue" is printed in the 1775 edition of the comedy.

LXIV David Garrick 19 December 1774[1]

Bath ½ past Six oClock
Monday

My Dear Friend

I write to you now while my Trial is sub Judice, if the Day passes as ill in Town with my Affairs as it has done at Bath with me, The Choleric Man is now the damned man. I have done dining with the most noisy illbred set of fellows I ever fell in with; a Gentleman of a very recent acquaintance pressed me to his House, and I am come home thoroughly fatigued and not well. I cannot abstain from writing to you, if it be only to give my testimony to your Care and friendly attention to my play, let its fate be what it will, and to desire that if the Public liking is not with it, that you will not strain the Interests of the Theatre in my behalf, but that you will give me up with as much candour as you took me. If my attendance could have alleviated yours, I should be content to share the burden; else I am most heartily glad to be clear of the Affair, as my Health and Spirits are ill able to stand any extra-ordinary Exertion. I find every thing affects me too sensibly, and being much wounded of late, I am easily hurt[2]-- Dont misinterpret my impatience about the prologue; and above all things dont think I can misunderstand the friendly motives of your writing it;[3] nothing could be kinder--but I am very anxious to avail myself of the conciliatory turn which my prologue has taken by your advice, and as I am apt to wish ardently, when I do wish, I have written to you perhaps too warmly on the Subject; I thought so, which made me subjoin my last short Letter.

If I do not come to Town on Thursday, Mrs. Cumberland certainly will, but I have no Spirits to face a theatre. I am ever affectionately yours

Richd Cumberland

I desire to be remembered to Mr. Beckett;[4] I have received his Letter, and approve of the Conditions entirely.

Source: British Science Museum. The manuscript is not in Cumberland's hand.

1. The date is determined by the date of the performance of *The*

Choleric Man, on Monday 19 December 1774.

2. Cumberland's father had recently died, a fact which had an unusually sobering effect on the dramatist.

3. See his letter of 17 December.

4. Thomas Becket (1721?-1831). He published *The Choleric Man*.

LXV   David Garrick   About 28 January 1775[1]

My Dear Sir

Having been disappointed of finding Mrs. Abington at home, I have written her a Letter to the Effect you wished.[2] I have told her the very unpleasant situation I was thrown into by having exceeded my powers from a wish to gratify her Inclination, and I have represented the high displeasure you had conceived both against her and myself from the attempt upon what is justly inherent in you alone. In short not to repeat what I have said, I can not doubt her continuing in her part without putting you to the trouble of saying what must finally decide the Question, if my Intervention fails.

Your Letter to Henderson is so fair and so full, I will send it as it is unless you wish any thing otherwise.[3]

I am Yours

Richd Cumberland

Source: British Science Museum. The manuscript is not in Cumberland's hand.

1. The date is determined by the date of the letter from Garrick to Mrs. Abington relative to the same subject on 28 January 1775.

2. I have found no copy of Cumberland's letter to Mrs. Abing-

ton. Cumberland's comments on *The Choleric Man* in his *Memoirs* make no mention of this incident. In his letter to Mrs. Abington of 28 January, Garrick complains of his being affronted by a recent letter from her stating that she had "settled the matter" of her part "in the new Comedy" with Cumberland. He seems also to have been angered by the fact that she chose to correspond through William Hopkins (d. 1780), the prompter. Mrs. Abington's letter to Hopkins is located in manuscript in the Folger Shakespeare Library, and is dated Friday, January 20th: "Mrs. Abington sends the part of Latitia, in the Choleric Man to Mr. Hopkins, in order to his receiving Mr. Garrick's Commands as to the person he is pleased to give it in study to, for the next representation of the play: Mr. Cumberland has obligingly given his Consent to her resigning of the part: and Mrs. Abington flatters herself that Mr. Garrick will have the goodness and complaisance to relieve her from a character so little caled (sic.) to her confined stile of acting.

Mrs. Abington has been Ill for some days past, but would not Importune Mr. Garrick with complaints as she saw there was a necessity for her exerting herself till the new Tragedy was ready."

3. This letter is not included in Garrick's letters edited by Little and Kahrl.

LXVI Roger Pinckney 28 July 1775

Tetsworth, near Biggleswade, July 28, 1775

Dear Sir,

Your letter of the 10th of May, after a silence of so long standing, gave me much satisfaction, and I should have received much more from it, if your zeal for America and its cause had allowed you room and disposition to have informed me of yourself and your affairs. You are silent as to your family, and all that concerns a friend and well-wisher to hear; but you are very particular and diffusive in your description of the action at Concord,[1] and the inhumanity of your late countrymen, the English troops. One enquiry, however, I had at heart, which by implication your letter answers, and that is, when your friends in England may expect your return; this I can plainly see will not be till Mr. Hancock and Mr. Adams[2] take lodgings at St. James's, for you are as true an American as ever I met with, so thoroughly have you assimilated yourself to the soil and sentiments to which you have been transplanted. I make no reply to the list of savage enormities, the rapine, plunder and barbarous indignities to the mangled bodies of the dead, with which your information loads the military, which, in general, is composed of the most humane, and always of the most brave amongst your countrymen and mine; time must have cleared up the truth to you in this particular, even through the medium of New England misrepresentation; and you will now have another account to lament over of the action on the 17th of June,[3] in which the same tale of horror will be repeated, and the same *Te Deums* sung by the victorious Bostonians; but I still repeat to you, that time will clear your error and alter your sentiments. To give you my ideas, wide as they stand off from your own, would be quite useless and laborious to us both, I deplore the situation of America in every vein of my heart; I think the measures which have inflamed and misled them, have not originated with themselves; they have conceived the idea of disobedience and disorder in all its fatal extent, from the conduct of certain politicians in the heart of this realm;[4] but those politicians have been opposers, and not abettors of administration; I pity the deluded throng who rouse at the call of liberty, (though it is like the shepherd's-boy in the fable, who cried wolf when there was no wolf), but I have also, and you, dear Sir, it is presumed once had, some bowels of consideration for those murderers (as you call them) *who are sparing neither sex, age, or condition, tearing down, burning, and destroying every thing in their way, and with rapine and plunder of the poor inhabitants, enriching themselves.* And is it possible you can lend a serious ear to this nonsensical rhapsody, excusable in no one but a New England field preacher; and can you seriously transcribe so ridiculous a calumny, and send it to me as authentic news? Have not you known the temper and nature of your own brave countrymen in times past?--Have you never lived with English officers, or recollected the transactions of the late war in all its branches? When they conquered the empire of America for the Americans, did they exhibit any instances of this blood-thirsty disposition, which seems copied from a Grub-street paper of a *horrid, bloody, and inhuman murder?* Our natural enemies never had it to accuse us of what our natural friends now charge us; and that through the medium, not of an American, but of an English gentleman, who has left his country not many years past, and in that time, to my knowledge, been spectator of many very disorderly proceedings and insurrections in which there was no English soldier to be found to bear the blame; I believe when you went your progress into the interior of South Carolina, you would not have been sorry to have had a file of British grenadiers in your suite.

I have troubled you and myself much too long upon this painful subject; I have no desire to wean your partiality from the place you are in, and the people you are with. It is in some respects a most convenient and happy partiality; and it is a pity to awaken reason and judgment when they are buried in so sweet and innocent a slumber.

I have been at Peterborough lately, where I saw some late friends of yours, some bloody Englishmen, who I suppose would roast and eat you for an American, if you was to come amongst them again. This you may at least expect, that there is plenty of tar and feathers provided for you, but I am apt to think they would rather give you the fowl than its feathers.

I do not shew your letter to Mrs. Cum. or any of your old friends; she would not thank you for your character of the *king's troops*, having lately lost the bravest and best of brothers, (but joy be for the Americans!) he was an inhuman Englishman, and one of the *king's troops*. I have never worn a cockade, so I may conclude myself, as usual,

Dear Sir,

Your most faithful friend,

And obedient Servant,

Richard Cumberland.

Source: Mudford.

1. On 18 April 1775, General Gage had sent a force of soldiers to seize a magazine of arms at Concord and on the way they fired on a much smaller group of American volunteers gathered at Lexington.

2. John Hancock (1737-1793), a wealth Bostonian, and probably Samuel Adams (1722-1803), who had been a leader of the Boston Tea Party.

3. The Battle of Bunker Hill (or more accurately Breed's Hill), in which the British under General Howe suffered considerable casualties in dislodging the rebels.

4. "Stephen Sayre (an American but formerly sheriff of London) was sent to the tower on charges of plotting to seize the King. Radicals of Wilkes's stamp faced charges of disloyalty. There was indeed a massive strengthening of Lord North's political position. The suspicion, long felt, that the Rockinghams were factious received confirmation from across the Atlantic" (Watson, *The Reign of George III*, p. 203).

LXVII   George Romney   July or August 1775[1]

Tetworth Wednesday

Dear Sir

I returned home the day before yesterday from Warwick Castle, where I had passed a few days with Lord
Warwick, and in which time I took an opportunity of
talking over with him at leisure all that you desired me relative to your disappointment in not executing his Commission and your readiness to have
gratified him in it, if you had found any pieces of
art worth bringing home.[2] We had frequent discours-
es about you (the more especially as we were alone)
and I had the happiness to find an elegant friend
who went equal lengths with me in giving testimony
to your genius and the hopes of your future fame,
advanced by travell and experience. Lord Warwick is
possess'd (as no doubt you know) of a magnificent
Castle, and is disposing his furniture and pictures
to the taste of the building; He has collected some
very respectable pourtraits, cheifly of Vandyke, and
has reserved a place in his principal Apartment for
a Companion, where he wishes you to try your
strength in the same bow with the best Masters of
pourtrait painting; but as he woud not fetter your
fancy by any fixt subject he leaves the object to
your own Chusing and all Circumst[an]ces about it,
only it must be female, as I beleive it is to Companion with Cha[rles] the first's Queen by Vandyke.
It is his wish that you woud work upon this picture
at the Castle, and he proposes to give you possession of an entire Tower, where you will have choice
of Light, a most delightfull workshop, bedroom,
study, books and Closets for your Tools with all
peace and Content that solitude and serenity can
give you; You will not doubt this plan being adapted
to your disposition when I tell you it was the joint
result of our Councils, and we have laid the time as
well as Scene when Lord Warwick will be entirely a-
lone, and when I can meet you, provided your business in Town can spare you for a fortnight in the
month of October, in the beginning of the month. My
Lord and I propose going to Kiswick for a short tour

on the 10th of October, so that if you can meet me at Warwick on the 8th, we can leave you in possession of your Tower, and at our return shall expect to find something in forwardness.[3] This is our project, and if meets your approbation and consent, let me know by letter and I will apprise my friend of it, and unless a Call of Parliament absolutely prevents our whole Scheme, I think we shall have something Capital from you, as I perswade myself you will be ravish'd by the Scene, notwithstanding all you have so lately view'd: We take an Artist with us to Kiswick, so that we shall have something to show you on our return.

I have set my heart upon your apporving this little plan of my amiable friend's and am with true esteem

My dear Sir,

Your sincere and

faithfull friend and servt

Richd Cumberland

Source: Yale. Addressed "To George Romney Esquire"

1. Romney returned from Italy to London on July 1, 1775. Reference to his not having brought home paintings for Warwick suggests that this letter was written shortly after that date. Chamberlain puts it as a few weeks after his return home (p. 80).

2. Romney evidently did not comply with the requests of Warwick mentioned in Cumberland's letter of 14 August 1774.

3. Romney evidently did not accept the commission offered and Chamberland questions whether he knew Warwick well: "nor is there any evidence that he ever paid a visit to Warwick, although Ronald Sutherland Gower states in his book that he was a frequent guest there" (p. 80).

LXVIII   Henry Wilmot?[1]   After 16 January 1776[2]

I do hereby certify, that the Board on the 16th of January last Order'd the Hearing between the Parties interested in the Claims set up by the Colony of Connecticut to lands within the reputed boundary of Pennsylvania, to be postponed to Tuesday the 30th day of April next, and notice thereof to be given to the parties.

Richd Cumberland

Secrty

Office of Trade
and Plantations

Source: Historical Society of Pennsylvania

1. Henry Wilmot, Agent of the Proprietors of Pennsylvania, was the likely recipient of this letter.
2. This matter had previously been considered on 6 July and 30 October 1775. The record of the meeting of 16 January 1776 is contained in the *Journal of the Commissioners for Trade and Plantations, January 1776-May 1782* (London, 1938, p. 1).

LXIX   David Garrick   20 January 1776

Dear Sir

The manner in which the public prints announce your having disposed of your Patent, confirmed by what I hear, leaves me no room to doubt but that the Theatre has lost it's brightest Ornament.[1] The moment therefore which puts my sincerity beyond the reach of misconstruction conveys to you the gratefull Acknowledgements of a Man, who fairly owes to your Judgement a share of the little fame he has gather'd from the drama, and to your friendship many kind and obliging offices, which subsequent misunderstandings cannot obliterate.[2] The Muse may have refinements which the Man disclaims; While you continued in the Administration of the Theatre, I shoud have continued to have esteem'd you without telling you so. Now that you have quitted your Vocation, I throw off my reserve and seize the first opportunity of wishing you all possible happiness and assuring you that I am with real affection, Dear Sir, Yr most faithfull and obliged Servt

Richd Cumberland

Queen Ann street
Saturday 20 Janry 1776

Source: British Science Museum. The letter is endorsed by Garrick: Mr. Cumberland a conciliatory Letter."

1. Garrick retired after thirty-five years as an actor and manager of Drury Lane at the conclusion of the 1775-1776 season. "By mid-January the town was aware that Garrick had sold his share in the patent and would leave the stage forever in May or June" (*The London Stage*, Part IV, ed. Stone, p. 1907).

2. Cumberland's first major quarrel with Garrick seems to have been over the "new scheme" mentioned in the dramatist's letter of 30 June 1773. There are good reasons to believe this was the promotion of Goldsmith's comedy, *She Stoops to Conquer*. Subsequently he showed irritation over the prologue to *The Choleric Man*, which evoked the following comment from Garrick to George Colman on 28 December 1774: "...it was impossible for you to satisfy Cumberland, had ye rack forc'd from you as much falsehood, as he has vanity--I am very glad you have prepar'd him for Me, had you been as Mischevous, as you were sincere with him, You might have sent him so high Senason'd, & stuff'd so full with conceit, that I should have had much ado to lower him; he has behav'd so disa-

greeably with me, that I must have a pluck at his feathers, whether they belong to Terence, Shadwell, or are of his own growth" (Little and Kahrl, #875, p. 973). The reference to Terence and Shadwell are to the supposed models of *The Choleric Man* that had been produced on 19 December. Cumberland also, at this time, irritated Garrick by his efforts to convince Garrick to hire the actor John Henderson. Cumberland notes in his *Memoirs*: "Truth obliges me to say that the negociation in all its parts and passages was not creditable to Mr. Garrick, and left impressions on the mind of Henderson, that time did not speedily wear out" (I, 389-390). Garrick did make reasonable proposals to Henderson and had clear reservations about his quality as an actor. See Garrick to Cumberland, 20 January 1775 (Little and Kahrl, #889, p. 986) and Garrick to George Colman, 15 April 1775 (Little and Kahrl, #903, p. 1001).

LXX   Sir Grey Cooper   1 February 1776

Whitehall Febry 1, 1776

Sir,

Governor Patterson[1] having presented to my Lords Comm[o]n for Trade and Planta[tion]s a General State of the quitrents arising from grants of lands in the isl[an]d of St. John; and having in a letter to Mr. Pownall[2] desired that Mr. Allanby, Receiver of the said quitrents[3] may be instructed to pay into his hands the money already collected, (which by the annex'd State appears to be 889:2) and to continue so to pay in future as he collects it; I am directed to transm[i]t to you Copies of the abovementioned papers for the information of the Lords Comm[o]n of His Majesty's Treasury, that such Order may be had thereupon as to their L[or]ships shall seem proper.

I am Sir,
Yr most obedt

138

Hum Servt

R cumberland

Sir Grey Cooper Bart.[4]

Source: Library of Congress

1. Walter Paterson, Governor of St. John's.
2. John Pownall, Secretary of the Board of Trade.
3. In the *Journal of the Commissioners for Trade and Plantations January 1776-May 1782*, Allanby is not further identified.
4. Sir Grey Cooper (d. 1801), Secretary to the Commissioners of the Treasury.

LXXI George Colman 17 February 1776[1]

Queen Ann Street

A friend of mine I beleive has made you acquainted with a Rejection I have met from the propr[ietor]s of Covent Garden theatre.[2] I have not presumption enough in my own behalf to say they are not warranted in what they have done, neither am I attempting to traverse any Right, which is in them, and which they may properly exercise. At the same time I woud in no period of my life desert what may prove to be for the Interests of Literature in general, what Ridicule soever may fall upon me in the upshot. In this light I ask you, as a Scholar and an Author of Genius, if you have any objection to read and judge my piece. The rejection was peremptory, general, and prohibitory of any Reply; I moved in Ernest of Judgement, which I had too much reason to call in queston condider[in]g where it was lodged, but was denied an Appeal by the very Gentlemen, who not a week before had exhibited *The Man of Reason*.[3] My tragedy cost me great pains and much attention; hath been many years in hand, is entirely original in plan, popular in it's subject and free of all Imitation. The Opinions of Men exceeding high in the Republic of Letters have been unanimous and more than warmly in its favour. You will not wonder if such Authority makes me hesitate about acquiescing under the *Veto* of a Junto of Proprietors, whose education has not started with the Muses, and whose habits have been little calculated to make them Critics in literature. I shoud add that my Peice was accepted by Mr. Garrick and had a place for this Season, but was withdrawn by me for reasons not worth troubling you with.

I have faithfully told you its history, and wait your Decision with the respect with which I am, Sir,

Yr most obedient
Hum Servt

Richd Cumberland

Source: The Historical Society of Pennsylvania.

1. The date is conjectured from the reference to *The Man of Reason*, produced on 9 February 1776. Cumberland speaks of the rejection of his drama a week after that presentation, which would have been 16 February. The next Saturday was the 17th. This would assume characteristically fast action by Cumberland.

2. There were five proprietors of Covent Garden for the 1775-1776 season, Thomas Harris (d. 1820), Henry Dagge (d. 1795), James Leake, Mrs. Fisher, and Thomas Hull (1728-1808). See *The London Stage*, Part IV, ed. Stone, p. 1909. The play they rejected was probably *The Battle of Hastings*, Cumberland's first tragedy, produced at Drury Lane on January 24, 1778.

3. Hugh Kelly's comedy was performed only once on 9 February.

4. See Cumberland's "conciliatory letter" of 20 January 1776.

LXXII   David Garrick   16 June 1776[1]

Tetworth near Biggleswade Bed
Sunday Noon

My Dear Sir,

Your kind Note[2] followed me thither, which I answer by the first opportunity. I wish'd to congratulate you on your honourable Release from public
business,[3] and I took the first day in my power for
the purpose, but I could not send you notice of my
design before the morning, which I did as soon as my
business allowed me to call the day my own. In truth
I have been so thoroughly employed, when I have been
in Town, that I have been as great a stranger to my
own family, almost, as I have to my friends. Amongst
the latter there is truly no attraction more pressing than that which points to you, but you will not
measure my love by my company for I have been in a
manner proscribed from Society. At length I have got
a few Holidays, and now for a little Strength, if I
can pick it up in these Shades upon the back of my
Mare, and in the bosoms of my family, who are my
second soul, more purified than the first and clear
of the Body's Encumbrance. Accept now, tho late, the
warm Congratulations of a friend, who loves your
fame, but who would not have you buy a sprig of Laurel at the price of contentment, ease and good
Health. Enjoy the affluent fortune you have made,
but in general dont trust any part of it to West India Mortgages;[4] if you have any dealings with a set
of Adventurers in Grenada, I believe I may say they
are honest, and their Affairs thank God are flour-
ishing; but if you are as generous in lending to
some, as you was to them, your Security may chance
to be not quite so good. When I come to Town again I
shall hope to find a day to spare, and you at Hampton. Mrs. Cumberland joins me in the best wishes she
can form both for you and Mrs. Garrick. My daugh-

ters desire their respects, and I am, My dear Sir,

Ever yours most faithfully

Richd. Cumberland

Source: British Science Museum. The manuscript is not in Cumberland's hand.

1. The date is conjectured from the fact that the letter was apparently written the first Monday following Garrick's retirement.

2. This note is not contained among the letters in Little and Kahrl.

3. Garrick's last performance was as Don Felix in Susannah Centlivre's comedy, *The Wonder: a Woman Keeps a Secret*, on Monday, 10 June 1776.

4. Cumberland's employment at the Board of Trade may have given him some insights into the value of investments in the West Indies.

LXXIII John Robinson 11 November 1776

Whitehall Novr 11 1776

Sir,

Having communicated to my Lords Commissioners for Trade and Plantations your Letter to me of the 6th instant, and the Copy of the Treasury minute therein contained, I have their Commands to transmit to you the inclosed Estimate for the Civil Establishment of the Island of St. John,[1] which My Lords have prepared with as much Oeconomy as they concieve the necessary Service of the said Island will allow of, and which I am to desire you will lay before the Lords Commissioners of His Majesty's Treasury.

I am,
Sir,
Your most humble servt.

Richd. Cumberland

John Robinson Esquire[2]

Source: Library of Congress

1. See the *Journal of the Commissioners for Trade and Plantations, January 1776-May 1783* (London, 1938), p. 53.
2. John Robinson (1727-1802), Secretary of the Treasury from 1770-1782.

LXXIV Henry Wilmot[1] 19 November 1776

Whitehall Nov. 19. 1776

Dear Sir,

Having reminded the Lords Commissioners for Trade and Plantations, that the hearing upon the Claims to Lands between the Colonies of Pennsylvania and Connecticut stands adjourned to the 30th instant,[2] I am directed by their Lordships to acquaint you that, whenever those Colonies return to their Allegiance, they will be ready to proceed in hearing the parties concerned in the said Claims.

I am,
Dear Sir,
Your most obedient
humble Servant,

Richd Cumberland

Source: The Historical Society of Pennsylvania.

1. Henry Wilmot, agent for the Proprietors of Pennsylvania, was the person with whom correspondence regarding the Pennsylvania boundary was conducted. See *Journal of the Commissioners for Trade and Plantations, January 1776-May 1782* (London, 1938), p. 54.

2. Postponement of consideration of this case was made at the meeting of the Commissioners on 3 April 1776 (*Journal*, p. 21).

LXXV   **Thomas Cadell?[1]   29 December 1776**

Drayton near Thrapston
29th Decr 1776

Sir

I inclose you a rebel Gazette of the 25th of Novemb[e]r from Boston: It is generally beleiv'd that fort Washington is taken by storm, and that the Event happen'd on the 16th of Novem[be]r:[2] You will observe a short paragraph in the inclosed gazette, which countenances this report; at least the shy manner in which they mention it encourages us to credit the good news. Other particulars may possibly be selected proper for publication. I observe with satisfaction that your paper leads the others in all the particulars, which we have communicated with each other upon. Your Letter to me has given great satisfacton to those where I have confided it.

I shall pass the remainder of this week at this place, where of course we shall have the earliest notice, when the General's[3] express arrives; of which you shall hear;   at least such particulars as may be proper to be made public, and which will not militate with the gazette Account.

I am, Sir, Your most obedt servant

144

R Cumberland

Source: The Historical Society of Pennsylvania.

1. The recipient of this letter is conjectured to be Thomas Cadell (1742-1802), the publisher, with whom Cumberland correspond-
ed on matters that could usefully be passed on to the public.

2. Fort Washington was taken on this date by the Hessian, General Knyphausen, with the aid of Brigadier General Mathew and
General Cornwallis.

3. Possibly General William Howe (1729-1814), the Commander-in-
Chief in America.

LXXVI   Thomas Cadell?   After 29 December 1776[1]

Sir

If you carefully examine the inclosed Gazettes, I
believe you will find a great deal of curious matter
very interesting to the Public. The General's[2] dispatches do not give us the name of the Rebell Officer who commanded at fort Washington;[3] This, with
the Summons and the terms agreed to, you will find
in the inclosed gazettes.

I came to Town this afternoon, & receive these papers within these few minutes: a day or two will
probably furnish me with fresh commun[ication] for
you.

I am, Sir, &c &c &c

R Cum.

QAS friday Evening

Source: The Boston Public Library.

1. This letter seems to be a follow-up to that of 29 December

1776.

2. Probably General William Howe.

3. According to the *Annual Register for 1776* the rebel officer was Colonel Magaw (p. 179).

LXXVII   Ozias Humphry   Probably about 1777[1]

Dear Sir

I was charged with Mrs. Montagu's[2] best Thanks to you;   she has sent to the Duchess of Portland[3] and I hope she will obtain the Box;   but, as I told her of your partiality to the Spirit of her Countenance, in it's present state, she was willing to submit to your Art, what she woud not have done to any other man's; and if two Sittings (viz. Once this Evening and once on Thursday morning) woud have sufficed, she coud have waited upon you--but alas! I find you not at home, so that those hopes are blasted, and the Box seems the only anchor, unless it should fall within the Compass of your Art to take her features at one Sitting on Thursday, which doubtless would be preferable to the best Copy of the best pourtrait. At all Events, Dear Sir, I will contrive, if possible, to make her bring you the box, and I will inform you of the Hour--Woud Eleven on Thursday morning find you disengaged? pray favour me with a Line. I see and am persuaded that your friendship does not start at difficulties. I am Yrs

Richd Cumberland

2 oClock

Source: Princeton.

1. The date of this letter is conjectured from the fact that

Ozias Humphry (1742-1810) had returned from a trip to Italy with the artist George Romney, a friend of Cumberland, in 1777 and was establishing himself as a portrait painter. It is characteristic of Cumberland that he would attempt to assist him at the start of his venture.

2. Elizabeth (Robinson) Montagu (1720-1800), a member of London society.

3. Cumberland's eldest daughter, Elizabeth, had married Lord Edward Bentinck, brother of the Duke of Portland.

LXXVIII   Richard Brinsley Sheridan   9 January 1777[1]

Sir

I am informed by Mr. Garr[ick] that you have been so obliging as to express a readiness to receive a tragedy of my writing and to give it a representation, if you find it deserving. This unfortun[ate] production is under such peculiar Circumst[ances] that I cannot omit expressing to you that I am tendering a peice rejected at the other theatre,[2] yet I think myself bound to remind you of this particular in it's disfavour; and so absolute were the terms of it's dismission, that I ought and shoud have despaired of it's merits, if I had not had a pretty long and intimate acquaint[ance] with the stage and what produces stage-effect, if I had not given infinite pains and attention to this composition for very many years, and above all if I had not been supported by the unanimous suffrages of every person to whose judgement I have committed it. I really say this to you not for the sake of parade, but in the way of excuse for persisting in any degree of self opinion, after I had rec[eive]d judgement ag[ain]st me; I beseech you therefore, Sir, to read it with as much malice as you are capable of, considering that an author is an ill judge in his own cause. Before I conclude I shall do justice to the Prop[ri-

etor]s of Cov[ent] Gar[den] Theatre so far as to
say, that the peice hath undergone corrections and
amendm[en]ts since it passed thru their hands, tho'
to no considerable extent. I beg leave to add, that
as this peice ought always to be consider'd as
standing in a doubtful predicam[en]t, I shall consider myself in honour engaged not to draw any profits from your treasury, till I am convinced your
Treasury is profited by it.

Source: British Science Museum.

1. This is a copy of Cumberland's letter to Richard Brinsley
Sheridan (1751-1816), the new manager at Drury Lane, which the
dramatist sent to Garrick. It bears the note: "Copy of my letter
to Mr Sheridan of the 9th of Jan. 1777." It is endorsed by Garrick: "Mr. Cumberland to Mr. Sheridan."
2. The Battle of Hastings had been rejected by Covent Garden.
See Cumberland to Colman, 17 February 1776. The tragedy was ultimately produced at Drury Lane on 24 January 1778.

LXXIX David Garrick 18 January 1777

Queen Ann-street, Jan 18th, 1777

My dear sir

I am thankful to your horse and to the serentity
of our climate for the relief they have brought you,
I propose to myself much happiness in the evening of
our days, if Heaven shall give us good health and
peace of mind. I have been four hours on my legs in
the Drawing-room, which was as full as loyalty could
cram it; the women were charimingly dressed, and so
uniform in their style, that you would have sworn
they had all been equipped by the hands of one and
the same milliner; not a feather in the Court, but

as fine as could be; how amazingly has that taste
advanced in my time, which has no very long retro-
spect! The men were in general plain and under-
dressed: the richest habit at Court was Lady Warwick's:[1] Sir George Warren had his order snatched
off his ribbon, encircled with diamonds to the value
of 700 *l.* Foote was there, and lays it upon the parsons,[2] having secured (as he says) his gold box in
his waist-coat pocket upon seeing so many black
gowns in the room. The dramatic literati and the A-
merican refugees made a large corps. The King and
Queen both spoke particularly long to Mrs. Montagu.[3]
Mr. Colman[4] was there, and I had an opportunity of
thanking him for a copy of his dramatic works in
four volumes, newly printed by Beckett;[5] the present
surprised and at the same time pleased me; it *surprised* me, because I understood he is the author of
a very clever copy of verses entitled *Bath*, &c.[6] in
which I am honoured with a satirical couplet; and it
pleased me, because peace is become so valuable and
so necessary to my composition, that I cannot endure
a face of hostility on a human pair of shoulders;
nay I have not even nerves to quarrel with my dog.
Colman talked to me about his theatre, and asked me
naturally enough about my tragedy,[7] which he had
heard was in Mr. Sheridan's hands;[8] I told him the
short story, and what you had done;[9] I was forced
to add, that having written a letter on Friday se'n-
night to Mr. Sheridan[10] in the most candid and fair
terms I could devise, he had not to this moment acknowledged the receipt of it, and we both agreed
that such a conduct must be altered, or would operate to his disgrace and ruin; in my particular it is
of small consequence, though it is not easy to put a
case where his politeness was more called upon: let
his reply come when it will, it comes with no grace.
I beseech you not to molest yourself one moment
about it; but my experience with the world assures
me that there is no man who can keep his place in
the good-will and esteem of those he has to deal
with, if he so totally throws off the forms of po-

liteness, which even a prime-minister cannot dispense with, and which we shall only excuse in him from his ignorance of good breeding. What can I do about Sir Thomas Oberbury?[11] What I cannot do I well know, and that is, I cannot refuse what you request; but I must see the tragedy; I will send to Mr. Woodfall and endeavour at a prologue,[12] though I think, upon reading Dr. Johnson's account of Rivers,[13] that he was a bad man, and one for whose memory I have no idolatry.

Every ship that comes from the continent of America brings tidings of comfort: we have letters which inform us of a great defection in the colony of Georgia from the banners of rebellion; three entire companies laid down their arms and submitted. Bullock,[14] the rebel governor of Georgia, with a number of converts to loyalty, signed a petition to the King for mercy and signified their submission. This is a pin out of the scaffold, and the whole edifice of revolt seems tottering to its fall.

Farewell!--if you stay any time in the country, write to me. Thanks to your good consort for her box; we kept peace, and were well entertained with a full house.

I am yours,

R. Cumberland

Sunday 19th, 1777

I have just received a note from Mr. Sheridan, calling me to a conference. I do not know when you come to town, so I shall appoint him to come to the office tomorrow evening, if it is convenient to him.

Source: Boaden, Vol. II, pp. 206-207.

1. The Earl of Warwick, Fulke Greville, toured the lakes in Cumberland with the dramatist, a trip which inspired an ode pub-

lished by Cumberland in 1776.

2. Samuel Foote (1720-1777), the actor. Although Foote was undoubtedly engaging in his usual satiric pranks, there was reason
to be apprehensive of thieves. The *Annual Register* for 1777 records that at the drawing room of St. James "a sharper found means
to cut off from Sir George Warren's ribbon the ensigns of the order of the Bath, ornamented with diamonds" (p. 163).

3. Mrs. Elizabeth (Robinson) Montagu (1720-1800), a leading
member of London society.

4. George Colman, the elder.

5. Thomas Beckett.

6. These verses do not appear in Colman's *Prose on Several Occasions with Some Verse* (London, 1787).

7. *The Battle of Hastings*.

8. Sheridan produced the tragedy on 24 January 1778 at Drury
Lane.

9. Garrick had interceded with Sheridan on Cumberland's behalf.

10. See Cumberland to Sheridan on 9 January 1777 and postscript
to this letter.

11. *Sir Thomas Oberbury*, an alteration by Richard Woodfall
(1746-1803) of Richard Savage's play was acted at Covent Garden
on 1 February 1777.

12. Cumberland wrote an epilogue, rather than a prologue for the
play. The prologue was composed by Sheridan.

13. In Samuel Johnson's *The Life of Richard Savage* (1744).

14. Archibald Bullock (1730?-1777) was Governor of Georgia in
1776 and 1777.

LXXX Edmund Burke 15 February 1777[1]

Planta[tion] Chambers 15th Feb.

Dear Sir

In last Thursday's Public Advertiser a malevolent
reviler lampoons me in an Ode, which woud have fixed
very little sting in my peace, if he had not charged
me with being the Author of a Letter signed *Cross
purposes* in the paper of the preceding Thursday,

wherein you are made the subject of a very silly Ode.

I flatter myself there can be little Occasion for me to assure you that I am incapable of mentioning your name but with respect and esteem; I sincerely entertain both for Mr. Burke and give you my honour that neither on this imputed Occasion, nor on any other, have I ever committed your name, or the name, politics or performances of any living Creature to the public papers; It is a business I so perfectly abhor, that I never meddle with it myself, nor can endure those who do. I have the honour to be with true regard Dear Sir, most obediently and faithfully Yrs

R Cumberland

Source: Sheffield City Library. Wentworth Woodhouse Muniments.[2]

1. The year of this letter is determined by the references to the material in *The Public Advertiser.*

2. With permission of Olive, Countess Fitzwilliam's Wentworth Settlement Trustees and the Dir. of Libs. Information Services.

LXXXI David Garrick 23 May 1777[1]

Friday 23d May

My Dear Sir

I think it an Age since we met, and have made every Effort to see you that my indispensable Occupations would admit of. Day after day has carried me down the same Road to Pall Mall and Whitehall, without the variation of a turning.[2] As a proof how I have been engaged, it was not till last night that I could wait upon Mr. Sheridan's Muse and now I am enchanted with her;[3] I think there is a vast deal to admire: much true wit, natural Character and sound Moral. If I was not so much pleased I should have no fault to find, but there are parts so prominently brilliant that I occasionally felt too strong a Contrast of Shade. His Judgment may yet overhaul some few things that the rapidity of his Genius has left inaccurate--But, dear Sir, my Women have not seen the Comedy, and the Theatre gives them no hopes. Have you a night to spare in your box? I need not say any more, but that (which is still more needless) I am ever

affectionately yours

Richd Cumberland

Tomorrow night only my Ladies have an engagement incompatible with the Comedy.

Source: British Science Museum.

1. The year is determined by reference to Sheridan's *The School for Scandal* which was presented at Drury Lane first on 8 May 1777.

2. Cumberland was employed at the Board of Trade.

3. For a different account of Cumberland's reaction see Stanley Williams, *Richard Cumberland*, p. 144.

LXXXII   John Robinson   23 July 1777

Whitehall July 23d. 1777

Sir

I have laid before My Lords Comm[o]n for Trade and Plantations the memorial of Mr. Desbrisay transmitted in your Letter to me of the 9th instant,[1] complaining that his name as Secretary of St. John's hath been omitted in the Returns to Treasury of Arrears due upon Salaries payable out of the Quitrents of that island, and I am directed to acquaint you for the information of the Lords Comm[o]n of His Majesty's Treasury, that no Civil Officer being by the King's Instructions intitled to any part of his Salary or Allowance, unless he be resident, excepting only when he shall be absent by leave under His Majesty's Signet or Sign Manual, or by Order in Privy Council, and Mr. Desbrisay not having resided on the is[land] nor produced any Leave of Absence, My Lords submit to the consideration of the Lords of the Treasury, whether it may be proper in his particular to recede from the established Regulations.

I am
Sir,
Your most obedient
humble Servant

Richd Cumberland

John Robinson, Esq.

Source: Library of Congress

1. Thomas Debrisay, Lieutenant Governor, Secretary and Register upon the Provincial Establishment of St. John's See *Journal of the Commissioners for Trade and Plantations 1776-1782*, p. 100.

LXXXIII **William Woodfall**[1] **8 November 1777**[2]

Drayton. 8th Novr.

Dear Sir

If you think the enclosed worth a Column in your paper at any time, when you have a dearth of Correspondents, it is at your service: Nothing coud excuse such a trifle, but a leisure hour upon a rainy morning.

I think the principal parts of our favorable Reports will turn out to be true, and it is now full time to hear from Philad[elphi]a, if we are to beleive the General possess'd himself of it on Sunday the 14th of Sepr.[3] Lord George and I perused your Wednesday and Thursday Morning's paper,[4] and he was extremely pleased with your Conduct in several particulars, applicable to the present Crisis; Indeed if the Minister can overlook your merit with Government it will be a greater neglect than I can readily suppose him capable of.

Lord George returns on Wednesday, if no Express summons him before; and I shall be in Town for the winter on Saturday next at farthest.

Your hostile Brother[5] has favour'd me with another Ode, which I enclose; it is foul play to attack a peice before it is produced, and which the author of the verses never has seen in all human probability; however as I have sanguine hopes that the Tragedy[6] will be very successfully represented, I am not in the least molested by these squibs, on the contrary perhaps am more obliged by Mr Woodfall, than he ever meant I shoud be. It rather puzzles me why he shoud chuse to admit such scandalous personal invectives against one, who is neither big enough, nor base enough, to be obnoxious; and how he can think it worth his while to put a lasting Affront upon a man, whom he does know, to gratify the rancour and Envy of an anonymous Scribbler, whom he does not know: This I think is not good policy, and I fancy he will find it so before long. For the present I wish you woud be so kind to send him the following Lines, to be inserted by way of reply in his paper.

I am Dear Sir

Yr most obedt

Humble Servant

R Cumberland

Mr W. Woodfall.

Source: Yale.

1. William Woodfall (1746-1803), journalist and dramatist.

2. The year is determined by the reference in the letter to the tragedy, *The Battle of Hastings*, and to the capture of Philadelphia.

3. The British, under General Cornwallis, took possession of Philadelphia on 27 September 1777.

4. William Woodfall was on the staff of the *Morning Chronicle* from 1774-1789.

5. Henry S. Woodfall (1739-1805), editor of the *Public Advertiser*. He printed the letters of Junius.

6. *The Battle of Hastings* was successful and received "with uncommon applause" according to the *London Magazine*. See *The London Stage* (Part 5, ed. C. B. Hogan, p. 143).

LXXXIV David Garrick About 15 December 1777[1]

My Dear Sir

If you was one to whom I coud refuse any thing I shoud send you two lines of excuse instead of twenty lines of Epilogue, but tho' I have neither leisure, nor any line to follow, for what you desire, I have not the heart to say you nay. I will meet you at the Theatre tomorrow Evening with something or other for one of the Ladies no matter which, and little matter what, so long as I can approve myself, what I really am,

most truly your's

R Cumberland

Queen Ann Street

Sunday Evening

Coud not you have written the Epilogue almost as soon as you did the Note?

Source: Harvard.[2]

1. The date of this letter is conjectural. Cumberland wrote two epilogues in 1777 that Garrick comments on in his letters. The first was for William Woodfall's revision of Richard Savage's play *Sir Thomas Overbury* produced at Covent Garden on 1 February 1777. Garrick observes to Woodfall on 1 February: "I am Easy about your Prol: & Epil:--" (Little and Kahrl, #1078, p. 1152). The second was for William Shirley's *The Roman Sacrifice*, acted at Drury Lane on 18 December 1777. Garrick writes to his brother George on 15 December, "Mr Cumberland has written an excellent Epilogue for it..." (Little and Kahrl, #1148, p. 1205). If this letter concerns either of these, it seems more likely to be *The Roman Sacrifice*. Cumberland speaks of Garrick's request for a prologue for Woodfall's play in his letter of 18 January 1777. This seems to be a different request.

2. Harvard sources are by permission of the Houghton Library.

LXXXV David Garrick 19 December 1777[1]

Friday Evening

My dear Sir

Inclosed I send you my Tragedy,[2] as far as the 68th page, which includes the 3d Act, and a small part of the 4th. Some little alterations which I coud not yet write in, prevent my sending you the whole, which tomorrow's post shall bring. I wish the

Copy had been better written and more deserving your perusal; I coud have sent a fairer transcript, but I thought my handwriting rather more intelligible.

I send you the Article from the Morning Post respecting the Tragedy; at the foot you will see an Acco[un]t of the Epilogue.[3] Be assured there is no man from whom I shoud be so free to borrow, or to whom I shoud be more proud to approach, than Mr. Garrick, but in serious truth I do not recollect the purport, much less the letter, of your Prologue to the School for Scandal, which in general terms only I have ever heard extolled. I wrote on this head to the Editors of the Morning post, and stated in effect as above; I wrote as civilly as I coud, and as humbly as I ought; but I contended for my Right, which I will ever maintain, of being, (tho' an unimportant) an independant Author; nor do I know that I have a debt to any dead or living Author more than the general obligation, which every man of education owes to the Classics of Antiquity. I was glad of this occasion to put in my plea with the editor of this extensive publication for an impartial scrutiny of my succeeding Peice; I told him the time and pains it cost me, and wished him to point the artillery of his Press against Translation, not personally, but generally, with a public view of supporting the native original Genius of Britain against the lazy Imitation of the French stage. I do not know whether I have done prudently in this, but I have done it honestly for the good of that Cause to which my latest wishes will be addressed, and to which my best thoughts shall at some future period be dedicated.

A brave Man like Bates must in certain respects be an honorable one;[4] I beleive you think him so, and I hope you will therefore excuse me for referring to the pleasing testimony you was so good to give for the *originality* of my little paltrty Epilogue,[5] which coming from the Author himself from whom he says I drew my plagiarism was a case in point.

Beleive me to be ever most affecty Your's

R Cumberland

I will give you what news there is stirring tomorrow. I am now going to enquire after your Letters at the Adelphi.

Source: Folger.

1. The date is conjectured from the reference to Cumberland's epilogue to Shirley's *The Roman Sacrifice*, acted at Drury Lane on 18 December 1777.

2. *The Battle of Hastings*, Drury Lane, 24 January 1778.

3. To *The Roman Sacrifice*.

4. Henry Bate (1745-1824), editor of *The Morning Post*.

5. See reference to a letter from Garrick on this subject in Cumberland's letter of 22 January 1777.

LXXXVI David Garrick 22 December 1777[1]

Monday Evening

10 oClock

My dear Sir

I was favour'd with your letter, and hope you will be under no apprehension about the matter of the epilogue, having burnt your letter long ago, and not endanger'd any misunderstand[ings] relative to what your partiality was so kind to say about that trifle. My remonstrance drew a very handsome Letter from the Editor, with assurances of candour and impartilaity &c &c and excuses for his point-blank Charge of plagiarism;[2] I have so many just debts to you, that I scorn to pick your pocket besides.

I read the Tragedy[3] in the Ears of the performers on friday morning; I was highly flatter'd by my audience, but your Successor in Management[4] is not a Representative of your polite attention to Authors on such occasions, for he came in yawning at the 5th Act, with no other apology than having sate up two night running. It gave me not the least offence, as I put it all to habit of dissipation and indolence, but I fear his office will suffer for want of due attention; and the present drop in the theatre justifies my apprehensions. The poor Author of the *Roman Sacrifice* had the thinnest house on his 3d night that perhaps was ever assembled on any exhibition;[5] such a spectacle was never seen; but I beleive Mr. Sheridan has been very generous to him, of which he seems truly capable. In the meantime the Author seems to have suffer'd without the pity of a single soul, not being blest with the fairest fame.

Mr. Smith[6] made good my apprehensions, and refused taking any part in my Tragedy but that of Edgar. He was disposed to take this step with some small accompaniments of asperity, but as I wished not to give him offence so I laboured hard to prevent his taking any, and we parted as I hope in perfect friendship and good understanding. Mr. Bensley plays *Harold*, Mr. Palmer *Edwin*, Mr. Brereton *Waltheof* and Mr. Aickin *Northumberland*. Miss Young is *Matilda* and Mrs Yates *Edwina.*[7] So stand my forces.

I have no news of a public nature; abund[ance] of proposals and subscriptions for raising Troops. Lord Galloway[8] has subscribed to the City purse for Recruiting the sum of 1000 Guineas. A great many fine matches in the matrimonial way. Lady George Germain[9] is alarmingly ill with the Measles caught by nursing her Children. The Duke of Dorset[10] has got a sore throat inclining to the putric kind, which is very epidemic. I hope you and your good Lady with all the noble Household about you enjoy health and recreation. I and my women are perfectly well, God be thanked.

I am most affectionately
Yrs

R Cum

Source: British Science Museum.

1. The date is conjectured from Cumberland's reference to the third performance of *The Roman Sacrifice*, without mention of the fourth. Genest records the fourth and last on the 22nd of December, and the first on the 18th. Since there were no performances on Sunday, this letter was probably written on the Monday on which the tragedy was last performed.

2. See Cumberland's letter of 19 December.

3. *The Battle of Hastings*.

4. Richard Brinsley Sheridan.

5. The third night, or first author's benefit for William Shirley, Saturday 20 December.

6. William Smith. Edgar was played by John Henderson.

7. Robert Bensley (1738?-1817?); R. Palmer; William Brereton (1741-1787); James Aickin (d. 1803); Elizabeth Younge (1744?-1797); Mary Ann Yates (1728-1787).

8. John Stewart (1736-1806), Lord Galloway.

9. Lady George Germain (1731-1778), the wife of George Sackville (1716-1785), who was Secretary of the Board of Trade. The disease was fatal and she died on 15 January 1778.

10. John Frederick Sackville became the third Duke of Dorset in 1769.

LXXXVII   David Garrick   4 January 1778[1]

Sunday Evening 4th January

Dear Sir

Nothing can be kinder than your Opinion so candidly given about my Epilogue; You are perfectly right in your Judgement; it is a poor thing ill-conceived, and I thank you for your rejection. I don't know whether I have much mended it by the inclosed,[2] as I wrote it post haste, directly upon reading your Letter; Such as it is, I send it; fearing however that I intrude too much upon your better time, and pester you with nonsense and bad verses.

I consider myself doubly honoured to be heard by such an Audience and read by such a Master. I expect your correction with impatience, for tho' your applause woud highly flatter me, your emendations woud profit me, and in my present situation scruple which to prefer. We have as yet had no Rehearsal, nor can I tell when we shall.[3] Thank you for your advice; I persuade myself I have anticipated it, and shall certainly not lose the battle for want of temper; without some prudence and patience I shoud never have got the Ladies cordially into their business, nor shoud I not only have avoided a jar with Mr. Smith,[4] but so far have impressed him in my favour as to draw an offer from him, (tho' too late) of taking the part of *Edwin*; but it was in other hands; and the kindness with which these good people have engaged themselves to me, woud make any reversal *unpardonable*. I am ever most faithfully

Your's R Cumberland.

No news whatever.
Pray burn the Copy of my Epilogue.
Lady George Germain is extremely ill and in much danger.[5]

Source: British Science Museum

1. The year is determined by the reference to *The Battle of Hastings*, produced 24 January 1778.

2. This prologue was published as part of the 1778 London edition of *The Battle of Hastings*.

3. Of *The Battle of Hastings*.

4. William Smith.

5. See Note 9 to 22 December 1777

162

Monday Evening

I beg you, my dear Sir, to receive and to render
ten thous[an]d thanks from the Author of the Tragedy
which has been so highly honour'd.[2] There is both
pleasure and profit in your friendship; pleasure in
your approbation, and profit in your correction. I
am greatly flatter'd by the last; there is nothing
gratifies like the condid censures of a real judge,
and on the score of criticism you know I am more endebted to you than to any man living. The whole
which you recommend is done. Edwina's simile of the
Tower (Act the 1st) is made very empassioned; the
Conclusion of the 4th Act was before your Criticism
came to hand entirely reformed, and I owed the Correction to Miss Young's[3] Protest against the Simile
of the Lightning; your observation tallying with
what I had done was particularly pleasing. In the
close of the 5th Act, out of 53 lines which followed
after the death of Matilda 29 only remain, so that
all things are now settled, and what gives me infinite comfort settled with your judgement at my side.
We are advertised for next week, viz. Saturday. Henderson[4] returns Saturday next, and we shall have
three practices this week. I called yesterday on
Mr. Sheridan[5] and quickened him, but all in good humour and perfect harmony; having strictly followed
your good advice in all particulars. John Home comes
out on Saturday,[6] so we escape a Collision; which I
am very glad of on all accounts; it is not pleasant
at my time of life to be running races with rival
authors, where everything is risqu'd and little can
be gained. How rejoiced shall I be when you come to
Town. I have. this moment rec[eive]d the Copy safe
and sound and I thank you for the most obliging
note. What can I say to your fair and amiable Audience? If their fine eyes have been obscured, it is
not my doing; the whole fault is your's, and if you

had recited the Roman Sacrifice[7] I beleive you woud still have been irresistable. My women will be very good, and are in high good humour with their parts.

I am interceding with Mr. King[8] to speak my Prologue.

I have no news for you of a public sort. Lady George[9] continues most dangerously ill, and I have little hopes of her recovery; nothing can exceed the distress incident upon her loss; her Truth of character, Charity and domestic Virtues are almost without parallel, but being a latent character without any brilliancy they are only known to those who feel her merits and live under their influence. My time is painfully employed in continual attend[an]ce on Distress. Adieu. May Heaven keep such Misfortunes from you and your's. I am ever Yrs R.Cum.

My good woman and the dear Girls send Love and Comp[liment]ts.

Source: British Science Museum

1. The year is determined by reference to the tragedy of John Home (1722-1808), *Alfred*, that Cumberland believes was to be performed the following Saturday. Its appearance was delayed until Wednesday, 21 January 1778.

2. *The Battle of Hastings*, which Garrick corrected.

3. Elizabeth Younge, who acted Matilda.

4. John Henderson played Harold.

5. Richard Brinsley Sheridan, then manager of Drury Lane.

6. See note 1.

7. *The Roman Sacrifice* by William Shirley was acted at Drury Lane on 18 December 1777, and lasted for only four performances.

8. Thomas King. The prologue was spoken by Henderson.

9. Lady George Germain. See letter of 22 December 1777.

LXXXIX   David Garrick   13 January 1778[1]

Tuesday Evening

I have this morning, my dear friend, rehears'd the *Battle*,[2] and a brave Battle we made. Madam Yates[3] rehears'd without book her whole part; all was Harmony, Zeal and good will. Nothing lagg'd or hobbled in the whole; and the new Corrections, (especially the *finale* to the 4th Act) was   applauded. The 5th Act, which was long, is now very brilliant, and I am well contented to take my trial. Saturday ten'night is fixed as the latest day; Alfred comes out next Saturday.[4]

So much on the side of comfort; the reverse is very melancholy, at least on the score of friendship. I am just come from Lord George's[5], where I almost live; I fear there are small hopes for this excel[len]t woman, and what his sufferings must be, I can only judge from w[ha]t they are. Adieu. Pray present my humble but earnest respects to Lady Spencer.[6]

Turn over[7]

R Cum.

Source: British Science Museum. It bears Garrick's endorsement: "Mr. Cumberland's Letters to me when at Althorp in Decr. 1777 about the Battle of Hastings-- A true picture of the man." All of the letters were not written in December.

1. The date is determined by reference to *The Battle of Hastings*, and the projected performance of John Home's *Alfred*.

2. *The Battle of Hastings*, acted at Drury Lane 24 January 1778.

3. Mary Ann Yates.

4. *Alfred* was acted on Wednesday, 21 January 1778.

5. Lord George Germain. His wife was seriously ill at this time. See Cumberland's letters of 18 December 1777 and 12 January

1778. She died on 15 January 1778.

6. Margaret Georgiana (Poyntz) Spencer (1736-1814), the wife of John Spencer (1734-1783), the first Earl Spencer.

7. On the reverse side is a curious bill for plumbing to Lord Craven, apparently in Cumberland's hand.

XC   George Germain   21 January 1778[1]

Wednesday Evening
Eight oClock

My Lord

The Board sate this Day from ten till past five, in which time many witnesses were examined touching the Complaints against Macnamara;[2] the result of which was the clear demonstration of most scandalous Impositions upon Government in the course of his Trade; a more enormous scene of Villainy and more fully establisht was never laid open. This hearing is to be followed by Memorials ag[ain]st Governor Clarke,[3] so that there is no end to crimination and recrimination. Six Lords attended, who joined in the most respectfull and affectionate Enquiries after your Lordship. I understand from Mr. Eden[4] that Lord Suffolk[5] intends writing to Yr Lordship tomorrow. My Heart is not at rest upon that subject. Sir T. Mills[6] came with enquiries and fine speeches from Lord Mansfield.[7] Mr. C. Greville woud have told me the Warwick transaction,[8] but he made the tale so tedious, that I coud make nothing of it, except that Lord Warwick[9] is gone to the King this day with his proposals, and that there seems to be a pro and con between him and Lord Hertferd,[10] which must be cleared up, and in which the King is a party.

I have this from all Hands—that every man's eyes are upon you, and every man's will in your favour. You are ardently expected. The Duke of Dorset[11] is much better.

I have the honour to be, My Lord, Yr. most devoted and most faithful Serv[an]t

Richd Cumberland

Source: Michigan.

1. This letter is postmarked 22 January 1778. Wednesday was the 21st.

2. Matthias McNamara, Lieutenant Governor of the Province of Senegambia, against whom charges had been made as early as 1776. The records of the Board of Trade for Friday, 20 September 1776 indicate that two memorials were presented against him, one by Robert Browne, and the other by "the merchants and other adventurers in the trade to Senegal (*Journal of the Commissioners for Trade and Plantations, January 1776 to May 1782*, London, 1938, pp. 48-49). It is apparently these same charges that were discussed at the meeting of Wednesday, 21 January 1778 (*Ibid.*, pp. 153 ff.).

3. John Clarke, who had been appointed Governor of Senegambia in 1776. Among the papers presented to the Board of Trade at its meeting on Tuesday, 27 January 1778 was a memorial against Governor Clarke by Matthias McNamara (*Journal of the Commissioners for Trade and Plantations, January 1776 to May 1782*, p. 155).

4. William Eden (1744-1814) became first Lord of the Board of Trade in 1776.

5. The Earl of Suffolk (1739-1779) was Secretary of State for the Northern Department from 12 June 1771 until his death.

6. Sir Thomas Mills whom Cumberland credits with introducing him to a social group that met periodically at the British Coffee House (*Memoirs*, I, 343).

7. William Murray (1705-1793), first Earl Mansfield.

8. Charles Francis Greville (1749-1809) was during this period involved in a scheme "to attract a large American colony to the magnificent natural harbor of Milford Haven. This was indeed a stimulating design" (John Ehrman, *The Younger Pitt*, London, 1969).

9. Fulke Greville (1746-1816), second Earl of Warwick.

10. Francis Seymour Conway (1719-1794), first Earl of Hertford.

11. John Frederick Sackville (1745-1799), the third Duke of Dorset.

XCI William Eden 1 April 1778

Mr. Cumberland presents his Respects to Mr. Eden[1] and sends him Vol. I and II of the *Atlantic Neptune*, *American Atlas*, and *Atlas des Indes*. If there are any other Maps or Charts which Mr. Eden requires, he will be pleased to signify his Commands.

Plant[ation] Chambers
1st April 1778

Source: British Library

1. William Eden (1744-1814) became First Lord of the Board of Trade in 1776.

XCII George Germain 31 August 1778[1]

31st August

My Lord

I have returned the Bahama Instructs to Mr. Goddard,[2] and as the Code was more than usually correct, I am humbly of opinion they may pass with very few alterations and the omission of two or three preambles only to some of the Articles. These I have mark'd in the Copy and they will be submitted to Y[ou]r Lordship's Approbation. I am to thank you for your great goodness in sending this paper to me, but

I hope your Indulgence will never be extended to me to the interruption of any attendance on my part, with which I can express my duty and obedience to your Commands.

I am not yet able to tell Your Lordship that Mr. Harford[3] has declar'd himself, tho' I have little doubt of his Intention. I write to Lady Crosbie[4] by this post with a particular Account of our situation. We have the Duke and Duchess of Cumberland here.[5] His Royal Highness has given me two batches of poliitics of near two hours each; they would have been more tedious and ininteresting to me, if he had not releiv'd them both by the most honorable encomiums on that person, for my attachment to whom I am always flatter'd to be distinguisht.[6] He last night unfolded his situation in terms far above my idea of his Capacity, commenting that all his tenders of Service in the line of his profession had been revolted, and concluded by asking me very pressingly what I woud advise him to in the present Crisis;[7] When he related at the same time how you had aided his Negotiation, and how much he owed to your friendly Agency, tho' it did not meet success, it was evident to me that he wish'd to find himself again under the same protection, and that it woud not be an unacceptable breach of secrecy, if I repeated to you what he said on the subject. I have this night had another tete a tete, as long as the two former ones, and nearly on the same topic.

From what has this Evening passed between Mr. Harford and my daughter, since I began this Letter and was interrupted in the writing it, I have every reason to conclude upon their certain, tho' not speedy agreement.

I am with most sincere affection and respect,

> My Lord, Yr Lordship's
> most devoted Servt
>
> Richd Cumberland

I will postpone for a post or two writing to Lady Crosbie as something determinate may soon occur.

Source: Michigan.

1. The year 1778 is assigned because of the reference to "the present Crisis." See Note 7 below.

2. Probably a clerk at the Board of Trade.

3. Harford did not marry Cumberland's daughter as he expected.

4. Germain's eldest daughter, Diana (1756-1814), married William Crosbie (d.1781), Viscount and Earl of Glendore.

5. Henry Frederic (1745-1790), Duke of Cumberland, and his wife.

6. George Germain, himself. He had been since George III's accession favored and trusted by the King, despite the disgrace he suffered following his court-martial after the Battle of Minden.

7. General John Burgoyne's surrender at Saratoga on 16 October 1777 brought storms of opposition against Germain, and the General's return the following May precipitated bitter controversy over the blame for the disaster. This is likely the crisis referred to.

XCIII   Decimus Reynolds[1] 13 January 1779

Queen–Ann–Street
Monday 13th Jan. 1779

Dear Sir,

I received your letter by the conveyance of Major George Reynolds,[2] and in obedience to your commands have resigned into his hands all your title deeds, entrusted to my custody. I would have had a schedule taken of them by Mr. Kipling for your better satisfaction and security, but as your directions were peremptory, and Major Reynolds, who was ill might have been prejudiced by any delay, I thought it best to put them into his hands without further form, which he assured I have done without the omission of one, for they have lain under seal at my banker's ever since they have been committed to my care.

Whatever motives may govern you, dear Sir, for recalling either your confidence, or your bounty, from me and my family, be assured you will still possess and retain my gratitude and esteem. I have only a second time lost a father, and I am now too much in the habit of disappointment and misfortune, not to acquiesce with patience under the dispensation.

You well recollect, that your first bounty was unexpected and unsolicited: it would have been absolute, if I had not thought it for my reputation to make it conditional, and subject to your revocation: perhaps I did not believe you would revoke it, but since you have been induced to wish it, believ me I rejoice in the reflection, that every thing has been done by me for your accommodation, and I had rather my children should inherit an honourable poverty, than an ample patrimony, which caused the giver of it one moment of regret.

I believe I have some few papers still at Tetworth, which I received from you in the country. I shall shortly go down thither, and will wait upon you with them. At the same time, if you wish to have the original conveyance of your lands, as drawn up by Sir Richard Heron,[3] I shall obey you by returning it: the uses being cancelled, the form can be of little value, and I can bear in memory your former goodness without such a remembrancer.

Mrs. Cumberland and my daughters join me in love and respects to you and Mrs. Reynolds, whom by this occasion I beg to thank for all her kindness to me and mine. I spoke yesterday to Sir Richard Heron and pressed with more than common earnestness upon him to fulfil your wishes in favour of Mr. Decimus Reynolds in Ireland. It would be much satisfaction to me to hear the deeds are safe to hand, and I hope you will favour me with a line to say so.

I am, &c. &c.

R. C.

Source: *Memoirs*

1. The Reverend Decimus Reynolds was the son of Bishop Reynolds and Cumberland's aunt. The story of his leaving the legacy mentioned in this letter to Cumberland is recorded in Cumberland's *Memoirs*, I, 323 ff.
2. The nephew of Rev. Decimus Reynolds.
3. Sir Richard Heron (1728-1805) was chief Secretary in Ireland.

XCIV   Samuel Farr[1]   26 January 1779[2]

Queen Ann Street 26th Janry

Sir

My Son George, serving as Midshipman on board the Milford, informs me of his having been under your Care in the Hospital: He says his Complaint was bilious, but from the length of his Confinement I apprehend he has not apprised me of the worst: I beg you will favour me with a Line on the subject, and I have confidence that your humanity as well as your skill will be exerted in the case of a youth, who has every goodness of heart to recommend him to your protection.

Any comm[an]ds you may signify on the Occasion, or any expences incurr'd on his Acco[un]t I shall thankfully defray, and shall ever remain, Sir

Yr most obedt and obliged Servt

Richard Cumberland

Source: British Library.

1. Samuel Farr, M. D. (1741-1795).

2. The year of this letter is not certain, but is very likely 1779. Cumberland's second son, George, mentioned in this letter, enlisted in the navy and was killed at the siege of Charleston in the Spring of 1780. All four of the dramatist's sons enlisted in some form of military service about the same time, probably late in 1778 or early 1779, since this fact is mentioned at about that point in the *Memoirs*.

XCV General Frederick Haldimand[1] 1 April 1779

1st April 1779
Plant[ation] Chambers

Dear Sir

Mr. William Drummer Powell is the bearer of this Letter; He is a student in the Law, educated here and upon the point of being called to the Bar; He is the Son of a loyal Gentleman of Boston, a refugee from rebellion in this Country having left the Town when General Howe evacuated it.[2] This Young Gentleman is seeking his fortune in the line of his Profession in the province of Quebec, and having been recommended by common friends to the protection and favor of Lord George Germain,[3] I am directed by his Lordship to introduce him to your Countenance and support, trusting that you will be pleas'd to grant him your Licence to practice, and will give him such further protection in his Undertaking as he shall merit and your Goodness shall be disposed to confer.

I beg leave by this Conveyance to tender you my sincere respects, assuring you of my constant Esteem and that I shall be at all times happy to recieve and obey your Commands. I have the honour

to be, Dear Sir,
Yr most faithfull
and obedt Humle Sert

Richd Cumberland

Source: British Library

1. Sir Frederick Haldimand (1718-1791). He replaced General Sir Guy Carleton (1724-1808) as ranking General in Canada on 27 June 1778.

2. General William Howe (1729-1814) evacuated Boston on 17 March 1776.

3. George Germain, Cumberland's superior at the Board of Trade, and at this time Secretary of State for the American Colonies.

XCVI George Germain 19 November 1779

19th November 1779

I waited on Mr. H[ussey][1] this morning after I had seen your Lordship; and began my Conversation by telling him that perfect credit was given him for the purity of his motives in the proposal he had made thro' my means--I premised to him that what I was about to say to him must be rec[eive]d, not as the concurr[en]t sense of King's ministers, but rather as Your Lordship's observ[ations] upon his Ideas express'd in the proposal--That it must be known to him that G[reat] B[ritain] had not sought a rupture with Spain, but that the Court of Madrid was altogether responsible, as the undeniable Agressor, for the interruption of that harmony which subsisted till the departure of the Span[is]h Ambass[ador][2]--Mr. H[ussey] gave full assent to this--I pro-

ceeded to observe to him, that upon this position,
it coud not be doubted but that if the Co[u]rt of
Spain was to signify a disposition for accommodation, she woud be met with like sincerity in that
disposition, and if he (Mr. H[ussey]) woud undertake
a Journey to Madrid for the voluntary purpose of
bringing to this Court testimonials of the pacific
disposition of Spain, I did presume it coud not but
be acceptable to H[is] M[ajesty]s Ministers--Mr.
H[ussey] replied that he clearly conciev'd the Idea
and was ready and willing to undertake the errand,
being so empower'd--That as to the mode of empowering him he shoud not presume to dictate, so that
it was done with suffic[ien]t care to distinguish
him for what he really was, a disinterested Mediator, and not a Spy--That this might be done by a
Letter from Y[ou]r L[or]dsh[i]p or L[or]d N[orth]³--
He added that he sh[oul]d wish the letter might be
so couched, as not to ground his going upon previous
Conversation with him, or overture from him, as it
might raise some Suspicion or offence ag[ain]st him
on the other side the waters, as being too forward
and intrusive; and he instanc'd a Case in point--To
this I observ'd that if the Letter had not some
foundation of that sort, it woud carry evident Appearance, that G[reat] B[ritain] was making Suit to
Spain for a negotiation, which I presumed coud never
be expected from her after suffering an attack so
unprovoked on her part--There was no Evid[en]ce
wanting of her good faith, let Spain offer the like,
and the business woud at once be put in train--To
this reasoning he absolutely yielded and submitted
the wording the Letter entirely to the Minister,
wishing however that I might apprise him of the purport before it came to his hands. This I promis'd
woud be done, if the transaction reach'd that
point--In conclusion he referr'd himself to Y[our]
L[ordship] and the Ministry without reserve--He had
wrote a Note to me and left it at my House this
morning, saying that particular Reasons made the
time very pressing--He explain'd those Reasons, to

be first the Chance of some reciprocal   Article or Treaty with France upon the separation of the fleets, by which Spain might bind herself not to make peace without France.[4] Secondly, *That he had secret Intelligence that it was now in Agitation to send a Man from Spain to the Congress, and that the late Secretary of the Embassy was talk'd of to go--*

I observ'd to him that if he was now possest of any authentic Intelligence, which led him to ascribe to Spain pacific disposition at the present moment, it woud advance the business to exhibit that authority and so get rid of a preliminary Inquiry;   He declar'd solemnly, that if he had those proofs he woud exhibit them, but that he spoke from Opinion only, strong indeed, but not commission'd.

Our Conversation led us to speak at a distance of terms as far as related to his former Assertion of Gibraltar being the Sine qua non of Spain; he repeated that assertion, as to his opinion, but added that he woud not expose himself to the egregious folly of bringing to G[reat] B[ritain] a   Requisition of the Cession of that important fortress, unless he brought ponderous Equivalents in the opposite Scale--I told him *that it was ridiculous in the extreme for Me to say a word on such a Subject, but if he had heard anything agitated upon that Idea by the Spanish Ministers of any description, I sh[ou]d not be sorry to hear what they conceiv'd woud invite G[reat] B[ritain] to gratify the uncontrollable propensity of H[i]s Catho[lic] Maj[esty] on that Article*; He answered readily enough that he had heard it agitated, more than once (*and if I did not mistake him by Flor[ida] Blanc[a]*)[5] and he said *that Spain woud give us strong footing on the Mosq shore, and upon the Coast of Barbary Oran,*--but he added she *woud not part with Ceuta*--he added that she *woud give Money*, and he *bel[ieve]d almost without limitation.* Your L[or]dsh[i]p will readily beleive I made no reply.

R. Cum.

Source: Michigan.

1. Abbé Thomas Hussey (*Memoirs*, II, 54ff.).

2. On 16 June 1779 a "hostile manifesto" was "presented by the Marquis D'Almodovar, the Spanish ambassador" (*Annual Register for 1780*, p. 17). The Aambassador was then withdrawn. Spain declared war the same month.

3. Lord Frederick North (1732-1792), First Lord of the Treasury from 1770-1782.

4. France and Spain had in April 1779 signed an agreement that no peace woud be concluded until Gibraltar was restored to Spain (Lecky, *England in the Eighteenth Century*, V, p. 6).

5. José Monino y Redondo conde de Floridablanca (1728-1808).

XCVII George Germain After 19 November 1779[1]

Queen Ann Street
Saturday 4 o'Clock

My Lord

I send your Lordship inclos'd the heads of my Converation with Mr. H[ussey][2]--It was a long one, but it was principally so made on his part. He express'd an ardour for being employ'd in any overtures tow[ar]ds pacification, that was little short of enthusiasm, to which tho' he gave a religious cast, I coud not but ascribe a proportion of Policy, which I think arises from the Instruct[ion]s of the Spanish Minister,[3] who cordially detests the French Alliance.

The Anecdote of what dropt from the King to Count Florida Blanca is recorded in my minutes and is worth attending to; He did not mention it to you it seems, and I thought he was rather vex'd that he had open'd himself so far to me.

Spain seems to dread offensive Operations next year upon her Colonies, and thinks we shall withdraw from Amer[ic]a with the whole force of the well-affected on that Continent to descend upon the Settlem[e]nts of Spain in So[uth] America; and Mr. Hussey says she despairs of Gibraltar--and he even insinuated that the K[ing]s obstinacy in persisting to reach at that unattainable object might throw H[is] Maj[esty] into a Convent for Life, or end in an assassination--Nay, he pointed at the parties, but this I don't commit to a letter.

It is not likely therefore that Mr. H[ussey] is instructed to make this effort of obtaining by negotiation, what they despair of enforcing by Arms, and the attempt of which leads to such dangerous Consequences.

France has made a very high demand for Naval supp[lies] furnish'd to the Spanish fleet at Brest.[4]

I am My Lord ever most devotedly

R Cum.

Source: Michigan.

1. Reference to the Spnish fleet at Brest places this letter after 1779. Its content suggests it followed the conversations recorded in Cumberland's letter to Germain on 19 November.

2. This material is contained in the Historical Manuscripts Commission edition of the Stoppford-Sackville papers, Part III (London 1884).

3. Count Florida Blanca.

4. In June 1779, the French and Spanish fleets, numbering more than sixty ships, united and dominated the English Channel, frequently moving close enough to the coast of Britain to threaten a possible invasion. They did not, however, succeed in engaging the British fleet, and in September retired to the port of Brest.

XCVIII **George Germain** 21 April 1780

Portsmouth Friday morning
21st April 1780

My Dear Lord

The Milford frigate, which was on a Cruize upon my arrival, yesterday Noon came up to Spithead in company with the Hussar, after having chaced a privateer of 30 guns into Havre. Sir Wm. Burnaby[1] is preparing with great alacrity and good will to receive us on board, and I hope we shall be under weigh before Sunday morning. The wind at present is west with a point to the South, and there lies your St. Helen's fleet bound to Quebec. Sixteen Sail of the Line, including the *Rothec, Monarca* and *Diligente* lie at Spithead; the last of these is said to be a very bad ship. About five Line of battle ships are getting ready in Dock, of which two are the Barfleur and Union of ninety Guns each. Everything here that floats, floats upon Copper; I walk'd Mr. Hussey purposely thro the dockyard and minutely; It exhibited a wonderfull display of stores.

Accept my most gratefull thanks for your kind protection and advice to the Ensign;[2] his Letter sets my mind entirely at rest.

The Ladies present their Respects to Your Lordship and the young Ladies; I have the honour to be with the most affectionate esteem, My Lord,

Yr Lordship's most
devoted and oblig'd Humb Servt

R Cumberland

Source: Michigan.

1. Captain of the Milford frigate.

2. Cumberland's third son, Charles, had enlisted as an Ensign
in the Tenth Regiment of Foot Guards. His eldest son was in the
First Regiment, and his two other boys were in the Navy (*Memoirs*,
I, 399-400).

XCIX   Lord William Hillsborough   19 May 1780

My Lord,

When Mr. Hussey[1] waited on Count Fernan Nunez[2]
yesterday for his passport, he woud have made his
commission for the exchange of prisoners the pretence for his journey into Spain, but the ambassador
gave him plainly to understand he was confidential
with Count Florida Blanca in the business upon which
we are come. This being the case, Mr. Hussey thought
it by no means necessary to decline a conversation
with the ambassador under proper reserve. He was
soon told that his arrival was anxiously expected at
Aranjuez. No expression of good will to him, to me,
and to the commission I am entrusted with was omitted. It was proposed by the ambassador to pay me the
honour of a visit, if acceptable, in any way I
liked best; but this Mr. Hussey without referrin to
me very properly and readily prevented.

He entered into many pertinent enquiries as to the
state of the ministry and the manner, in which Lord
North had been pressed in the House of Commons;[3] he
woud have stirred the question of an accommodation
with France, but was plainly answered by Mr. Hussey
that he had no one word to say upon that subject;
the channel was open, he observed, but ours was not
that channel--

The conversation then closed with such assurances of a sincere pacific disposition on the part of
Spain, that if Count Fernan Nunez reports fairly and
is not imposed on, our business seems to be in an
auspicious train--

Source: *Memoirs*. This is an extract of the letter.

1. Abbé Thomas Hussey.

2. Count Fernan Nunez was the Spanish Ambassador to Portugal.

3. The ministry was being pressed to defend its actions in regard to its orders to General Howe and General Burgoyne, who, through the inept handling of the situation by Germain, had been granted an inquiry into their conduct. See Alan Valentine, *Lord George Germain* (Oxford 1962), pp. 350 ff.

C   **Lord William Hillsborough   20 May 1780**

May the 20th 1780
Milford frigate off Belem

My Lord,

I cannot let this opportunity go by without expressing to your Lordship, and through you to Lord Sandwich,[1] my most thankful acknowledgments for indulging my wishes by putting me on board the Milford under the care and command of Sir William Burnaby, whose unremitted kindness and attention to me and my family, I can neither duly relate nor repay. Throughout a long and an eventful passage, whether we were struggling with a gale, or clearing ship for action, both he and his officers uniformly conducted themselves with that harmony, temper and precision, as seemed to put them in assured possession of success; the men themselves have been so long attached to their officers, and all of them to the ship itself, that the severest duty is here directed without an oath, and obeyed without a murmur.-- Though we have been encumbered with such a crowd of prisoners, many of whom seemed to possess the spirit of mutiny in full force, our discipline has kept all in perfect quiet, and such humane attention has been paid to their health, than not a single prisoner has sickened or complained.

I take the liberty of intruding upon your lordship
with these particulars to introduce a suit to you,
which I have most anxiously at heart, and in which I
am joined with equal anxiety by my friend Mr. Hussey;[2] it is, my lord, to beseech you to promote the
application made by Sir William Burnaby to Lord
Sandwich in behalf of his first lieutenant Mr. William Grosvenor[3] to be made master and commander; an
officer of ten years standing, well known in the
navy and distinguished for activity, sobriety and
professional skill and ability: he went round the
world with Admiral Byron,[4] and is highly respected
by him; he has been in this ship during the whole
war, and assisted in the capture of near four-score
prizes, by which he has acquired very little more
than the approbation of his captains, and the love
and reverence of the men.

Had our prize been a king's ship Mr. Grosvenor
would have come home in her, and his promotion would
most probably have followed in train; however, as
she is a very fine new frigate and will I dare say
be reported fit for the king's use, the opportunity
is judged favourable for recommending Mr. Grosvenor's pretensions, and as the Milford may be said
to be now acting under your lordship's orders, I
flatter myself you will take her under your protection by granting your good offices with Lord Sandwich in Mr. Grosvenor's behalf; an obligation, that
I shall ever gratefully carry in remembrance.

I have the honour to be, &c. &c.

R. C.

Source: *Memoirs.*

1. John Montagu (1718-1792), fourth Earl Sandwich, was First
Lord of the Admiralty from 13 January 1771 to 30 March 1782.

2. Abbé Thomas Hussey.

3. Sir William Burnaby was captain of the Milford frigate.

182

"This letter produced no advantage to Mr. Grosvenor," Cumberland comments in his *Memoirs*, II, 6.

4. Admiral John Byron (1723-1786) sailed around the world in 1764-1786 and later became Governor of Newfoundland.

CI **George Germain 25 May 1780**[1]

25 May. Buenos Ayres,
Lisbon

My dear Lord

The thermometer for several days has never been below 80° in the shade, and the Sun's action is intense. Lisbon is built of the whitest stone and without the shade of trees, the soil also is white and the hills are steep, with deep vallies, where Circulation of air is scarce perceivable; Under these Circumstances part of the City is almost insupportable and as the heats are premature and sudden without great drought, the Town is becoming sickly and replete with bilious fever and cholics-- My wife is a sufferer to a great degree of this description, and I am advis'd to remove her either to Cintra or on board the frigate. Cintra is describ'd to me as a spot of enchanting beauty; it's admirers prefer it to everything in Europe of the natural and romantic cast; I cannot hear this, and not take a view of a place within five leagues of me, I have therefore made a party with Sir William Burnaby and Captain Payne of the Cormorant (Brother to Sir Ralph) for Tuesday next, and shall write to you some description of Cintra, if it deserves one.

There is a good deal to see in and about Lisbon, but Curiosity is a dangerous passion to indulge in this climate. Every thing that is great or striking has Pomball[2] for it's author; His fountains, Streets, Squares, bridges, aqueducts and public Edifices are monuments of a lofty mind; they are now suspended or very feebly pursued and the melancholy habits of superstition cast a gloom over the whole city and state; In Pombal's day, processions of monks and friars scarce dar'd to show themselves, he drove thro' them, or even over them, without reverence to the Host; now they parade the streets with impunity; Yesterday exhibited His Majesty of Portugal[3] with the Prince of Brazils[4] walking the streets, bareheaded in the flaming meridian sun, without a conopy, following the cardinal Patriarch of Lisbon bearing the Host, in vestments of white damask and silver embroider'd with gold and spangles underneath a cloth of Gold supported by six mitred Abbots and preceeded by the Knights of Christ with all the religious Orders bearing Crucifixes, Images and chaunting as they walk'd; The train was near five Hours in passing, with very little intermission, thro' lines of Troops, which to my utter surprise made a most respectable appearance; two entire Regiments pass'd me under arms, which to my Judgement, as to men and accoutrement, were excellent, the whole Corps was prostrated in the dust at the passing of the Host, and the attitude of the men with the Action of the Musquets with fixt bayonets resting over the arm, and pointed into the earth, had a touching Effect; the queen[5] did not walk, but sate very stately and erect in the Church, never speaking to any of her train, nor even to the Prime Minister who with her Confessor attended at her back; She was fine in jewels, particularly pearls, but dressed in an ill stile both of cloathes and head-dress. Her equipages of Horses are fine and without number and the Liveries are stately; I saw seven Zebras in her stables of exquisite shape and beauty, and in her gardens at Belem she has an Aviary of Brazil small birds of incomparable plumage; The Gardens are disposed in strait walks between hedges of Myrtle, Portugal Laurel and yellow Jasmin over arch'd and centering in stars; the Quarters being planted with Limes, Citron and Oranges now in high Season. The parterres are neglected, and in general the whole is dishevell'd and wild, but the flowers are luxuriant in excess, particularly Carnations of a Patagonian expanse. I was quarter'd during yesterday's grand procession at a window with Count D'Oegras, eldest Son and Heir of old Pombal; This young Man is a close resemblance of John Yorke,[6] with the advantage of some years; he wears the gold key, at the time when prosecutions are going on against his father, and the Prime Minister[7] avowedly hostile; his abilities are moderate, and his passions in great government; in short he has the character of a worthy prudent man; He enjoys Pombal's whole fortune, which is about 12000 per annum, mostly in Houses within this city, built since the Earthquake;[8] It was a grand object with him to encourage the rebuilding of Lisbon upon a magnificent plan and in a grand stile of disposition; he granted Ground at very low Rents, and in several spots erected Houses upon his own adventure, which he now lets out at what appear to me very high Rents; Mr. De Visme our Countryman, who has the contract for Brasil wood, pays him £600. per annum for the house he lives in; Pombal during his Administration purchas'd several Ground plots and built Houses, and now the late Ground owners are prosecuting him for making usurious bargains below the value; He has made over all his Estates to the Count d'Oegras and lives upon his Court appointments, which the Queen continues to him. The present Minister is a very inferior Character, and seems distinguishable for no passion but that of making money. The Dutch Consul has the lucrative Contract for diamonds, all within a certain weight the King sells to him at a fixt rate, and all above that weight are kept in the royal treasures; the Collection is immense; It is lodg'd in the Arsenal in iron Chests where there is a great Sum of Gold; I am in hopes of being admitted to see this Treasure. The Square which Pomball projected is truly magnificent. It is built upon Arches with cloisters like Covent Garden only much loftier and more spacious; the River forms one side and the approaches to it are form'd by magnificent Arches of the whitest stone rais'd upon Ionic Columns of fair proportion and in a grand gusto; the whole was to be dedicated to public Offices; A Colossal Equestrian statue of the late King[9] fronts the River in the Center of the Square; It is the work of a Portuguese Artist; the statue is of brass and the Emblems round the Pedestal are of stone; these latter are of much superior workmanship, and both in execution and design have great merit; a medalion with the head of Pomball was fixt under the royal Arms in front; This is now cut out and a bronze bas releif of a ship fixt in its place; a guard is mounted upon the statue day and night.

Source: Michigan.

1. The year is determined by the time Cumberland was in Lisbon.

2. Sabastiao José de Carvalho e Melo (1699-1782), who rose to Chief Minister in 1755 during the reign of King José I. He was a ruthless individual, but was responsible for rebuilding much of Lisbon following the great earthquake of 1 November 1755.

3. Pedro, the husband of Maria I (1734-1816). She married her uncle, Pedro III (d. 1786), in 1760 and became Queen-Regent in 1777.

4. José (1761-1788), son of Maria I.

5. Maria I.

6. John Yorke (1728-1801), Clerk of the Crown in Chancery.

7. The Marquis of Angeja (d. 1788).

8. The earthquake of 1 November 1755 destroyed much of Lisbon and caused the deaths of between 5,000 and 15,000 people.

9. José I (1714-1777) reigned from 1750 until his death. The statue was erected by Pombal who held the real power during most of his reign.

CII   George Germain   26 May 1780

26 May 1780
Milford Frigate

I have   now moved Mrs. Cumberland and my eldest Daughter on board the frigate: the former was so ill, that I am persuaded she woud have stood three nights more on shore, being reduced with flux and fever to the lowest state; She revives to a wonder in this Climate,[1] and the friendly solicitude of these dear and gallant creatures from the Captain down [to] the Cook's mate is not to be described; I wonder at myself for standing the heat, as I do; The flies cover the table as we sit at our meals, and the bugs and fleas are another plague of Egypt. My Heart however is so fixt upon my business, and my hope of Success is so warm, that I feel no difficulties and fear no dangers. I am closely watch'd, but I know it and know the Spies that are set upon me; Thus forewarn'd, I am forearm'd, and tho' I have no Soul to advise with, apprehend nothing either for myself or my business: Of a certain I shoud be delighted, if I coud slip into your Cabinet for one Hour and avail myuself in this exigency of that clear and candid Judgement which at once possesses me of both Head and Heart, and give both comfort and counsel at the same time--But my Lot has fallen upon other ground, and I must be silent. I beseech of God to bless you and your sweet family, whom I love with the tenderest respect and affection. I beg you will bear my kindest wishes to the friends of your Household. I need not name them. Lisbon affords no one Article that can be convey'd to the young Ladies; its fruits and flowers woud perish and as for manufactures, it has none, the scourings of our shops form the chief ornaments of their's, but they are not shops, they are hogstyes hung with penny ribbands.

I am with sincere affection, My Dear Lord,

Ever your's most truly,

R Cumberland

Source: Michigan

1. Mrs. Cumberland gave birth to her seventh child, Frances Marianne, while in Spain.

CIII Lord William Hillsborough 6 June 1780

Lisbon June 6th 1780

My Lord,

In my letter No. 1. I informed your lordship of my arrival here on the 17th of last month at six in the afternoon, and of Mr. Hussey's departure for Aranjuez on the 19th following at eleven o'clock in the forenoon. I have now the honour of transmitting to you a letter, which I received yesterday morning by express from Aranjuez, addressed to your lordship, and I inclose one also, which I had from Mr. Hussey of the 31st of last month by the same conveyance.

The letter of my instructions is explicit for my returning to England, or advancing to Spain, as that court shall make or not make the cession of Gibraltar the basis of negociation. The simple resolution of this question formed the whole purport of Mr. Hussey's journey, and as I well know it was clearly understood on his part, I expected a reply in the same style of precision with these instructions: the case is now unexpectedly become exceedingly embarrassing and delicate. As he does not say that Spain stipulates for the cession aforesaid; I do not consider myself under orders to return; on the other hand as he does not tell me that she will treat without it, I am doubtful whether I am warranted to advance. He says the minister *is very desirous of finding means of bringing things to a happy conclusion,* and I have not only his authority, but good grounds from private information, to give credit to his assertion: I am also furnished with the necessary passports from the minister of Spain[1] and from her ambassador at this court.[2] It remains therefore a question with me, and a very difficult one I feel it, whether I should wait at Lisbon and require a further explanation, or proceed without it.

If I take the first part of this alternative, I must expect it will create offence to the punctilio of the Spanish court who have given me their passport for myself and family, have not only provided me with every convenience of coaches and relays through Spain, but have directed their ambassador here to give me every furtherance from hence, that can accommodate me to Badajoz, and I have this day received Count Fernan Nunez's passport with a letter of recommendation to the Marquis de Ustariz, intendant of Badajoz. By the terms, in which Count Florida Blanca has couched my passport, it is set forth that I am travelling through Spain towards Italy for the extablishment of my health: under this pretext it is in my power to take my route as a private traveller, and by no means deliver to the minister your lordship's letter until I have explicit satisfaction in the leading points of my instructions: should I find the court of Spain acquiescent under these particulars, success will justify a doubtful measure; whereas if I withstand the invitation and advice of Mr. Hussey, sent no doubt with the privity of the minister, and expressive of his good wishes and desires for an accommodation, I shall throw every thing into heat and ferment, ruin all Mr. Hussey's influence, from which I have so much to expect, and at once blast all his operations, which in so fair a train for success, and which probably have been much advanced since Daly's[3] departure. In short, my lord, I regard this dilemma as a case, in which personal caution points to one side, and public service to the other. In this light I view it, and although Mr. Hussey's letter to your lordship, (for it was under a flying seal) is as silent on the same material point, as that to me is, I have after full deliberation thought it for his majesty's service that I should no longer hesitate to pursue the advice of Mr. Hussey, but resolve to set out upon my journey for Spain.

The high opinion I entertain of Mr. Hussey's understanding weighs strongly with me for this measure, because I know he has intuition to penetrate chicanery, and discretion enough not to expose me to it; and though he does not expressly say that there is no obstacle in my way, yet this I am persuaded must be his firm assurance and beleif before he would commit me to the journey. The verbal message he has sent me by his servant Daly that *all is well*, is to me a very encouraging circumstance, because it is a concerted token and pass-word between us, agreed upon when we were together in the frigate. The underlined espressions in the memorandum for my journey have not escaped my observation, and I inclose you the original for your inspection: he says, I am impatient to tell you a thousand things, *which I do not write*. This marks to me an embarrassment and reserve in his letter, which probably arose from the necessity of his communicating it to the subminister Campo,[4] or to the minister himself. The letters to your lordship and me were couched nearly in the same words, and these so much out of his style of expression, that they seem either shaped to meet another man's thoughts, or to be of another man's dictating. He tells me in the same memorandum, that at Aranjuez, *every thing else*, as well as his heart, will be ready to receive me: these expressions from Mr. Hussey I know to be no trivial indications of his thoughts, and though I am sensible my duty instructs me to take clearer lights for my guidance than side-way hints and insinuations can supply, yet such circumstances may come as aids, though

190

not as principals, in the formation of an opinion.

I think it material to add that I have reason to believe the dispatch, which the Spanish ambassador received from the minister by the hands of Daly, Mr. Hussey's servant, is expressive of the same disposition to a separate accommodation with Great-Britain, and accords with what is stated by Mr. Hussey in his letter to your lordship.

Through the same intelligence I have discovered the channel, by which the propositions fabricated in this place were conveyed to the Spanish minister, and am to the bottom made acquainted with that whole intrigue. I can only by this opportunity inform your lordship, that it is a discovery of much importance to me in my future proceedings, gives me power over, and possession of, an agent in trust and confidence with the minister of Spain, as well as with the ambassador here, and that the deductions I draw from it strongly operate to incline my judgment to the resolution I have now taken of entering Spain.

I have the honour, &c. &c.

R. C.

Source: *Memoirs.*

1. Count Florida Blanca.
2. Count Fernan Nunez.
3. Frederick Daly, Abbé Hussey's servant and messenger.
4. Bernardo del Campo.

CIV **Lord William Hillsborough 7 June 1780**

Lisbon June 7th 1780
Wednesday morning 5 o'clock

My Lord,

I am sensible I have taken a step, which exposes me to censure upon failure of success, unless the reasons, on which I have acted, shall be weighed with candour and even with indulgence. In the decision, I have taken for entering Spain, I have had no other object but to keep alive a negociation, to which any backwardness or evasion on my part in the present crisis would I am persuaded be immediate extinction. I know where my danger lies, but as my endeavours for the public service and the honour of your administration are sincere, I have no doubt but I shall obtain your protection.

Though I dare not rest my public argument so much on private opinion as I am disposed to confess to you, yet you will plainly see how far I am swayed by my confidence in Mr. Hussey, and this will be the more evident when I must fairly own that Mr. Walpole's[1] opinion is not with me for my immediate journey into Spain: I owe this justice to him, that, if I fail, it may be known he is free from all participation in my error. I have delivered your letter, and in general opened the business to him as I was directed to do, but I have disclosed to him no other instruction, except that, on which Mr. Hussey's errand turns. He appears to me totally to discredit the sincerity of Spain towards any accommodation with Great-Britain, and this opinion certainly coloured his whole argument upon the subject: had we agreed in this principal position, it is not likely we should have differed in deductions from it.

I have written to Mr. Hussey, and beg leave to send you a copy of my letter. I had fully purposed, in conformity to what I said to your lordship, that my family should not accompany me upon my journey, but the nature of the passport and the circumstances, that have arisen, make it indispensible for me to take them with me, not only as an excuse for my delay upon the road till Mr. Hussey shall meet me, but also as a cover for my pretence of health, should I find it necessary to pass through Spain without an explanation with the minister, &c. &c.

R. C.

Source: *Memoirs.*

1. Robert Walpole, the British representative in Lisbon.

CV Abbé Hussey 16 June 1780

Talevara la Reina, Friday 16th
June half-past 5 evening

My dearest friend,

Your consolatory letter meets me at the end of a long and laborious journey, and like a magical charm puts all my cares to rest at once. Say not however *how could I suspect*--Had that been the case, how could I advance? Yet I am come at every risque, upon the reliance, which I am fixed to repose in your honour and friendship upon all occasions.

I have entered on an arduous service without any conditions, and I fear without securing to myself that sure support, which they, by whom and for whom I am employed, ought to hold forth to me; but you know full well who is, *and who is not*, my corresponding minister,[1] and if success does not bear me through in this step, which I have taken, my good intentions will not stand me in much stead. Still, when I saw that my reluctance would affect your situation, dash every measure you had laid, and annihilate all chance of rendering service to my country in this trying crisis, I did not hesitate to risque this journey, even against the advice of Mr. W[alpole].

We are not long since arrived after a most sultry stage, and have been travelling all night without a halt. I dare not but give Mrs. Cumberland an hour or two's repose, and shall not take my departure from hence till midnight. I shall stop at La Venta de Olias to relieve my party from a few hot hours, and shall be there tomorrow morning about ten or eleven. I shall set out from thence at seven o'clock in the evening at latest, and reach the ferry at Las Barcas de Azecar at nine that evening—There if we meet, or whenever else more convenient to yourself, it will I trust in God be remembered as one of the happy moments, that here and there have sparingly checquered the past life of your

Affectionate R. C.

Source: *Memoirs.*

1. George Germain, a close friend of Cumberland, was Secretary of State for the Colonies and seems to have been instrumental in arranging Cumberland's mission. He could therefore be expected to be sympathetic to him. His actual superior, however, was Lord William Hillsborough, Secretary of State for the Southern Department, who was far less tolerant of Cumberland's shortcomings.

CVI **Lord William Hillsborough   26 June 1780**

(Extract from dispatch to the Secretary of State)

[In this dispatch I observe to the Secretary of State] That although I relied upon his lordship's kind interpretation of my motives for leaving Lisbon, yet it was no inconsiderable anxiety that I suffered till my doubts were satisfied upon the points which Mr. Hussey's letter had not sufficiently explained. As it appeared to me a case, where I might use my discretion, and in which the inconveniencies incidental to my disappointment bore no proportion to the good, that might result from my success, I decided for the journey, which I had now performed, and flattered myself his lordship would see no cause to regret the step I had taken.--

Had I not made ready use of my passports and relays, I had good reason to believe my hesitation would have proved decisive against any treaty; whereas now I had the satisfaction of seeing many things point to a favourable and friendly issue.--

[Speaking of a probability of detaching Spain antecedent to the news of the disturbances in London, I tell the Secretary of State--] That the moment for detaching Spain is now peculiarly favourable; she is upon the worst terms with France;[1] not only the King of Naples,[2] but the Queen of Portugal[3] have written pressingly to his Catholic Majesty[4] to make peace with England, and since my arrival a further influence is set to work to aid the friends of peace, and this is the Duc de Losada,[5] who on behalf of his nephew the Duc d'Almodovar has actually solicited the embassy to England, and been favourably received. These and many other circumstances conspire to press the scale for peace; in the opposite one we may place their unretrieved disgrace in the relief of Gibraltar,[6] their hopes in the grand armament from Cadiz on the 28th of April,[7] their over-rated success in West Florida,[8] and their belief that your expeditions to the South-American continent are dropt, and that Sir Edward Hughes's[9] condition disables him from attempting any enterprise against the Manillas--

[I then recite the circumstance that gave a check to my negociation, state the measures I had since taken for resuming it, and transmit a summary of such points in requisition as require answers and instructions, and conclude with suggesting such a mode of accommodating these to the punctilio of the Spanish court, as in my opinion cannot fail to bring the treaty to a successful issue--] If this is conveyed, in mild and friendly terms towards Spain, who submits the mode to the free discretion of Great Britain, and requests it only as a salvo I think I have strong grounds to say her family compact will no longer hold her from a separate peace with Great Britain--

Source: *Memoirs.*

1. Both France and Spain seem to have regretted their overt entrance into the American war. Spain had not obtained Gibraltar as she had hoped, and France was suffering economic difficulties because of it. See Lecky, V, p. 88ff.

2. Ferdinand IV (1751-1852) son of Charles III of Spain.

3. Maria I.

4. King Charles III of Spain.

5. The Duc de Losada was a favorite companion of the Spanish King.

6. The siege of Gibraltar had continued unabated since July 1779, and in early June, 1780, the Spanish had attempted unsuccessfully to destroy the English fleet and garison. The English, moreover, had been recently relieved by additional naval forces under Admiral George Rodney (1719-1782).

7. The Spanish dispatched a fleet to the West Indies during the spring of 1780. Joining with the French fleet, they captured the combined English East and West Indies convoys in August.

8. During 1779 and 1780, Galvez, the Governor of the Spanish colony of Louisiana, had been successful in the reconquest of much of West Florida. However, Pensacola, the last British stronghold, was not surrendered until 9 May 1781.

9. Rear Admiral Edward Hughes (c.1720-1794).

CVII Lord William Hillsborough 26 June 1780

[I tell his lordship in my letter of the 26th of June 1780--] That after the first civilities I put into the minister's[1] hands his lordship's letter, which I desired he would consider as conveying in the language of sincerity the mind of a most just and upright king, who in his love of peace rejoices to meet similar sentiments in the breast of his Catholic majesty,[2] and who has been graciously pleased to send me to confer with his excellency, not from my experience in negociation, but as one confidential to the business in all its stages, and zealously devoted to conduct it to an issue--[I proceed to say--That] as this visit passed wholly in expressions of civility, I shall observe no further to your lordship upon it, than that I was perfectly well pleased with my reception.

Source: *Memoirs.*

1. Count Florida Blanca.
2. King Charles III of Spain.

CVIII George Germain 5 July 1780

Madrid 5th July 1780

My Dear Lord

Tho' I am prep'd in time for making up my Letters to Lord Hillsborough by this Conveyance, I cannot omit the Opportunity of presenting to you my cordial congratualations on our Successes at Charles Town;[1] an event which I hope gives you absolute satisfaction, and reflects in my opinion great lustre on your administration; It is needless for me to suggest to your sagacity how it operates in this quarter of the World, and what consequences may be deriv'd from an improvement upon these advantages. I forbear to attempt a description of what I have felt upon the intelligence of your dreadfull Commotions in London;[2] I am anxiously a- waiting a confirmation of the happy prospect which has open'd upon me of the State of Affairs on the 13th of June,[3] at which period my Intelligence stops--No Letter has yet reach'd my hands from England and I suck my politics thro' the corrupted strainers of the Courier de l'Europe.

I am here in a very peculiar situation indeed: Determin'd that my good Intentions and Industry shall deserve your protection, I assure myself of it: Upon the strictest review of my conduct in every hour of it since I left your Room, I bless God I have not one Act to reproach myself with; and I am vain enough to think there are some occurrences in which I have kept life in a negotiation, of which all the world despair'd; How my strength and Spirit have been upheld thro' such fatigues of mind and body, as I have surmounted; I can only account for by referring them to that protecting Being, who has blest me above my deservings and to whose gracious superintendance I earnestly commend the man I most love and honour upon earth and the dear Children and friends that belong to him.

I know your goodness to me will extend itself to the gallant, but perhaps inconsiderate, Youth I have left behind me.[4] I am sure he did his duty in the tumults--To love one's Sovereign as one ought, it is necessary to come into these arbitrary states, where the virtues of our monarch are so strongly contrasted, that my respect for him in England has become Idolatry in Spain.

I am ever with the truest and most affectionate sincerity, in every sense of the word, devotedly Your's.

R Cumberland

Source: Michigan. A second copy in Cumberland's hand is at Columbia.

1. On 20 May 1780, the American forces under General Lincoln had surrendered to the British over fifty-five hundred soldiers and one thousand seamen.

2. The Gordon Riots. On 2 June 1780, Lord George Gordon presented a petition before Parliament protesting supposed Roman Catholic influence. He was supported in his effort by a large mob outside Parliament. Eventually the crowd grew out of control and indulged in widespread burning, looting and killing. It was not until 12 June that the rioting was brought under complete control, and only after hundreds had been killed or wounded.

3. Word of control of the mob may have reached Cumberland by the 13th, for by the 9th the crowd was being contained and Lord Gordon had been taken into custody. According to his *Memoirs,* Cumberland received firm information on 24 June (II, p. 38).

4. Probably Cumberland's third son, Charles. His youngest son had enlisted in the Navy. See 21 April 1780, note 2.

CIX Bernardo Campo 23 July 1780

Madrid 1 oClock Sunday
23d of July 1780

Dear Sir

I am favored with your letter of yesterday signifying to me that intimation has been received from Your minister at the Court of Russia of a formal overture made on the part of that Court proposing to his Catholic Majesty the good Offices and mediation of the Empress[1] in your misunderstanding with Great Britain, and that the said proposal has been made in the most friendly terms, showing the most sincere dispositions to interfere in this important business for the good of Mankind, You observe that in a fortnights time, I may expect some account in answer to my last dispatches and you are so good to inform me that His Excel[len]cy Count Florida blanca is willing to suspend his answer to Russia till that time in the hopes of getting some intelligence about my Courts way of Thinking on the aforesaid Mediation.

I am happy to receive this instance of his Excellencys attention to my Court, and as I am persuaded that My Court, having entered upon a Negotiation with Spain separate from and independent of every other power in Europe, will not, pending the Negotiation, refer herself to the Mediation of any such power without the concurrence of Spain to her previously signified, So I shall beleive that the Minister of Spain is too well disposed to reconcile the differences unhappily subsisting between our respective Courts, not to observe a reciprocal conduct by waiting for the concurrence of Great Britain, before he Answers to the proposals of Russia. In the mean time I should wish to know whether the Mediation of Russia is confined to Great Britain and Spain only, or extends to France also, likewise where the Scene of Negotiation is proposed to be laid.

As the Mediation of Russia if accepted by the Belligerent powers will of course superceed the separate treaty, which I have the honor to open, I desire to know if his Excellency Count-florida blanca expects that I should proceed to treat separately with him upon such Answers as may in the mean time arrive from my Court touching the Negotiation already in train.

As this business is of the greatest moment, it appears to me highly proper that we should confer upon these points personally and upon such measures as may necessarily result therefrom: With that view I propose setting out for S[a]n Ildefonso tomorrow in the afternoon. If this visit should be acceptable I beg you will be at the trouble to procure me an Apartment for myself and Servant, Our friend the Abbé[2] will take care of the Ladies at home. If any thing intervenes to make my visit incommodious, let me be met by this Messenger at any one of the Houses of relay on the road: In the mean time accept my thankful Acknowledgements for Your most obliging Enquiries after me and mine; the Ladies are well and join in best regards. My boy[3] that came into Lisbon is I believe gone out to Sea again immediately, As for me Whether by Sea or by Land, at Madrid or at London, I am and ever must be

Most obediently and
faithfully Yours

R C

You wont be affronted at my telling you that you write English like a Native.

Source: British Library.

1. Queen Catherine II (1729-1796), Empress of Russia.

2. Abbé Thomas Hussey.

3. Probably William, Cumberland's youngest son, who joined the Navy and sailed for America under Sir Richard Hughes. George Cumberland, who also joined the Navy, was killed in the siege of Charleston.

CX   Bernardo Campo   24 July 1780

Madrid 2 past 4 o'Clock
Monday Afternoon
24th July 1780

Dear Sir,

My Servant returned with your Letter of this day, in time to prevent my setting out for San Ildefonso. When I tell you that it is with pleasure I accommodate myself to the wishes of Count floridablanca[1] I not only consult my own disposition, but I am persuaded I conform to that of my Court and of the Minister under whose immediate Instructions I am acting.[2] The reconciliation of our respective nations is an object which I look to with such cordial devotion, that I would on no account interpose myself in a moment unacceptable to your Court for any consideration short of my immediate duty. I am persuaded there is that honor and good faith in the councils of Spain, and in the Minister who directs them, that I shall not suffer in his esteem by this proof of my Acquiescence; and I know too well the Sincerity of my Own Court to apprehend for the part I have taken.[3]

If it should be inconvenient to Spain to wait the return of my Answer by the circuitous Channel of Lisbon, I submit to Count florida blanca whether it would not be adviseable for him to advertize Lord Hillsborough of the proposal of Russia[4] by special express thro France.

I beg you to present me and my best services to His Excellency and to believe me with sincere esteem D[ea]r Sir

Your most obedient
and humble Servant R C

At the same time that I signify to you my acquiescence as above stated, I think my predicament thereby becomes such as to require an immediate report to my Court, and I desire you will request of His Excellency Count Florida Blanca to send me a blank passport to be filled up by me with the name of such person, as I may find convenient to Dispatch to England through Lisbon.

Source: British Library; *Memoirs.*

1. The Spanish Minister.
2. Lord William Hillsborough.
3. The next two paragraphs do not appear in the *Memoirs.*
4. See letter of 23 July 1780.

CXI **George Germain 4 August 1780**

Madrid 4 August 1780

My Dear Lord

I shoud have written to your L[or]dsh[i]p last
post, but have been laid up with a fractur'd arm accompanied with a terrible contusion, occasion'd by a
fall I got ten days ago from a Mule which I brought
out of Portugal.[1] As I know what you have already
said to yourself on this subject, I forbear to justify myself for riding this Animal circumstanc'd as
I then was; for these Creatures are excellent when
duely work'd, but are too apt to abuse indulgence,
and mine was such a favorite that he fed every day
at my table after Dinner upon the bread and fruit
that was left, and I had in my reveries even
destined him for a Tender to your Use as he walks
above five miles an hour, without ever offering at a
trip, and is perfectly beautiful. He is so compleat
that I refused 100 Moidores for him, and now he has
repaid me after a sorrowful fashion. My wife was in
the Berlin by my side, when the Mule took fright at
some cursed creaking waggons, ran out of the road,
and instantly a great Spanish Bitt snapt in two.
This added to his terror. He ran to the extreme Edge
of a precipice, turn'd short on his forelegs and
saved my neck, ran into the Pardo road am[id]st a
hundred Coaches and Six, avoided them all within a
hair's breadth, and at last by a sudden turn laid me
sprawling. I had life enough to get into my Chaise,
where my poor Wife sate petrified with terror. I got
home without fainting, was soon attended by a Succession of Surgeons. The first pronound'd my Arm
broke at the Elbow, which bled vehemently; the second broke at the Shoulder, where the chief contusion
was, and the third declared it a Contusion only. An
Argument ensued and no Question of Experimental philosophy was ever sifted more thoroughly, than my
miserable Limb, the different Surgeons by turns

moulding and pulling it to the purposes of their theory. This Lecture upon fractures lasted a full hour without a remonstrance on my part, when a worthy old priest belonging to my Neighbour, the Duc D'Ossuna,[2] put an end to it by deciding for the fracture at the Shoulder in favor of the Surgeon of the Body Guards, and in this train I have been treated. It is a miracle to relate that I am alive, and what encreases the wonder I am doing well, and Mrs. Cum[berland] who is within a few weeks of her time, has not miscarried with the fright,[3] but I am reduced to the Anatomy of a Monkey, and nearly to the Colour of one. I woud not enter your Room without apprising the ladies at least, if not you, of my coming. The Sensibility of your sweet daughters I am sure woud suffer at such a Spectacle, knowing, as I trust they do, how much that Spectacle loves, and must love them, whilst it has breath. In the meantime we have had ten days insufferable Heat with the Glass thro' the night at 86°. I have the good luck to be charmingly lodg'd. My House is very Spacious, well adapted to the Climate, stands high and faces the North gate of the City and opens to the Mountains. This has been the saving of our Lives. My Wife just exists. The Girls enjoy themselves tolerably, but Sophia the best. They are much carest, and are the spectacle of the place, and have set the English fashions for every tittle of their Dress from the Princess of Asturias downwards.[4] The Abbé Hussey chaperons them, for their Mother can't stir out. The Duchess d'Osuna and the Old Countess of Benevento make parties for them continually. They have been to one bull-fight but suffer'd more than words can relate. Three Combatants and seven generous Horses lost their lives. Shocking Spectacle! Shall I reserve a box for Lady Crosbie and Miss Sackvilles?[5]

I have been now near 4 months absent, and have not yet heard from the Minister.[6] The Intervention of the Riots was critical ag[ain]st my business.[7] A communication of their issue from authority would

have been a very useful Exhibit. I have in the meantime not omitted by every post writing to the Minister besides special conveyances, and shoud communicate more, if my letters were secure, and to send
Expresses upon every occasion wou'd be an insufferable Expence. As to Mr. W[alpole][8] at Lisbon, his
Correspondence is too trifling and ridiculous to put
up with; I shall hold on with that Gentleman no
longer--I hope I am guilty of no breach of Duty when
I say to [Your] Lordship, that if I do not egre-
giously flatter myself, I must think I see my way
clearly thro' this business and coud almost warrant
for it's Issue; but my Instructions must be my rule,
for I have neither powers, nor discretion. I can
hardly expect my son[9] to come out with the instructions in answer to my dispatch by Daly;[10] however,
if my hopes in this particular shoud be so much better'd, as to find him with me, I shall receive it as
a great indulgence and particular gratification. I
have many reasons to wish him here, some on my own
Account, some on his, and some for the business,
which I cannot now explain. The Imperial Ambassador,
Count Kaunitz,[11] with whom I have formed something
more than Acquaintance, wishes to have my Son with
him to Vienna, where he is soon returning. He tells
me he shall live with him in his father the Minister's House, and enjoy the benefit of his daily Society. A more Amiable or more elegant Man, than
this Amb[assado]r, I never saw, and I think a little
time so bestow'd woud be of unspeakable Advantage to
my Son. If your L[or]dsh[i]p can assist me towards
this object, I perswade myself you will. The Mode I
forbear to suggest, as your judgement will best direct that with due attention to his Duty. It has
given me no small delight to hear that he was upon
Guard at your House, and I trust and hope he did his
Office, as my Son ought to do in the case of my Benefactor. He was reported sick before the tumult, yet
attended his duty, and was 14 Nights without going
to bed or taking off his boots. I hear it has shaken
his Health. May not this furnish an honourable plea

for leave of absence out of England?--And will not
my Situation supply some occasion for sending him
with fresh Instructions?--for instance in the affair
of the Russian Mediation.[12] A Complaint is a sorry
thing, and yet I think had Mr. De Grey[13] and I
chang'd Situations, he woud have heard something of
me in all this time. If our friends knew the joy of
a Letter (which I have not yet tasted) they woud not
be unkindly indolent.

I am with every possible Regard Affection and Respect

R Cumberland

Source: Michigan.

1. A more detailed account of this incident is given in Cumberland's *Memoirs* (II, 108-110).

2. The Duke of Osuna was the Commander of the Spanish Guards.
Cumberland tells the story in his *Memoirs* of the Duke's satis-
fying his vanity by granting a pension to the famous gypsy actress, La Tiranna, although he had never met her (II, 108).

3. Mrs. Cumberland gave birth to her seventh child, Marianne,
while in Spain.

4. Cumberland says in his *Memoirs* that, at the time they were
written (1806-1807), she was the Queen of Spain. Charles IV
(1748-1819), who became King of Spain in 1788, married Maria
Louisa of Parma (b. 1751).

5. Germain's eldest daughter, Diana (1756-1814), had married
Viscount William Crosbie (d. 1781). Elizabeth (b. 1762) and Caroline (d. 1789) were not married at this time. Caroline did not
marry. Elizabeth married Henry Arthur Herbert of Muckross near
Killarney in Ireland. She left her husband and two sons and became notoriously promiscuous in London.

6. Lord Hillsborough, Secretary of State from 24 November 1779
to 27 March 1782. Most of Cumberland's official contact was with
Hillsborough.

7. The Gordon Riots had created the impression in Spain that
the American revolution was spreading to England. Cumberland's
bargaining position was further weakened when on 8 and 9 August

1780 the Spanish and French fleets seized 55 of 63 vessels in the combined East and West Indies convoys.

8. Robert Walpole, the British representative in Portugal.

9. Probably Charles, who had enlisted in the Army. All four of Cumberland's sons saw military service. George, who was killed at the siege of Charleston, and William joined the Navy. Richard, like Charles, joined the Army. He later died at Tobago while seeking civil employment.

10. The servant of Abbé Hussey, who acted as Hussey's messenger.

11. The Austrian Ambassador, Count Joseph de Kaunitz, is said to have formed a romantic attachment to Cumberland's oldest daughter, Elizabeth, while she was in Spain.

12. See letter of 23 July 1780.

13. Thomas De Grey, later Lord Walsingham, an undersecretary in Germain's office.

CXII Lord William Hillsborough 4 August 1780

[Extract from my Letter to Lord Hillsborough]

Madrid 4th August 1780

Mr. Hussey imparted to you by last post my Correspondence with the Subminister Campo on the matter of the Russian Mediation.[1] You will observe that Condo Florida Blanca stands pledged to wait your answer on this proposal before he Speaks for Spain and it will not escape Your Lordships notice that this Engagement was drawn from him by my Letter to Senor Campo against the tenor of his first report. I have no information to add on this Subject. Mr. Hussey made an Observation in his Letter to Your Lordship on the proposal of the Court of Vienna in September last.[2] I was not apprized of this before I quitted England, but learnt the particulars in this place. If the Wisdom of the British Cabinet should decide for accepting the mediation now offered by her Czarist Majesty, it may perhaps be held adviseable to communicate with the Imperial Court on that Subject.

Source: British Library.

1. See 23 July 1780.

2. After the Peace of Teschen (10 May 1779) which concluded the war of the Bavarian succession "both Austria and Russia made a serious effort to mediate between the beligerent Powers. They proposed that, in order to save the pride of England, the negotiations with America should be conducted independently of those with the European Powers, but on the understanding that the two peaces should only be signed conjointly, and they also proposed that an immediate truce should be established; but no party was prepared to accept the terms" (Lecky, V, p. 88).

CXIII   Lord William Hillsborough   11 August 1780

Madrid 11th August 1780

My Lord

Mr. Hussey has written to the Minister Campo for passports to return to England by way of Lisbon,[1] and has this day received for answer, by Count florida-blanca's direction, that he shall not move the King of Spain on this subject, until Mr. Hussey shall receive permission from Your Lordship to return; observing in conclusion, that it cannot be for his reputation in the present state of the business to desert his Situation.

It may seem wonderfull to your Lordship, when I declare that I am at this moment absolutely uninformed of the immediate motives of Mr. Hussey's return: I have this hour lived with him in the most uninterrupted cordiality; and yet he has written his letter to Senor Campo without communicating it to me; and I think it a measure so directly to the prejudice of the business committed to my care, that I have held it my indispensable duty to write the inclosed to Senor Campo, of which I have apprised Mr. Hussey.

Mr. Hussey has shewn me a Letter, which he designs to forward to Your Lordship this evening: I have express'd to him my total disapprobation both of the measure, and of the mode he has taken of demanding of your Lordship his recall--Whether his mind has been opprest by the long interval of four months, which has passed since our departure from England without a Line from your Lordship, or whether his reception here, (which has been much inadequate to his merits) may have disgusted him, or that his spiritual concerns in England press upon his conscience for his return, I know not; but so it is, and under these circumstances of disquietude, I am equally anxious with himself for his safe and speedy departure; convinc'd that with the Minister of Spain he has given the last blow to his influence by the demand of the passports.

For these reasons I hope your Lordship will forward his recall, in case he solicits it: otherwise you will permit this letter to be understood as private communication.[2] I have the honor to be with all possible respect,

My Lord, Your Lordship's
Most obedient and
Most humble servant

Richd Cumberland

Source: Columbia.

1. This event is described in Cumberland's *Memoirs* (II, 64 ff.). He recounts a sudden and unexplained change in Abbé Hussey's attitude: "...from the warmest and unreserved attachment, that man ever professed to man, [he] took up a character of the severest gloom and sullenness, for which he would assign no

cause, but to all my enquiries, all my remonstrances, was either obstinately silent, or evasively uncommunicative."

2. Cumberland indicates that Hussey did not write to Hillsborough on this occasion (*Memoirs*, II, p. 65).

CXIV George Germain 30 August 1780

Madrid 30 August 1780

My Dear Lord

You coud not give me a more gratefull testimony of your kindness, than by the Letter I had the honor to receive from you thro' the hands of Daly.[1] To find myself in your remembrance is a consolation to my mind, and I woud add that it will be a spur to my Zeal, if that admitted of encrease.

After some observations, which must naturally result from an Understanding like your's, reasoning upon the requisition of Spain, you remark, (but with great tenderness towards my feelings) that you are sorry I committed my sentiments in writing before the Minister gave me the outlines of his ideas; The truth is, My Lord, I did not commit one sentiment to the Minister;[2] I extracted from the treaty of Paris the Articles relative to Spain, and this I was positively instructed to propose, whereby to sound his disposition towards peace; the only difference is, that to accommodate Count Florida-blanca, I gave it in writing thro' the hands of Mr. Hussey, upon his promise to return it to me, which he directly fulfill'd; This was suggested by him, merely to avoid a repetition of our Interviews, which at Aranjues in particular were exposed to observation and discovery:[3] I flatter myself I committed no indiscretion in falling in with this proposal; the paper is in my hands and will speak for itself, being correctly within my Instructions: Had I set out with an

unaccommodating spirit by insisting upon Conferences, instead of managing by the means of Mr. Hussey,
I think the consequences woud have been unpleasant;
and until I was officially told to the contrary,
this very Circumstance was one, in which I thought I
had some little merit; As for the Letter to Count
florida-blanca (which, being argumentative, was in
fact a sketch of my Instructions) I am exculpated
and by implication approved of by the Minister.

It is not easy, even for your Lordship, to conceive the managements necessary in transacting business here: I do assure you I came upon very bad
ground, tho' I will not presume to say who made it
such. I shall attend to your cautions with the
strictest care; and I pledge myself solemnly to you,
that a want of temper and forbearance shall never
be my error; As for my Judgement I can only tender
it to you for what it is. The Crisis is now become
exceedingly arduous and intricate; The Intrigues
that have started up since my Arrival, and the
circumstances of Solano's Junction and Cordoba's
success[4] have so chang'd affairs, that I retract
from my confidence and coincide with your suspi-
cions: My friend Hussey writes to you by this post
and I refer to his letter for other reasons of dis-
couragement.

I explain'd myself ill as to my reception being
public and with eclat; I assure you I have
sequester'd myself entirely: My Girls have visited
in the houses of Osuna and Benevento, but I was present only at one visit: The Imperial Ambassador[5]
comes here frequently and without form, but I don't
go to him.

The Minister Campo enquires much after the Ensign
and why he did not come out, You will easily apprehend his reason;[6] I can only explain it by his want
of health, but such excuses seldom serve. I hope I
am rightly inform'd of his good Conduct in the
Riots. I have conceal'd from Mrs. Cum[berland] the
death of her Son George,[7] whom she has endeavor'd to
replace with a fine Girl,[8] born on Sunday last.

I flatter myself I am sufficiently recover'd to encounter the change of climate, and am setting out for San Ildefonso; I am preparing warm cloathing for what we call a sharp air, but what at Stoneland Lodge we shoud deem insupportably hot. I woud fain have written to your Lordship by last post, but Daly's Arrival on post-day put it out of my power.

I send Lord Hillsborough by this Conveyance an authentic Journal of Solano's fleet from their departure from Cadiz to the 29th of June; a paper which perhaps is well worth your Lordship's perusal.

I beg your Lordship to accept the best respects of my women and I hope you will be good enough to remember me to the amiable Circle, within which my best hours have passed, and where perhaps I may one day find myself again--but appearances are against Me.

If Mr. Thompson[9] will bring his Frigate to Lisbon in February, I shall [be] happy to embark with him for Falmouth: Wherever the Girls go, they are sure of a fight and a good prize.

I have the honour to be with the most ardent attachment, My Dear Lord,

Your ever faithfull
and devoted Servant

R Cumberland

I rejoice to hear of Lady Crosbie's[10] Return: We have planted the Laurel, if Spain will water it, she shall have a branch.

Source: Michigan.

1. Frederick Daly.

2. Count Florida Blanca.

3. Cumberland describes his negotiations at Aranjues in his *Memoirs*, II, 34 ff.

4. Admiral José Solano, sailing with a large fleet from Havana,

captured much of Florida in the spring of 1781. Juan de Cordoba, the Spanish Admiral who intercepted the combined East and West India fleets.

5. Count Joseph de Kaunitz.

6. Cumberland's son, Charles. The suggestion seems to be that Campo was probing for information regarding conditions in London following the Gordon riots.

7. George had been killed in the seige of Charleston.

8. Frances Marianne, Cumberland's last child.

9. Possibly Benjamin Thompson (1753-1814), later named Count Rumford, who had acted on Germain's part as a scientific aid and observer to Admiral Sir Charles Hardy (1716?-1780) and Admiral August Keppel (1725-1786).

10. Germain's eldest daughter, Diana.

CXV George Germain 24 September 1780

Madrid 24th Sept. 1780

My Dear Lord

My worthy friend Mr. Hussey delivers this to your Lordship. After a long Negotiation with the Minister of Spain,[1] we are convinc'd that the Politicks of this Court have been greatly warp'd by late Events in favour of their French Connections; and in the multiplicity of matter which now occurs to be reported to you, we have judg'd it most adviseable and satisfactory for Mr. Hussey to repair to England; This he has willingly undertaken, and having with great address engaged the Minister to adopt our Idea, and take the proposal on himself, he comes to you in full possession of the Mind and Opinions of the Court of Spain.[2]

Your Lordship's Sentiments respecting Mr. Hussey are so just and withal so friendly, that I forbear to add those testimonies, which in Duty to his character and conduct I shoud else be bound to give: I am satisfied therefore that you will grant him your full confidence and protection, and I am sure you will receive from him in return such Communications, as will be both pleasing and important to you.

This being the case, I shall refer every circumstance to his relation, observing only as a matter too essential to pass over, that if it shall be found consistent with the dignity of the State not to withdraw from the Negotiation, this advantage will accrue from it's continuance, that Spain, who has declar'd and avow'd her resolution of acknowledging Mr. Jay[3] instantly on my departure, will not, till that Event takes place, enter into alliance with the rebel Colonies; and as the great Events of the War are now at issue both in the West Indies, North America and Gibraltar, it is more than probable a short course of time may as effectively dispose the Court to peace, as her late Success and other Causes have for the present conspir'd to turn her from it.

I am with the sincerest respect and esteem,

My Dear Lord,
Your Lordship's most
faithfull and devoted
Servant

Richd Cumberland

Source: Michigan.

1. Count Florida Blanca.

2. See *Memoirs*, II, 55.

3. John Jay (1745-1829), one of the Americans negotiating in Paris.

CXVI   Lord William Hillsborough   3 January 1781

No. 18

Madrid Jany 3rd 1781

My Lord,

Having found means to obtain some papers, the authenticity of which may be relied upon, I have the honor to transmit them to your Lordship by express to Lisbon.

Their Titles are[1]

No. I.   Traduction d'une lettre du Comte de florida blanca a Mr P. Normande, chargé des Affairs d'Espagne en Russie.

II.   Premiere lettre de M[r] de florida blanca au Ministre de Russie du 24e Oct[re] 1780.

Traduction de la lettre d'avis de l'ambassadeur d'Espagne a Lisbonne qui etoit incluse en copie dans la precedente datee le 19 Octobre 1780.

Traduction d'une Seconde Lettre de M*r* de Comte de florida blanca au Ministre de Russia, datee le 2[ne] de Novembre 1780.

III.   Traduction d'une troisieme lettre de M*r* de florida blanca au ministre de Russia datee du 25[e] Nov[re] 1780.

All these Translations, My Lord, are literal and Correct, and as the first in particular appears to me of consequence I beg leave to inform your Lordship, that on the 20th of December last, the Russian and Danish Ministers here resident, in conformity to the convention of armed neutrality, presented Copies of that Convention to the Court of Spain, Sweden having fulfilled that condition some time in the Month of October.

On the 23d of December Mr. de Zinowieff had the conference with Count florida blanca alluded to in the Letter No 1, in which conference after stating to the Minister the unpropitious aspect of the Af-

fair, in colours somewhat stronger than the recital
sets forth, it was with particular reserve and caution he proceeded to open the idea of a Mediation in
very general terms, not offering on the part of Russia any overtures to Spain further than to the other
beligerent powers, nor carrying his Advances beyond
those agreed to be made by Denmark and Sweden in the
like terms. This indeed may be collected from Count
florida blanca's recital, but I have more particularly addressed my enquiries to the Establishment of
the fact, for reasons which your Lordship will an-
ticipate, observing without doubt, that if the Court
of Russia had been as explicit in her late overture
to the Spanish Chargé des Affaires at Petersburgh,
as we were told she was, Co[un]t F[lorida] Blanca
writing confidentially to that very Chargé des Affairs, would not have failed alluding to those Advances, which Russia had made thro' his Channel and
which the Subminister Campo in his letter to me
terms a formal overture.

This Letter therefore of Count Florida blanca to
Mr. Normande offers to your Lordship strong presump-
tive evidence of an artifice in the instance of the
Russian overture, pretended to be made to Spain, and
in that presumption, I beg leave to reassure your
Lordship of my having closely adhered to the instructions I received upon that Subject; suffer me
to add that from the first I possest myself with a
suspicion of the Artifice. If your Lordships information from Petersburgh has put this fact out of
doubt, or if the Evidence I now inclose shall have
the effect, and in consequence it may be thought a
reasonable moment to urge this Circumstance against
the Spanish Interest at the Russian Court, I beg
leave to refer Your Lordship to Mr. Campo's Letter
to me of the 22nd and 24th July inclosed in Mr. Hussey's to Your Lordship of the 28th of the same
month, in which it is plainly asserted, that Russia
had made a formal overture of her Mediation.

As to what degree of influence Spain may really
have with Russia and the other confederated neutral

Powers, Your Lordship must be so much better advised in that particular, that I shall not presume to offer any thing in the Subject further than to observe, that the idea of Spain's having no other interest at the northern Courts, than what is Secondary to and dependant on her french Alliance has the more authority with me, Since I have been given to know that this Consideration, jointly with the hopes inspired into her of reducing Gibraltar by the Assistance of the fleet of France, were the Arguments, with which Mons[ieu]r D'Estaing in his conferences at S[a]n Ildefonso combated the effects, which France apprehended from the Negotiation, with which I was charged;[2] Since the separation of the fleets and the pointed opinion given by Mons[ieu]r D'Estaing from Cadiz of the impracticability of covering the Blockade of Gibraltar against relief by Sea,[3] it appears to me that French Politicks here have declined from their ascendancy, and on the other hand France imputes the loss of one naval Campaign and the anticipated Sacrifice in part of another[4] to the measures she was obliged to keep with Spain, whilst a treaty with Great Britain was on foot, and if the Ambassador here talks the language of his Court he is as little Satisfied with her rebel Engagements, and the enormous ballance of Millions outstanding in her Trade against the Colonies in her Alliance.

The Letters comprized under the Article No II contain a remonstrance on the part of Spain, which, tho' Shaped with some management and precaution, will I guess not improve her good understanding with Russia, coloured as I think it has been in its passage thro Mr. de Zinowieffs hands at the same time.

The Letter No III will afford your Lordship an instance of the high stile in which Spain resents the conduct of Denmark in agreeing to the Arrangements with G[reat] B[ritain] respecting contraband Articles in time of War, a Copy of this Letter has been furnished to the Danish Minister[5] by Mr. de Zinowieffs and transmitted to Copenhagen, but as it will arrive in Petersburgh posterior to the remonstrance contained in the Article No II it is not to be expected that Spain will reap much fruit from her Appeal.

After concluding the above I am this instant honored with your Lordships letter of the 9th of December sent forward by Mr. Hussey upon his arrival at Lisbon and as your Lordship therein directs me to acquaint you with any further intelligence I may obtain concerning the mediation said to be proposed by the Empress Queen of Russia,[6] I hope the particulars herein contained, may in some degree answer your enquiry. I have no further information to add on the Subject.

In obedience to that part of your Lordships Letter now received in which you tell me you do not yet signify the Kings command for my return, tho' you see little utility in my remaining at Madrid, I shall continue to hold myself in such readiness, that I may with as little delay as possible obey His Majesty's recall, when it shall be signified to me; In the meantime it will be my faithful Study to fulfill his Majestys most gracious Expectations by the Strictest Adherence to my Instructions without any deviation whatsoever.

I have the honor to be &c
My Lord.

Source: British Library.

1. These documents are in the British Library.

2. Charles Hector D'Estaing, the French admiral, arrived at San Ildefonso while Cumberland was attempting his negotiation and greatly influenced Spanish attitudes. Cumberland comments on this in his *Memoirs*, II, 44 ff.

3. Cumberland indicates in his *Memoirs* (II, 58) that D'Estaing left Cadiz, separating himself from the Spanish fleet, against Spain's wishes, and thus forfeited his popularity with them. He also complains of the English fleet's failure to engage D'Es-

taing as he left, since his ships were in poor condition, and thus vulnerable. He was, perhaps, correct in his attitude toward Gibraltar, for the English Admiral Darby succeeded in relieving it in April 1781.

4. In 1780, the French fleet had failed in its first expedition with Count Rochambeau's forces to bring about the capture of New York, and the second expediton with the remainder of Rochambeau's army, which was essential to success, was confined to Brest by a British blockade (Lecky, V, 33-4 ff.).

5. Count Reventlau. Cumberland speaks of his friendship with him in his *Memoirs*, II, 101-102.

CXVII Lord William Hillsborough 18 January 1781

No. 19

Madrid January 18th 1781

My Lord,

In consequence of a letter, which Mr. Hussey will receive by this conveyance from Count Florida Blanca, I am to conclude, that he will immediately return to England, without coming to this court. In the copy of this letter, which his excellency has communicated to me, he remarks, that, in case the negociation shall break off upon the answer now given, my longer residence at Madrid will become unnecessary: and as I am persuaded that your lordship and the cabinet will agree with the minister of Spain in this observation, I shall put myself in readiness to obey his majesty's recall. In the mean time I beg leave to repeat to your lordship, that I shall strictly adhere to his majesty's commands, trusting that you will have the goodness to represent to his majesty my faithful zeal and devotion, how ineffectual soever they may have been, in the fairest light.

Understanding that the king had been pleased to

accept from the late Prince Maserano a Spanish horse, which was in great favour, and hoping that it might be acceptable to his majesty, if occasion offered of supplying his stables with another of the like quality, I desired permission of the minister to take out of Spain a horse, which I had in my eye, and his excellency having reported this my desire to the King of Spain, his Catholic Majesty was so good as to give immediate direction for twelve of the best horses in Andalusia of his breed of royal Cribaneers to be drafted out, and from these two of the noblest and steadiest to be selected, and given to me for the above purpose. I have accordingly received them, and as they fully answer my expectations both in shape and quality, and are superior to any I have seen in this kingdom, I hope they will be approved of by his majesty, if they are fortunate in a safe passage,[1] and shall arrive in London without any accident.

Don Miguel Louis de Portugal, ambassador from her most faithful majesty to this court, died a few days ago of a tedious and painful decay. The Infanta of Spain is sufficiently recovered to remove from Madrid to the Pardo, where the court now resides.

I have the honour to be, &c. &c.

R. C.

Source: *Memoirs.*

1. The horses were safely conducted to England.

CXVIII   Lord William Hillsborough   31 January 1781

No. 20

Madrid 31st Jany 1781

My Lord,

My Courier being returned from Lisbon I have the satisfaction to find that he safely delivered to Mr. Walpole[1] my dispatch No 18 of the 3d instance, and that it was forwarded by the Packet to Your Lordship two days after its arrival at Lisbon.

By the paper No III therein contained Your Lordship is possest of the Complaints of the Minister of Spain against the Conduct of Denmark stated to the Russian Minister Mr. De Zinowieff for the information of his Court, these Complaints have been followed by a decree of His Catholic Majesty of the 31st of December signified to the Departments of Marine[2] of which I inclose a literal french translation.

I took the liberty of suggesting in my Letter No 18. that Spain would probably reap little fruit from her Appeal to Russia. I am since well informed that Russia both at Petersburgh and at Copenhagen hath signified her acquiescence in those Arrangements of Denmark with G[reat] Britain,[3] of which Spain complains and that France has in express terms signified to the same effect, agreeing to defer her claim to a reciprocity, until the Conclusion of the War, so that Spain stands alone in her remonstrances and these being reported, have occasioned strong instructions to the Danish Envoy here, who in a conference with Count Florida blanca on Saturday last delivered to him the Substance of those instructions, wherein his Danish Majesty asserts in very high and independant terms, his right of making those Arrangements with G[reat] Britain in conformity to his Engagements, declaring his resolution of abiding by any Consequences, that may ensue, and requiring at the same time reparation of Damages sustained by his Subjects from those of the Catholic King.

Count Florida blanca received this Communication with much impatience, interrupting the recital of it more than once, observing that there was no occasion to speak of the Arrangements, they were concluded and Spain had taken her part in Consequence, and all Europe regarded them with Astonishment and Scandal.

If France had acquiesced, France's Conduct was no rule or example for that of Spain, the Danish Minister having concluded his Message tendered the paper, from which he had recited it, but without date or Signature; This Count florida blanca declined to receive, saying that his Memory served him for the whole, yet he would report to the King, and upon his receiving his Commands, C[oun]t Reventlau[4] should have his answer; that Answer will depend upon the return made to his Appeal by the Court of Russia, and the Declaration of that Court above mentioned puts it out of doubt what reception this Appeal will meet with there.

Such, My Lord, has been the Management of Spain towards one of the neutral powers, the whole proceeding is reported circumstantially to the King of Denmark, the word *Scandal* used by the Minister of Spain is certainly a very strong expression, and as such has been stated, and I shall not wonder if the envoy's dispatch shall be followed by some very peremptory instructions; these particulars may be depended upon, of which I will give you some proofs by another Conveyance; In the mean time if they shall convey any useful information to Your Lordship at this critical conjuncture, I shall be sincerely happy.

An Express from Vienna brought to Count Kaunitz[5] in the evening of the 27th instant the important particulars relative to the Medilation of his Imperial Majesty, jointly with the Empress of Russia,[6] the Court being at the Pardo, the Ambassador took the next day for communicating with Count florida blanca, and yesterday a courier arrived from Paris, with the instructions of that Court to Count Montmorin[7] on the Subject. When the Minister of Spain shall deliver the sentiments of his Catholic Majesty to the German Ambassador, which will take place on the day after tomorrow, they will probably be found conformable to those of France, of which I find Count Kaunitz already possest. I shall think it my duty to apprize your Lordship of any particulars that may come to my knowledge proper for your information.

Since Count Florida blanca's dispatch of his Express to Lisbon, I have not heard from Mr. Hussey, as I understand your Lord-ships last letter, as an express restriction not to interpose in this part of the Negotiation I have obeyed it. I know nothing of Mr. Hussey's Commission but what Count florida blanca's answer opens to me, and as I must believe that in great part a finesse I cannot but lament that it has not been prepared by Discussion.[8]

Whenever the King commands me to quit this Court I hope your Lordship will interceed to allow of my bringing my family thro' France as the state of their health makes the journey from Lisbon to be apprehended.

I have the honor to be &c.

Source: British Library.

1. Robert Walpole of Lisbon.

2. The text of this decree is in the British Library.

3. Probably those regarding the seizure of contraband on the high seas.

4. Count Reventlau.

5. Joseph de Kaunitz, the Austrian ambassador.

6. Catherine II (1729-1796).

7. The French ambassador to Spain.

8. A slightly different version appears in the *Memoirs*, II, p. 123.

CXIX   Lord William Hillsborough   3 February 1781

No. 21

Madrid 3d Febry 1781

My Lord

An opportunity offers of sending this letter by the Courier of Count Kaunitz[1] as far as Bruxelles where I have referred it to the care of Mr. Fitzherbert.[2] I beg leave therefore to transmit to your Lordship Copies of my Letters No 18 of the 3d and No 20 of the 31st of January with their respective inclosures. I further add a paper containing the Message delivered to Count florida blanca by the Danish Envoy on the part of his Court, to which I refer in my letter No 20. The answer of Spain to the proposition of the Emperor's mediation was made on the day mentioned in that letter, and as I then beleived it would conform to that of France, so in effect it has proved with this further circumstance, that in future reference is to be made to the ambassador of Spain at Paris, who in Concert with the Minister of France is to speak for his Court being instructed in all cases for that purpose.[3]

Extract from the Same.

As the French Court have hinted at the mode, which Russia took of explaining herself upon the proposition of a Mediator, if required, by a Message *verbally* delivered at Paris, whilst in London, Mr. Simolin[4] gave it in *writing*, your Lordship will be pleased to observe that Mr. de Zinowieff[5] here delivered himself also *verbally* and Count florida blanca took no other method of answering, than by Communicating to him his Letter to D[o]n Pedro Normande encangado de negocios at Petersburgh, copy of which is in your Lordships hands; as for the *formal overtures* of Russia, fabricated by the Minister of

this Court, the proofs of that Chicanery are too
gross to escape detection, and the purposes of it
too apparent to require an explanation: My Early Intimacy with the Imperial Ambassador at this Court[6]
where Correspondence not only with the Minister his
father,[7] but with the emperor himself,[8] is carried
on in terms of the Closest and most equal friendship
opened to me such presages of an equitable and pacific disposition, that I could not abstain from expressing my wishes in my Letter No 8 of the 4 of August, which I hope pleaded its excuse; that the good
offices of the imperial Court, might maintain their
precedency before those of any other, and I am well
assured it was owing to the knowledge Russia had of
these overtures, made by the Imperial Court that she
put her propositions to the Belligerent powers in
terms so guarded and so general, as should not awak-
en any jealousy in the first proponents; the Instructions of Mr. de Zinowieff I know were so pre-
cise on this head, so far removed from all ideas of
the formal overture pretended by the Spanish Minister, that I think he would hardly have been induced
to deliver any *writing*, as Mons[ieu]r Simolin at
London did, altho' it had been so delivered.

I beg leave to add a word in explanation of what I
observe at the conclusion of My Letter No 20 touching the answer made to Mr. Hussey Viz. that it were
to be wished, it had been preceded by a discussion
this I said My Lord, because that answer was no
sooner settled and dispatcht, than a disposition evidently took place to have reconsidered and modified
the Stipulataion of Gibraltar, now so glaringly inadmissible; but this and every other observation
touching our negotiation, traversed by so many un-
foreseen Events, will for the future as I hope find
its course in a more general and successful channel.

I have the honor to be with all possible respect

My Lord

R C

Source: British Library.

1. Count Joseph de Kaunitz.

2. Thomas Fitzherbert (1747-1822).

3. In his *Memoirs*, Cumberland provides a slightly different version of this letter. These differences are not material, except for the following lines inserted at this point, and not contained in the British Library manuscript: "Upon this arrangement I observe that it is made--'As well to sooth the jealousy of the French court, who in their answer glanced at the separate negociation here carrying on with Great Britain, as for other obvious reasons--'" (II, p. 125).

4. The Russian ambassador to England.

5. The Russian ambassador to Spain.

6. Count Joseph de Kaunitz.

7. Wenzel Anton von Kaunitz (1711-1794), Austrian State Chancellor from 1753 to 1792.

8. Joseph II (1741-1790), who was the sole ruler of the Habsburg lands after the death of Maria Theresa (1717-1780).

CXX   George Germain   3 February 1781

Madrid 3 Feb. 1781

My Dear Lord,

Mr. Hussey, who has not advanc'd beyond Lisbon, has nevertheless convey'd to me the happiest Intelligence I can receive, viz, the Assurance of my being still continued in Your friendship and protection: With what degree of sensibility I receive this Intelligence I will not attempt to express; I know the Occasion I have had for your support, and I foresaw it; but as your Lordship's Judgement of an Absent Man's Conduct is not to be guided solely by the degree of his Success, I do not doubt to prove to you that if I have not obtain'd all the Objects of my Commission (which by the way was from the

first regarded as desperate) I have faithfully perform'd it's duties; The Effects resulting from it
have not been conspicuous, but by consequence they
have operated to very solid Uses.

As I send this Letter by Count Kaunitz's Express,[1]
which is waiting for my Dispatches, that are pretty
considerable, I have not reserv'd more time than to
repeat to you my most cordial and gratefull thanks
and to pledge myself to you that I will not disgrace
your protection in any act of my Life, so far as my
Understanding enables me; I entreat you also to present my Love to Mr. Thompson,[2] who I am told has exerted much zeal and friendship in my behalf; on what
occasion, or in what manner, my Informer does not
tell me, but I can readily believe the Information
and have conceiv'd all the gratitude towards him,
that a Heart conscious of no Offence and sensible to
many Injuries, can conceive. I beg your Lordship to
be at the trouble of perusing my Letters to the Ministers of the Department number'd 18, 20 and 21; the
Intelligence I have fortunately establisht at this
Court is such that I flatter myself few Things of
any importance can be stirr'd, of which I shall not
have speedy and correct information; but being
strictly restrained to a very narrow scale of Commission, I am fearfull of excceeding by Communications beyond the limits of my Instructions. My wom-
en join in most sincere Respects to your family, including Mr. Sackville and Mr. DeGrey.

I have the honour to be with the truest affection
and most perfect Esteem, My Dear Lord,

ever and more than ever
Your most devoted

R Cum.

Source: Michigan.

1. Count Joseph de Kaunitz.

2. Probably Benjamin Thompson (1753-1814).

3. Germain had two sons, Charles (1767-1843) and George (1770-1836). Thomas De Grey was an aid to Germain.

CXXI Abbé Hussey Before 11 February 1781[1]

Dear Sir,

The Minister has had the kindness to communicate to me a Copy of the Letter he writes you by this Conveyance,[2] as it is a matter extraneous to my Commission, I have no remarks to make upon it either to this Court or my Own, I may be allowed however to observe to you that there are two objects held forth by Spain as essential in a pacification Viz. an Exchange for Gibraltar and a Management with France respecting the Colonies. With respect to the first, if Spain requires a secret article, coexistent with the preliminaries, whose execution shall keep pace with the execution of other points therein contained, how does this differ from an open Stipulation, and where is the Salvo to Great Britain by leaving it out of the preliminaries? She might as well have opposed the conditon to me at Lisbon nine months ago as at the present moment, but you and I know that altho this was always the object of her wishes, it was not always or at least equally the object of her demand. Events which I need not enumerate, and some circumstances of which perhaps you are not informed, have turned that to a peremptory and present requisition, which before She contemplated as a distant hope; In my poor opinion the proposition for Spain to make wou'd have been to *stipulate for the cession of Gibraltar upon a stated equivalent, (under a secret Article perhaps) and that exchange of equivalents not to take place until G[reat] B[ritain] had ratified an accomodation with*

her Colonies that G[reat] B[ritain] will be disposed
to cede Gibraltar at any period or upon any terms,
far be it from me to take upon myself to say, but
this I will presume to say that there is no period
which I can devine so probable as the above, when
the popularity of a long wished for reconciliation,
and the Arrangements incident thereto shall capaci-
tate the minister to effect and dispose the people
to endure the measure. By affixing the Cession to
this period G[reat] B[ritain] has always in hand the
strongest hostage to guarantee the Sincerity of
Spain for promoting an accomodation with the Colonies, which upon other principles it will be her
policy to obstruct and if such a proposition might
appear insecure to Spain as doubting if G[reat]
B[ritain] would fulfill it at the stipulated time,
the Mediators of the present peace, which present
themselves amongst the neutral powers, might guarantee the condition.

As to the second point and all her reasoning upon
it, which occupies most part of the Minister's letter to you, I am persuaded that it is a finesse entirely secondary to the object first in view. Was my
Court to be found in the disposition to accord to
the projected exchange for Gibraltar, Spain would
find no difficulty in arranging with France upon her
American Alliance fully convinced as She must now be
that France is weary of that Alliance and of the
debt outstanding from the Colonies upon her Commerce
prepared withall as   She is to throw off that alliance when either her honor or her interest shall admit of it; and knowing also that the Colonies hold
as loosely with her on their part. Of this reciprocal disposition in both France and the Colonies I
have little cause to doubt for reasons that at present I forbear to give, but I should think they cannot be unknown to Spain. If therefore you shall find
(which I am far from saying or expecting that you
will) a disposition on the other side of the water
to give any opening for hope upon the former requisition I do not beleive that you will find any ob-

stacle here as to the expedient required by Spain touching the Colonies and France.

Source: British Library.

1. In his letter of 11 February 1781, Cumberland calls the attention of Germain to "the Ultimatum carried home by Mr. Hussey." It should also be noted that Cumberlan refers to being in Lisbon "9 months ago," *i.e.* May 1780, when he was beginning his Spanish mission.

2. The manuscript is endorsed: "My Letter to Mr. Hussey on occasion of the preceding *Paper*." The reference is to the ultimatum given Hussey by Florida Blanca, the Spanish minister, which worked toward destroying the effectiveness of Cumberland's efforts.

CXXII George Germain 11 February 1781

Feb. 11th. 1781 Madrid

My Dear Lord

A secure Conveyance offering itself, I trouble Your Lordship with a few words to repeat my thanks for your continued friendship and protection, of which I am assur'd by Mr. Hussey. I hope you have perus'd my Letters No 18, 20 and 21: As they lay open the situation of this Court with Russia and Denmark in a very interesting transaction, I trust they have convey'd material information to the Cabinet; and the rather, as the exposition of Russia's pretended overture of mediation, formally offer'd to Spain, was so critical in point of time with respect to the Emperor's[1] interposition: I hope it will also be thought of some importance to my Court to be in-

formed, as they are by my letters No. 20 and 21, of
the arrival here and reception of the Emperor's declaration and of the reference made by Spain to her
Ambassador at Paris in answer thereto, also of the
allusion made by France to my negotiation in her reply to the proposal: If I stand in need of any justification for having stept beyond my Commission in
a business not yet communicated to me, I flatter myself your Lordship at least will think my conduct
deserves it. By this information I have proved the
trick and chicanery of the Court, which I always
suspected, as to Russia's mediation; And by Count
florida blanca's letter to Mons. de Zenowieff, and
by Count Reventlau's message to the Minister, it is
evident that Denmark is upon such terms with Spain,
as present a fair opportunity of drawing her into
alliance with Great Britain, if the war is to be
continued; And if it is to close upon the Emperor's
accession to the Mediation, I perswade myself that
your Lordship's candour will give me some credit for
having adverted to the measure so early as the month
of August, and stated the friendly disposition of
the Imperial Court, to which the correspondence of
the Ambassador[2] here with his Father and the Emper-
or, particularly since his accession, has not a little contributed.

If the Ultimatum carried home by Mr. Hussey is
what the Minister communicated to me, I may expect a
short and speedy Answer with my recall from a residence, which is now continued upon the sufferance of
this Court, and it is not improbable but they will
send me my Passports of their own accord, seeing me
here in no manner of confidence or correspondence
with my own Court. If Mr. Hussey had come through,
or if I had authority, I coud have modified the Ultimatum to an Idea, which I think woud have fitted
the purposes of G[reat] Britain, of which I will inform Your Lordship when we meet. When I reflect
upon the consequences, which have resulted to France
from my coming to Spain, and the sacrifice she has
made of a whole year's Naval operations to her Man-

agements of this Court for the prevention of my negotiation,[3] I flatter myself the Experient has had it's uses, and the charge I have unavoidably incurr'd has not been thrown away.

An example yesterday from Cadiz announc'd the sailing of the fleet under Don Vicente Doz on the 6th instant. Whatever you may have heard of the Affairs of the Pern cannot easily fall short of the truth. I think I have some grounds to say, that a Certain person, here employ'd on the part of the Rebel Colonies,[4] woud not be deaf to reason, if he was properly applied to; as the importance of the object does not strike me any public view, I have taken no step, and probably shall take none.

It is true, My Lord, I have not much encouragement to pursue the line of Negotiation from the Specimen I have yet had, nevertheless I cannot withold from saying to your Lordship, and that with all diffidence in myself, that if the Emperor's Mediation shall bring on a Congress of the Belligerent Powers at Vienna or elsewhere, and if Great Britain shall appoint Commissioners to the Convention under His Imperial Majesty's mediation, I think that my connection with the House of Kaunitz,[5] and the insight I have acquir'd in Spain, render me serviceable as one in the Commission: I shoud not offer such an idea to your Lordship, if I did not know in what place the report of Count Kaunitz had put me with his Father and his Court, and what had passed between them and him on that occasion: The daily intercourse of Count Kaunitz in my family, and his personal Correspondence with the Emperor, warrants me to say what otherwise I shoud not have said.

The King's Horses are not yet set out on their Journey thro' France, being in waiting for their passports; If they arrive in health and safety, they will do honour to the Country from which they come. My wife and Girls are in good health and desire me to present to Your Lordship and family their most respectfull and affectionate good wishes: We hope Lord and Lady Crosbie[6] are returned to London and in good health. I beg to assure your Lordship that I have the honor to be with the most entire respect and attachment,

My dear Lord,
Your Lordship's most faithfull
and most devoted Servant

Richd Cumberland

Source: Michigan.

1. The Austrian Emperor, Joseph II.
2. Count Joseph de Kaunitz.
3. This may be something of an exaggeration, but the French Admiral Charles D'Estaing found it necessary to spend time in Spain in an effort to counter Cumberland's presence.
4. Possibly John Jay (1745-1829) mentioned in 24 September 1780.
5. Cumberland's daughter had been the object of the romantic attentions of de Kaunitz, but the romance came to nothing.
6. William Crosbie and Diana Sackville.

CXXIII George Germain 2 March 1781

March 2d. 1781. Madrid

My Dear Lord

I think it proper to inform your Lordship that the Speech of your new Member Mr. Wraxall[1] has rais'd a flame here amongst the Diplomatique body that is extremely unseasonable: The Comments and Insinuation of Mons[ieu]r Montmorin[2] have been artfully applied to enflame the Parties, who resent the several Insults to their Sovereigns and States, particularly the Imperial and Danish Representatives;[3] The Ministers of this Court second these unfriendly offices with more Success, than one sh[oul]d suspect coud be drawn from so despicable an Occasion. As I live in daily intimacy with Count Kaunitz and Count Reventlow (the latter of whom is the Danish Minister) it has been in my power to remove any Impressions on their Minds, individually consider'd; and as they are both well informed Men, acquainted with the Constitution of our Parliament, it is easy to bring them to hear and to talk reason; but each apprehends the mischeivous Consequences that may attend the Circulation of so infamous a Libel, when the Dutch papers shall join the Courier de L'Europe in spreading the poison. Contemptible as I know Mr. Wraxall to be, both in his Writings, Opinions and person I cannot help being very uneasy for the Consequences of his Speech, unless some healing Measures are taken by Lord North[4] and Lord Stormont,[5] especially towards the Danes, against whom no Invective could be more critical and ill-tim'd. I hope some of the young Danish Volunteers in our fleet will have the Spirit to give this silly Incendiary a proper personal Chastisement, which he so fully merits.

Your Lordship will have the goodness to pardon my troubling you on this subject, in which I confess I have no other object in view than to vent my chagrin, perswaded as I am that the prudence of Administration will use all proper preventions on the occasion.

I have the honour to be with all sincerity and respect My Lord, Your Lordship's

most devoted and
most obliged Servant

R Cumberland

Source: Michigan.

1. Sir Nathaniel William Wraxall (1751-1830).

2. Count Montmorin, French Minister of Foreign Affairs.

3. Count Joseph de Kaunitz and Count Reventlau.

4. Lord Frederick North (1732-1792) was First Lord of the Treasury from 10 February 1770 to 27 March 1782.

5. David Murray (1727-1796), Lord Stormont, the second Earl of Mansfield, was Secretary of State for the Northern Department from 27 October 1779 to 27 March 1782.

CXXIV John Robinson[1] 8 March 1781

Madrid 8th of March 1781

Sir,

My banker informs me of a difficulty, which has arisen in replacing the bills, which I have had occasion to draw upon him for the expences of my commission at this court.

As I have not had the honour of hearing from you on this subject, and as it does not appear that he had seen you, when he wrote to me, the alarm, which such an event would else have given me, is mitigated by this consideration, as I am sure there can be no intention in government to disgrace me at this court in a commission, undertaken on my part without any other stipulation than that of defraying my expences. I flatter myself therefore that you have before this done what is needfull in conformity to what was settled on our parting. Suffer me to add, that by the partition I have made of my office with the gentleman, who executes it,[2] by the expences preparatory to my journey, all which I took on myself, and by many others since my departure, which I have not thought proper to put to the public account, I have greatly burdened my private affairs during my attendance on the business I am engaged in.

That I have regulated my family here for the space of near a twelvemonth with all possible economy upon a scale in every respect as private, and void of ostentation, as possible, is notorious to all who know me here; but a man must also know this court and country to judge what the current charges of my situation must inevitably be; what the *occasional* ones have been can only be explained by myself; and as I can clearly make it appear, that I have neither misapplied the money, nor abused the trust of government in any instance, I cannot merit, and I am persuaded I shall not experience, any misunderstanding or unkindness.

I have the honour to be, &c. &c.

R. C.

Source: *Memoirs.*

1. John Robinson (1727-1802) was Secretary of the Treasury from 1770-1782.

2. Mr. Grey Elliott who acted as Secretary of the Board of Trade in Cumberland's absence.

CXXV   Lord William Hillsborough   15 March 1781[1]

My Lord,

On the 11th instant I had the honour of your lordship's letter, dated the 14th of February, and in obedience to his majesty's commands, therein signified, I took occasion on the same day of demanding my passports of the minister of Spain.[2] Agreeably to the indulgence, granted me by His majesty, I yesterday took leave of Count Florida Blanca at the Pardo, and this day my family presented themselves to the Princess of Asturias[3] at the convent of Santo Domingo el Real, who received their parting acknowledgements with many expressions of kindness and condescension. I am to see the King of Spain[4] on Sunday, and expect to leave Madrid on Tuesday or Wednesday next.

The ambassador of France[5] having in the most obliging manner given me a passport, and your lordship's letter containing no directions to the contrary, I propose to return to Bayonne and Bourdeaux, to which route I am compelled by the state of my health, and that of part of my family.

I have the honour to be, &c. &c.

R. C.

I hope your lordship has received my letter No. 18, also those numbered 20 and 21, which conclude what I have written.

Source: *Memoirs*

1. The date is indicated in Cumberland's *Memoirs*.

CXXVI **Bernardo Campo   20 March 1781**

Madrid March 20th 1781

You have done all things, my dear Sir, with the greatest kindness and the politest attention. I have your passports, and as my baggage is now ready to be inspected, I wait the directions of the Minister Musquiz,[1] which I pray you now to dispatch. Tomorrow in the forenoon at 11 o'clock, or any other hour more convenient to the officers of the customs will suit me to attend upon them.

You tell me that no more could be done for me, were I an ambassador; I am persuaded of it, for being as I am, a dependant on your protection, and entrusted to you by my country, how can I doubt but that the Spanish point of honour will concede to me not less, (and I should not wonder if it granted more) than any ambassador can claim by privilege.

I have never ceased to feel a perfect confidence in my situation, nor ever wished for any other title to all the rights of hospitality and protection, than what I derive from the trust, which my court has consigned to me, and that which I repose in yours.

I bring this letter in my pocket to the Pardo, lest you should not be visible at the hour I shall arrive. I beg to recommend to you the case of the English prisoners, who have undersigned the inclosed paper.[2]

I hope to set out on Friday; be assured I shall carry with me a lasting remembrance of your obliging favours, and I shall ardently seize every occasion in my future life of expressing a due sense of them.

If your leisure serves to favour us with another visit at Madrid, we shall be happy to see you, and I shall be glad to confer with you on the subject of the Spanish prisoners, and apprize you of the language I shall hold on that topic upon my return home.

On all occasions, and in every place I shall conscientiously adhere to truth. Let me say for the last time I shall speak of myself, that no man ever entered Spain with a more conciliating disposition, and I hope I leave behind me some proofs of patience.

Farewell! ever faithfully yours,

R. C.

Source: *Memoirs.*

1. Probably Rafael de Musquiz, later the confessor of Maria

Louisa, the wife of King Charles IV.

2. In his "Memorial" to Lord North, printed in his *Memoirs* (II, 169), Cumberland notes: "That upon the capture of the East and West India ships by the enemy, your Memorialist was addressed by many of the British prisoners, some of whom he relieved with money, and in all cases obtained the prayer of their Memorials. Your Memorialist also, through the favour of the Bishop of Burgos, took with him out of Spain some valuable British seamen and restored them to His Majesty's fleet; and this also he did at his own cost."

CXXVII George Germain 28 April 1781

Bayonne 28 Apr. 1781

My Lord

Mr. Secr[etar]y Robinson[1] not having replaced my bills on my Bankers Messrs. Crofts and Co. of Pall Mall, they have sent back a Bill of £100. protested for non acceptance, which may probably be follow'd by some others. This is an effectual stab to my Credit and Repose; The misfortune has overtaken me here at Bayonne, where I have been at death's door with a violent fever; I was just setting out for Bordeaux on my return, when I found my Credit totally stopped there and at Paris, and myself and family without money or means to extricate myself from my distress: What effect this may have upon a skeleton, scarce convalescent; God alone knows--Were it not for these beloved Dependants around me, I woud meet the decision without regret; providentially I found a friend[2] to answer for me and to enable me to pass my vagrants to England. I entreat your pardon for this trouble and have the honour to be, My Lord, Your Lordships

most affect. and devoted servant.

R C

Source: Michigan.

1. John Robinson.

2. Signor Marchetti, who accompanied Cumberland when he left Spain (*Memoirs*, II, 161).

CXXVIII   **William Petty[1]   29 March 1782**

Portland Place. 29th March
Friday morning

My Lord,

If it is a measure resolved upon to abolish the Board of Trade[2] and incorporate the Records of that office in those of the Department your Lordship now fills, I hope you will not think it an unbecoming presumption in me to take this opportunity of saying, that if my experience in office and such services, as the best exertion of my faculties can render, shall be thought acceptable by your Lordship at this most important crisis, I beg leave to lay them at your feet without reserve or any view to interest, but entirely upon principles of public zeal, flattering myself that I could be usefull and most ardently praying that your distinguished abilities and those of your colleagues in power may effect the rescue of this sinking Empire.

I have the honour to be with great respect, My Lord,

Your Lordship's most obedt. and most humble Servant

Richd. Cumberland

Source: Library of Congress (a typed copy).

1. Sir William Petty (1737-1805), second Earl of Shelbourne and first Marquis of Lansdowne. He became Secretary of State for home and colonial affairs in March 1782.

2. Edmund Burke had succeeded in his motion in Parliament to abolish the Board of Trade on 13 March 1782, and it was eliminated in June. Cumberland was not given a new position.

CXXIX   George Germain   3 December 1784[1]

St. Albans Street friday Evng
My Dear Lord

I find there is no way so effectual to give me some Consideration with myself, as to suppose that you take some little Interest even in my dramatic Concerns, therefore I take the liberty to tell you that The Carmelite[2] was triumphantly receiv'd, and I am now sitting in a little dirty lodging (*not Mr. Lackington's*)[3] over a smoaky Chimney by myself under the shade of my Laurells. Mrs. Siddons[4] was divine, and crown'd with unceasing peals of applause; Mr. Palmer[5] and Mr. Kemble[6] excellent, Mr. Smith[7] Execrable; if any thing coud have tempted you to Sacrilege, you would have crackt his shaven Crown with your Cane for being such a bellowing Carmelite. I found Sir Charles Thompson[8] with Mrs. Siddons this Morning and was vastly flatter'd by him, posted between Actress and Author he scarce knew which way to turn: Lord Loughborough[9] was there and all the fine people in Town; Poets, Painters, Printers, Writers, Devils and Demireps from all quarters.

The Drayton Comedy[10] comes out in three Weeks, for we strike whilst the iron is hot. I saw Wraxall[11] in the morning, but neither he nor *My Lord* were with Mrs. Siddons at Night. Father Hussey[12] was with me in the Manager's box and wept streams, but he anathematized his brother Monk, and said he acted like an Atheist preaching Christianity. I took Henderson[13] into the Green Room, where he was the Life and Soul of the party, adoring Mrs. Siddons and cheering every body around him; Her brother Kemble was applauded thro' the House and his likeness to Mrs. Siddons, whose Son he is in the Play, was greatly felt.

I am excessively happy to hear Mr. and Mrs. Herbert[14] are with you at Drayton, and beg my best remembrances to them; I dare say Mrs. Herbert found her little ones grown and improv'd, and that so many good Peaches and Pears have not been bestow'd upon Bessy[15] for nothing; If I saw her, I coud tell her that *William Henry Edward Cavendish Bentinck*,[16] tho' he does not own many more nonths than names, begins to sing *Malbroock*[17] most divinely, so that I am thinking of sending him my Prologue and Epilogue, hoping they will go pretty well to that tune: Therefore I take it to be high time for a young Lady of her standing to cry something else besides Peaches and Pears.

I beg to be most respectfully remember'd to Miss Sackville[18] and the Ladies: I was sorry for Miss Leighton's[19] sake to find Lord Derby with Lady Paragon,[20] when I came with my book under my Arms to read her part: We are great friends however, tho' rivals, and I was afraid he woud have jump'd out of a three–pair–of–stairs Slip last night for joy of the Carmelite, and I really doubt if he woud not, had not the spikes of the Orchestra been in his way; He made it up with screaming. Sheridan[21] behav'd like an Angel both to me and the performers, and even Will Woodfall[22] grinn'd a ghastly smile.

What nonsense have I been chattering to you. If I read it over I shall not venture to send it. My only Consolation is that it will arrive in a December Evening and as Miss Jane has nothing to do of a Sunday Night, she perhaps will read it, if nobody else will.

Lackington's daughter is recovering fast.

I have the honour to be, My Lord,

Your Lordship's most oblig'd
and most devoted servant

Richd Cumberland

Source: Michigan.

1. The date is determined by the reference to *The Carmelite* and the indication of the day of the week.

2. A new tragedy by Cumberland, acted at drury Lane on 2 September 1784.

3. George Lackington (1768-1844), publisher of Cumberland's *Memoirs*.

4. Sarah Kemble Siddons (1755-1831) played Matilda in *The Carmelite* with great success.

5. John Palmer (1742?-1798), one of the best general actors on the eighteenth-century stage, played Lord Hildebrand.

6. John Philip Kemble (1757-1823) played Montgomeri.

7. William (Gentleman) Smith acted St. Valori.

8. Sir Charles Hotham Thompson (1729-1794).

9. Alexander Wedderburn (1733-1805), the first Lord Loughborough.

10. The Drayton Comedy undoubtedly was *The Natural Son*, produced at Drury Lane on 22 December 1784. Cumberland's curious name for it probably refers to the estate, Drayton House, which Germain inherited from Lady Betty Germain in 1769. It was a requirement of the bequest that Sackville adopt the name Germain. The comedy deals with Blushenly's receiving an inheritance from his natural mother, Mrs. Frances Latimer, who would not acknowledge him during her lifetime. The story does not closely parallel the life of Germain, but he was unusually interested in it and made suggestions regarding its composition. See Stanley Williams, *Cumberland*, p. 190.

11. Sir Nathaniel William Wraxall (1751-1831).

12. Abbé Hussey.

13. John Henderson.

14. Germain's daughter, Elizabeth, and her husband, Henry Arthur Herbert of Muckross, Ireland. They were married in 1781.

15. Elizabeth's children had apparently been staying with Germain at Drayton.

16. Cumberland's eldest daughter, Elizabeth, who had been with him on his mission to Spain, shortly after their return married Edward Bentinck, brother of William Henry Cavendish Bentinck, the third Duke of Portland. The jest about the name of their child reflects Cumberland's obvious pleasure in this society marriage.

17. "Malbrook" was the French version of a popular song about Marlborough taught in the schools. It was frequently taught in French and the title as used here suggests that Cumberland's grandchild had mastered that version.

18. Germain's youngest daughter, Caroline (d. 1789), who never married.

19. Possibly the daughter of Sir Charles Leighton (1747-1784).

20. Edward Smith-Stanley (1754-1834), the Earl of Derby, ultimately married Elizabeth Farren (1759?-1829), who played Lady Paragon in *The Natural Son*.

21. Richard Brinsley Sheridan, manager of Drury Lane.

22. William Woodfall (1746-1803). He was on the staff of *The Morning Chronicle* at this time.

CXXX   Richard Sharp[1]   5 December 1785[2]

T Wells. 5 Decr.

My dear Sir

Your trouble is renew'd, and my acknowledgements ought to be repeated: As for my gratitude and esteem for you, it is not easy to augment them. By this morning's Coach I send our worthy Dilly[3] a pacquet, containing seven Numbers, all upon the Greek Middle Comedy, and the whole which will be given to that Subject, in the volume now in the press. The matter behind will consist of miscellaneous pap[e]rs, which I have studied to make as amusing as I can; some Critiques on Jonson, Milton and relatively on Shakespear; and a tract upon the proofs of Reveal'd Religion, in which I controvert the point with David Levi--The Critical peices to *The Fox* of Jonson, and a Comparison of his witches in *The Queens* with those in Macbeth; That upon Milton to his drama of *Sampson Agonistes*: I beleive I shall touch upon Fletcher's *Elder Brother*, and Massinger's *City Madam*, but this is in embryo only. Tell me your opinion of my Contents.

It was unavoidable in the pap[er]s on the Greek State, that I have here and there dipt into the Greek text--Let me beg you to look close to the press in the learned Languages. Errors there woud be some blots in our Scutcheon.

Dilly sent me three Vol[ume]s of Essays, intitled *Winter Evenings*; I am charm'd with them as far as I have gone. I think it a moral, manly and learned work: I take them to be Mr Knox's,[4] and if so I am happy to see an Author raise himself so high in his progress. They are toto Coelo beyond his former Essays.

I am affectionately Your's

R Cumberland

Source: Yale.

1. Richard Sharp (1759-1835) is identified as the recipient because of his involvement with Cumberland and Dilly in the publication of the *Observer*, and because of what seems a follow-up letter addressed to Sharp on 13 December.

2. The year is established by reference to the publication of the *Observer* in 1786.

3. Charles Dilly (1739-1807), who published *The Observer*. Cumberland had attempted to print the work on a press at Tunbridge Wells, but he found the results so unsatisfactory that he obtained the services of Dilly. Sharp corrected the sheets as they came from the press. See *Memoirs*, II, 200-201.

4. Rev. Mr. Vicesimus Knox (1752-1821), master of Tunbridge School from 1782 to 1812, mentioned by Boswell as one of those who imitated the style of Samuel Johnson.

CXXXI   **Richard Sharp**[1]   **13 December 1785**[2]

December the 13th

Dear Sir

I cannot express how gratefully I feel your kindness to me, nor the comfort I receive by your Letter; for I am asham'd to say how much this attack annoy'd my mind, as it is the first that ever struck at my principle, tho' very many have been levell'd at my productions. I have no wish to know from what dirty hand the Arrow came, tho' I can easily guess, if I woud indulge myself in following Circumstances, that cannot mislead: I beleive you are mistaken in the name you hinted at, but of this no more--of my remembrance no end, but that of life, as far as you are related to the affair.

Pray shew my Letter to Mr Whitefoord,[3] whom I know to be [a] man of strict honour; and as for conceiving him in any unbecoming character of anonymous defamation, I shoud think it an affront to him to say any thing that implied a possibility of suspicion in me, else I woud have written to him myself, and as for exculpating myself from any Acquaintance with the person who signs himself *Draco*, I shoud be asham'd of such a condescension. I am happy to be able to say with truth that I never nam'd any one man [person] or his productions or his politics in a Newspaper in my life, nor ever will.

I am charm'd with the type and paper of The Observer, and never saw anything more correct than the first sheet, may I request of you to tell Mr Dilly[4] to send me down the other sheets when they amount to three or four at a time, by the Coach, that I may collect a Copy and at the same time be a judge of the progress of the Work, how it advances--I mean not to trouble you to speak to Mr Dilly, till it falls in your way.

I am, Dear Sir, with the truest Esteem
Your most faithfull
and most obliged Servant

R Cumberland.

Source: Yale.
Addressed: Richard Sharp Esquire, Monument Hill,
London, and postmarked Tunbridge Wells, 14 Dec.

1. Richard Sharp 1759-1835.
2. The Year is determined by reference to publication of *The Observer*.
3. Caleb Whitefoord (1734-1810).
4. Charles Dilly.

CXXXII George Colman[1] 30 April 1787[2]

My Dear Sir

I send you the Comedy, which I have intitled the *Country-Attorney*. I think the Cast as far as respects the leading Characters points itself out in your Company, but when I put it into your Hands, I consign it to one whose Judgement needs no assistance, and upon whose candour I can implicitly rely. I flatter myself it is as safe in all points as any manuscript I ever tender'd to a Theatre; if it proves acceptable to you, and succeeds on your Stage, it will give me great Satisfaction and I hope establish a closer Correspondence between us in future. If your opinion shoud revolt against it, I repeat to you my assur[an]ces that however I may be disappointed in my wishes to enlist myself as your author, I shall not cease to be your friend and very faithfull Servant

R Cumberland

30th April. T Wells.

I had almost forgot to say that your Letter will find me for a fortnight to come at Lord Edward Bentinck's,[3] Micklefield Green, Watford, Herts--under cover.

Source: Harvard.

1. George Colman, the elder, (1732-1794) managed the Haymarket theatre from 1777-1792.

2. The year is determined by reference to "The Country Attorney", which was acted on 7 July 1787 at the Haymarket.

3. Cumberland's eledest daughter had married Lord Edward Bentinck.

CXXXIII John Bannister[1] 14 July 1787[2]

Saturday 1 oClock

My dear friend

Your kind and cordial note gave me infinite pleasure, and I thank you for it. Be assur'd my spirits are not in the least depress'd, tho my hopes are in some degree disappointed. I am not conscious that my Comedy can disgrace either the Theatre or myself, and I reflect with high satisfaction that it has given you one more opportunity of displaying those powers of acting, and proofs of feeling, that place you where you have a right to be in the hearts of your audience and the gratitude of your author.

I had determin'd to call on you this morning, but I am not in a state of health to face the weather, neither was I yesterday well enough to visit the

Theatre. I shall, if I am fit for it, come this evening, but I have a vile hemoroidal attack, that fixes me to the fireside.

I am to dine tomorrow at Mr Rogers's[3] Chambers in the Paper buildings Temple, where Sharpe[4] and my Captain[5] will also be. Let me beg of you to make him and me and the rest of your friends and admirers happy by dining with us at $\frac{1}{2}$ past 4 oClock: It will be charming to us all--but if you can't dine with us from prior engagem[en]t, do give us your company in the afternoon, if you possibly can--These friends of mine love you much and are worthy of you.

I render back in exchange with perfect truth your own kind and expressive words assuring You that I am *your's*

in truth of heart

R Cumberland

Source: Yale

1. John Banister (1760-1836) may be identified as the recipient from the context of the letter. He acted the role of Jack Volatile in "The Country Attorney", which was replaced by John O'Keefe's The Son-in-Law on Saturday, July 14, after having been announced in the playbill of the previous day.

2. The play is dated by that of the replacemant of the comedy.

3. Samuel Rogers (1763-1836), the poet.

4. Richard Sharp.

5. Cumberland's son, William.

CXXXIV   George Colman   Before 7 July 1787[1]

My Dear Sir

I have just rec[eive]d your Letter, dignifying

Miss Farren's Comm[an]ds for transposing her Introductory Scene to the Second Act.[2] Be it so! But I conclude it will be done with the hand of a Master-- or in other words, that You will transpose it yourself--therefore I rest in peace.

For Heaven's sake write her an Epilogue; I have plung'd from thought to thought in the profound of nonsense and can fix upon nothing--

One sense is left me, the sense of your kindness.

farewell.

R Cum

Tuesday 11 oClock

Source: Folger.

1. The date "The Country Attorney" was acted.
2. Elizabeth Farren acted Lady Rustic in "The Country Attorney."

CXXXV   **Frances Abington   Before 8 May 1789**[1]

Tunbridge Wells
Sunday Noon

Dear Madam

I thank you for the kind favor of your Letter, and I flatter myself we shall now renew our dramatic friendship and connection with mutual satisfaction and pleasure. I have reform'd the passages you pointed out, and since I have been here have written a prologue, which contents me much, and an Epilogue for you, which does not so easily satisfy my ambition of doing something not unworthy of the Elegant Representative: However we will sit in e-qual and strict judgement upon it.

The time I own is pressing, and the man I also own is precarious[2]--yet under the shelter of your sheild--I defy auguries. I submit to you, if it may not be proper to let Mr. Harris know his Author, and if he will meet me on Tuesday Night (the day after you receive this) and you will let us settle our business over a Cup of your Tea (shoud it be convenient to you and your engagements) the business might be put in trim, and the copy deliver'd to the transcriber.

I flatter myself we shall be successful, and as we started with the Bishops blessing, we shall plead benefit of Clergy in arrest of judgement. Recollect, my dear Madam; that the play is got up with no other difficulty, than what arises from the long and laborious part of the Widow, and that will be in the hands of a lady, who, whatever you may have to say in the case, is in my opinion of persons the very first Ornament of the English stage, and that in a period when it abounds with Genius. I have the honor to be that Lady's

most devoted Old Poet
and oblig'd Humble Servant

Richd Cumberland

Source: British Library.

1. The date of the first performance at Covent Garden of "The School for Widows," the subject of this letter.

2. Thomas Harris (d. 1820), then manager of Covent Garden.

CXXXVI   **Frances Abington   17 May 1789**[1]

Tunb. Wells. 17th May

My Dear Madam

I cannot express to you how kindly I feel your Sensibility towards me, and how much oblig'd to you I am for both your flattering and consolatory Letters. If I shoud deprive myself of the happiness of other favors of the same sort by declaring to you that I neither do, nor ever did, experience any real vexation for the treatment I have rec[eive]d from Mr. Harris,[2] I shoud lose a great pleasure for a small vanity--but in truth and sincerity I must say no treatment from that party, nor any dramatic disappointment can now disturb my temper. Time was (I confess it to my shame) when success was too much the object of my wishes; that anxiety has now lost it's edge, and I take events as they fall without murmur or complaint. I enter upon these undertakings with hopes of so low a pitch, and with resolutions so well fortified against miscarriage, that I am never taken by surprise.--But in the present case, what Have I lost? How have I suffered? at what should I repine? I have had a peice well approv'd, and you have been the supporter of it's introduction, representation and success.[3] Coud I for a moment state the case, that your opinion had fallen from me by the exhibition, that I confess woud have been a wound; but on the contrary of this, I have gain'd the most pleasing proofs of your friendship, zeal and affection for my peace of mind as well as credit, and the acquisition of such a friend is more to me than I will undertake to tell you, tho' I shall not be so scrupulous in speaking of it to others.

I don't wonder at Mr. Conway's[4] withdrawing from the flames, he must have been a salamander coud he have liv'd in such a climate. Now indeed we are

252

dropt 20 degrees on the scale, and winter is come back again in floods of rain. I have the happiness to see my beloved wife far onwards towards a recovery, but alas! I must be prepar'd ag[ain]st relapses: The rest of my circle are well, except my daughter Cum[berland],[5] who has got so strong a cold and cough, that she will not venture up to Town upon her Sisters weddings, both which are to take place on Thursday next.

Farewell, my dear Madam; need I say how truly I am what I shall ever esteem both as an honor and happiness, Your most obliged Servant

and very faithfull friend

R Cumberland

Source: British Library.

1. The year is determined by reference to "The School for Widows" that was produced in 1789.

2. Thomas Harris, manager of Covent Garden.

3. The "School for Widows" was produced on 8 May 1789 and performed only three times.

4. The Honorable Henry Seymour Conway (1721-1795), whose play *False Appearances* was acted at Drury Lane for the last time on Saturday 16 May 1789.

5. Probably Albinia, daughter of the Duke of Buckingham, who had married Cumberland's eldest son. She was a widow at this time.

CXXXVII   **Frances Abington   21 May 1789**[1]

21st May

Dear Madam

I shoud make an ill return to your kind and zealous negotiation, coud I do otherwise than highly approve of what you have done for the credit of our play,[2] and heartily thank you for it.

A renovation of this Comedy in another season will be the probable consequence of giving it another Night or two before this is over: such a rally will be most pleasing to me, and when we compare our fate with that of our neighbours, we have no right to complain nor any call upon us for a blush. Mr. Conway's[3] is indeed a doleful drop of the curtain; and I think Mr. Harris[4] woud hardly have told this in your ear, if he had not reconcil'd himself to a further acquaintance with our widow. I have no kind of backwardness to writing to him, but with submission to your advice I cannot help thinking it will be best for me to persist in patient silence and conformity; for whilst I have such a friend to act for me, why shoud I put in my oar? I shall be in Town next week and will attend your Exhibition[5] as I hope; I have only to wish that the House will have so much consideration for me as to quit the play with a short paragraph, which will cost them nothing, and may rescue it from the illnatur'd conclusions of such newspapers malice as the World and other public prints of the Day are too ready to announce, when a play is laid aside for the season.[6]

I little doubt your making a respectable Hand with proper afterpeices to uphold you.

> I am, Dear Madam, your most faithful
> and obedient Servant
>
> R Cumberland

Source: British Library.

1. The year is determined by the reference to "The School for Widows."

2. "The School for Widows," Covent Garden, 8 May 1789.

3. See note 4 of the letter of 17 May 1789.

4. Thomas Harris, manager of Covent Garden.

5. Mrs. Abington did not act in "The School for Widows" again, as Cumberland hoped.

6. "The School for Widows" was not acted in subsequent seasons.

CXXXVIII   Reverend John Romney[1]   18 April 1790

Tunbridge Wells
Sunday 18 April
1790

Dear Sir

I beg you will assure your worthy Father of the perfect sense I have of his kindness, and at the same time of the little need there was to make any thing like an Excuse for his forbearance, whilst he was engag'd in so interesting a work as the completion of his great Composition for the Shakespear Gallery.[2]

When he indulg'd me with a sight of that noble work he effectually forestall'd every occasion for an Apology to his friends, if any of them coud be stupid enough to stand in need of any explanation of the cause of his sequestering himself from the distractions of Company. He has done enough to justify himself to the most captious and querulential, if any such can be found in his list of acquaintance, for when they see the Operations of his Art, they cannot fail to judge of the exertions of his Mind, and of the necessity he was under to keep it collected and in force. Had he let in the world upon his work, their very praises woud have been unreasonable and an interruption of the progress of it. In my Opinion therefore he did perfectly right in holding the door against all Observers, and myself (tho' one of the most anxious and I flatter myself the least intrusive) amongst the rest. I now assure myself of his success, and have a fellow-feeling in the satisfaction, which his laurels will bestow.

I am coming to Town on Tuesday and shall stay only that night and Wednesday, and on Thursday set out with my friend Dilly[3] to Bedfordshire with a view of paying a visit to my old relation Mr Reynolds,[4] whom I have not seen for some time, and who is at the end of life or very near it: I have accepted Mr. Dilly's kind offer of a bed at his House, and we shall be accompanied by Mr Boswell[5] on our journey.

I hardly flatter myself I can get to Cav[en]dish Square from the Poultry, as my time is laid out in business; but if I can, I do not want for inclination and attraction. Accept the best Comp[limen]ts and good wishes of your Guests Mrs Cum[berland] and Sophia[6], and beleive me most sincerely and affect[ionatel]y Your's

R Cumberland

I shall return on Monday following, and if you will favor me with your Company hither we shall be most happy to make this place agreable to you, and flatter ourselves you will not regret the favor you confer upon us.

Source: Yale.
Addressed: The Reverend Mr. Romney at George Romney's Esq. in Cavendish Square London. It is postmarked 19 AP 90.

1. Rev. John Romney (1758-1832), the son of the painter, George Romney.

2. George Romney, beginning in the winter of 1786, was engaged in the painting of a scene from Shakespeare's *Tempest* for John Boydell's Shakespeare Gallery, which was devoted to illustrating the works of the dramatist. A second painting on the *Tempest* was projected by Romney, but not executed.

3. Charles Dilly (1739-1807), the publisher.

4. The Rev. Decimus Reynolds, "the son of Bishop Reynolds by my father's aunt, and of course his first cousin,..." (*Memoirs* II, 323). See also Cumberland's letter to Reynolds of 13 January 1779.

5. James Boswell (1740-1795). Dilly was a friend of both Samuel Johnson and Boswell. Cumberland speaks of his friendship for Boswell in his *Memoirs*, II, 228.

6. Cumberland's second daughter.

CXXXIX   Edmund Burke   11 November 1790

Tunbridge   Wells. 11 Novr. 1790

Dear Sir

I have been so charm'd with the perusal of your incomparable publication,[1] that I must plead the impulse of gratitude and affection for intruding upon you with my thanks, tho' I have no words that can express what I feel towards an Author, who has taught his fellow-subjects to reason rightly on the conduct of their neighbors, to avoid the contagion of enthusiasm and to preserve the purity of their own invaluable constitution, whilst all the world around them is running mad after levellers and innovators.

It has been your happy fortune to encounter an occasion fitted to your talents, to seize a subject in dignity not unworthy of your genius and no less lofty than your own sublime imagination; And it has been your happy art to employ upon that subject a splendor of diction, which woud ornament the brightest work of fancy, together with a force of argument, which investigates and establishes truth to a mathematical certainty and precision. The only possibility I foresee of anything occurring, which may in the smallest degree confute your positions, is the chance (and I hope a very improbable one) of your fellow subjects falling off from those sober principles, for which you have credited them and in which you have taken such patriotic pains to fix them: If ever this nation shoud be intoxicated with metaphysical rhapsodies and the visionary doctrines of Natural Rights to the ruin of society and good government, they woud sorrowfully prove that you had pronouc'd too favorably of their Understandings; but even in that event, (which God avert!) your's would be the glory of having done your best to stem the torrent, and so long as there shall be one sound head and honest heart surviving in the Country, your name will live in it's remembrance.

Permit me to assure you, that I am with the warmest affection and most unfeigned respect,

Dear Sir,
Your most faithful and devoted servant

Richd Cumberland

Right Hon. Mr. Burke

Source: Sheffield City Library. Wentworth Woodhouse Muniments.[2]

1. In 1790, Edmund Burke (1729-1797) had published his *Reflections on the Revolution in France*. Burke responded to this letter; see *Memoirs*, II, 272-3.

2. With permission of Olive, Countess Fitzwilliam's Wentworth Settlement Trustees and the Dir. of Libs. Information Services.

CXL Lady Edward Bentinck[1] About 1 December 1798[2]

Chas Street St Jas Square
Wednesday

My beloved Daughter

You will be pleas'd to hear that your brother William is on the point of being promoted to the rank of post-Captain by the special application and desire of Princess Amelia,[3] and I hope thro' the same means will have a ship. His attention was certainly very great and he merited the very great favor with which that amiable Sufferer regarded him and his services. I visited him twice and occasionally went out with him upon short trips; I flatter myself no example of nautical perfecton ever went beyond the discipline and good Order of the Fly.[4] Nothing else coud have sav'd her in these dreadfull gales upon that cursed Coast. He has however brought her safe, tho' crippled, to Spithead, and I fancy his promotion was settled yesterday at the Board. I hope the same good fortune will speedily attend Captain Thompson, and that he will not much longer be wedded to the Savage Sloop. Cavendish[5] I dare say is grown a fine fellow, and a bit of a seaman; William tells me he fell in with him. Bentinck[6] I hope is recovering, tho' I am sorry to find not yet able to return to his quarters in Dean's yard. I heard with infinite concern Lord Edward[7] had receiv'd a fall, but when I heard it, I was told of his being safe and about again. Pray, my dear. satisfy me how he, and you, and your dear children all are, and direct hither to Lackington's.[8] No news of poor Charles;[9] when may we look for him? Your mother and Marianne are well at home; I am also well, and with every affectionate good wish and blessing to your babies remain my beloved Daughter's

Most fond and faithfull father

R Cumberland

Source: Yale.
Addressed to Lady Edwd B.

1. Lady Edward Charles Cavendish Bentinck. Elizabeth, Cumber-

land's oldest daughter.

2. The date is conjectured from an entry in the diary of Mme. D'Arblay for 1 December 1798 that mentions Princess Amelia going to Worthing in the hope that bathing in the sea water would relieve a painful lameness. The letter indicates that Cumberland's son, William, was at that time at Worthing in command of the Fly.

3. Princess Amelia (1783-1810), the fifteenth and last child of King George III.

4. Cumberland's expectations were based on the service his son performed for Princess Amelia at Worthing. He "kept guard upon that station, prepared to accomadate her Royal Highness with his boats or vessels in any excursions on the water she might be advised to take" (Memoirs II, 295).

5. Cumberland's grandson.

6. William Henry Cavendish Bentinck (1738-1809), third Duke of Portland.

7. Cumberland's son-in-law, Edward Bentinck.

8. George Lackington (1768-1844), who published Cumberland's Memoirs.

9. Cumberland's son, then serving as an army officer.

10. His daughter Frances Marianne.

CXLI   Unidentified   20 January 1799

Tun. Wells. 20 Janry. 1799

My dear Sir

Accept my thanks for the favor of the letter forwarded to me from Mr. Winslow of Quebec.[1] I am disappointed to find it contains no remittance for any salary as Agent,[2] by him receiv'd in part and that it signifies to me at the same time that payment is stopt in the province until Certificate of Life shall be given in. I presume at this time there is no mode which I can take to forward this Certificate to Mr. Winslow, nor any other measures on my part to pursue, which your kindness can recommend at present. If there is I trust that friendship so long experienc'd will dictate them to me; in the meantime I seize the occasion to reassure you with the warmest sensation of gratitude and esteem that I am, My Dear Sir, unalterably and

faithfully yrs

Richd Cumberland

Source: Harvard.

1. Probably Joshua Winslow (1727-1801), who before the American Revolution was Paymaster General for British forces in North America. He settled in Quebec after the war.
2. Cumberland was Crown Agent for Nova Scotia.

CXLII Richard Dennison Cumberland[1] 6 February 1799

Dear Cousin

Accept my most sincere thanks for your kind Letter, and your care of me in the case of Mr. Phillip's publication.[2] I shall be in Town in a few days, and will not fail to call upon him in St. Paul's Church Yard. I own to you I am not very studious about the correctness of these fugitive Characters of literary men; I have found myself in two of this description already, and am the less anxious to correct their errors in point of fact, inasmuch as I am employ'd in preparing a detail of my own humble memoirs, to be given to the world when I have left it.[3]

As no dramatic writer of this nation ever wrote so much, and few of any description so variously, I thought it justice to my-self and posterity to leave this account behind me faithfully executed.

I rejoice to hear of your domestic happiness, and that your large family are blest with health and content. It seems to me a very wise measure in you, as a father of so many children, to turn your land into money, if the times suit for that purpose, of which you are well qualified to judge.

I am glad you amuse yourself with composition, but I am surpriz'd to hear that you are at a loss to fix upon publishers, for when your Copies are out of the printer's hands and all exp[en]ces paid, the whole trade of retailers is open to your choice, any one will gladly deal with you, and their terms are settled and the same throughout.

I shall be happy to be favor'd with a copy of your romance,[4] and if you will send it to me directed at Mr. Lackington's,[5] Charles Street Saint James's Square, it will come safe to hand, and I promise myself much entertainment in reading it.

Mrs Cum. and my daughter[6] join in best wishes and regards to you and your's, and I beg you to beleive me with sincere esteem

Dear Sir, Your affectionate Cousin
and faithfull Servant

R Cumberland

Feb. 6th 1799

Source: British Library.

1. Richard Dennison Cumberland was related to the dramatist through a parallel line of the family dating back four generations.

2. Probably Sir Richard Phillips (1764-1840), who established the *Monthly* magazine in 1796.

3. Cumberland's *Memoirs* were published in 1806, five years before his death.

4. There is no record of this work in the British Library Catalogue.

CXLIII **Richard Dennison Cumberland 21 August 1799**[1]

Dear Cousin

Your delicate attention to avoid any literary mistakes from the coincidence of names may be the means of saving yourself from disgrace and excluding me from praise that I do not earn or deserve. I shall dispose your printed Catalogue in the public library.[2] I congratulate you on the interesting accession to your family, and thank you for the flattering encomiums you are pleas'd to bestow on my unmarried daughter.[3] She joins with Mrs. Cumberland and me in best [comp]liments to you and your's.

I am with sincere esteem Dear Sir,
Your faithfull and affect Servt

R Cumberland

21st Augst.

Source: British Library.

1. The year is conjectured because of the exchange of letters earlier in 1799 between Richard Dennison Cumberland and the dramatist concerning publishing. See 6 February 1799.
2. There is no record of this in the British Museum Catalogue.
3. Frances Marianne.

CXLIV   Sir James Bland Burgess 10 January 1800[1]

friday Evening

My dear Sir James

We shall rehearse the Music &c. tomorrow at Twelve,[2] and if it suits you to waste an hour in hearing what we are yet not quite perfect in, your company will be most acceptable to your faithful Servant and you will meet Mr. and Mrs. Pitt[3] and Miss Cum[berland].[4] You will come to Brandon's door in Hart Street, where I shall leave orders for your reception. I have taken the box for our *Literary* brethren in your name for Thursday next.[5] Must I order beefstake at the Shakespeare at 4 oClock.

Ever

R Cumberland

Source: Folger.

1. The date is calculated from that on which *Joanna of Montfaucon* was produced, Thursday, 16 January 1800.
2. For *Joanna of Montfaucon.*
3. Probably William Pitt (1759-1806). In his *Memoirs,* Cumberland suggests, however, only a slight acquaintance with him: "I never was in a private room with Mr. Pitt but once, and that was a few minutes only at Burlington House" (II, p. 317).
4. Frances Marianne.
5. Burgess and Cumberland were members of a literary club that met frequently for dinner. The box was for the first performance of *Joanna of Montfaucon.*

CXLV **Sir James B. Burgess Before 10 January 1800**[1]

My dear friend

I have your manuscript with me,[2] and will take care to send it over by a safe hand, unless I am happy enough to see you in person, which I am unwilling to despair of. I purpose to stay the whole week; and hope to shake off a London Cold, that has hung upon me ever since we last met. Hen[ry] Fry[3] came down with me; else I shoud be much more solitary than I have been in London, where my friends were kind enough to feed and maintain me very liberally.

Writing for singing men and singing women is not a very enviable task, tho I have escap'd with less trouble, than many of my brethren, that have preceeded me.[4]

I am now upon the point of sitting down here once more for the remainder of my days; it is not a delectable prospect, for my old friends are dispers'd, and I have no great temptation to look out for new ones. I come entirely at the request of my volunteers, and I purpose to devote my leisure time to them. I have recruited some new officers, and am about to raise a fifth company to compleat my establishment, if I can succeed in it.

Capt. W[illiam] Cumberland[5] has brought the Leyden home from the Tagus, and I am happy to hear that young Crouchley[6] is very well, and has work'd very closely at his navigation under the Master: My son describes his passage as very boisterous, and that he has carried away most of his yards, and leak'd very much. Capt. Thompson has the good fortune to have got The Minotour, and is confirm'd in his command of that fine ship. I hope Captain Beresford will soon be re-appointed for the sake of my friend Wentworth.[7] If Charles[8] is with you, give my love to him, and let me be respectfully remember'd to Lady Burges and your amiable daughters.

Camis[9] tells me he can recommend a Servant to you for Fabry's place, who I am told has left you and come up to London. If you are therefore in want of a butler, you will let me know, and I hope let me see you at the same time. Beleive me ever, My dear friend,

affecty your's

Rd Cumberland

Source: Harvard.

1. The date is conjectured on the basis of the date of the production of *Joanna of Montfaucon* on 16 January 1800. Cumberland was still at Tunbridge Wells when this letter was written but he was in London by the 10th of January. See 10 January 1800.

2. Probably Burgess's poem *Richard I*, which was published in 1800 with "corrections and emendations suggested' by Cumberland.

3. Henry Fry, a close friend, who did legal work for Cumberland. Cumberland died at his house.

4. *Joanna of Montfaucon*, a melodrama interspersed with music and song was produced at Covent Garden on 16 January 1800 with some success. Genest calls it "one of the best of those irregular Dramas which have been so frequent on the stage of late years." but he found the genre "unworthy of Cumberland" (VI, 476).

5. Cumberland's youngest son.

6. A "Mr. Crutchley of Clifford's Inn" was a "worthy and respectable partner" of Henry Fry (*Memoirs*, II, 343). This reference may be to his son.

7. Probably a member of the family of Charles Watson Wentworth (1730-1782), second Marquis of Rockingham. The family were friends of Burgess.

8. The son of Sir James Bland Burgess.

9. Cumberland's servant, Thomas Camis.

CXLVI   **Sir James Bland Burgess**   22 May 1800

22 May 1800

My Dear Sir

Many thanks for your's of the 19th. I perceive you ascribe the events of last Thursday to design, and indeed I fear with truth, Particularly in the case of the pistol. If it is so, I trust it will be develop'd upon the trial of the Assassin.[1] Fearfull times they surely are at home and abroad. I bear you all possible respect for the part you are supporting as a Commander of Volunteers in the Capital, and so near the person of the Sovereign, and I honor him for his fortitude in persisting to present himself to his Subjects in our public Theatres, for what security can he find in avow'd timidity, and what man living can defend his person from the enthusiasm of a Desperado? I fear our German Campaign does not open auspiciouly for Austria, and I doubt if Melas will not loiter before Genoa till the Consul's succours will releive the place, and reverse the Scene of affairs even there.[2]

Miss Cumberland's situation is still very distressing, but I hope it will mend in time for me to come to Town and leave her before our last meeting of the 5th of June.[3] I am very sorry we shall not see our good Neighbour in the interim, but I can readily understand the propriety of your stay at this particular period.

My Son the Captain was married last Saturday week by our friend Mr. Gordon at Tonbridge Church, and that morning brought his bride elect from Town, when Mrs. Cum[berland] and I met her at the Church and were present at the Ceremony.[4] They have ever since inhabited a pleasant little Cottage near Chalke Hall, and liv'd with us. Every prospect of happiness seems to open upon them, and every hour that has pass'd since their union seems to endear them more and more to each other, and each of them to us. Her temper is angelic, and her manner truly amiable and elegant. I humbly hope that Providence will befriend and protect them.

They join in the most affectionate regards and good wishes to you, with many acknowledgements for all your past kindnesses, and your obliging endeavors to find them out in Town. They say it woud be a most pleasing addition to their happiness if they coud see you and enjoy your Company.

I do not understand our brother Boscawin's Criticism,[5] and therefore only consider it as a mark of his sincerity and confidence in your candor; He can hardly expect your compliance. I forgot to speak to you of Sir Sotheby's drama,[6] which in point of diction I think has great merit, tho' in contrivance glaringly defective. That writer has the powers of sublimity; Time I hope will give him judgement: It is a Genius that has need of discipline, but I fear it is not very obedient to correction. More of all these matters when we meet. Farewell.

Ever most sincerely and
affectionately your's

Richd Cumberland

Source: Harvard.

1. The attempt was by one James Hadfield. *The Annual Register for the Year 1800* records that it took place on 15 May 1800: "In the evening a most alarming and extraordinary circumstance occurred at the theatre royal, Drury Lane. At the moment when his majesty entered the box, a man in the pit, near the orchestra, on the right hand side, suddenly stook up and discharged a pistol at the royal person" (p. 14). At his trial at the Court of the King's Bench on June 26, the jury declared him "not guilty, being under the influence of insanity, at the time the act was done." He was, however, kept in custody (p. 19).

2. Steven Watson describes this stage of the war against

France, and his view generally supports Cumberland's fears. Pitt had decided not to respond to Napoleon's overtures for peace in December 1799: "Napoleon, denied peace, carried war to his enemies. He took the Austrians, who had been methodically preparing to push the French from Genoa, in their rear. By mid-June 1800 Bonaparte's victory of Marengo had turned the tables once more. The Austraians were no longer meditating a thrust northwards but were, on the contrary, concerned to hold on to fragments of their gains (*The Reign of George III*, p. 381).

3. Probably of the literary club of which he and Burgess were members.

4. William Boscawin (1752-1811).

6. Probably William Sotheby's tragedy, *The Siege of Cuzco*, published that year. Allardyce Nicoll also tentatively ascribes another drama, *The Cambrian Hero; or Llawelyn the Great*, to Sotheby (*A History of Early Nineteenth Century Drama 1800-1850* (Cambridge 1930) II, 395).

CXLVII Mr. Barker[1] 10 October 1800[2]

Sir

Let the prologue stand exactly as it does; the Italics and Note are much more flattering to me than any lines I can substitute.[3]

Yrs

R Cumberland

T Wells. friday
N.B. Vide the Erratum Line 7

Source: Folger.

1. The letter is addressed to "Mr. Barker, Bookseller, Great Russel Street, Covent Garden."

2. The date is determined from the postmark, 11 October 1800. The previous Friday was the 10th.

3. The prologue to *Joanna of Montfaucon*, published by Lackington, Allen and Company.

CXLVIII   George Cooke[1]   4 January 1801

Jan 4th. 1801 Tunbridge Wells

Sir

My worthy friend Sir Ja[me]s B. Burges informs me that in a conversation he had the pleasure to hold with you at your lodgings, you told him that it was in contemplation to bring my play of *Torrendal*[2] upon the stage of your Theatre.

I confess to you it woud give me great satisfaction to know that such was the design, wishing as I do to have that production on which I have expended my best efforts committed to your care, and supported by your talents. Have the goodness therefore to tell me what you know or beleive to be the intention of Mr. Harris[3] in the case of Torrendal, and you will much oblige, Sir,

Your most obedt
Humble Servt

Richd Cumberland

Source: Historical Society of Pennsylvania.

1. George Cooke (1756–1812?) was acting at Covent Garden in 1801.

2. *Torrendal* was not acted, but was published in *The Posthumous Dramatic Works* of Cumberland.

3. Thomas Harris, manager of Covent Garden.

CXLIX   Robert Hobart[1]   5 January 1801

Tunbridge Wells Jan 5th 1801

Sir

Tho' the letter I have now the honor to address to you, looks back to a business long since past, and for which I cannot have the smallest claim upon your justice, yet as I conceive myself to have suffer'd by my service to a most severe extent, the pressure of which now lies peculiarly heavy upon me in my old age, I think I may venture to refer myself to your candor and benignity, and presume to hope you will take the following case into your consideration upon motives, that cannot but be congenial to a mind so dignified as your's.

In April of the year 1780 I was sent to the Court of Spain upon a secret negotiation: I was directed to take my family (viz my wife and two daughters) with me as a cover for my journey: I had also Mr. Tho[ma]s Hussey, (now titular Bishop of Waterford) associated with me in that mission: I had no specific allow[an]ce granted for my expences, but was instructed to draw bills upon my own banker accompanied by letters of advice to John Robinson Esqr., then Secretary of the Treasury, who engaged on the part of the Minister Lord North to replace them: Encumber'd as I was with a family, and bound to defray all Mr. Hussey's expences, who was to separate from me at Lisbon and travel into Spain before me, I was limited to no calculation, neither was I restrain'd in the article of Secret Service, but had discretionary credit for all such charges as I might necessarily incur in the Service I was employ'd upon.

On the faith of these assurances I went to Spain, and was absent fourteen months: I solemnly declare I incurr'd no expences but what to my conscience appear'd unavoidable, and I kept correct and authentic vouchers of every article that belonged to the account: I had to follow the Court thro' the whole toure of the Setios, journies to take and lodgings to provide at Aranjuez, St. Ildefonso, the Escorial and Madrid: I had Mr. Hussey's separate journies and separate establishments to defray: I employ'd my own confidential Servant as my Courier,[2] and paid his charges: I transmitted home some important papers and communications obtain'd at an expence: The East and West India Convoy was taken by the Spanish fleet, whilst I was in the Country; I found means to redeem several seamen prisoners, and at my own charge forwarded them to Lisbon:[3] I had the honor to receive from the King of Spain two Horses, selected as the finest in his whole stud, and given me to present to the King my Sovereign: I employ'd and paid two Spaniards to lead them from Madrid thro' Paris to London on foot: during my whole residence in Spain I drew my bills on my banker Mr. Crofts of Pall Mall thro' the medium of Mr. Devisme at Lisbon, accompanying every one with the prescrib'd regular letter of Advice to Mr. Secretary Robinson, who to all the applications of my Banker answer'd only by evasions, and never replac'd a single draft.

I was order'd home and on my return thro' France fell ill at Bayonne; here whilst I remain'd without hopes of life, in a delirious fever, the bones piercing thro' my skin, attended upon by my wife and daughters, my bills came back protested by Mr. Devisme; I had exhausted my credit with my banker; my Employers had broken faith and were deaf to all remonstrances, and from hence I coud not have departed, had not a Gentleman in the Spanish service,[4] who was travelling to Paris with me generously supplied my necessities, and by the loan of five hundred pounds enabled me to reach London.

After my return home I pass'd ten months in solicitation for payment, tendering all my vouchers fairly authenticated and arranged: In that period I had one audience only of a few minutes with Lord North,[5] and neither gain'd admission, nor a single answer to my letters afterwards; I had strictly fulfill'd my duty; there was not the smallest charge against me; the King was graciously pleas'd to approve of my service, and to accept of the Royal Horses. What Lord North left unpaid his Successor Lord Shelburne[6] woud not look at, and my case devolv'd upon the humanity of the Duke of Portland,[7] who referring it to Mr. Fox[8] then Secretary of State, and he reporting instantly in its favor, I had Order for the sum of about £1300, which was all I then ventur'd to pray for, intimidated and desponding as I was by such a course of disappointments.

In the meantime I had sold my Wife's jointure to replace my exceedings in account with my Banker; My place of Secretary of the Board of Trade was abolish'd, and I was compensated to the amount of about half its value: My family bore hard upon me; the Marraiges (sic) of son and daughter only encumber'd me with fresh demands, and I have from that period to the present, tho' divesting myself of every thing that can be call'd superfluity, been struggling to uphold myself and family against the pressure of the time, with the painful reflection ever present to my mind, that at the advanc'd age of near seventy years, I am departing out of life without leaving any provisions for a wife, whose jointure I was oblig'd to sacrifice in the extremity of my unmerited distress.

If you have read thus far, Sir, forgive me I entreat you. I can have no claim but what your own nobleness of Soul may consent to create and feel for a Man, unknown to you, but honoring you in heart and truth. You have generously protected the Widow and Children of my son in the persons of Lady Albinia and her daughters. I now lay myself and my wife at your Mercy--we are both near the end of our days--

I have the honor to be with truth and respect,

Sir,

Your most obedient

and most humble servant

Richard Cumberland

Source: New York Public Library: Henry W. and Albert A. Berg Collection. The New York Public Library. Astor, Lenox and Tilden Foundations.

1. Cumberland's eldest son had married the daughter of the Earl of Buckinghamshire, Albinia, whose brother, Robert Hobart, became the fourth Earl of Buckinghamshire in 1804. He was at the time this letter was written Baron Hobart, and was to become Secretary of War in the Addington administration, formed in February 1801. This letter is conjectured to have been written to him on the basis of the reference to his protection of Lady Albinia and her daughters. It also suggests that Cumberland had information suggesting that Hobart was to become Secretary of War, a position from which he could assist him in his claim for compensation for his Spanish mission.

2. Probably Thomas Camis, whom Cumberland mentions in his *Memoirs* as accompanying him to Spain (II, 143). He might possibly refer to Frederick Daly, Abbé Hussey's servant, who on occasion acted as a courrier for him.

3. See Cumberland's "Memorial" to Lord North, in the dramatist's *Memoirs*, II, 169.

4. Signor Nicolas Marchetti of the Corps of Engineers, a Sicilian in the Spanish service, who accompanied Cumberland throughout his Spanish journey.

5. Frederick Lord North (1732-1792), the First Lord of the Treasury.

6. William Petty (Fitzmaurice) Shelbourne became Secretary of State for Home and Colonial Affairs in March 1782, and First Lord of the Treasury in July 1782.

7. William Henry Cavendish Bentinck (1738-1809), the third Duke of Portland, who became First Lord of the Treasury in April 1783. Cumberland's oldest daughter, Elizabeth, had married his brother Edward Bentinck.

8. Charles James Fox (1749-1806).

CL   **Sir James Bland Burgess 30 January 1801**[1]

Jan. 30th

My Dear Friend

A thous[an]d thanks for your letter; it brought me, as your letters are ever apt to do, fresh marks of kindness and friendship of a character rare in these times.

My Son holds himself everlastingly beholden to you for your efforts in his behalf, and as he knows, loves and honors Adm. Dacres,[2] he declares to me with sincerity that nothing in the objects of his profession coud give him more true pleasure than to enjoy the honor you have been seeking for him.

I rejoice to hear well of your Richard in his out-set;[3] contemporary praise is not always the lot of Merit to obtain; your claim is of so striking a sort, that I little doubted of your gaining present fame, and I was perfectly sure your work woud secure future fame to itself, when jealousy and cavil had exhausted their spite. Something of this species I guess will be aim'd at you and your friends in this Eleventh Edition of The Pursuits.[4]

You have got a poet, who compliments you with his printed works, alas![5] I have got two unknown Correspondents, who desire my judgement of their Manuscript ones--the first a Youth, who writes Epistles in prose; the latter a girl of seventeen, who writes tragedy, as I guess, and probably neither in prose nor verse.

I rejoice in Cooke's[6] recovery, which will be happy indeed for the dramatic world, if it produces an adherence to advice of his Doctors, and a new system of sobriety on his part. I hear nothing from him on the question of Torrendal.[7] If therefore I do not hear any thing on that point, or hear (what I am most likely to hear) nothing to encourage me to come to Town, I shall not take the trouble and expence of a Journey, but request of you to tender my apology to the Members of the Club on Wednesday next. The fact is, William and his little Wife are very pleasant to me[8] and the Corps[9] is just now in the crisis of receiving their second supply of arms, and second lot of officers, when my presence becomes usefull at least, if not necessary.

Mrs. Cum[berland] thanks you for your kind wishes; she is somewhat better. Elisa presents her best regards and Will[ia]m tenders you his most cordial thanks.

I beg my respects to Lady Burges with every good wish to Miss Burges and Charles, and I need not add that I am ever

and ever shall be, Your's
most truly and affecty

R Cumberland

I have advanc'd very far in my projected defence of Revelation against the Patrons and Professors of the New Philosophy.[10]

Source: Harvard.

1. The year is determined by reference to Cumberland's letter to Cooke of 4 January 1801.

2. Admiral James Richard Dacres (1749-1810). What honor Burgess was seeking is not clear, but it was probably preferment for Cumberland's son, William, who was a Naval officer.

3. Burgess's *Richard I*, published in 1800.

4. The eleventh edition of *The Pursuits of Literature*, a four dialogue satiric poem, was published anonymously in 1801. Its author was Thomas James Mathias (1754-1835). Cumberland is right in conjecturing that there would be a reference to Burgess, although it is not to *Richard I*. In the Second Dialogue (p. 121, l. 2) there is the following line: "And like Sir James Bland Burgess murmur love." This is footnoted: "I allude to Sir James Bland Burgess's Poem, entitled, 'The Birth and Triumph of Love.'" The

extended note criticizes Burgess for prudishness about love. Cumberland also receives mention in the poem (Dialogue Four, p. 442): "For Athens Cumberland seems born alone." The footnote to the line is complimentary, with the exception of criticism of Cumberland's novels.

5. This very likely refers to the author of *The Pursuits of Literature*. It is a matter of interpretation whether or not the reference is "complimentary."

6. George Cooke who was acting at Covent Garden.

7. Burgess had suggested that Cumberland write to Cooke regarding the possible presentation of his drama, *Torrendal*, at Covent Garden. It was never acted. See 4 January 1801.

8. Cumberland's son, William, and his wife Eliza. See 22 May 1800 for an account of their wedding.

9. Cumberland had organized a corps of volunteers for local defense against a possible French invasion.

10. Cumberland published his defense in *A Few Plain Reasons Why We Should Believe in Christ and Adhere to his Religion*, London, 1801.

CLI Sir James Bland Burgess[1] 10 February 1801[2]

Tuesday feb. 10th

One line, my best friend, to tell you that my poor Woman survives and rallies under reiterated blows. She has come down stairs, dines with us, is gay and unshaken in spirits and in courage. William and Eliza[3] are of unspeakable comfort to us both, and judge you if we do not need a comforter, when I tell you that my Grandson Cavendish[4] was among the lamented Crew that perish'd in the Rabet. Alas! it is a sad blow, but it is God that strikes, and who shall murmur? I attend my Volunteers every evening as usual, and find amusement in my duty.

Accept our united Love and good wishes for yourself, your excellent Lady, and dear Children.

Ever your's unalterably and truly

R Cumberland

Source: Folger.

1. The content of the letter clearly suggests that Burgess was its recipient.

2. The year is conjectured from references to the illness of Cumberland's wife. In addition, 10 February fell on a Tuesday in 1801.

3. Cumberland's son and daughter-in-law.

4. Probably the son of Cumberland's daughter, Elizabeth, who had married Lord Edward Bentinck.

CLII George Lackington?[1] 31 March [1801][2]

Dear George

What is become of the pamphlet, which I beg you to send us down? I desir'd two dozen; but I think a dozen will serve. Not seeing it advertis'd, I am half inclin'd to beleive the Parties concern'd stop'd publication; but I think I shoud have heard from you, had this been the case.

Very truly Your's

R Cumberland

March 31st. Tws.

Source: Princeton.

1. This letter is addressed only to "Dear George." From the content it seems likely that it was to his publisher, George

Lackington. The only pamphlet published for Cumberland by Lackington and his associates was *A Few Plain Reasons Why We Should
Believe in Christ and Adhere to his Religion*, London, 1801, which
is probably the subject of this letter.

2. The year is conjectured from the reference to the pamphlet
in question and from the fact that March 31 was a Tuesday in
1801.

CLIII Sir James Bland Burgess June or July 1801[1]

My dear friend

I am quite delighted with every particular, which
your kind and most welcome letter contains. I most
heartily hope you will obtain your wisht-for purchase in that enviable Country and Climate,[2] where I
have ever wish'd to end my days, and escape the
frosts that chill the veins of age and decrepitude.
I rejoice in the just applause which the Critical
Reviewer has bestow'd upon your excellent poem,[3] and
I am asham'd of the duplicity of Parson Nares,[4] who
coud blow hot and cold in the shameful way he took,
quibbling with that in publick, which he had inspected and reveiw'd in private as a friend. You have
pleas'd me very much by your temperate answer to
those unhandsome paragraphs, which spoke untruth
about the motives for the disolution of your Companies.

But above all things I am rejoic'd to hear you
mean to come to us next week, and I hope it will be
on Monday. I have been quite dishearten'd by your
tedious absence. Lord Hobart[5] is here, and has
lodg'd himself at the next door, which we call Mrs.
Wogan's, exactly between our houses. Some few pleas-
[an]t characters are with us, many are with us that
we coud do without. I write in haste to save the
post but small space serves to convey the true assurance that I am, and ever shall be, yr affection-

ate

Rich Cumberland

Thursday 7 oClock

Source: Harvard.

1. The date is determined by the reference to the review of *Richard I* in *The Critical Review.*
2. Burgess permanently moved to Beauport in Battle, Sussex, in 1803.
3. *Richard I.*
4. Reverend Edward Nares (1762-1841).
5. Robert Hobart (1760-1815). Baron Hobart succeeded his father as the Earl of Buckinghamshire in 1804. His sister had married Cumberland's oldest son, Richard, who had died at Tobago before the date of this letter.

CLIV   Sir James Bland Burgess[1] Probably Early 1801[2]

My dear friend, I have now Mrs. Cumberland with me in the room so ill in Spirits that she cannot bear up, even if my best friend comes into the room, excuse me therefore, and pity me, if I beg to come to you for a few minutes in my way to the Drill, at, or very soon after, 9 oClock.

Your's ever

R Cum.

Source: Folger.

1. The recipient is conjectured to be Sir James Bland Burgess, Cumberland's close friend at Tunbridge Wells.

2. Mrs. Cumberland became seriously ill early in 1801, and died that year.

CLV   Sir James Bland Burgess   1 January 1802

My Dear friend

I know you too well to trouble you with any apology for my long silence. I have met nothing worth telling you. The Chancellor[1] has not help'd us much as to the past, the future I beleive will be better for it. I have had a good deal to do with Sheridan,[2] and we have talk'd much together; I have sold him a penny worth of my brains, and am just now come from reading *The False Demetrius* in the Green Room;[3] It pass'd without reference to any Judge, open or secret, and possess'd itself of the Stage suo jure; Kemble takes the part; how he will treat it time may show; I can't guess. I am also preparing an Opera in 3 acts,[5] in which Billington [6] is to take a part; I take the best of the old brick out of the Jew of Mogodore to run up my hasty building, but there is no fear there; My danger lies in *The False* Demetrius.

Many thanks for your troublesome search; You sent me the very MS I wanted, but I found the 5th Act am[ong]st my papers here.[7]

I long to see your poem in advance;[8] You have been worthily and happily employed; I have been drudging like a daylaborer, and doing dirty work for dirty lucre, which in the event may disappoint me. I shoud ask you for a few lines of prologue, but the task is below you, and you shall not write but *with* me pari passu.

As I go hence on Monday to carry Marianne home from Ramsgate, we shall not meet--Alas! I am sorry--Recollect Mr. Todd on Wednesday;[9] I commit him to your protection, and I assure him to you as a man deserving of your esteem and friendship.

I have read our venerable Master Vincent versus Meath and Rennel:[10] He is excellent, unanswerable, inimitable; Not a word more than you and I coud wish; not a word less than his Subject demands. Nares[11] has already review'd him--so, so! not quite amiss, not very brilliant--Westm[inste]r may be proud of it's Master; Our Club may be proud of their Member.

I have found time for my Annual Prayer, and shall send it to *The Sun.*

The british Critic says he is surfeited with Epic poems; how will his queasy stomach bear our double dose?[12]

If by chance you do not come up to the next Club day, pray take care that Mr. Todd is nam'd for ballot at the next meeting.

My respects to your excellent lady; Love to Charles. Need I say I am Your's

R Cum.

Brunswick Row
Queens Square

Jan 1st 1802--Many and Happy!

Source: Harvard.

1. On 5 January 1801, Cumberland had appealed to Lord Hobart, who was to become Secretary of War and who was the brother of his widowed daughter-in-law, Albinia, for aid on the basis of his Spanish mission of 1780. The reference here may be to Henry Adddington (1757-1844), Chancellor of the Exchequer.

2. Richard Brinsley Sheridan of Drury Lane.

3. *The False Demetrius*, published among the *Posthumous Dramatic Works* of Cumberland was never produced. Apparently Sheridan desired revisions of the fifth act, and while they were being made used the sets designed for its production for another play. Genest suggests that this so piqued Cumberland that he laid the play

aside (VIII, 396).

4. John Philip Kemble (1757-1823).

5. This musical play was produced as *The Jew of Mogodore* at Drury Lane on 3 May 1808.

6. Elizabeth Billington (1768-1818), a much sought after singer. Sheridan writes to his wife in June 1801: "If I had left Town on Sunday I should have lost Billington and now I have *secured* her which I am truly delighted at" (*The Letters of Richard Brinsley Sheridan*, ed. Cecil Price, II, p. 153)

7. The fifth act was not published in the *Posthumous Dramatic Works*. Cumberland's daughter, in publishing it, suggests that the fifth act was not finished. This letter indicates that it was, but is apparently not extant.

8. Probably *The Exodiad*.

9. Henry John Todd, Archdeacon of Cleveland, and editor of *The Works of Edmund Spenser*, 1805.

10. William Vincent (1739-1815) was a contemporary of Cumberland at Westminster School, of which he later became the Master. He rose to Dean of Westminister and spoke the funeral oration over Cumberland's grave. He replied to attacks by Thomas Rennell (1754-1840), Master of the Temple, and Thomas Lewis O'Beirne (1748?-1823), Bishop of Meath, who had charged that headmasters were neglecting their duties in *Defense of Public Education*, 1801.

11. Reverend Edward Nares.

12. They were to collaborate on *The Exodiad*.

CLVI Sir James Bland Burgess Probably 1803[1]

W Hatting 9 oClock
Tuesday Morng

My Dear Friend

I am desir'd to present to you the joint wishes of the whole Mess of your friends and my brother officers that you and our respected Lady Patroness[2] with as many of your fair Daughters as shall be so dispos'd, will honor us with a visit on Thursday next, and as soon in the morning as you see fit and convenient to the ladies, if you have any wish to see us out. We can give you comfortable beds in the Abbey, now occupied by our ladies, who have done us the honor to visit us.

I am my dear friend,
for Self and Co, affecty Your's

Richd Cumberland

Source: Harvard.

1. The date is determined by reference to the Corps of Volunteers.

2. The wife of Sir James Bland Burgess acted as patroness of Cumberland's Corps of Volunteers. The Corps, originally formed in 1801, was disbanded following the Treaty of Amiens of 27 March 1802. It was, however, revitalized by 1803.

CLVII Sir James Bland Burgess Before 8 January 1803[1]

Friday

My dear friend

I am returning to T[unbridge] Wells tomorrow, not well; nor yet much worse than I ought to be at my age. Your see, and I suspect with some degree of surprise, what a project I have set my name to. I know your judgement did not favour it, and if you have not alter'd it, I lose the prospect of my best support. We are provided for a great circulation of our plan, as we have already printed 30,000 of the prospectus. I will not despair of your name am[ong]st others of respectability, upon whom I may

depend.[2] The World has read us in one title-page,
and where an opening offers for a liberal stand to
be made against anonymous illiberality, I will persuade myself you will be found am[ong]st the fore-
most in zeal as you are in talents. Ever afftly
Your's

R Cumberland

Source: Harvard.

1. The date is conjectured from reference to the "project" that
Cumberland has "set his name to," which is very likely the publication of *Pic Nic*, Colonel Henry Francis Greville's periodical
published beginning 8 January 1803.

2. Burgess was one of the contributors to *Pic Nic*. The periodical attempted to shed a new light on theatrical criticism which
was largely laudatory because the press depended on the theaters
for advertizing. *Pic Nic* attacked the deterioration of theatrical
productions caused by the monopolies held by Drury Lane and Covent Garden.

CLVIII   Richard Sharp[1]   31 January 1803

Jan 31st. 1803 TWells

My Dear Friend

In your last favour you hinted at a probability of
our next Installment, which now stands for the 5th
of March next, being again procrastinated.[2] Let me
request you to tell me what your opinion now is on
that point, for I do not perceive that our property
has much encreas'd, tho our produce has been abundant. If Mr. Addington[3] is applied to for more time,
I presume he will grant it, our plea being so
strong, and our sufferings unredress'd.

I hope you enjoy your health: I beg to be kindly remember'd to Mr. Rogers,[4] when you see him.

Ever beleive me,
My Dear friend,
Most affecty and truly
Yours

R Cumberland

Source: Harvard.

1. Richard Sharpe (1759-1835) was a close friend of Cumberland whom the dramatist credits with suggesting to him that he write his *Memoirs* (II, 230).

2. There seems to have been difficulties in publishing on time. The issue for 5 March did appear.

3. Henry Addington (1757-1844), first Viscount Sidmouth, First Lord of the Treasury at this time. The Government had apparently pledged support for *Pic Nic* and its successor, *The Cabinet*, in exchange for favorable political articles. For this reason, Addington would have been impatient with delay in publication.

4. Samuel Rogers (1763-1855), a minor poet.

CLIX Sir James Bland Burgess After April 1803[1]

Thursday 1 o'Clock

I write to you, my dear friend, from Baylis's Den of Devils.[2] Witness the paper, on which I write. It was doubtful to me if the poor Cabinet[3] woud have been kept open, unless we put our hands to the work with activity; I did not hesitate to brush up my old brains for it's support. You will see I have new modell'd Napoleon's Feast, and soften'd its personality without sinking the little portion of vivacity, which belong'd to it. I have also sent in some prose, such as it is; and what is more to the pur-

pose, James Smith[4] has sent in an admirable Essay
with an Epigram in it of great merit. There are some
verses by Maddox,[5] that are very creditable to him
on the score of genius and originality, tho' not extremely correct and clear in their conception.

I am now on my way to Kemble,[6] and have your Manuscript between my waistcoat and my breast, with the
cause of the Author very warmly at my heart. I have
seen nothing of our friend Greville[7] since his writing me to give up the copy of his Appeal to the
Committee. I am anxious to hear from you about your
correspondence with Col. Dyke.[8] I understand from
Mr. Pugh, one of the firms who are Agents to Henry
Fry, that it is at the option of Mr. Lambe to make
good his purchace of Beauport or to desert it, if
he sees fit.[9] If he is a willing Purchaser he may
safely take it on it's title; if he is not, there is
a loop-hole to creep out of--But all this, no doubt
is better known to you, than to me or my informer. I
shoud be apt to conjecture that Mr. Lambe will consult the times, and avail himself of the occasion to
be off. How think you?

I can't say when I shall come down, but it will be
the first day that I can. Love to all around you. I
don't write by this post to Marianne.   Adieu! ever
Your's

R Cumd

Source: Harvard.

1. The date is determined from the fact that the periodical,
The Cabinet, a successor to Pic Nic, came into being in April
1803.

2. Probably a printer involved in producing Pic Nic or The Cabinet.

3. The Cabinet went through twelve issues before being abandoned in July.

4. James Smith (1775-1839), one of the anonymous contributors
to Pic Nic and The Cabinet.

5. Possibly Frederick More Maddox, the author in 1828 of the melodrama *Frederick the Great*.

6. John Philip Kemble (1757-1823), the actor and at this time a part owner of Covent Garden. Cumberland was probably bringing him Burgess's play, *The Rhodian*.

7. Colonel Henry Francis Greville, originator of *Pic Nic*.

8. Probably Colonel Dyke of the Coldstream Guards, the son of Sir John Dyke.

9. Henry Fry, Cumberland's friend and attorney. Burgess at this time sought successfully to purchase Beauport, in Battle, Sussex.

CLX Thomas Greene April [6 or 8] 1803[1]

My Dear Sir

Charles Cumberland[2] desires me to tell you that he writes by this post to Mr. Dunn to repeat to him, (what he has often repeated) his entire acquiescence in the propos'd refer[en]ce to You and Him of the trifles in dispute between him and Mr. Mathew.[3] He is not less persuaded than I am that what you decide will be strictly equitable.

It was a claim, as I understand it, started and pursued in such a stile and in such terms, as might well have led to a worse issue even than a lawsuit, if certain circumstances had not interven'd to divert it into the course it is now in.

I am quite asham'd to confess my long delay in executing your wishes with respect to our friend Romney, but in truth I am not in fault. To write without materials, whereupon to build any thing worthy the man, who is the object of the undertaking, is to me a most revolting task. The Memoirs of a celebrated Artist demand a review of his Works, I have no documents before me. The life of a man, whose habits were of that retir'd cast, which mark'd the character of Mr. Romney, is very unproductive of events, and the narrative must be uninteresting. Furnish'd as I am, I do not see the substance of ten pages in what is in my hands, for when I have said he was an eminent painter bothe in the historical and pourtrait branches, I have no proofs to refer to, nor any means of dilating upon the subject as a subject of Art. I must therefore put a paper out of my hands, known to be mine, of which I shoud be a-sham'd. I trust you will feel for me in this dilemma, and acknowledge it is not without reason that I shrink from the undertaking.

I am, my dear Sir, with unalterable esteem, Your very sincere and affect Servt

R Cumberland

Tuesday noon
TWs.

Source: Oxford, Bodleian Library, MS. Autogr. c. 9, fols. 155r–156v.

1. The letter is postmarked April [6 or 8 (illegible)] 1803. Cumberland's account of his friend, the painter George Romney (1734-1802), which is discussed below, appeared in *The European Magazine* for June 1803.

2. Charles Cumberland, the dramatist's third son.

3. Possibly a relative of General Mathew, whose daughter Charles married. The nature of the dispute is unknown. Thomas Greene (1769-1825), one of the mediators and the recipient of this letter was a friend of J. Mitford, editor of the *Gentleman's Magazine*. He was also a contributor to both the *Gentleman's* and *European* magazines. In his *Memoirs* (II, 214-215), Cumberland states that he published a short account of Romney in a "magazine" at the request of Mr. Green of Bedford Square.

CLXI Sir James Bland Burgess 26 June 1803[1]

My dear friend

I beg leave to say in confidence to you that I have no wish to turn out again upon such Propositions, as are now made; and I see the business of Volunteering in so different a light from what it was before we broke up, and am so perfectly unable to uphold the outgoings of the Corps at my own expence, that if the men are not resolute to stand forward and as a full company, I shall be most entirely content to stay at home.[2]

I trouble you with this private intimation, lest your friendship shoud be betray'd into recommendatory measures upon the idea that my wishes point to new engagements. Not one of the Company coud be cover'd from the levy, as no exemptions take place in Corps accepted posterior to the 16th of this month. You will hint as much of this as you see fit to Knight[3] for his government.

Greville[4] is more wrong-headed than I gave him credit for. I think as you do that he will attempt to go on; Herries[5] saw him this morning, and it was then his purpose; He means to see him again before we meet this night at Hatchard's; I don't expect Greville will come. I shall correctly follow you step for step, whether it be to go on, or to give over. With Greville I cannot act any more than you can, so it is no compliment to say I am as you are in that connection. I will take care not to commit you in the slightest degree; I think myself bound in common with the amiable Smiths to the twelve papers, guarantee'd by Government.[6] Beyond that, my answer to any speculation will be simply, that I will do as Sir J[ame]s Burges does.

My heart overflows with love to Marianne, bless her and kiss her for me.

Ever your's

R Cumberland

Source: Harvard.

1. This letter is dated by reference to Cumberland's letter of 27 June 1803 which describes the results of the meeting mentioned here.

2. "The patriotic volunteers found, therefore, that when they rushed to help their country, they were coldly received, their expense allowances reduced, and a pike at most put into their hands. Not unnaturally there were loud cries against such ineptitude" (Watson, *The Reign of George III*, p. 416). Cumberland did, however, re-form his corps of volunteers.

3. Probably Peppard Knight, at one time Major of the Fourth Foot Regiment. He was appointed an inspecting field officer of yeomanry and volunteer corps on 13 October 1803 with the temporary rank of Lieutenant Colonel.

4. Colonel Henry Francis Greville, founder of *The Cabinet*, which he apparently wished to continue.

5. John Herries (1778-1855).

6. James and Horace Smith. *The Cabinet* contained a number of political papers favorable to the Government. This seems to have guaranteed twelve issues.

CLXII Sir James Bland Burgess 27 June 1803

Tuesday Morning

My most dear friend

We had a meeting last Night, at which Mr. Greville[2] attended, and signified his intention of carrying the Cabinet[3] on upon his own account, and at his own risque. He brought an Irish man with him, who wrote the Essay in the last No sign'd N., who seems likely to be his chief coadjutor. With the ensuing Number therefore we conclude: It was the sense of The Committee to fill it up on the Spot, and it is full. Combe is dismiss'd from being Editor,[4] Mr. Herries[5] is exonerated from any future pledge on the part of Government; and thus this poor misguided Gentleman has quitted his best hold, and thrown himself upon new friends and new Chimaeras, which can only lead him into fresh disappointments. He does not visit me, so I have no opportunity of speaking my sentiments, or offering my advice.

A word more with regard to the Volunteers—I wish to be honourably excus'd from ingaging in that service; It is not only in itself a service now no longer usefull to the Country, or desirable to the Undertakers of it—but also, since I wrote to Mr. Knight,[6] I must say to you in confidence and secrecy, that I find that the times and my circumstances will dictate to me such a reform, as will make a residence in Tunbridge Wells no longer prudential for me; I must break up and remove.[7] The consideration of my most beloved Marianne, and the charge of the dear Children[8] are what occupy my thoughts, and where to fix them is the arduous question. If I betake myself to a distant solitude, I am lost to all the solace of society, or the aids of friendship; I am buried before death: If I settle them in London under those circumstance that close oeconomy will impose, what will be the situation of my amiable daughter? Shoud I put her fortitude to such a proof? Yet London itself, or a nearer access to London than Tun[bridge] Wells, seems to be the only alternative, which is properly at my choice; for it is to London I must look, and thither I must resort for occasions, that cannot be dispens'd with. The Badcocks have a house at Leatherhead, and it is about to be vacant; I coud not have a better landlord than my own Grandson: It is a suggeston worth attending to. If I were to fix in London, I know no House like Dilly's,[9] but that I have no grounds to suppose attainable. I confide these melancholy meditations to your friendly bosom; I have not nerves just now to write them to Marianne—but I request of you to impart them to her, (*and her only*) in your own tender and considerate manner. It is for her, and in her that I live: I know her constancy of mind, but I woud fain mix as much comfort with her lot as I can, and I wish to receive her counsel and advice;

that from all the situations now before us, she might choose that, to which she coud best reconcile her feelings. I know she will quit the Wells without regret, since you are going, and a certain family at my gate are come:[10] I also know her generous nature will direct her to consult my health, and am prepar'd to expect her remonstrance against London; but I beleive wherever my mind woud be easiest, my health woud be most secure; and to put my mind at peace, she must point out that station, to which she coud be best reconcil'd. Whilst Lady Edw[ar]d[11] lives, she will always have that resource at times to resort to. I have now put the most sacred of all commissions into the hands of the most delicate and best of friends.

Need I say I am entirely Your's?

R Cumberland

Source: Harvard.

1. The letter is postmarked 28 June 1803. The previous Tuesday was the 27th.

2. Colonel Henry Francis Greville, the founder of *Pic Nic* and its successor *The Cabinet* during the first half of 1803.

3. *The Cabinet* was not continued beyond twelve issues.

4. William Combe (1742-1823) had edited both *Pic Nic* and *The Cabinet*. See his biography, *Dr. Syntax* by Harlan Hamilton (Kent State University Press, 1969).

5. John Charles Herries (1778-1855) was a link with the administration. Both *Pic Nic* and *The Cabinet* included pro-government articles. Under the Addington administration he became private secretary to Nicholas Vansittart (1766-1851), who was Secretary of the Treasury.

6. Probably Peppard Knight. See 26 June 1803, note 3.

7. Cumberland remained in Tunbridge Wells and participated in the formation on another corps of volunteers.

8. Probably the children of Cumberland's daughter, Sophia, and her husband, William Badcock.

9. Probably that of Charles Dilly (1739-1807), the publisher.

10. Burgess seems to have decided to settle permanently at Beauport.

11. Lady Edward Bentinck, Cumberland's daughter.

CLXIII   Sir James Bland Burgess   About July 1803[1]

My dear friend

Many thanks for your kind letter, the same to my beloved Marianne. I did not expect you, tho' the sight of you woud have been a cordial, but I was not selfish enough to wish it. It is now within a quarter of 4 o'clock, and I have not conjur'd up spirit enough to meet the Club, as you will not be there. I rejoice to hear of Beau-port.[2] You say nothing of Captain Burges,[3] whether he has join'd. I woud to Heaven Peggy[4] had join'd too, and fil'd in with the Nottinghams. So Charles stays another week at Ramsgate--Well! Merry may they be. I beg you will tender my best thanks to Colonel Gould.[5] This you can say, my friend, but how much I lament not to be where you are, and to be where I am, you cannot say. If I were on the Grampian hills,[6] I scarce coud be more lonely--but no matter--*The Mind is its own place.* Pray don't demean yourself to waste a word of anger or resentment upon Greville.[7] Such follies are but feathers in the scale of a substantial mind. I never knew a wise man right in arguing with a silly one. Kemble I know nothing of, but I predict duplicity;[8] I shoud be very happy to be wrong.--Tell my dear Child I think I may assure her, she will not fail to find me in her arms on Monday, or on Tuesday at the farthest. I stay because I woud be free to go to Ramsgate, and not necessitated to return. I know you will communicate this letter as soon as you have read it, that she mayn't think I have neglected her.

What is there at the Club that I shoud covet? Vincent[9] is not in Town. I shall walk over to the

Theatre. I understood from Greville he meant to have no XIII Number;[10] but He is no authority in his own case. Farewell!

Your's Ever

R Cumberland

Wednesday 4 oClock
Warren's.

There is a chance *I may* return this week.

Source: Harvard.

1. The date is approximated from the reference to Greville's not intending to have a thirteenth number of *The Cabinet,* which was discontinued about this time, after twelve issues.

2. Sir James Bland Burgess's residence in Battle, Sussex.

3. One of Burgess's sons.

4. Possibly Lady Margaret Fordyce, Burgess's sister.

5. Possibly the son of Sir Charles Gould (1726-1806).

6. A range of low mountains in Scotland.

7. Colonel Henry Francis Greville, founder of the Pic Nic Society and of the periodical, *Pic Nic.*

8. John Philip Kemble, who managed Drury Lane under Sheridan from 1788 until 1801, purchased a sixth share of Covent Garden and undertook its management in 1803. Reference here may be to an effort by Burgess to have one of his dramas produced there.

9. William Vincent, Dean of Westminster.

10. See Note 1, above.

CLXIV Robert William Elliston[1] 11 October 1803

Tun. Wells 11th Octr. 1803

Dear Sir

Mr. Thomas Younger, of Mrs. Baker's Comp[an]y of Comedians,[2] gives me a plea for troubling you with a Letter. He was promis'd a situation on the stage of Drury, but is put by till next season, and seems to drop all thoughts of the Engagement. Mr. Younger is a very sensible, well behav'd, worthy man; better educated than most in his line, and very capable of filling in a respectable manner parts of grave and sentimental Character, such as Aikin,[3] late of D[rury] Lane, us'd to personate. But perhaps his better recommendation to the Bath Stage woud be his Irishman, in which I have repeatedly seen him with pleasure and approbation. He makes famous battle in Brulgruddery, and the Wags of Windsor &c. &c.[4] If you want him, I can recommend him, and I dare say you will find him in all respects what I have describ'd. His direction is at Mr. Tassell's Mill Lane, Maidstone.

How much I lament the disappointment of my hopes for seeing you on the stage of Drury,[5] I need not attempt to say. It is their loss, and they will have cause to lament it. Pray tell me if you have any temporary engagement with them for some part of the season, and for which.

I have finish'd the Comedy[6] to my own satisfaction, at least, and as the part is pointedly compos'd for you, have so strong a wish that you shoud bring it out, that I am almost tempted to devote it to you upon the Bath stage, if I coud preserve a transferable right in it to act it at Drury Lane, where it has never been seen, and from which I still hold it, till I hear from you in consequence of this idea, telling me what terms and conditions I could make with your Proprietors upon the Idea above stated.

I am, Dear Sir,
Your sincere admirer
and faithful friend

R Cumberland

Source: Folger.

1. Conjectured from the fact that Elliston was acting at Bath during the 1803-1804 season and reference to his not appearing at Drury Lane.

2. Mrs. Baker headed a theatrical company at Tunbridge Wells. Thomas Younger apparently was not hired at Bath, nor did he appear at Drury Lane during the following season.

3. James Aickin (d. 1803) acted at Drury Lane from 1767 until he retired in 1800.

4. Brulgruddery was a character in George Colman's (1762-1836) play, *John Bull; or an Englishman's Fireside*, produced at Covent Garden on 5 March 1803 and, according to Genest, acted forty-eight times. Colman's afterpiece, *The Review; or the Wags of Windsor*, was first performed on 1 September 1800 at the Haymarket.

5. Elliston joined the Drury Lane company for the 1804-1805 season.

6. *The Sailor's Daughter*, produced at Drury Lane on 17 April 1804.

CLXV George Hardinge[1] 30 October 1803

Sunday 30th Octr. 1803

My dear Sir

Tho' I am conscious the praises, you have so elegantly bestow'd upon me, are not merited on my part, yet I confess I am delighted with them, and regard them as a sample of so much genius in both languages, that I really know not which I shoud give the preference to.

It was for your sake I was tempted to communicate them to Dr Knox,[2] tho' I ought to have blush'd for my vanity; but it is amongst the finest arts of a poet to elevate mean objects, and dignify an humble being, whom it is his pleasure to encourage. Had such a tribute ever been offer'd to me in my earlier years, I woud have been more carefull of my literary fame, and with your lines in my memory woud not have sent mine into the world with such precipitation and indifference.

I am now too old to speak of the Future, and therefore do not presume to make any promises for time to come, except that of faithfully remaining,

My dear Sir,
Your most oblig'd friend
& affect humble Servant

Richd Cumberland

George Hardinge Esqr. &c &c

Source: Yale.

1. George Hardinge, Esq. (1743-1816), author and jurist.
2. Likely Rev. Dr. Vicesimus Knox, master of Tunbridge School.

CLXVI   Unidentified   About 1803[1]

Tunb[ridg]e Wells Sunday 12 oCk

Dear Sir

I write by this post to my Attorney Mr. Spearing in Wallbrook No 19 and inclose Your Letter. I am an unpaid Author, and of course one of the Corps, whom the subject of your Communication does very much concern, for they are several hundred in default with me.

I shall be at my friend Dilly's[2] in Brunswick Court Queen's Square Holborn on Wednesday next. I wish you may make it convenient to call on me there on Thursday morning after your Breakfast. I shoud be glad to consult with you. My Dear Sir,

ever most faithfully Your's

Richd Cumberland

Source: Folger.

1. The approximate year is conjectured by reference to the Corps of Volunteers.

2. Charles Dilly (1739-1807) was one of Cumberland's publishers and a close friend.

CLXVII Sir James Bland Burgess Late 1803[1]

TWs. Tuesday 1 oClock
Incessant rain.

My dear Friend

I have been in expectation of a letter from you this long time, and just now Henry Fry tells me, what he had not told me before, that you wait to hear where I am. This is so natural, tho' I stupidly did not advert to it, that I take shame to myself, and sincerely ask your pardon. You are beginning now I hope to feel yourself settled, tho' I understand not completely furnish'd and arrang'd within doors: In a house like Beauport and a family like your's this cannot be accomplish'd very speedily;[2] but I trust I shall hear that as far as you have gone every thing is auspicious to your happiness and their's who belong to you--God grant it!

I am here solitary in a croud, for Marianne is gone to Ramsgate, and I have nothing left but the two boys,[3] and the favor of my friends, who ask me to their tables. We have abundance of rich and noble folks. Charles's house is taken by the Duke and Duchess of Rutland,[4] and Mrs. Wagan's by the Duke of Portl[an]d.[5] The Kenmores are very sociable, and the Jerninghams give me excellent french dinners and good music;[6] Here is all the old set besides and several new ones. Fothringham is with his wife at Cheltenham, and wearied out the patience of Jasper Sprange,[7] who opens his room for a ball this evening, tho the Clouds pour down torrents, and declare against all that cannot come in carriages. Capt H. Fry[8] is to do the honors vice MS.

So much for our foolish History, and now I want to hear what you are doing; how my lady proceeds in her department, and you in your's; in other words how the garden and the farm go on. Charles gave me a friendly call, and it pleas'd me much to see how stout and athletic he had become: I flatter myself you have every reason to rejoice that he has struck into the very line most suitable to his feelings and honorable to his character. I conclude you dedicate some portion of your time to composition, and I long to know what you are upon: Above all I wish to hear what is decided as to the Tragedy.[9] Dowton[10] says that Mr. Graham[11] is coming here for a day or two on his way to Portsmouth, where he has something to do about the sea-fencibles. How happy it woud make me if you coud step over and meet him, provided I am inform'd of the day, which he promises me I shall be. Charles writes word he will be here on the 19th, about which day I hope Lord Romney[12] will come his round of reviews: Woud not that be a good time for you to ride over, and look upon us, when he comes from General Mathews[13] to play his cricket match. Then also I can probably return with you and pay my son William a visit into the bargain.

I desire to be most gratefully and affectionately remember'd to Lady Burges, and that you will be so good to assure her that her Corps is not likely to disgrace their patroness, as I have every reason to

be gratified by their conduct and good order. My
best regards to the Young ladies and friend Wentworth.[14]

Ever, my dear Sir,
Truly and unalterably yr's

R Cumberland

Source: Harvard.

1. In Cumberland's letter of 27 June 1801, he mentions the departure of Burgess from Tunbridge Wells.

2. Burgess had apparently rented Beauport in previous years,
for Cumberland addressed a number of letters to him prior to
this.

3. Probably the children of Cumberland's son, William.

4. The house of Burgess's son Charles was rented to the Duke
and Duchess of Rutland, John Henry Manners (1778-1857) and Elizabeth Howard (1750-1825).

5. William Henry Cavendish Bentinck (1738-1809), the third Duke
of Portland.

6. Edward Jerningham was a member of the original Committee to
Form the Literary Fund of which Burgess was an officer from 1797
to 1802.

7. Possibly J. Sprange, the author of *The Tunbridge Wells
Guide*, 1780.

8. Henry Fry was Captain of one of the companies of Cumberland's Corps of Volunteers.

9. Probably Burgess's tragedy, *The Rhodian*.

10. Probably the actor, William Dowton.

11. Possibly Thomas Graham (1748-1843), a military man.

12. Charles Marsham (1793-1811) became Earl Romney in 1801.

13. Cumberland's son, Charles, married the daughter of General
Matthews.

14. Probably a member of the family of Charles Watson Wentworth
(1730-1782), the Marquis of Rockingham, and Frederick Thomas
Wentworth (d. 1799), who was Earl of Strafford 1791-1799. Burgess
had been married to the sister of Lord Wentworth, Elizabeth Noel,
who had died on 30 October 1778.

CLXVIII Sir James Bland Burgess   Probably 1803–1804[1]

Tuesday 6 oClock

My Dear Friend

I have staid this long before I coud bring myself
to say to you that I must decline the happiness I
had propos'd to myself of dining with you and our
friends tomorrow;[2] I was packt up and prepar'd but
having undergone more fatigue than my strength coud
bear yesterday, I am so rheumatiz'd and lumbago'd
today that I cannot think of undertaking a journey
to Town without more risque than I ought to undergo.
We had a day of rejoicing Yesterday, and I was from
morning till late at night upon my legs. Without
exaggeration I assure you my Volunteers perform'd to
admiration, nothing could exceed their firings of
all descriptions. In the place of illumination I
rais'd a contribution of meat and bread for the
poor, and this morning our butcher brought ten fat
Ewes at £28, with part of our subscription. I wish'd
for you most sincerely, as it was really a day of
triumph. As soon as I have recover'd my strength I
shall come to Town; at present I am quite unfit to
move, and beg you will present my respectfull apolo-
gies to the Club, assuring them truly of my most
sincere regret.

I am ever, my Dr. Sir,
most affecty your's

R Cumberland

Source: Historical Society of Pennsylvania.

1. The content of the letter suggests Sir James Bland Burgess
as its recipient, and the reference to the Volunteers suggests
late 1803 or early 1804.

302

2. Probably one of the regular meetings of the literary club of which Burgess and Cumberland were members.

CLXIX   Sir James Bland Burgess   Probably 1804-1805[1]

Sunday TWells

My dear friend

A few days ago, when I was in Town, I din'd tête à tête with Mr. Graham,[2] and took that opportunity to enquire into the proceeding relative to your tragedy of the Rhodian.[3] He spoke to me openly and I am persuaded with unreserv'd sincerity as to his opinion of that piece; which he said he had read three times through with encreas'd gratification and delight. That he consider'd it as a drama, that it would be his particular object to bring forward, if he had the power of selection, which at present rested with Mr. Sheridan,[4] who had treated author's productions with such neglect and indecision, as to have stopt all business, and effectually ruin'd all hopes of a successfull season, unless immediate measures were taken to wrest that office out of his hands, which if not done, he woud throw up all concern with the Theatre.

It woud be of little use to detail to you our whole conversation, but, as I am sure he did not know the intimacy that subsists between you and me, I have no hesitation in beleiving the respect he express'd for you, and the high opinion he gave of your Tragedy, were what he really and truly felt. I hope therefore you will not withdraw the peice in disgust, nor beleive that the delay in answering your offer proceeded from any negligence on the part of Graham, but merely from the circumstances above mention'd, so severely felt by all, who have concerns with D[rury] Lane.

Of this I am persuaded that if ever Mr. Graham has a voice in the choice of peices for representation, yours will be most cordially accepted, if you are so dispos'd, and will permit them to perform it.

I think it right to inform you of this, and I beleive you may depend upon what I have reported.

Henry Fry[5] has told you what I am about to do, and that I am on the point of migrating.[6] I forbear to say more on the subject, as I woud but vex your tranquility, but wish you to think no otherwise of me, but as one, who can never fail to be with unalterable esteem Your affectionate and faithfull

friend and servant

Richd Cumberland

Source: Harvard.

1. The year is identified by reference to Burgess' tragedy, *The Rhodian*, which Cumberland mentions in dated letters of that time.

2. Aaron Graham (1753-1818) became head of the management of Drury Lane in 1802.

CLXX   **George Cumberland[1]   23 January 1805**

Ramsgate 23d Janry 1805

Dear Cousin

Your favor after a circuit to Tun. Wells came to hand yesterday with its enclosure, the poem of my old Acquaintance De Salas, whose kind recollection of me is very flattering, and I beg you to present my thanks to Mr. Hill[2] for the communication of it.

It is true that I am in the decline of life, and more deeply sunk into it than you, yet as my age has

not so chill'd my zeal as to prevent me from standing forward in my Country's cause as Commandant of
one of the most respectable Corps in West Kent,[3] it
is plain that you and I think very differently about
the character of our Native Island, and that I regard *her Conduct to all Nations* by no means deserving of the terms you affix to it--*anti-christian and
unjust.*[4]

May you long enjoy the domestic tranquillity you
describe, and may reflection inspire you with juster
notions of the Country in which you live.

This is the sincere wish of Your affect Cousin

R Cumberland

Source: British Library.

1. George Cumberland was the descendant of a parallel line of
the Cumberland family, dating back four generations. The family
is traced in detail in *The Cumberland Letters*, ed. Clementina
Black (London, 1912), which deals with the correspondence of
George and his brother, Richard Dennison.

2. Possibly George Hill (1750-1819), who authored many works at
Edinburgh, notably *Lectures in Divinity*, ed. Alexander Hill,
1833.

3. Cumberland commanded a corps of volunteers.

4. A reply to this letter by George Cumberland, defending his
position, is in the British Library.

CLXXI   George Cumberland   30 January 1805[1]

Ramsgate 30 Jany

Dear Cousin

I am very much oblig'd to you for your admirable
good letter, not only as it clears away every thing

that gave me pain in your former favour, but as it justly reprooves me for a flippancy, which I am now asham'd of, and for which I beg your pardon.

I shall never cease to express what I feel, but I cannot fail to acknowledge conviction, whenever it meets me.

I must say at the same time that I see nothing in the public character or conduct of our Country, that merits reprehension, but on the contrary much for an Englishman to be proud of; and as to our proceedings towards Spain, it appears to me that they are perfectly justified by the Declaration.[2] I write in great haste, but woud not miss the post.[3]

Affecty Yrs.

R. Cumberland

Source: The British Library.

1. The year is determined by reference Cumberland's previous letter to George Cumberland on 23 January 1805.

2. Regarding Spain, Watson observes: "As for Spain, she was Napoleon's ally in all but name. In October 1804 Captain Moore with *The Indefatigable* and three other frigates fell in with Spanish frigates escorting the main Spanish treasure convoy from the American mines to Cadiz. The escort was sunk and all the bullion seized; this without declaration of war. This action, reminiscent of Drake was justified by the claim that the gold would have ended in the service of France. It helped to drive Spain into open war" (*The Reign of George III*, pp. 422-423).

3. A conciliatory reply from George Cumberland is in the British Library.

CLXXII   George Lackington   Before 24 March 1805[1]

Dear George

It strikes me from your calculation that you put me on a compass, that will nearly, if not quite, embrace the whole, or as much, of my life, as I may chuse to give, and that one full Quarto may comprise it all.[2] In the mean time, tho' your proof page has not one line too many, it has more (take notice) than Hayley's 3d Vol.[3] It occurs to me that you shoud put two Guineas on your book, and to do that with an easy conscience, you may give a print of the great Bish[o]p Cumberland[4] in front, where it begins with his memoirs, another of Dr. Bentley,[5] where I begin to treat of him, and a third of Me opposite the page that records my birth. I have fine prints of both my Ancestors above mention'd.

If they are in, I won't strut into Company before my superiors. Turn this in your thoughts, and calculate if ½ a guinea per Copy won't pay you well for 2 prints.

Your's

R Cumberland

I say again and again 1250 are too few.

Source: Harvard.

1. The date is determined by material in this letter referred to in Cumberland's to Lackington of 24 March 1805.

2. The first edition of the *Memoirs* was in one volume (1806), but was expanded with a supplement into two volumes in 1807. George Lackington (1768-1844) was its publisher.

CLXXIII   George Lackington   24 March 1805[1]

My dear George

You rightly conclude that I am sincerely interested in your happiness, and of course rejoic'd to hear that you have so fair a prospect before you in the choice you have made of a friend and partner for life.

Remember, George, that the felicity of the married state turns upon very small circumstances in the outset of it, and is frequently overthrown before the contracting parties are come to a right understanding of each others tempers and dispositions. Every body has some habits and humours, which education, prejudice or custom have impos'd upon them, and these oftentimes take such hold of the mind as to become what may be call'd second nature. In the delicacy of managing and reconciling either these habits to our own, or our own to them, the whole art of living happily with husband or wife consists. Temper will do everything; there is a province for the woman, another for the man; these shoud be kept sacred and distinct. They cannot be invaded without discontent. I am persuaded your judgem[en]t does not want to be advis'd of this, yet in good will I offer you the result of my experience.

I shall be in Town on Tuesday, and at Warren's[2] if he can receive me; I shall stay till Sunday, and go to T[unbridge] Wells for a few days. I wish you coud call on me on Tuesday evening at 7 oClock, and bring the first quire, which I want to make a little addition to before it goes to press. My picture will come up to you by the Hoy directed to you in Finsbury Square. Of B[isho]p Cumberland and Dr. Bentley we will talk further,[3] for if you resolve ag[ain]st 2 quires, I don't see why you shoud take that expence upon you: One print will be quite sufficient, and I am anxious that you shoud make so good a bargain, that you may consider it as my wedding favour.

I begin to fear that I shall not get out of the way of your press, if it follows me so fast; but you will hardly publish in the Summer recess, and I must not disgrace my work by overeagerness to conclude it. It must be done well, or I shall not act justly either by you or myself. Adieu!

All joy attend you and your bride, to whom present my best regards.

Your's very faithfully

R Cumberland

Ramsgate. Sunday

Source: Michigan.

1. This letter is postmarked 25 March 1805. The preceding Sunday was the 24th.

2. The hotel where Cumberland habitually stayed.

3. This refers to the inclusion of pictures of Cumberland's forebears in his *Memoirs*.

CLXXIV Sir James Bland Burgess 29 March 1805

Lond March 29th 1805

My dear friend

I have your favour of the 24th, for which I thank you, but am sorry to hear you do not meditate a trip to Ramsgate.

I write to our friend OGrady,[1] and hope he will show you my letter. I have been told that my last remonstrance was angrily and contemptuously receiv'd. I hope he won't treat this in the like way, and if he is inclin'd so to do, I trust you will advise him better. I shall look for him on Sunday evening, or by noon on Monday, as we have a march to make, and must start early.

I left Capt. Burges well,[2] when I came from Ramsgate, tho' he had had an attack of his Ague, which

Lord Edward[3] charm'd away with a plaister on his wrist, a recipe of Lady Stamford's.[4]

I very much fear I cannot come to you this time, as I must return to Town for a few days in my progress homewards; besides, if OGrady slights my summons, I shoud not chuse to discuss the point under your roof; that must be refer'd to my Commanding Officer.[5]

I am not at all surpriz'd that you are writing a Comedy with music, because I am perswaded you can accomplish it in both it's branches. I wish to hear of the Tragedies;[6] I conceive Cook's benefit cannot be far off.[7]

I shall bring my memoirs down to the time of writing them, but my difficulty is how to comprise them in one quarto Volume.

Marianne has not been well of late, but I hear a better account of her: The Children are in perfect health. William outward bound on foreign service; Fanny at School in London, and Jonathan going to Mr. Kemble after the Easter holidays.[8]

My best respects ever attend your excellent Lady, with kind remembrances to all your family I am, My dear friend, ever truly and affecty your's

R Cumberland

Source: Harvard.

1. This letter has not been found. O'Grady's identification and his role among the Volunteers is not clear. He may have been Cumberland's adjutant. See 26 August 1805.

2. One of Burgess's sons.

3. Probably Lord Edward Bentinck, Cumberland's son-in-law.

4. Lord Stamford (1737-1819) had been married on 28 May 1763 to Henrietta Bentinck (1736-1827).

5. Probably the Earl of Romney, the Lord Lieutenant of the County, through whom Cumberland first received "His Majesty's commission" to command the Volunteers with the rank of Major Commandant (*Memoirs*, II, 290).

310

6. In his *Dramas*, 2 vols., 1807, Burgess includes a number of
serious plays, among them the tragedy *The Knight of Rhodes*. No
tragedy of his appears to have been produced, however.

7. George Frederick Cooke (1756-1812). Genest does not indicate
the date of his benefit in the spring of 1805.

8. Marianne was Cumberland's eldest daughter, not yet married.
The children are probably those of William Badcock, who had married Cumberland's daughter, Sophia. His grandson Badcock, is mentioned in 25 August 1805 as having written to Cumberland from
Cork about being about to leave for a cruise "off the Western
Isles." Jonathan may have been undertaking a theatrical career
with John Philip Kemble, then at Covent Garden. See *Memoirs*, II,
339. Badcock had been an actor.

CLXXV Sir James Bland Burgess 26 August 1805[1]

Warren's Hotel
Monday

My dear friend

I had a tedious passage by sea of 48 hours with a
foul wind, which is a way it has of being always in
my teeth. We rashly adventur'd through the Narrows
at low tide in a dark night, when we coud not see
the buoys, and got ashore upon the Land call'd The
Spaniard. Our situation was unpleasant, to say no
worse of it, and I do not feel ambitious to encounter it again.

I am setting off for Ramsgate tomorrow and have
collected nothing in Town, that can either inform
you or amuse. The Naval Manoeuvres of our Enemy seem
to puzzle us, and opinions here seem prevalent for
invasion; the majority expecting it in Irel[an]d,
and some, but not many, on our own shores.[2]

OGrady[3] is order'd to join his Skeleton Corps of
the 3d batt[alio]n 60th foot in the Isle of Wight: I
tried to hold him a little longer at his 8 p[e]r

day, but coud not obtain leave. I am now striving to
get George Fry[4] into the pay of Adjutant, and do not
despair of success. I have waded through my onerous
memoirs to page 600 ms, and begin to descry land.

I long to see your Opera and hear your music;[5]
When will you come to us? Tis easier for you to move
than for me upon many good and substantial reasons;
yet when I come next to the Wells, I will with God's
leave present myself at your Castle gate.

I cannot wonder that at the present moment you
prefer to keep your dramas under lock and key. Elliston[6] does not hold the station, that I wish'd him
to be found in; he is vain, intemperate and over
self-sufficient. Master Betty has an early engage-
m[en]t at D[rury] Lane at 100 per night, whilst Harris, more wise, has contracted with him for half the
surplus after 300 is deducted: He'll beggar one and
balk them both.[7]

I agree with you in your opinion of L[or]d Melville's speech:[8] He has hurt himself by it very
much; the sketch he read to me in manuscript was
very difficult. What induc'd him to depart from it
so widely I cannot devine. I have only to assure you
not a syllable of it was mine.

I have a letter from my grandson Badcock,[9] who is
come in with the Loire to Cork, and is going out for
a three months convoy and cruize off the Western
Isles.

I look'd for a line from you, but none has arriv'd.

My best respects to Ly Burges--
I am oblig'd to conclude in haste
but in truth most affecty your's

R Cumberland

Source: Harvard.

1. This letter is postmarked 26 August 1805, which was a Mon-

day.

2. On the threat of an invasion of England in the summer of 1805, Watkins notes that Napoleon's plan to invade England "was completely destroyed by the movements of Austria and Russia. As late as 3 August 1805 when the emperor heard that Villeneuve was back at Vigo, he at once ordered him to put to sea again, to liberate more ships from the blockade, and to hasten to clear the British from the Channel." However, within a week Austria entered the war against France, and Napoleon abandoned plans to invade England (*The Reign of George III*, p. 426).

3. The context of the letter suggests that he might have been Cumberland's adjutant.

4. Probably a relative of Henry Fry, Cumberland's attorney.

5. No play by Burgess was produced at this time. A comic opera of his, *Tricks upon Travellers*, was produced at the Lyceum Theatre on 9 July 1810.

6. Robert William Elliston.

7. William Henry West Betty (b. 1791), a boy actor, who, after his first performance at Belfast in 1803, was recognized as a prodigy and was able to achieve rapid fame and fortune. He appeared at both drury Lane and Covent Garden during the 1804-1805 season. After a few years he left the stage and in 1808 attended Christ's College at Cambridge. When he returned to the stage in 1812, it was with only minor success.

8. Henry Dundas (1742-1811), first Viscount Melville, who was First Lord of the Admiralty.

9. Cumberland's daughter, Sophia, had married William Badcock. See 29 March 1805.

CLXXVI Sir James Bland Burgess 3 September 1805[1]

Sep. 3d. Ramsgate

My dear friend

My diary is so barren of events, that I have had nothing to communicate, and of course have not written to you. I do nothing without doors, and care little about what is passing. A few pages comprise the labour of the day, and the memoirs creep towards their conclusion, having touched p. 85. The printer of the Octo edition drives on a merry pace, and will be upon my heels, if I do not speedily wind up.

In the meanwhile I am going to my old friend Higgs in Suffolk,[2] and the gallant Alderman Sir Wm Curtis[3] carries me in his private Yacht by long sea to Woodbridge, or perhaps Harwich, well victuall'd and well man'd. My daughter Marianne goes with me and takes faithfull Mary and my little grandchild Emma. We are off, (Deo volente) on Tuesday next, and have only to hope no french row-boat will spoil our party.

I have been but poorly, and do not rally as a veteran shoud; but my spirits do not flag, and my head is not quite worn out. We have abundance of fine folks and fine singers, but I am like old Barzillai;[4] yet I am well pleas'd to listen to the inimitable Miss Guns, and they are but two doors from me.

I beg my respects to Lady Burges, and be pleas'd to tell her that when I turn'd out the Corps, whom she has honour'd with her patronage, not a single man hesitated to stand by their Colours, and towards the latter end of Oct[obe]r I purpose to be at The Wells, and work out my thirteen days, when I hope we shall meet, if life is granted to me.

Marianne joins in best compts to the ladies and you. Beleive me ever faithfully and truly yr's

Rd Cumberland

Source: Harvard.

1. The year is conjectured by the date of publication of the *Memoirs,* 1806.

2. Reverend John Higgs, a friend of Cumberland since they were rivals for a fellowship at Cambridge in their youth. Cumberland notes that it was at Higgs' residence that he completed his epic poem, *Calvary,* and wrote the "Supplement" to his *Memoirs* (*Mem-*

314

oirs, II. 397.

3. William Curtis, Baronet (1752-1829).

4. A benefactor and favorite of David. He rejected David's invitation to accompany him to Jerusalem because of his old age (2 Kings XIX, 31-38).

CLXXVII Sir James Burgess About 18 September 1805[1]

My dear friend

I had the pleasure of hearing of you by my friend Captain Bates, who was highly gratified by the visit he paid you at Beauport, and the very kind reception he met with there. He is a good and amiable man, and well deserves the countenance you are so kind to shew him. I must go to Town in a very few days, and if I can possibly come on to you thro' The Wells, I certainly will wait upon you and your Lady, whom I can never cease to love and honour, whilst I have life. I hope you will nurse up a few figs for me, for Bates says you abound in fruit and all good things--May your abundance never fail; and may health and content continue to you all those blessings, which alone can give a relish to your comforts!

I live as I have long done; in my stile and habits of life there is no change: I enter very few doors but of the house at the Corner, and there I never fail to meet a filial welcome.[2]

I think I write more than ever, and of course worse than ever, but I do not court company, and for exercise and fresh air I have little taste and no great call: A turn upon the pier satisfies me; and as far as Marianne can accompany me, so far, and no further, I am well pleas'd to walk: She is however to my great comfort wonderfully better, and upon her unceasing attentions and truly filial care of me I depend for every thing like happiness, that I have

now to look to. Bentinck is with his father and
mother, and Captain Thompson[3] is gone to Hampshire,
where his Mother lies sick and in a dying state.
Meyers is at present inmate in the Corner House, and
there is good harping, and much harmony both mental
and instrumental.

If I live to see you I wish you woud prepare yourself by a revision of our Exodiad[4] to put that work
in further train, for I am now within two or three
days of closing up my book, which upon the printed
copy has now turn'd above five hundred pages, which
is a full hundred more than by my written contract I
engag'd for, and my publishers in consequence have
put another half guinea upon the selling price,
which to the gentleman purchaser is now to be two
guineas. Whether I have done only what your partiality will excuse, or what in fact your Judgement will
approve of, I cannot presume to say. I am writing
without books, for I have none about me, but I have
descended into times, where memory wants no written
aids.

The sight of the Downs has been wonderfull and is
still a wood of Masts; in short the whole sea is a-
live, and my windows embrace one of the greatest
spectacles that can be conceiv'd. We have lost our
friendly West Kents, and the regiments of Perthshire, Lanerk and Renfrew are now quarter'd with us
and about us: Lord Mansfield[5] commands the Perth,
and lodges within a few doors of us. The 13th Dra-
g[oons], who live with us as friends, are on the
wing, being under orders to be ready. I find OGrady[6]
has been with you; I take for granted he has join'd,
if not remember me to him--Above all to your domestic Circle and beleive me ever

Your affectionate and oblig'd

R Cumberland

Marianne sends her best regards.

316

Source: Harvard.

1. This letter is postmarked 18 September 1805.
2. Cumberland's son, William, a naval officer, resided with his wife Eliza at Tunbridge Wells. Edward Bentinck and Cumberland's daughter, Elizabeth, also were frequently at Tunbridge Wells. The "corner house" may have belonged to either of them.
3. Captain Norborne Thompson.
4. Serious work on this poem began after the publication of Cumberland's *Memoirs* in 1806.
5. David William Murray (1777-1840), Earl of Mansfield.
6. See 26 August 1805. O'Grady had been ordered to join the Third Battalion, 60th Foot Regiment.

CLXXVIII Sir James Burgess After 18 September 1805[1]

Sunday TWells

Your letter, my dear Friend, afforded me very sincere gratification, and I thank you most heartily for it. In my solitude, where the spectacle of a beloved Child,[2] sickening in the flower of her age is ever in my eye, and weighing on my heart, the affectionate remembrances of a kind friend come with encreased delight to my relief.

I have been closely engaged upon our Exodiad,[3] and I tell you without flattery that the abundant supply of your Genius gives me entire satisfaction, and encourages me to work upon the poem with spirit. I have made a progress in the first book of about 300 lines, meaning to make a complete copy according to my own idea in the manner you have done, and not to touch your's with my pen in the meanwhile. From the two manuscripts we may hereafter agree upon our corrected copy for the press, and this I conceive will be as severe an ordeal as we can put our joint production to. You have done admirably, and when I come to sift your work I find very little but here and there a redundancy, and sometimes, but not often, a prosaic phrase. To lift therefore now and then, and to compress has been my attempt, and I find so much excellent matter, that I really think the poem, as it clears itself, comes out beyond all my hopes.

I am highly flatter'd by your approbation of The Observer.[4] The Story and Diary of Chaubert is to a single word my own, invented and written, and I can say the same of every Chapter in the six volumes. The story of Nicolas Pedrosa is more suspicious than Chaubert and the Reviewers charge it upon me as a positive translation from a Spanish author; It is every syllable and every thought my own--so is that of the Portuguese, who is tried by the Inquisition.

Eliza[5] has written some beautifull airs, and longs to sing them to you. Marianne sends her best regards. Present me to your excellent lady--Love to Cha[rle]s and the family of Ladies.

I am ever your's

R Cum.

Source: Harvard.

1. The date is conjectured from his reference to revising *The Exodiad.* The preceding letter, postmarked 18 September 1805, refers to their returning to *The Exodiad* project.

2. Marianne, his eldest daughter.

3. The first part of *The Exodiad* was published in 1807.

4. Cumberland's *The Observer* was published in its final form in six volumes in 1798.

5. Eliza was the wife of Cumberland's son, William.

CLXXIX **Sir James Bland Burgess 4 October 1805[1]**

At Capt Camfield's
Friday morning.

My Dear Friend

I beg to return you and Lady Burges my best acknowledgements for your kind reception, and the pleasant days I pass'd with you at Beauport.

Yesterday was a day of infinite fatigue, for from five in the morning till four in the afternoon I pass'd most of the hours under a canopy of water, incessantly pouring down upon us. The whole Corps, (Camfield's[2] company inclusive) were drawn up at six, and waited till near ten for Lady Buggen's funeral,[3] which we follow'd for some short distance on the London Road; After which we attended the body of one of our own Grenadiers to the grave at Speldurst, wet to the skin and ankle deep in mud.

I din'd and slept in this comfortable house last night, and am alive and very little the worse for work, tho' I can acknowledge a few remembrancers in the back and head, for I am not as I have been. My new Adjutant[4] gave me great satisfaction, and as he is highly acceptable to the men, I think he will prove so to me.

I have fixt upon Thursday the 24th for my Inspection, when, with God's leave, I shall attend, and take my departure for Ramsgate: Let me therefore suggest to you a partnership in a post chaise, which you will have much use for at Ramsgate. I will accord myself to your route, and if you prefer to meet me any where rather than at TWells, I will be govern'd by your choice.

I have written very fully to Ramsgate about our German friends, and have no doubt of their receiving a hospitable welcome. You will answer this to me at Warren's Hotel, for I shall leave the Wells on Sunday.

Ever affecty Your's

R Cumberland

Source: Harvard.

1. The date is determined by reference to Lady Buggin's funeral. She died on 29 September 1805. The following Friday was 4 October.
2. Camfield headed one of the four companies that at this time made up Cumberland's Corps of Volunteers.
3. The *Annual Register for 1805* records that at Tunbridge Wells, the lady of Sir George Buggin of Great Cumberland place died and that her remains were interred by torch-light at St. Dunstan's in the East (p. 500).
4. Probably George Fry. See 26 August 1805, note 4.

CLXXX   Sir James Bland Burgess   Fall of 1805[1]

Warren's Hotel
Tuesday

My dear friend

I must be at T[unbridge] Wells the day after to-morrow and be inspected on friday; I shall therefore be happy to meet a letter from you there, and much more happy coud I meet you than your letter. I shall return through London to my long-deserted home.

It occurs to me that the moment is seasonable for the production of your Rhodian at Covent Garden, and I cannot form my mind to suspect that it's merits woud not command acceptance. It woud be a fine tragedy to oppose to the young Roscius at D[rury] Lane.[2] What can prevent your stepping up to Town, and consulting Kemble[3] on the subject? It will also fall in with your first Wednesday at the Club, and then we

320

may go down together to Ramsgate.

I have devoted every leisure minute to The Exodiad, and am making a corrected Copy of the Two first
books with very many alterations, which I hope you
will approve of. It has seiz'd me very strongly, and
I flatter myself I am doing well.

I hope you have put the last hand to the Rhodian.
That Composition will do you high honour. The Memoirs are very near the birth, and the Engravings are
said to be very good:[4] I have reserv'd proofs for a
few dear friends like you.

My best regards to Lady Burges, and your Circle.
Adieu, Ever your's

R Cumbd.

Source: Harvard.

1. The year is conjectured from both the reference to the appearance of Master Betty (the young Roscious) and to the near
completion of the *Memoirs*, which were published in 1806.

2. *The Knight of Rhodes* was not acted, but published in Burgess's *Dramas*, 2 vols., 1817, Master Betty had an early engagement at Drury Lane in the fall of 1805. See 26 August 1805. His
first appearance that season at Drury Lane was on 16 December,
and at the rival theatre Covent Garden on 23 December (Genest,
VII, 704, 716).

3. John Philip Kemble of Covent Garden.

4. The engravings of his great-grandfather Bishop Richard Cumberland of Petersburgh and of his grandfather Richard Bentley,
which, in addition to his own portrait, were published in the
Memoirs.

CLXXXI   Sir James Bland Burgess   Late 1805 (1)[1]

My most kind friend

I have just time to request you will have the great goodness to send me three bottles of your Hock by the Coach for Mr. Badcock, who is here—and can swallow nothing else. I have one left and it has chear'd him—He is all but dead.

Marianne is better.

Ever yrs

R Cum

Wednesday.

Source: Harvard.

1. The date is conjectured from the reference to the illness of William Badcock, the husband of Cumberland's second daughter, Sophia. He died early in 1806.

CLXXXII Sir James Bland Burgess Late 1805 (2)[1]

Tuesday 2 oClock

My Dear friend

Accept my sincere thanks for the Old Hocke,[2] which is every thing I coud wish, except in quantity much above my wants, for this poor exhausted dying mortal can apply to it but very few times more, before his lips are clos'd. Marianne,[3] I bless God, is surprizingly recover'd, and I now seriously perswade myself she will be completely reestablish'd, as every symptom, that threaten'd danger and even death, is so wonderfully withdrawn, that it is next to a miracle what Pullen and his steel-pills have effected.

I am much pleas'd with your Jewish researches,[4] and shall be curious to see the translation of the passage. I have not got Eusebius, but somewhere or other I have met with the names of Jamones and Mambres, which are familiar to me.[5] I shall be thankful for your kind Extracts.

Nothing gives me greater pleasure than what you tell me of the affair of the Literary fund, that the King sees your conduct in the right light, and of course estimates that of your opponents as they ought to be estimated.[6] What can be more acceptable than to elect Mr. Bernard, if he acceeds to it? It is highly proper and becoming of the Club.[7] I hope it will be proposed. As you know my excuse I pray of you to tender it on my behalf to the Gentlemen assembled.

I give you hereby joy of your Norfolk purchase: I will execute your message to Henry Fry.[8]

We are welcoming the good news in our noisy way of being merry. Lord Boyne[9] and I have a military Council about our Gala which is to take place on friday next, D[e]o V[olent]e. How I long for you!

My best respects to your excellent Lady, and my best wishes to Charles and Arile.[10]

Ever most affecty

R Cumberland

Source: Harvard.

1. The date is determined by reference to the dying Badcock.

2. In a previous letter, Cumberland had requested three bottles of Old Hocke for his dying son-in-law, William Badcock.

3. Cumberland's youngest daughter.

4. In regard to their joint poem, *The Exodiad*.

5. Eusebius of Caesarea (c.350), an early Biblical scholar; Jannes and Jambres (Mambres) were traditional Jewish names for the two magicians mentioned in Exodus 8-13. See also II Timothy, 3:8.

6. Originally proposed in 1773, The Literary Fund was established on 18 May 1780 to aid poor authors and their widows and

children. The King provided a house for its permanent location in 1805. At this time there was some controversy about the details of incorporating the fund, which did not take place until 1818. Burgess was an officer of the Corporation from 1797 to 1802. See *Royal Corporation of the Literary Fund*, London, 1847.

7. Thomas Bernard (1750-1818), who wrote on the treatment of the poor and who was made a member of the Club. His biographer, the Reverend James Baker (*The Life of Sir Thomas Bernard, Baronet*, London, 1819) notes: "In this year [1808] he was also occupied with another plan of a different nature to any thing in which he had hitherto been engaged--the formation of a new Club. He was a Member of a Club comprising many of the first literary characters in this country, which met once every month at the Thatched House" (p. 87). Baker goes on to indicate that the new Club prohibited gambling, drinking and party politics. It was ultimately successfully established in January 1809 and called *The Alfred*.

8. Cumberland's close friend and attorney.

9. Gustavus Hamilton, eldest son of Frederick Hamilton, who succeeded to the peerage of Frederick's father, Gustavus (1639-1723). See Lodge's *Irish Peerage*, V, pp. 174-178.

10. Burgess's son and wife.

CLXXXIII Sir James Bland Burgess   1 November 1805[1]

Warren's friday

My dear friend

I must write to you again to say you are not correctly inform'd as to my tendering any thing to Mr. Harris,[2] which coud be put into competition with your drama,[3] or coud in any degree bias his Judgement with respect to it.

My offer was simply of an old Comic opera call'd the Sicilian Banditti, and founded on The Armorer,[4] which he no sooner read with one hand than he return'd to me with the other--So that nothing coud stand more clear of your course than mine.

I am indeed getting up a scrap of a thing to be sung and recited after Nelson's funeral,[5] but it is only gone to Cov[en]t Garden because D[rury] Lane coud not take it in.

I must be at T[unbridge] Wells on Tuesday, and shall be inspected on Thursday.

I write in great haste, but am ever your's

Affecty

R Cumberland

Source: Harvard.

1. The date is determined by reference to the piece regarding Nelson's funeral, perfeormed on Thursday, 7 November 1805. The preceding Friday was the 1st.

2. Thomas Harris, manager at Covent Garden.

3. Probably *The Knight of Rhodes*, not acted, but published in Burgess' *Dramas*, 2 vols., 1817.

4. "The Sicilian Banditi" as a version of "The Armorer" is not extant. A text of "The Armorer" (Covent Garden, 4 April 1793), a musical version of Cumberland's "Richard II," is available in manuscript in the Larpent Collection at the Huntington Library.

5. "An Occasional Attempt (A Melodramatic Piece) To Commemorate the Death and Victory of Lord Viscount Nelson," was licensed on 8 November 1805 for performance at Drury Lane. It was, however, performed according to Genest (VII, 714) at Covent Garden on 7 November 1805. The manuscript is in the Larpent Collection.

CLXXXIV Sir James Bland Burgess 5 November 1805[1]

Thursday. Warren's Hotel

My dear friend

I shoud have been happy if my proposal had accorded with your conven[ien]ce, but if we ultimately meet, my disappointment as to the means will be the less.

I am concern'd to find that 1400 of our Hanoverians embark'd yesterday from Ramsgate pier, and 1500 this day from the same spot. The whole amount in the course of the week will be 7000.[2] Of this I am inform'd by a letter from Marianne just now receiv'd.

I am persuaded your remarks upon our friend Todd's life of Spenser are strictly just, but I have not read him, and only glanc'd upon that passage, in which he names your poem.[3] By imitation he can merely allude to the stanza, and as that is peculiar to Spenser, or at least not so general as blank verse or the rhiming couplet, he was I suppose led to the expression, which if it convey'd any idea but that, woud be perfectly misapplied. I never read Turner's three first volumes, which I understand are in point of stile by no means equal to the 4th, lately publish'd, and which seems to me a work of such great merit.[4]

I mean to correct and transcribe afresh the two first books of The Exodiad, which I think will allow of still further amendment and compression, by which part of the 1st will bear into the 2d, where it will have a better ending, and I am resolv'd with God's leave to give diligent attention to my portion of the work to the best of my abilities.

I was yesterday present at the Commitment of Patch for the suppos'd murder of Blight. I heard the whole Evidence read, and Mr Graham's[5] reasons for committing him very clearly detail'd, and am persuaded of his guilt.

I am, my dear friend, most affecty your's

R Cumberland

Source: Harvard.

1. The date is determined from the reference to the commitment of Patch for the murder of Blight which took place on 4 November 1805.

2. "By June of 1807 the German legion (8,000) men had been sent by Britain to aid Sweden and thus, indirectly, Russia. But an end was put to this by Napoleon's destruction of the Russian army at Friedland on 14 June 1807" (Watson, *The Reign of George III*, p. 455).

3. Henry John Todd (1763-1845), *The Works of Edmund Spenser*, 1805. In his *Memoirs*, Cumberland notes: "I was greatly pleased to see that the learned and judicious Mr. Todd in his late edition of Spenser has spoken of this poem [*Richard the First*] in such handsome terms, as I can never have a stronger confirmation of my own opinion, than when I find it coinciding with that of so excellent a critic" (II, 234).

4. Sharon Turner (1768-1847), an antiquarian and scholar.

5. Aaron Graham, Esq., one of the magistrates of Bow Street, who committed Richard Patch to Newgate on 4 November 1804. Isaac Blight had been shot on 21 September 1805 and died the next day. Circumstances pointed to Patch, who was tried and convicted on 5 April 1805.

CLXXXV Sir James Bland Burgess 6 November 1805[1]

My Dear Friend

We are not hardy enough to encounter such Crowds and Clamour, as we shoud fall in with tomorrow,[2] neither is Marianne quite fit to sleep with tallow candles in her bed room, as she must do, if we were to think of reposing ourselves in Charles Street.

Once more therefore permit me to desire you will allow us to wait upon you on Saturday, if conven-[ien]t to Lady Burgess, for I had engag'd myself on friday to friend Dilly,[3] who has made his party.

We shall come up on friday, and dine in Brunswick Row at 1/2 past 4 oClock. I dismiss'd my men yesterday[4] in a heavy shower of rain, not the only water that was shed.

> Adieu, my most worthy friend! Yrs
>
> R Cum

Wednesday 3 oClock

Source: Harvard.

1. This letter is dated by a likely reference to Admiral Nelson's funeral. See Note 2, below.
2. Tomorrow is probably 7 November 1805, a Thursday, the date of Nelson's funeral. Cumberland's musical piece commemorating his death was performed at Covent Garden on that date.
3. Charles Dilly (d. 1807), Cumberland's friend and publisher.
4. See 1 November 1805, in which Cumberland refers to the inspection of his Corps to be made the following Thursday, 7 November.

CLXXXVI Sir James Burgess After 14 November 1805[1]

> Warren's Hotel
> Wednesday

My very dear friend

I lose no time in answering your most kind and welcome letter. I have said nothing of your tragedy[2] but what I really think, and having fix'd my opinion of it, I am always prepar'd to say it over again to any body, that is prepar'd to hear me. I shall see Mr. Harris[3] here tomorrow at 11 oClock by appointment, and I shall think it for your interest and repose to call upon him for his decision upon your tender. I know nothing of his mind, but upon my asking Kemble[4] en passant if your tragedy was given in, he told me it was with Mr. Harris, and that he had not seen it nor had any voice in the acceptance of it, pro or con—*Credat Judeus*—My expectations on the subject point naturally to the repelling pole; for the man, who took Reynold's Delinquent,[5] ought consistently to refuse your Knight of Rhodes, and tho' I am prepar'd to hear him on one side, I am re-solv'd he shall hear my full opinion on the other.

This only I answer for, that you are not a writer and a gentleman, who ought to be, or shall be, rude-ly treated. For the issue I care so little, that I only wish it to be acted, because you seem to wish it; otherwise I shoud never wish to commit your feelings to the getting up a play, so located. Cook[6] is come in again. The infant Miss you see is put to bed with a good whipping, and I have grounds to think you conjecture rightly about the Quiz upon the forthcoming Master Betty: I guess he is in some dan-ger, temper'd as the Public now is.[7] If Mr. Harris returns your play, and I live till next season, I shall hope to see it on the stage of Drury.

After all, if you will take my advice, you will put your body into the Hastings Stage, and come up like a man to see with your own eyes a variety of things, interesting to you as a man of talents, but which I cannot detail to you by letter. Take your bed here, and I shall be ready for you, and have much to say to you. The *Memoirs* will be out in two or three days—[8]

Ever affecty your's

R Cumberland

Source: Harvard.

1. The date is determined by reference to *The Delinquent; or Seeing Company* by Frederic Reynolds' (1764-1841), produced at Covent Garden on 14 November 1805.

2. *The Knight of Rhodes*, never acted, but published in Burgess'

Dramas, 2 vols., 1807.

3. Thomas Harris, manager at Covent Garden.

4. John Philip Kemble.

5. Genest comments: "--this is a very poor C[omedy] by Reynolds--it was acted 9 times--but several better plays have been damned on the 1st night--..." (VII, 715).

6. George Frederick Cooke (1756-1813).

7. Master Betty, who in the 1804-05 season was received with great favor as something of a prodigy, did not meet with as general approbation for his appearances during the 1805-06 season.

8. *The Memoirs* are dated 1806, but were very likely printed late in 1805.

CLXXXVII **William Smith**[1] **27 March 1806**[2]

Tunb. Wells 27th. March

My Dear Sir

Your Letter of the 12th inst did not reach me till this morning, having lain here during my absence thro' the neglect of those, who sh[oul]d have sent it to me at Ramsgate, where I now reside. It woud have been impossible for me to fail in my acknowledgements for so friendly, so candid and so elegant a letter by the first opportunity, and I beg you now to accept my cordial thanks for the honour you confer upon me so much above my deserts.

Your honorable and honest nature takes to itself something as a motive on my part for discontinuing our intimacy, which I solemnly assure you I cannot interpret, nor can I call to mind any passage in your life, or in my own, when there was either cause on your part, or caprice on mine, on which I can ground a reason why our friendship seem'd to intermit. I can only ascribe it to those chances and changes in a life like mine, that might very possibly divert my attentions to some other objects, without impairing the esteem, in which I always held you.

I have never been in the habit of keeping letters, but I must preserve your's as being, without flattery, one of the most amiable pictures of the human heart, that I have ever met with. It is at once so generous on your part, and so highly flattering to me, that I have every inducement to prize it, and to preserve it--I only wish I may live to meet and embrace the writer before I die, and to assure you with what unfeign'd sincerity I am, and ever shall be, My dear friend,

Your most affectionate
and oblig'd humble Servt

Richd Cumberland

My best respects
to Mrs Smith.

Source: Yale.
Addressed to: William Smith Esquire, Bury St Edmund's.

1. William "Gentleman" Smith (1730?-1819), who acted at Drury Lane from 1774 until 1788.

2. This letter is a response Smith's letter of 12 March 1806.

CLXXXVIII Sir James Burgess Before April 1806[1]

I have return'd to our poem, My Dear friend, with recruited energy from the necessity I found myself under of a temporary relaxation, whilst certain melancholy Events were taking place in my family.[2] To confess the truth the task of the Exodiad is no light one, and wherever I feel a wish to alter from your copy, the repugnance of changing your words, and the difficulty of finding any that I like better to substitute instead of them, makes the work move slow--for I woud fain let nothing pass into the world that is not worthy of your name, not to disguise the zeal I have towards my own reputation with posterity. Composition therefore of this sort is laborious, and, as I have not been in high health, requires the relief of lighter studies, which offer themselves in the person of DeLancaster.[3] The Poem however rolls on, and when we meet, will not convict me of gross idleness. I am extremely sorry to hear you talk of June when I had built my hopes on April. Can't you look upon us in the Holy Week, and pass a day or two? Marianne is quite well, and Lady Edward will be here.[4] Poor Badcock sleeps in his leaden House, and lies in my bookroom till I am ascertain'd where to inter his miserable remains. I have much to say on the subject of his death, and the helpless family he has left behind him, but I can't write it. I am quite tir'd and must conclude with an unalterable truth that

I am affecty Yrs

R Cum

Friday

Source: Harvard.

1. The date is determined by reference to *The Exodiad*, published in 1807, and his expected visit of Burgess in April.
2. The illness and death of William Badcock, the husband of Cumberland's daughter, Sophia.
3. Cumberland's novel, *John de Lancaster*, published in 1809.
4. Cumberland's daughter, Elizabeth, the wife of Lord Edward Bentinck.

CLXXXIX Sir James Bland Burgess Spring 1806 (1)[1]

Wednesday TWs.

My very dear friend

I am waiting for my orders of Dismission,[2] altho' it is necessary for me to go to Bath for the purpose of arranging the Affairs of my daughter Badcock,[3] who must take out Administration, as there is no will.

This being a pressing business I purpose to wait no longer than till Monday morning before which time if no order comes to hand, I must let the men stand fast till I am able to come back and dismiss them, an operation I shall not chuse to let pass by my proxy. My absence will involve three weeks.

Marianne[4] with God's leave will accompany me, and with Lady Burgess's leave and your's will eat your mutton on Monday next at $1/2$ past 4 oClock, and will not be later. If the Letter of office comes in the meantime and keeps me past Monday, I will write to you, and at all events you shall hear from me on Monday morning.

My worthy friend and brother–Officer Henry Fry accompanies me as my Solicitor.

It will go to my heart to order my men to the Right-about, as they are in perfect discipline, fit for service and ardent to serve.

All further conversation I postpone till we meet. Our best respect to your excellent Lady.

Ever your's

R Cum.

Source: Harvard.

1. The date is determined by Cumberland's reference to taking

care of the affairs of his daughter, the wife of William Badcock who died during the early months of 1806.

2. Of his Corps of Volunteers.

3. See Note 1 above.

4. Cumberland's youngest daughter.

CXC   Sir James Bland Burgess   Spring 1806 (2)[1]

My dear friend

I am determin'd to wait for my letter of dismission, and do what is needful before I leave this place; therefore with a thous[an]d thanks for your goodness I beg to postpone waiting upon you for a few days. If there had been nothing in the way but the Illumination, and your Avocation upon Monday,[2] I shoud have revok'd my journey for your sake and my own; tho' Marianne, who is perfectly well, says she shoud have enjoy'd the spectacle very much.

I shall be happy to shew you the progress I have made in our poem,[3] and consult with you upon it when we meet here. I have bestow'd my utmost pain and attention to it, for I thought it well deserv'd our best consideration. I transcribe as I go on, which will give us two copies, from which to form a third. I have not made one material departure from your MS, and I think mine exceeds your's in a vey few lines, if I have rightly counted your's. I am just now in a fit of intermission, having got to the ague of De-Lancaster[4] to cool myself after the fever of Verse, by these means I go to each with a better appetite. I study hard, but I don't turn out a great deal of work.

Adieu! Ever beleive me entirely Your's

R Cum

Friday 8 oClock

334

Source: Harvard.

1. The year is conje4ctured from his reference to *The Exodiad,* which was published in 1807, and from reference to his dismissing his troops, mentioned in the previous letter [Spring 1806 (1)].

2. Probably a reference to efforts to produce dramas written by Burgess, possibly his *Knight of Rhodes.* The first play Burgess produced was *Riches; or, the Wife and Brother,* an adaptations of Massinger's *The City Madam,* at the Lyceum Theatre on 3 February 1810.

3. *The Exodiad,* published in 1807.

4. *John de Lancaster,* Cumberland's third and last novel, was published in 1809. This letter is evidence of his having worked on it much earlier than has generally been supposed. See Stanley Williams, *Cumberland:* "In 1809 was written and published...*John De Lancaster*" (p. 275).

CXCI Sir James Bland Burgess Spring 1806 (3)[1]

Monday T Ws.

My dear friend

I dismiss and take leave of my Vol[unteer]s tomorrow, and on Thursday I begin my progress towards Bath. I am very desirious to see you and Lady Burgess in my way, therefore if you will give me meat at half past 4 on Thursday, and it does not interfere with any engagem[en]t, Marianne[2] and I will be at your door. Henry Fry accompanies me as Sol[icito]r for my poor widow'd Child; if he comes, I dare say you will throw him a bone; if not, he will go about his business, where it may call him; I have said nothing to him on the subject. I think to treat poor emancipated Marianne with a play, where it may be most to her mind, so you will forgive us Country folks, and perhaps we may be so happy to have you with us. Adieu My Dr Sir

R Cum.

Source: Harvard.

1. The date is determined by reference to his taking care of
the estate of his daughter, Sophia.
2. Cumberland's youngest daughter.

CXCII **Sir James Bland Burgess 5 May 1806[1]**

Monday 5 May

My dear Sir

I beg you will accept my Apology for not attending
your Summons on Wednesday next, as I am still detain'd by the very painfull duty of attending upon
my daughter,[2] who advances so very slowly, if at
all, in regaining her strength, that my anxiety remains as when I wrote to you last. She is now lying
on her Couch blister'd and in great pain from an affection in her side, which is suppos'd to proceed
from nervous and hysteric spasms, which debilitate
her to a great degree.

I look with impatience for your coming here, and
hope I shall be in condition to avail myself of the
enjoyment which your neighbourhood and friendly
kindness will afford me. I hope to see all your Alterations, and all your Criticisms.[3]

Adieu, I can only say I am most afftly yrs

R Cumberland

Source: Folger.

1. The date is conjectured from reference to alterations of the

Exodiad, published in 1807.

2. This reference may be either to Cumberland's daughter, Marianne, who was ill during the spring of 1806, or to his second daughter, Sophia, who had just lost her husband and was possibly in a nervous state.

3. Of *The Exodiad*, which they were jointly writing.

CXCIII   Sir James Bland Burgess   About 8 May 1806[1]

My dear friend

I find myself able to use my pen, and the first and best use I can put it to is to thank you for your very kind anxiety about my situation.

I think myself fairly convalescent, and am getting strength by degrees. By a skillfull effort on the part of Saunders[2] under providence I was snatcht from death.

I wish you woud come and see the shadow of your friend. It woud be very chearing to me, and very good and kind in you.

Ever yours
Affecty

R Cumberland

Source: Harvard.

1. Although blurred, the postmark of this letter seems to read May 8, 1806.

2. Probably William Saunders (1743-1817), author of *Observations on the Superior Efficacy of the Red Peruvian Bark in the Cure of Agues and Other Fevers* (London, 1782) and *A Treatise on the Structure, Economy and Diseases of the Liver* (London, 1793).

CXCIV   **Sir James Bland Burgess   Mid-1806[1]**

My dear friend

I send down by tomorrow's Coach a Copy of my Memoirs, which I entreat you to accept, and hope it may employ an hour in a winter evening with some degree of entertainment.

I am quite sorry to find you are so irremovably fixt in your chair, that we cannot tempt you to leave it and to look upon your friends at Ramsgate. My long delay'd departure will take place next Saturday.

I think we have some reason to expect that the enormous power of France is in train to be humbled, and the fortune of Bonaparte falling from him at last. If the Admiralty's Account of the action shoud be true, or even near the truth, it will be a grand event; but it is not confirm'd, and I don't expect it will be.[2]

May you and your Circle enjoy health and happiness! I am thoroughly fatigued with a very long walk, and have only time to assure you that I am affecty yrs

R Cumberland

Wednesday

Source: Harvard.

1. The year is indicated by reference to Cumberland's *Memoirs*. See also Note 2 below.

2. Steven Watson describes the events: "Meanwhile British forces from Sicily, the fleet under Sir Sidney Smith, and 4,800 men under Sir John Stuart, made an attempt to restore the Queen of Naples to possessions on the mainland from which Joseph Bonaparte had driven her. Sir John Stuart landed in Lower Calabria and attacked the French to the number of 7,000 who were encamped at

338

Maida on 4 July 1806" (*The Reign of George III*, pp. 451-2).

CXCV   Sir James Bland Burgess   After 23 June 1806[1]

Tuesday Ws Hotel

I wish my good friend, you had reproach'd me a little more, that I might not reproach myself so much for neglecting to inform you of an event so interesting to my happiness as that of Marianne's[2] perfect recovery.

Lackington[3] approves much of our books by detail, and recommends Qu° Numbers at 5s. each, which he thinks will go off to our profit, or if we prefer to treat for Copy-right he seems dispos'd to meet us. You perfectly agree with him and me in postponing the 1st book till the add[itiona]l mem[oir]s shall come out, and advertise the work.[4] It shall be in your hands the moment it is out of mine.

In the meantime I shall devote myself without avocation to complete the supplem[en]t, which is already far advanc'd. I have taken great pains with my remarks upon Mr. Hayley's charge,[5] and I hope you will approve of what I have done. I am very glad you meditate another Comedy, and that you propose-- celebrare domestica facta--*Perseverando vinces*--

I will be sure to tell Mr. Cooke to send you down his dramas.[6] He does me the honour to subscribe my name to Horry's Critique on the Busy body.[7]

Rae plays Mortimer with astonishing applause to crowded houses.[8] Impartially I think it the finest performance now on the Stage, including Kemble and Ellison &c.[9]

Marianne is very happy with Henry and his worthy dame;[10] she feels very gratefully your kind design of treating her with the Ice on her arrival, and desires to be remember'd to you, your Lady and daughters. Include my respects, and beleive me

Affectly Yours

R Cum

Source: Harvard.

1. The date is determined by reference to Rae's performance as Mortimer in *The Iron Chest*.

2. Cumberland's youngest daughter.

3. Geroge Lackington, publisher of Cumberland's *Memoirs* and *The Exodiad*.

4. Both the 2 volume version of the *Memoirs* and the first part of *The Exodiad* were published in 1807.

5. For Cumberland's reply to William Hayley's comments see *Memoirs*, II, 311 ff.

6. C. Cooke, the publisher of *The British Drama*, "A collection of the most esteemed dramatic productions, with biography of the respective authors, and critique on each play," ed. Richard Cumberland. It was published in fourteen volumes in 1817. Burgess wrote some of the critiques.

7. Probably Charles Lucas Pinckney Horry (1769-1830). *The Busie Body* by Susanna Centlivre was acted on 12 May 1709 at Drury Lane.

8. Alexander Rae (1782-1820) made his debut as an actor at Bath in the role of Hamlet on 28 January 1806. He first performed Mortimer in George Colman's *The Iron Chest*, at the Haymarket on 23 June 1806.

9. John Philip Kemble and Robert William Elliston.

10. She was probably staying with Cumberland's attorney, Henry Fry, and his wife.

CXCVI Sir James Bland Burgess Late 1806[1]

Ramsgate, Sunday

My dear friend

Whilst you have the consciousness of writing such

a play as *Welcome Home*,[2] you ought on no account to concern yourself about any measures, which the propr[ietor]s of a stage, devoted to spectacle alone, may take either against it, or for it. I am very glad they don't act, for I don't think it quite ripe for acting, and, if it was I do not think they are quite the people to perform it. You will complete it, and what is it to you how they estimate your genius, when you have just got into the vein.

Your argument about Korah's speech is very good,[3] but perhaps when you see the context you may not think it altogether inadmissible with some touches, that may make the hypocrisy of the speaker rather more apparent.

I am now with Jethro, which is not a very animating subject, but I hope it will carry on the book so as to wind it up with the delivery of the Law, and leave us two books for the sending out of the spies, and their journal. At all events you must consider what I am now upon as *rough Copy* to be alter'd or omitted as we see fit hereafter on perusal.

When everlasting war is denounc'd ag[ain]st Amalek, what is more natural for Cavillers and Blasphemers to take hold of than the cruelty of the denunciation? Tis no proof of their humanity, but it is a strong display of their hypocrisy and malice: However let it pass ad referendum.

I write in haste, and am, My dear friend,

Ever affecty your's

Rd Cumberland

Source: Harvard.

1. The date is determined from Cumberland's working on *The Exodiad* with Burgess. See Note 3 below.

2. This play was neither acted nor published.

3. This and the remainder of the letter refer to aspects of *The Exodiad*.

CXCVII   Sir James Bland Burgess   September 1806[1]

Grundisburgh, near Woodbridge
Friday noon

Many thanks, my very good friend, for your letter. I have now put the last hand to the supplement,[2] and when that has pass'd the Press, I shall be at your command to join with you in any measures, that upon consultation may seem best for us to take respecting the *Grande Opus.*[3] At the end of next month I must be at T[unbridge] Wells to attend upon the Vol[untee]rs. I depend upon our meeting then, and as the Mem[oi]rs will hardly come out before Xstmas, time will be before us.

I confess I am not quite convinc'd at present that it will be wise in us to sell our first experimental book, for the calculation, which publishers will make of the risque, will produce no tempting offer, and if we start with alienating a portion of the whole, we shall very much impair our property in the book, and come with great disadvantage to a second bargain. I do not think any judicious friend will counsel us to lose hold of the totality.

We have the pleasure of seeing   Captain Burges frequently, and always accompanied by his amiable friend Col. Dalton, who is wonderfully mended in health and spirits: Your Son is in high bloom of strength and youth; I have never seen him so well and so entirely as I coud wish him: His regim[en]t is to be review'd by the Duke of York[4] on Sunday next--of all days in the week--Which gives much offence to the friends of decency and order. The Corps is in the finest Condition, but, as you know, quite stript of Officers, which is all the better, as Dalton is in himself a host.

I shoud like to hear you on the Event of Fox's death, and the posture of public Affairs at this extraordinary Crisis.

Marianne desires her best respects to the ladies

and yourself. Believe me

ever most affecty yrs

R Cumberland

I have got the gout slightly but decidedly in my
foot. I think it has been of service to my general
state of health.

Source: Harvard.

1. The date is conjectured from reference to the death of Fox,
which occurred in September 1806.

2. To Cumberland's *Memoirs*, published in 1807.

3. *The Exodiad.*

4. Frederick Augustus (1763-1827), Duke of York and Albany.

5. Charles James Fox (1749-1806).

CXCVIII   Sir James Bland Burgess   3 November 1806[1]

3 Novr. Ramsgate

My Dear friend

According to my project for the 1st book of the
Exodiad[2] it comprizes 1100 lines, and as I am far
advanc'd in the second d° I am of opinion that it
will be well to send them into the world together--
This, and every thing that relates to their internal
fitness for publication will be refer'd to you, when
we meet and you take in hand the last revisal of the
work.

Without this accompaniment the portion wo[u]d
be too small, and with it we shall give a fair sample of our poem. I have fully talk'd the matter
through with George Lackington,[3] but it must lie

over for our joint decision whether we will print in Qu°, or in Oct°; the probability of sale is with the latter, but the greater respectability is on the other side. We must make no contract that can affect our Copyright, and therefore if we do not choose to take the risque upon our selves, we must consider whether it will be adviseable to let our publisher stand to profit or loss, which he is very ready to do, but which I can hardly think we shall be wise to agree with.

I have defer'd my visit to my Volunteers till the 1st day of Decem[be]r, when I shall with God's leave be at The Wells to take them out. I hope you will then make it convenient to meet me, and give your attention to the MS before it goes to Press. It will be ready for you. The Oct° Memoirs with the supplement[4] will be out in a fortnight, and I hope will prove instrumental as Advertisers of the poem, and smooth the way in some degree for its appearance. The printer will work it off in a very few days.

Give my best regards to Captain Burges;[5] he shew'd me and mine great kindness in Suffolk, and was a most agreeable companion on our toure; We felt his loss very sensibly. He is much belov'd by his men and officers, and you have great cause to be proud of him. Marianne meditates to pen him an epistle, but at present she is tormented with a head-ake and greatly indispos'd. She joins in regards to you and the Ladies. I have only to wish you wo[u]d put yourself in a Chaise with friend Charles, and come thither, where all will be happy to welcome you. What is the distance of a few stages to you. Adieu. Ever yr's

Rd Cumberland

You have made me yet no visit.
I find Marianne wrote yesterday to Captain Burges, of which I was not aware.

Source: Harvard.

1. The year is determined by reference to the publication of
the *Memoirs* with the supplement. This edition bears the date of
1807, but was undoubtedly printed late in 1806.
2. Their religious epic.
3. The publisher of Cumberland's *Memoirs*.
4. See Note 1 above.
5. Burges's son.
6. Another of Burges's sons.

CXCIX   Sir James Burgess   Before 22 December 1806[1]

Wednesday. Ramsgate

My dear friend

As I understand by Captain Burges's letter to Marianne,[2] that I am to have the happiness of meeting
you at T[unbridge] Wells, I trouble you with a few
lines to say I shall be there, deo volente, on Sunday to dinner, or early in the   evening. I shall
lodge with Jasper Sprange on the pantiles, that I
may have shelter from the skies, which are at this
moment giving a sample of what I may expect.
I shall of course bring with me the two first
books of The Exodiad for your inspection, and all
the MSS I have of your's on the same subject. The
line you trac'd out, has been my guide, and if I
have trode steadily I owe it to your support.
In haste, but not less truly, Your's

R Cumberland

Source: Harvard.

1. The date is conjectured by the reference to *The Exodiad*.

Cumberland's letter to Burgess postmarked 22 December 1806 discusses a stage of the writing in advance of that mentioned in
this letter.

2. Burges's son writing to Cumberland's youngest daughter.

CC **Sir James Bland Burgess** About 22 December 1806[1]

Temple of the Muses
Monday

My Dear Friend

I had your favour of this morning; As you express
a curiosity to see the specimen of our poem,[2] I send
you one inclos'd, without waiting for a frank.

The paper will be much better, and Lackington's[3]
spirit induces him to put himself to extra expense
for what is term'd *fine printing*.

We shall soon have it out, as it will comprise only 14 sheets, and you may depend upon every exertion
this house can make, who are in high good humour and
mean to be liberal.

I shoud recomm[en]d the general title to be--*By
the Authors of Calvary and Richard the First*-- instead of names.[4]

I have made a progress of above 200 lines in the
3d book, and very much wish you were at my elbow to
criticize it; You must absolutely not refuse to put
on your seven-league boots, and come to us at Ramsgate as soon after Xstmas as you can, and I flatter
myself Charles[5] will come with you; We may then confer at leisure, and I will return your visit early
in the year.

I leave Town on friday--take notice of that.

Ever afftly Your's

R Cumberland

Source: Harvard.

1. This letter is postmarked 22 December 1806, a Monday.

2. *The Exodiad*.

3. George Lackington.

4. Cumberland's epic *Calvary; or the Death of Christ*, 1792, and James Bland Burgess's *Richard the First*, 1800.

5. Burgess's son.

CCI Sir James Bland Burgess   About 24 December 1806[1]

Extract from Book III. Line 138 &c
(Korah addresses the Son of Peleth.)

Warrior, you see how fast the nations sink
Before our conqu'ring standard; you have heard
The doom of Amalek, by Him pronounc'd,
Who is our Israel's oracle, and seal'd
By Joshua on God's altar with an oath.
Not one must live of Esau's hapless race;
Nor age, nor sex, nor innocence can save,
But ev'n the harmless nurseling at the breast
Must perish with the mother--dreadfull doom--!
If this be so as Moses hath decreed,
And general carnage is announc'd from Heaven,
Where shall we look for mercy? Have these
                                   [plains
Not drank so deeply of their masters blood,
But we must drain from infants their small
                                   [store,
And wring the last faint drop from wrinkled age
To perfect a libation full and fit.
What shall I say?--for God? No; God forbid!--
For Moses, for a plume of deeper dye
To crown the helm of Joshua, and replace
That crest which Amalek's keen falchion cleft.
The sentence I have heard, but tell me now,
For I am yet to learn what is the sin
Of this unhappy people? In past time

Jacob did homage to them, brought them gifts,
As to his brethren of the elder stock;
They envied not his store; they had enough,
And, but for his entreaty, had declin'd
The tributary offerings of his flock:
They were the stronger then; his wives, his
[babes,
His All was in their pow'r; but they were kind,
And mercifull, and to our father's gave
That peace, which to their sons we now deny.
What if the Gods they worship be no Gods,
They do but follow where their fathers trode,
And what they taught beleive; if so they sin,
Then is Obedience guilt: Moses to them
Is not a Lawgiver, has not divulg'd,
As unto us, his conference with God
At Horeb's mount, and if he had, perchance
He might have found them of less easy faith
Than We, ye humblest of his subjects, are,
Not daring of ourselves to act, or speak,
Or think but as he wills, who makes revenge
A virtue, and to desolate mankind
A sacrifice acceptable to Heaven."
"Father, replied the Cheif, with me and some
Of Reuben's elder tribe, who weigh mens words,
All is not Oracle that Moses speaks.
When Cruelty is sanction'd, I must doubt
If what I'm taught to think that God abhors,
And human reason starts from, can be right.
Therefore my sword shall sleep within it's
[shell,
And Moses must not rail, if I refuse
To stab the wretch, that kneels to me for life,
Or mingle blood of babes with Mother's milk,
Altho' some young idolater may live
To sacrifice to Chemos. If the will
Of God had been to exterminate the race,
His pestilence had swept them from the Earth,
And cruelties more dire, than e're disgrac'd
The worshipers of Molock, had been spar'd.
I am my tribe &c &c.

I am tir'd my dear friend, and probably so are you, for this is only my rough copy, and has nor rec[eive]d the least correction.

I have avail'd myself of your pointing, which is quite right.

I set off for Ramsgate tomorrow--Adieu!

I will be diligent with my pen, that I may avail myself of your promise.

R C

Exodiad will soon be out.[2] It will certainly go to Stat[ione]rs Hall in course.

Source: Harvard.

1. This letter is postmarked 24 December 1806.
2. That is, proofs of the first part of the poem.

CCII   Sir James Bland Burgess   31 December 1806[1]

31 Decr. Ramsgate

My dear friend

I was told by George Isted[2] yesterday that our brother Sotherby [*sic*] has an epic poem in 8 books upon the subject of Saul,[3] which is to appear in May next. I receive this welcome news with joy, as I doubt not but the production of Sotherby's Saul will reflect honour on the age we live in, which from the date of Calvary[4] will have given birth to as many epics as the world can number for I know not how many generations.

I rejoice that our Countryman and brother poet has (like us) drawn from the Old Testament; His Subject is sublime, various and pathetic; yet I wonder, when

he was so near us, how he kept himself out of our
Preserve. I look for great things from him.

I shall be proud to show you my rough doings,
which grow under my hands the faster for having land
in view, where you have planted laurels to reward my
labours. I have 485 lines on my copy. If you retort
my own maxims upon me, I shall not wonder; but I
work very hard. I have had one entire sheet from
Wrighte,[5] who will not sleep in the business.

Your objection to Korah's comments shall be
heal'd, and in fact is already so in part; but nothing of course will stand, which in your judgement
ought to be expung'd. It is not so you treated me,
and it shall not be so, that I will act towards you.
You will find I have woven into the work the strongest vindication of Divine Justice for the extirpa-
tion of Amalek.[6] I hope you will meet me with *Welcome Home* totus teres atque rotendus.[7] I shoud blush
for your spirit, if you coud shrink from your career
upon that touch of a Torpedo. Shine on, and let them
wink, that cannot see the light.

The proper character of our National Genius is The
Epic, and the proper tone of our language is heroic
blank verse. Sotherby has found it out; Bowles possesses it, but Madoc has no ear.[8]

The old Year is now taking leave of us in one of
the brightest gleams of sunshine, that ever winter
sky coud boast of. The Sea is cover'd with ships;
Above 300 sail are within our peer, and the Spectacle of the Downs is amazing. A German General commanding 900 mercenaries occupies this important
post, and it justly gives offence: His band is now
serenading Lord and Lady Edward Bentinck,[9] and the
compliment is justly due, for every officer finds
hospitality and kindness there. We are going to dine
with them, and the little Badcocks[10] are to be of
the party; they are fine creatures, and I am very
proud of them.

My best respects to My Lady, and my Love to friend
Charles[11] and the amiable trio of Graces. Where is
the March, and If it is call'd a *Quick* one, why is

it so *slow* in coming?

Adieu. Ever yrs

R Cumberland

Source: Harvard.

1. The year is determined by reference to *The Exodiad*, published in 1807.

2. Probably a descendant of Ambrose Isted, who is mentioned prominently in Cumberland's *Memoirs*, I, p. 161ff.

3. William Sotheby (1757-1833), author of the religious epic, *Saul*, 1807.

4. Cumberland's epic, published in 1792.

5. John Wright (1770?-1844), the printer.

6. The preaceding sentence deals with specific aspects of the *Exodiad*.

7. "Welcome Home" a drama by Burgess seems not to have been produced or published.

8. William Lisle Bowles (1762-1850). His poetic works in two volumes were edited by George Gilfillan in 1855. I have not been able to identify Madoc.

9. Cumberland's daughter, Elizabeth, and her husband.

10. The children of Sophia Cumberland, the dramatist's second child.

11. Burgess's son.

CCIII Sir James Bland Burgess 8 January 1807

Jan. 8. 1807

My dear friend

The day before yesterday I concluded the 3d book, and have begun a fair copy, correcting it as I proceed. I ave given notice to Wrighte[1] our printer, that his publication will extend to three books, and told him to inform Lackington[2] of it. I have work'd hard. I find little if any Epic matter between the delivery of the Commandm[en]ts, and the sending out of the spies, so that our fourth book will not come upon your eighth, and the Journal of the Spies will form 5th and 6th. Korah's fate and the death of Moses may probably come within the compass of the 7th and 8th, if you fight no more battles, upon which question we need not now decide--I incline to wish more for Joshua--but of this hereafter. I am rather suspicious of the 4th book, as likely to be heavy unless we can make some use of Korah's vision, and at the same time I am alarm'd at the fabulous introduction of Chemos.

Wrighte has pull'd off 3 sheets, and I expect the 4th today. They are uncommonly correct. I trust we shall have nothing to fear now from Korah's humanity--

"For there are men so impiously perverse
They will arraign the providence of God,
When he forbears to punish; When he strikes,
Deplore His justice, and affect to find
In their own hearts more mercy than in Heav'n"

Were it not for the bar of the 4th book, we might have taken the whole journal of the spies into our first Number.

I hear nothing of the Supplement,[3] but I look for it every day. It is the Index halts it, but it is all the better for the Poem.

Ever affecty yrs

R Cum

Source: Harvard

1. John Wright, printer of *The Exodiad.*
2. George Lackington, publisher of *The Exodiad.*
3. To his *Memoirs.*

CCIV   **Sir James Bland Burgess   30 January 1807**

Janry 30th

My dear friend

I rec[eive]d your favour, and shall attend to your hints about the latitude of Midian, and be careful of Mount Pisgah.

I am glad to hear we have a contemporary at work upon the same subject with our's for it will very well carry double, and the only wonder is, that no body has been before both Mr. Hoyle[1] and us. I hope he will succeed; there are more bay-trees on Parnassus, than there are heads to be crown'd by their branches.

It is a good thing to keep the work warm, whilst we are upon it, but I see no spur to quicken us beyond our natural speed, that can have any reference to the Exodus of Mr. Hoyle. It woud be very easy to attach a 4th book to our portion in the press, for I am very near to the conclusion of it, and, having occasion to write to Lackington,[2] I consulted him upon it. He seems to think it a question entirely with us, but promises me his opinion in a future letter. I am well satisfied with it myself; but that is saying very little.

If you think it to be wish'd that the poem shoud be completed in two publications, we woud publish 4 books now, and 4 more when we are ready with them.[3] Otherwise we have enough in the press. This book will be shorter than the others, but still long e-nough, if we stuck at nothing else.

I shall be in Town on Thursday, and then you shall hear from me in a more particular manner, and give me your judgement.

Upon the whole I am inclin'd to think the sooner we can get before the public the better, and the sooner we can follow up with a second portion will be also the better; therefore I am ultimately for the 3 books, which will make 180 pages.

The sending out the spies is a most material incident, for upon their report it came to pass that God
punish'd their rebellion by a prolongation of 40
years in the wilderness. This will be a critical
period in our work, for we cannot blink it. There is
a way of doing it by the *Poeta loquitur* which may be
very solemn and sublime, but more of this when we
meet, which I hope will be upon my return. I have
prepared to meet this awful *hiatus* by the ominous
manner, in which I have consider'd the election of
the Ten spies, and the impression that it makes upon
Joshua: I have also combin'd it with what occurs to
Korah, when he meets the Evil Spirit in the Desert.
It is there I flatter myself that I have done well
and shall please you.

Adieu! I am ever affecy yrs

R Cumberland

I have had a very elegant letter from Sir Wm Pepys.[4]
My last proof goes to page 88.

Source: Harvard.

1. Charles Hoyle, author of *Exodus*, London, 1807.
2. George Lackington.
3. The poem was published in two stages.
4. Cumberland, in his *Memoirs*, says that Sir William Pepys
(1740-1825) was "one of the best classical scholars of his time,
and who, together with his learning, possessed a correct taste
and admirable judgment. When I lived with Johnson, Garrick, Dodington, Jenyns, and the wits of that period, I had the happiness
also of living with Sir Willaim Pepys" (II, 401).

CCV   Sir James Bland Burgess   Early 1807[1]

I have the pleasure to congratulate with you on my having now dispatch'd the last sheet, containing title page &c.[2] There has not been the smallest cause to complain of delay, for I have never had less than 3 sh[ee]ts the week. I think it will take a fortnight to get it out, and I don't expect it to be advertiz'd till it is fairly put into the hands of the subscribing retailers, which is consider'd as a point of honour in the trade.

All is done according to your orders respecting the Copies to be given.

I am very glad that you think there is something not much amiss in the little hasty specimen, that I sent you. Your Candour in every stage of our joint undertaking chears me in such portion of the work as falls to my share, and my task is decidedly the lightest, for I want no book but the bible and your MS, and, if I did, I have not got any.

I calculate that the 8th part of our remaining task is done, and as we may send to the press and keep it going a considerable time before the whole is done, I will not despair of seeing the entire poem within the year, and that will be a great thing to perform.

I have a letter from Sharon Turner,[3] which will not make me less industrious to deserve his good o-pinion, and that of The Club in general, of which he gives me a most pleasing assur[an]ce, for it includes you also.

Adieu, My dear friend! Write to me frequently: Your letters are inspiriting, and ever welcome.

Your's

R C

Source: Harvard.

1. The date is conjectured from reference to the advanced state of the publication of *The Exodiad*.
2. Of *The Exodiad*.
3. Sharon Turner (1768-1847).

CCVI Sir James Bland Burgess   Before 24 March 1807[1]

Ramsgate Sunday

My dear friend

I set out for T[unbridge] Wells tomorrow, and take Mr. Jansen[2] with me, who will go up to Town on Tuesday, and fall in with me on his return at Maidstone, to which we are on that day (vis Thursday) to march, and set up our quarters for ten days. Need I say what a gratification it woud be to me to catch a sight of you on Wednesday at T[unbridge] W[ell]s, were it not too long a journey for too small an object.

Thank you for your alteration, which I cordially approve of: Wright[3] must be very near his conclusion. I will take care of what you tell me about the critique. I am working on the novel.[4]

We have had a succession of magnificent spectacles. Some few Transports have come into harbour with horses and arms. Numbers have pass'd by, and some Danish line of battle ships. I have very pleasing tidings of the conduct and behavior of the Capt. of the Leyden.[5]

Our joint respects wait on Lady Burges, and we desire to be most kindly remember'd to your amiable Circle.

I am, my dear friend,
ever affecty yours

Rd Cumberland

Source: Harvard.

1. The date is conjectured from the advanced state of work on *The Exodiad*. Cumberland speaks of the completed book in his letter of 24 March.

2. Cumberland's youngest daughter, Frances Marianne, married a Mr. Jansen, who widowed her after a short time.

3. The printer of *The Exodiad*.

4. *John de Lancaster*, 3 vols., 1809.

5. Cumberland's son, William.

CCVII Sir James Bland Burgess 24 March 1807[1]

> Temple of the Muses
> Tuesday 24th
> 3 o'clock

My dear friend

Our book is one of the most beautiful Samples of the Art of Mr. Wright,[2] that was ever exhibited, and it is reckon'd very cheap.

I have turn'd over a few pages of *Saul*,[3] which comes out on the very same day and hour with us. You was right in your conjecture--too right, for I find the metre horrible, and the diction infinitely below par. He sells a Volume a few pages more than ours, but I shoud suppose fewer lines, for either a guinea or 18, not so well printed as ours.

I saw Walter Scott;[4] he comes out on the King's birth day. Murray[5] is laughed at for the price he has given. Sotheby's subscribing booksellers have not taken half our number. I will write to you again when I have more leisure. Farewell.

> R. Cum

Source: Henry W. and Albert A. Berg Collection. The New York Public Library. Astor, Lenox and Tilden

Foundations.

1. The year is determined by reference to publicaton of *The Ex-odiad.* March 24 was a Tuesday. This letter precedes that of 26 March 1807.

2. Printer of *The Exodiad.*

3. *Saul, a Poem in Two Parts* (London, 1807) by William Sotheby (1757-1833).

4. Sir Walter Scott (1771-1832).

5. John Murray (1778-1843), the publisher.

CCVIII   Sir James Bland Burgess   26 March 1807[2]

Thursday
Warren's

I thank you, my good friend, for your kind and prudent hint about the author of Saul:[2] I told Lackington,[3] whilst I was writing to you, that I was sure you wo[u]d wish to have it, but he hesitated about orders. Cadell and Davies[4] were the only booksellers, that w[ou]d not subscribe to us, and they are the publishers of Saul. I shall stay in Town all the next week, and most probably attend the Club. The Archb[isho]p of Canterbury[5] has given our friend Todd[6] a fine living of at least 600 p[e]r ann[um]. I am to dine with a large party of literati on Saturday at Israeli's: Sharon Turner[7] quorum unus, and probably Walter Scott, whom I met at Murray's,[8] and who devour'd me with Scottish flattery and affection. I am one amongst many more worthy, who are helping forw[ar]d Prince Hoare with his weekly essay, intitled The Artist.[9] I recollect a particular paper of your's about Criticism; it was one of your Man in the Moon: I wish you woud entrust me with those unpublisht essays, and if I find them convertible to his use, you will confer a great favor on him, Murray his publisher and on me. I won't make

358

any use of it, till I transcribe and send it to you.
Let us make friends of the Mammon.

I understand it will be very adviseable to send
two books[10] to the press as soon as we are agreed
upon the correction of them: They will be the better
it seems for lying by in the warehouse, and we shall
save time by stealing a march. I have brought the
whole Journal into Lib. V. and I send you a little
sketch of the outset of Lib. VI. viz--

Book VI

"No more, reposing on the mossy turf
In Hermon's soft recesses, on beside
The winding Jordan, must we sit and teach
His stream to murmur in melodious verse:
Horrors demand us now; a mournfull Muse,
Pall'd in funereal black, prepares to strike
The deep-ton'd harp, whilst on the topmost peak
Of Seir's high rock the boding Raven sits,
Scenting the Stygian blast, that o'er the camp
Of Israel, hovering to discharge it's plagues,
Rides in the morbid air. A thousand fiends,
Banding to rescue their devoted groves,
Spread their broad vans, and make a hideous might
From flank to flank of the o'er shadow'd host.
For till Rebellion's sin shall be aton'd
Years upon years must roll, and all the whilst
The great Arch-enemy of man shall hold
Usurp'd dominion over human minds:
Still Hell's dark legions shall enjoy a truce,
Still the avenging Angel shall persist
To stay the hand of Joshua from his sword
Till the fell Pestilence hath done his work,
And the deep chambers of the cavern'd Earth
Are ready to burst open, and engulph
Apostate Korah and his rebel crew--&c.

Ever affy yrs.

R C

Source: Harvard.

1. This letter is postmarked 26 March 1807, which was a Thursday.

2. An epic by William Sotheby.

3. George Lackington, publisher of *The Exodiad*.

4. Thomas Cadell (1742-1802) and William Davies (d. 1820).

5. Charles Manners-Sutton (1755-1828), Archbishop of Canterbury.

6. Henry John Todd became Archdeacon of Cleveland.

7. Sharon Turner (1768-1847).

8. John Murray (1778-1843), publisher and bookseller.

9. The dramatist, Prince Hoare (1755-1834). Cumberland contributed an essay, "On Dramatic Style," to the May 1807 issue of *The Cabinet of Polite Literature*. It had been originally published in *The Artist*.

10. Of *The Exodiad*.

CCIX Sir James Bland Burgess May 1807[1]

Royal Hotel. Wednesday

My Dear Friend

I am still here, and shall be here for the remainder of the week at least. Various concerns have arisen, which convince me that I must set up my staff in London for the short remainder of my days, provided I can make it tolerable to Marianne. Dilly's[2] house was my wish, and that is to be sold by auction this day; had it been in my power to have purchas'd it, I shoud have been a bidder, but he has not enabled me so to do, and I content myself without it.

You will have goodness to write by return post, and let me know the day you mean to come with your fair companion: I take for granted your son Charles wrote to you about lodgings at Robinson's in Piccadilly, and I think you will be comfortable there.

Our Poem[3] has not yet been review'd, but I suppose it will be notic'd on Saturday next. Saul[4] has been review'd by the Edenboro Critics, and tho' it has not escap'd censure, yet it has been treated with lenity, and the author prais'd for his other works; so that it is plain he was in favour with them, of which I was aware. Of us they say nothing.

We have had little circulation as yet, but not less than I expected; for the Town has had somethng else to do beside reading sacred poems. I have done a full quarter of the 7th book, but of course consider nothing done till you approve and correct. I have planted the Army in the plains of Moab, and when I have attended a Council of the hostile Gods upon Abarim, shall proceed upon your Interview with the Kings, and the splendid episode, which you have so finely sketch'd out of Balaam and Balak, and wind up the book. I have carried the poem over the 38 years interval in the best manner I coud devise, but I regret the loss of Korah and others, and am left with Joshua and Caleb, neither of them any longer young.

We were perfectly aware of this breach in our persons of the drama, and as it is a stubborn fact we cannot contend against it. There is fortunately a sufficient supply of new matter and character to substitute in place of what we have lost.

I hope you gentlemen of East Sussex will be able to carry your friend Fuller[5] through his poll, but it is such close running, that I am alarm'd for him.

I wish I coud have found a young man to suit your place, but it was not for want of pains that I miscarried. I will seek after Dilly's servant, whose character is unexceptionable. I sincerely hope Lady Burges has recover'd from her indisposition, and that the rest of your family enjoy good health. I beg to be most gratefully remember'd to them, and am with sincere esteem, My dear friend,

Most affecty Your's

Rd Cumberland

Source: Harvard.

1. This letter, postmarked MA 1807, is clearly subsequent to that postmarked 26 March 1807. There were no Wednesdays in March after the 26th.

2. Charles Dilly, who published many of Cumberland's works, including *The Observer*, was a close friend and a member of Johnson's circle.

3. *The Exodiad*.

4. *Saul* was reviewed in the *Edinburgh Review* for April 1807, pp. 206-217. Cumberland's characterization of the review is an accurate one. *The Exodiad* was listed among the "Quarterly List of New Publications" in the July 1807 issue of the periodical.

5. John Fuller was a member of the House of Commons representing Sussex in 1807. He was successful in his bid for reelection.

CCX Sir James Bland Burgess 18 June 1807[1]

Ramsgate, Thursday

My dear friend

I wish to my heart you were here amongst us to shake hands with some departing friends, who remember you with much affection, and desire me to convey to you their last respects. We are embarking German men and horses by thousands, and as the weather is serenely fine, the Spectacle is extremely brilliant. Five Companies of Col. Halkett's[2] light Infantry are far upon their way to Stralsund[3] under old Drecksel; Three Companies and the Major remain in barracks here, till their losses are repair'd: The Colonel will not go with them, but wait his orders for forming a new regiment. He and his brother are perfectly domiciliated with the hospitable house of Bentinck,[4] and so was poor Mackenzie, who departs this day to join the second embarkation, now at anchor in The Downs.

I have now corrected the 5th and 6th books,[5] and brought the latter to it's conclusion. I wait a safe opportunity of sending the 5th book to press, but will keep back the 6th till I see you here, which I hope will be soon. Marianne will be with me in a week's time, and if you can now come, you will make more people than me happy.

I hope Lady Burges and your amiable and ingenious circle of ladies are well. There is now such an opportunity of giving a naval education to your son Somerville, as perhaps the whole fleet cannot equal, under the care and tuition of Capt. Horton of the flag ship in The Downs:[6] He has done wonders for my little nephew Hughes,[7] and certainly makes his quarter deck the best School for his youngsters in all parts of instruction and science, that can any where be found on land or sea: Let me earnestly entreat you to think of this; to see it with your own eyes, and hear it with your own ears before you commit your charge to his care; experienc'd seamen assure me that your boy is not too young, especially for a ship at anchor; and I am authoriz'd to assure you that he will be accepted. Put the brave little fellow into your chaise, and bring him hither, and beleive me, as your friend, you will find cause to rejoice in the step you shall have taken: It is the very moment to start in. Youngsters never keep watch in Capt. Horton's ship; their school-room is a perfect Academy, and their books are constantly shown up to the Captain himself, who looks into every article of their diet, dress and behaviour, keeping them strict to all the manners of a well-born Gentleman. You will think I have said enough; I know I have not said a word too much.

Adieu, my most worthy
friend! I am truly Your's

R Cum.

Source: Harvard.

1. This letter is postmarked 20 June 1807. The preceding Thursday was the 18th.

2. Probably Colonel John Cornelius Halkett of the 55th Foot Regiment.

3. "The Russians in February 1807 had fought a drawn battle with the French at Eylau. This encouraged Prussia to continue her disastrous struggle. It brought more intense appeals for English aid. The place for this was the Baltic. France, refusing to allow Sweden to lurk in neutrality, invaded Swedish Pomerania and prepared to take Stralsund. This port had great importance for England as a means of economic entry into Europe and for shipment of raw materials in return. By June of 1807 the German legion (8,000 men) had been sent by Britain to aid Sweden and thus, indirectly, Russia. But an end was put to this by Napoleon's destruction of the Russian army at Friedland on 14 June 1807" (Watson, *Reign of George III*, p. 455).

4. Lord Edward Bentinck, Cumberland's son-in-law.

5. Of *The Exodiad*.

6. A naval school for boys. Horton is possibly Captain Joshua Sydney Horton.

7. The grandchild of one of Cumberland's sisters who had been widowed by a Mr. Hughes.

CCXI Sir James Bland Burgess 30 June 1807[1]

Tuesday noon

My dear friend

Were I to consider myself only, it is gratification enough, that my Zeal for your son is accepted by the father of him; but when I see you turn'd from the noble profession, to which his early Genius points, and dooming his fine spirit to a friar's frock, I lament as your real friend, that you can yeild up the rights of Education, and the duties of a father, to any influence, be it what it may Whose Judgement ought to superceed your own?--But I have done. Poor little gallant fellow! thou hast had a chance; but it is lost--The flagship is at this moment in my eye; but I cannot view her with the pleasure I might else have felt.[2]

Major Halkett and Mackenzie are in the Downs, waiting for a shift of wind. The two brothers Stigar, Swiss gentlemen of consideration and merit, are still on shore, with young Baron Tygal, a near relation of The Bentincks:[3] They are fine amiable lads, and live almost entirely at the great Corner House, which is the very headquarters of hospitality. I rejoice that my friend Captain Charles[4] is in train to wear Spurs; I prophecy he will one day have the regiment, if he persists.

Marianne is in Town, and will be here in a few days--You talk of weeks, and I must own to you that I despair of seeing you. I am old and weariness comes over me; you have strength, means and opportunities: Therefore I say farewell, and am affectionately Your's

R Cum

I am not well, and the Exodiad begins to weigh heavily upon me.

Source: Harvard.

1. This letter is postmarked 1 July 1807. The preceding Tuesday was 30 June.

2. This paragraph refers to Cumberland's suggestion that Burgesss' son, Somerville, become a student at the naval school of Captain Horton. See 18 June 1807.

3. Cumberland's daughter, Elizabeth, and her husband, Lord Edward Bentinck.

4. Burgess's son.

5. The second volume of *The Exodiad*.

CCXII   **Sir James Bland Burgess   8 July 1807**[1]

Wednesday, Ramsgate

My very dear friend

Nothing coud give me greater gratification than your kind Letter, which affords me so near a prospect of seeing you and your dear boy[2]--perhaps also one of the young ladies to take a corner in the Chaise.

I woud not write till I heard specifically from Captain Horton, that he was ready to receive and educate your beloved Child. I have this moment rec[eive]d his answer to me, and these are his words-- "It will give me great pleasure to receive Sir James Burges's son, with every disposition on my part to shew him every attention, and whenever he arrives at Ramsgate, shall be very glad to send for him, if I cannot give him the meeting--" I am happy to say I may now congratulate this young Adventurer on his admission into the very first Naval School either on sea or land, and I pray God to protect and bless him!

Lord Edward[3] and family are delighted to hear that you are coming to us: He also wrote to his friend Capt. Horton about Somerville,[4] and she hopes to have a bed at your service; but I shall decline it on your account, as I think it will put you out of your way, (at least whilst your son is with you) and I shall lodge you at Sackett's which is close at hand, and where you can be well attended at all hours.

I was at The Ball last night, and (wonderfull to relate) Lord Edward also; I was never so much pleas'd and entertain'd: The band of the 13th play'd country dances; Col. Halkett[5] and his officers were delightful, and danc'd admirably. The girls were very elegant and very gay, and I wish'd for your fair recruits to strengthen the Corps. Halkett hopes to see you, and begs you will expedite your journey, that he may shake you by the hand. I join him in this desire. Lady Edw[ar]d[6] sighs to see Miss Burges, and hopes you will bring her: For Heaven's sake do so: I flatter myself she will be highly amus'd, and my grand daughters I am sure will be happy.

The flagship now again looks gay, and the sight of her delights me. Capt. Horton has sent my Grand nephew little Hughes[7] to Capt. Thompson[8] in the Foudroyant, and he tells me he has had a letter from him at Plymouth, announcing his safe arrival.

I shall be happy to show you the progress of our poem,[9] which is now in the last book, and I have wound up the 7th with that mutual appeal, which you wish'd to be inserted, and I hope you will approve of it. Mariannne returns this week, and I beleive by sea. The House of Bentinck are quite well, and write with me in kind remembrances to Lady Burges, yourself and Circle. I write in great haste, and with blind eyes and an acking head, but am notwithstanding Ever truly your's

R Cumberland

The Sun is strong upon the glassy sea, and glares intolerably.
L[or]d Edw[ar]d has just now read to me Capt. Horton's letter, which is in terms quite as strong, and better express'd.

Source: Harvard.

1. This letter is postmarked 9 July 1807. The preceding Wednesday was the 8th.
2. Burgess's son, Somerville.

3. Lord Edward Bentinck, Cumberland's son-in-law.

4. Burgess's son was to be enrolled in Capt. Horton's naval school.

5. Possibly Colonel John Cornelius Halkett of the 55th Foot Regiment.

6. Cumberland's eldest daughter, Elizabeth.

7. The grandchild of Cumberland's sister.

8. Norborne Thompson.

9. *The Exodiad.*

CCXIII   Sir James Bland Burgess   3 September 1807[1]

Ramsgate 3d Sepr

My dear friend

I thank you for your kind letter of the 31st. Having had a severe indisposition, which chiefly affected my head, and for which I have been oblig'd to lose a good deal of blood which I coud ill spare, I must write briefly.

I have now nothing to do but to attend upon our Cheif personage in his last moments on Mount Pisgah, and conclude.[2]

I thank you for your offer about the Critiques—and shall be highly oblig'd to you to furnish them in the following order, as they stand for publication in the list I have had from Mr. Cooke, viz—[3]

1 Grecian Daughter.

2 Alzira.

3 Minor.

4 Love Makes a Man.

5 School for Wives.

6 Mistake.

I am sorry I have no better things to offer you, but they are about the best I coud pick out.

William Badcock[4] surpris'd me yesterday at dinner time with a visit: He arriv'd from Quebec in the

Downs in the night, and off the land's end the Croc-
odile, his ship, took possession of a Danish East
India man richly laden with silk &c. He is gone off
early this morning, and   I fear he is order'd to
Portsmouth; the detain'd Prize is in the Downs: He
is well, and, as usual, in high spirits.

Marianne sends her best comp[limen]ts. Jansen desires his respects to you.[5] I can't write any more;
my head is very weak and giddy. Farewell!

R Cum

Source: Harvard.

1. The year is determined by reference to details of the writing of *The Exodiad.*

2. In *The Exodiad,* Moses views the promised land from Mt. Pisgah.

3. Cumberland's edition of *The British Drama* was published by
C. Cooke in 14 volumes (London, 1817). Burgess supplied some of
the critiques that accompanied the plays. *The Grecian Daughter* by
Arthur Murphy, *Alzira* by Aaron Hill, *The Minor* by Samuel Foote,
The School for Wives by Hugh Kelly, and *The Mistake* by John Van-
brugh appeared in the collection. *Love Makes a Man* by Colley Cib-
ber did not.

4. The son of Cumberland's second daughter, Sophia.

5. Jansen married Cumberlands youngest daughter, Frances Marianne.

CCXIV   Elizabeth Walker[1]   26 March 1808[2]

Thank you, my dear good, andid, charitable Bessy!
Your efforts to serve a poor abandon'd fellow Creature upon earth will send you to Heaven, where no
good deed is forgotten.

Your money I shall return to you, when we meet,
for that can do no good, except to yourself for the

motives of the donation.

Present my thanks and best regards to Mrs Herries.[3] who flatters me much by desiring to be troubled with a worn-out guest. If however I have still some little talent in reserve, and some embers of past warmth in my bosom, the relicks of these blessings are owing to the friendly Zeal I have experienc'd from her excellent Son.[4]

>I write in extreme haste, but am
>deliberately and truly your's

>Richd Cumberland

Remember me to my dear
Isabella and her fair sisters.

Saturday

Source: Massachusetts Historical Society

1. Possibly related to John Walker (1732-1807), the actor, who was, along with Cumbeland, among Samuel Johnson's circle of friends.

2. The date is determined from the postmark.

3. Probably the wife of Charles Herries (d. 1819), Colonel of the Light Horse Volunteers of London and Westminster.

4. John Charles Herries (1778-1855), the son of Colonel Herries. He was active in politics, and under the Addington administration became private Secretary to Nicholas Vansittart (1766-1851), the Secretary of the Treasury.

CCXV C. W. Ward 1 August 1808[1]

>Monday night

Sir

I beg leave to assure you and the gentlemen of the Board of Management, that nothing can be more acceptable to me than the conditions stated in your Letter, in as much as they clear me from that responsibility, which if your proposal had not releiv'd me from, I never woud have committed myself to; for though my opinion of Mr. Rae is exactly what I have stated, it is only my opinion, and the Public may not confirm it.[2]

I beleive him to be the very performer that you stand in need of, and the one man to be found, who can more than balance the accession of strength, which Cov[en]t has gain'd by engaging Mr. Young.[3] But the trial you propose will either confirm or confute my judgement, and when I have receiv'd his answer, I will impart it to you.

I have the honour to be, Sir, Your most obedt Humle. Servt.

Richd Cumberland

Source: British Library.

1. This letter is postmarked 2 August 1808. The preceding Monday was the 1st. It is addressed to C. W. Ward, Esquire, Board of Management, Drury Lane Theatre.

2. Alexander Rae (1782-1820) made his theatrical debut at Bath as Hamlet on 28 January 1806. He played the role of Mortimer in George Colman's The Iron Chest at the Haymarket during the summer of 1806. He seems not to have been employed at Drury Lane in the 1808-9 season. Charles Young made his first appearance in the Covent Garden company on 10 November 1708 while the company was acting at the Opera House at the Haymarket following the Covent Garden fire of 19 September. Rae was among the performers at the new house when it was opened for the 1812-13 season.

3. Charles Young. Genest observes concerning him: "Young was a really good actor--his figure was unexceptionable--his fine voice--his countenance expressive--and his judgment excellent--he had no stage tricks" (IX, p. 536).

CCXVI   **George Townshend   21 December 1808**[1]

Warren's Hotel
Wednesday

My dear Townshend

It gives me great satisfaction to hear of your well-doing, and the many favours, that have been shewn to you at Cambridge,[2] particularly by your worthy tutor and the professor Smythe--[3]

You must never judge of my affection and solicitude by my correspondence, for I am so involv'd in various avocations, that it is with the utmost repugnance I can turn my pen from it's daily task to the digression of a letter.

I have been very strict in my enquiries ab[ou]t you, for I take on my conscience your fame, your character and your success in life. The reports I have of you better all my expectations, but you must be wary that flattery does not intoxicate and make you forward, vain and self-conceited. Remember modesty is the best test of merit; A man, who keeps silence, and listens, risques nothing, and has nothing to repent of in his solitary hour: A talker who advances crude opinions, will be heard, betray'd and ultimately brought to shame.

I charge and conjure you to nurse your embryo reputation with the nicest care. Plead poverty to those, who tempt you to excess; business to those, who wish to occupy your time, for my credit's sake; and virtue to the allurements of vice, in duty to your pious father, who trusts you to the world, in which I have been the means to plunge you.

As for your poetry, beware of publishing till all my hyper-criticisms are satisfied, and give you passport to the press.[4] You must strike hard, or spare your strength to wait upon your judgement.

If you are advis'd by your friend Mr. Javell to come up to Town, you will either find me here in my old hotel, or at Tun[bridge] Wells: In either place I shall be glad to see you.

Adieu! God bless you! I am truly your's

R Cumberland

I have no time for letter-writing, nor ever take my pen from the paper till it signs my name.

Source: Princeton.

1. This letter is postmarked 21 December 1808, which was a Wednesday.

2. According to Stanley Williams, Cumberland assisted George in entering Cambridge (*Cumberland*, p. 274).

3. William Smyth (1765-1849), who became Regius Professor of Modern History at Cambridge in 1807.

4. Townshend, the author of a number of religious books, tried his hand at poetry. In the first issue of Cumberland's *The London Review*, there is the plan of an epic poem in twelve books by Mr. George Townsend, to be called *Armageddon*. The first eight books of *Armagedon* were published (London, 1815), with a second edition in 1817.

CCXVII **Mr. Pratt[1] July 6, 1809?[2]**

Warren's Hotel. Chas Street
St James's Square
Thursday

Dear Sir

I am highly gratified by the Volume you have favour'd me with, and in a particular manner by what I have read in your introductory Observations.

I think you are fully warranted to augur well of

Joseph Blacket's genius, and from his Specimens I conjecture that it points towards Dramatic Composition. You can put him in the way to cultivate it, and if you find him faithfull to Nature, attach'd to none but to the best examples, and profiting by your instruction and corrections, you will approve yourself a benefactor not to Him only, but to the Age you live in.

That such may be the issue of your laudable adoption of this Child of Nature, is the cordial wish of, Dear Sir, Your most

faithfull and obliged Servt.

Richd Cumberland

Source: Yale

1. The editor of *Specimens of the Poetry of Joseph Blacket* (London, 1809) listed in the catalogue of the British Library, containing "an account of his life and some introductory observations." Also listed is *The Remains of Joseph Blacket*, "consisting of Poems, dramatic sketches, *The Times*, an ode, and a memoir of his life by Mr. Pratt (2 vols., London 1811).

2. July 6, 1809 is written on the letter but is not in Cumberland's hand.

CCXVIII   James Asperne   About 1809 (1)[1]

Warren's Hotel Chas Street
St Jas Square
Thursday

Sir

Your wish to insert my pourtrait in your publication, at this period of my life, can only exhibit human nature in decay: Yet if you chuse to have it, *Mr. Lane*, in Duke Street opposite Burlington House, can supply you with a copy. A few lines will suffice to announce so unimportant an Original, and those may be put together with very little trouble by any body, who may consult my *Memoirs*.

I thank you for your present of your Magazine and of the Engravings, both which do honour to your work. Your kind suggestion to my worthy friend Mr. Braithwayte is particularly obliging, and may give a circulation very serviceable to my Interest.

Beleive me, Sir with gratefull acknowledgement

Your most faithfull and hum Servt

Richd Cumberland

Source: Oxford, Bodleian Library, MS. Montagu d. 6, fol. 497u-v.

1. The letter is posted to Mr. Asperne, No. 32, Cornhill. It bears a close relationship the one following [About 1809 (2)]. The approximate date is indicated by the reference in that letter to *The London Review*, published by Cumberland in 1809. "June .09" is added in a diffferent hand.

2. The nature of this publication is not clear. The British Library catalogue lists only one publication by J[ames] Asperne, an edition of reprints of resolutions by the inhabitants of St. Mary Lambeth on 26 July 1803 favoring the formation of armed associations to repel the threatened invasion from France (London 1803).

3. Daniel Braithwayte is mentioned in Cumberland's *Memoirs* (II, 229) with some affection: "...in the company of the worthy Braythwaite I can enjoy the contemplation of a man universally beloved, full indeed of years, but warm in feeling, unimpaired in faculties and glowing in benevolence."

CCXIX   **James Asperne   About 1809 (2)**[1]

Warren's Hotel, Chas Street
St. James's Square
Tuesday Morning

Sir

I feel myself very highly oblig'd to you for what you have been pleased to say of me in your respectable publication,[2] and I thank you for the liberal present you have sent to me of the work itself, and also of the engravings.

As I have told the World quite as much of myself as the World most probably wish'd to be inform'd of, you have done well and wisely to make that story short, which you coud not render interesting or new. You have not withstanding candidly and judiciously notic'd the Undertaking I am concern'd in as Conductor of a Review. I acknowledge, and perhaps already experience, the force of your objections, but as I have never allow'd myself the indulgence of a Screne,[3] I did not chuse to resort to it in my latter days, when I bear no enmity, and dread no malice. I am conscious that my motive is exactly what it ever has been; and as I have been long exercis'd in labour, and well practic'd in forbearance, I am not easily exhausted by fatigue; or alarm'd by dangers; for I trust it shall never be in the power of any man living to convict me of being unfaithfull to the interests of sound literature, or backward in acknowledging the merits of those men of genius, who adorn the age in which it is my chance to live.

If this may not be thought an answer to your reasoning, I hope you will at least receive it as an apology for my error. I am Sir with the warmest sense of your kindness,

Your very obedient
and oblig'd humble Servt

Richd Cumberland

Mr. Asperne &c

Source: Oxford, Bodleian Library, MS. Montagu d. 3, fol. 10r-v.

1. The year is determined from the reference to *The London Review,* which Cumberland undertook in 1809.

2. See About 1809 (1), Note 2.

3. *The London Review,* attempted by Cumberland in 1809, survived only two issues. Its unique feature was to have the articles in it signed by the contributors, thus removing the "Screne" that protected them from hostile reviewers.

CCXX **Sir James Burgess   After 18 September 1809**[1]

Warren's--Monday

Your letter, my dear friend, is admirable, and exactly points out both the difficulties we have to combat, and the objects we might accomplish, if we overcome them.

What Mr. Sheridan's parliamentary influence can effect will be doubtless exerted against us; but when he talks of re-building Drury Lane, and erecting a third theatre, if occasion call'd for it, he must first extinguish or compromise a debt, which lies upon the ruins to the amo[un]t of £300,000, before he can execute the first object, and if he supposes that his dormant patent can enable him to do the latter he totally mistakes his powers.[2]

There is strong reason to beleive that Killigrew's patent cannot be sustained, and he has none other to act upon but one, that will expire in twenty years:[3] he cannot build on this, and I much doubt if he can build on either or both.

I can form no guess about the fate of Cov[en]t

Garden. Every day sinks them deeper in decay. The popular rage ag[ain]st Kemble[4] seems to shut him from the stage for a length of time, perhaps forever. I think the private boxes must be given up, and they produce £12,000 per ann[um]. They cannot now receed from their new prices, and whilst the mob persists, their treasury is tarv'd. The Lyceum[5] is the only theatre, that gentle folks can go to; but the government is of that mixt sort, which cannot act with decision, and such in fact as no man of talents can trust, or be concern'd with. Well may genius appear to be inert in a period like this.

My grandson Bentinck has gone to his Living in the north but keeps his residence at the Abbey for the whole month of January: He is a good and amiable young man. Lord Edward[6] has a house to seek, but seems wedded to Ramsgate, and I suspect will not listen to the proposals that have been made to him for residence elsewhere. I am, my Dear Sir,

Ever most sincerely your's

Rd Cumberland

Source: Harvard.

1. The date is determined by reference to the "popular rage against Kemble" which took place after the reopening of Covent Garden on 18 September 1809.

2. Richard Brinsley Sheridan of Drury Lane faced the problem of rebuilding the theater that had been destroyed by fire on 24 February 1809. It was not until 10 October 1812 that the new theater was built after a subscription for £400,000 had been raised. Sheridan and the other patentees each received £20,000. for their rights (Doran, *Their Majestie's Servants*, p. 277). In this connection, see Sheridan's letter to the editor of the *Morning Chronicle* on 20 October 1809 (*The Letters of Richard Brinsley Sheridan*, ed. Cecil Price (Oxford, 1966) III, p. 70, note 3. Henry Fry, Cumberland's close friend and attorney, with Cumberland, Burgess and others was attempting to erect a theater in competi-

tion with the efforts of Sheridan. They published a Prospectus for a National Subscription Theatre in the *Morning Post* of 7 October 1809.

3. King Charles II had granted theatrical patents to Thomas Killigrew and William Davenant. These eventually became the patents for Covent Garden and Drury Lane. Sheridan had discovered in 1792 that John Rich had in 1732 purchased patents to both theaters in order to secure a monopoly. In order to regularize the situation, Sheridan paid Thomas Harris of Covent Garden L20,000 for his rights to Drury Lane (E. B. Watson, *Sheridan to Robertson* (Harvard, 1926) pp. 21-22.

4. When John Philip Kemble opened the new Covent Garden theater on 18 September 1809, he did so with substantially raised prices. Audience riots followed this move.

5. The Lyceum was devoted primarily to English opera after its opening in 1794. However, the Drury Lane company performed at the Lyceum after their theater had been destroyed by fire on 24 February 1809.

6. Lord Edward Bentinck, who had married Cumberland's daughter, Elizabeth.

CCXXI   Sir James Bland Burgess[1]   6 January 1810[2]

Warren's Hotel 6 Jan. 1810

My dear friend

I am sure the Committee will feel themselves much beholden to you for a communication of Mr. Harris's[2] proposal, and I request the favour of you to inclose it to me at *Mr. Wyatt's in Picket Street, Temple Bar*; where, if I meet it on Tuesday, the Committee[3] will sit, and I shall have the honour of laying it before them.

We are in some hopes, that we shall hear of our Petition, which has been pass'd by the Secr[etar]y of State to the King in Council.[4] The project of the Charter was adopted as an expedient for avoiding

Parliament; it satisfied our Law Associates, and of course I had nothing to say upon a subject I did not understand.

You are right upon the point of location, and, if your theatre is to rise, it will be in the vicinity of the others. I have again since my return to town inspected Young Wyatt's plan,[5] which not in my opinion only, but in that of much better judges is perfect and complete. Every particular in form and construction has been studied for accommodation of distinctly hearing and seeing; and the avenues are calculated to provide against all interference with proper and improper company. The Vomitaries are of that expanse and facility, that the whole audience may extricate themselves, in case of alarm, almost momentarily. The grand front has a portico of fluted Ionic columns, and is correctly chast and pure. What will be effected within side will altogether depend upon what will be done by men of such classical talents as yourself[6] and others. There surely is dramatic genius in the nation, and, if the system is well conducted, it will draw it forth. As to the Actors &c, of them there is good store and well dispos'd to serve in their respective provinces. Nothing therefore is wanting but the Royal word to give the launch it's motion.

Farewell, ever affecty your's

Rd Cumberland

Source: Folger.

1. Burgess is surely the recipient of this letter.   See After 18 September 1809 to Burgess on the same subject.

2. Thomas Harris (d. 1820), proprietor of Covent Garden.

3. The Committee to build a new theater that resulted from the efforts of Fry, Burgess, and Cumberland as indicated in After 18 September 1809.   This should not be confused with the Committee to erect a new Drury Lane that was headed by Samuel Whitbread

(1758-1815). Whitbread's committee met for the first time on 1
March 1811 (*Letters of Sheridan*, ed. Price, III, 133, note 3).
Whitbread was successful in reconstructing Drury Lane and reopening it on 10 October 1812. Cumberland and his associates failed
in their efforts.

4. Probably Richard Ryder (1766-1832), the Home Secretary between 1809 and 1812. The Foreign Secretary during this period
was Richard Colley, the Marquis of Wellesley (1760-1842).

5. Almost certainly George Wyatt, author of *A Compendious Description of a Design for a Theatre Made in Persuance of an Order
from the Committee of Subscribers for Carrying into Effect the
Project of Erecting a Third Theatre in the Metropolis*, London,
1812. Benjamin Wyatt (1775-1850), the son of the more famous architect, James Wyatt (1747-1813), designed the rebuilt Drury Lane
theater.

6. Burgess had produced two plays at the Lyceum Theatre in
1810.

CCXXII   Celia Fry[1]   14 January 1811[2]

Monday

My dear Celia

I have to ask a favour of you, which I beg you
will only grant, if it is not greatly inconvenient
to you, and this is it. Fanny Badcock[3] returns to
Ramsgate with Mrs. Saffory on Monday next the 21st,
and of course we must send her up on Saturday, which
entails a whole day in Town to be pass'd at Furni-
val's Inn Coffee House by the poor Girl, unless You
in your benevolence can let her have the comfort of
being with you for the remnant of Saturday after her
arrival in the Coach, and keep her till Sunday evening, when Mrs. Saffory will give her a bed for that
night, and start with her the next morning. If this
can be done without much trouble to you, it will
make Marianne very happy, and add very much to the

many favours confer'd upon,

> My dear Celia,
> Your very affectionate
> and sincere friend

> Rd Cumberland

Source: Folger.

1. The wife of Cumberland's attorney, Henry Fry.

2. This letter is postmarked 15 January 1811. The Monday preceding was the 14th.

3. One of the children of Cumberland's daughter, Sophia, who had been widowed by William Badcock.

CCXXIII   Browne (Unidentified)   After March 25 1811[1]

The Comm[itt]ee[2] having taken into their consideration the shape, in which their application at present stands in consequence of what pass'd upon the day appointed for the second reading of their petition, were unanimously of opinion that the postponement for six weeks as agreed to in the debate of the 25th ins[tan]t, was a measure very judiciously taken,[3] and feel themselves highly oblig'd to Mr Browne for his very able exertions in Parliam[en]t on that occasion.

Source: Yale.

1. The date is determined from the date of the parliamentary debate, 25 March 1811.

2. Cumberland was involved with a Committee to build a new theatre. See 6 January 1810.

3. A second reading was debated and denied on 9 May 1811.

CCXXIV   **Elizabeth Walker**[1]   Undated

My dear Bessy

Your long silence alarms me, and I fear that illness has prevented you from writing to me as you promis'd. Tell me how you are, and if you are as well as I wish you, you are well indeed. I go to Tunbridge Wells on Wednesday, and am at home tomorrow till 3 o'Clock. I am tolerably well, but not to boast of.

Ever Yours

R Cumberland

Saturday afternoon
Warren's Hotel

Source: Boston Public Library

1. The letter is addressed to Miss Walker. See 26 March 1808.

Index

386

392

398